The Life of Toussaint L'Ouverture, the Negro Patriot of Hayti

Comprising an Account of the Struggle for Liberty in the Island, and a Sketch of Its History to the Present Period

By John Relly Beard

A DocSouth Books Edition
The University of North Carolina at Chapel Hill Library
Chapel Hill

A DocSouth Books Edition, 2012

ISBN 978-1-4696-0787-0 (pbk.: alk. paper)

Published by
The University of North Carolina at Chapel Hill Library
CB #3900 Davis Library
Chapel Hill, NC 27514-8890
http://library.unc.edu

Documenting the American South
http://docsouth.unc.edu
docsouth@unc.edu

Distributed by
The University of North Carolina Press
116 South Boundary Street
Chapel Hill, NC 27514-3808
1-800-848-6224
http://www.uncpress.org

This book was digitally printed.

About This Edition

This edition is made available under the imprint of DocSouth Books, a collaborative endeavor between the University of North Carolina at Chapel Hill Library and the University of North Carolina Press. Titles in DocSouth Books are drawn from the Library's Documenting the American South (DocSouth) digital publishing program, online at docsouth.unc.edu. These print and downloadable e-book editions have been prepared from the DocSouth electronic editions.

Both DocSouth and DocSouth Books present the transcribed content of historic books as they were originally published. Grammar, punctuation, spelling, and typographical errors are therefore preserved from the original editions. DocSouth Books are not intended to be facsimile editions, however. Details of typography and page layout in the original works have not been preserved in the transcription.

DocSouth Books editions incorporate two pagination schemas. First, standard page numbers reflecting the pagination of this edition appear at the top of each page for easy reference. Second, page numbers in brackets within the text (e.g., "[Page 9]") refer to the pagination of the original publication; online versions of the DocSouth works use this same original pagination. Page numbers shown in tables of contents and book indexes, when present, refer to the original works' printed page numbers and therefore correspond to the page numbers in brackets.

Summary

Toussaint L'Ouverture (1743-1803) won international renown in the Haitian fight for independence. He led thousands of former slaves into battle against French, Spanish and English forces, routing the Europeans and seizing control of the entire island of Hispaniola. L'Ouverture became governor and commander-in-chief of Haiti before officially acknowledging French rule in 1801, when he submitted a newly written constitution to Napoleon Bonaparte (1769-1821) and the French legislature for ratification. In response, Bonaparte sent an army to depose L'Ouverture, who was taken prisoner in June of 1802 and shipped to France to be held without trial in "the dungeons of the castle of Joux" until he died of pneumonia in April, 1803 (p. 233).

John Relly Beard (1800-1876) was an English Unitarian minister who wrote more than thirty books in his lifetime, including *The Life of Toussaint L'Ouverture* (1853) and several reference volumes on a variety of topics. He wrote in simple language and attempted to translate complicated foreign affairs—such as the Haitian struggle for independence—into terms that every reader could understand. Beard's biography of L'Ouverture was first published in London on the fiftieth anniversary of L'Ouverture's death. Ten years later, in 1863, Boston publishers reissued Beard's biography, replacing a brief history of Haiti's fight for independence after L'Ouverture's exile with the first English translation of a thirty-five page autobiography written by L'Ouverture and other related documents, including a transcript of his post-mortem examination. Beard's biography remained the authoritative English-language history of L'Ouverture's life until the late twentieth century.

In explaining his reasons for writing about L'Ouverture, Beard frankly admits that he does so in order to "supply the clearest evidence that there is no insuperable barrier between the light and the dark-coloured tribes of our common human species" (p. 1). Throughout the text, Beard compares L'Ouverture to famously successful white generals and argues for L'Ouverture's supremacy. L'Ouverture is superior to George Washington,

Beard writes, because L'Ouverture could have seized absolute power more easily than Washington, and "[t]he greater the opportunity the greater the temptation; nor can he be accounted the inferior man who overcame in the severer trial" (p. 142). Similarly, Beard argues that L'Ouverture is a better man than Bonaparte because "the two differed in that which is the dividing line between the happy and the wretched; for while, with Bonaparte, God was a name, with Toussaint L'Ouverture, God was at once the sole reality and the sovereign good" (p. 283). For Beard, L'Ouverture's ultimate failure to liberate Haiti and his untimely death are the product of unfortunate circumstances—not an indictment of his character or leadership abilities.

Beard suggests that L'Ouverture inherits his talent for governance from his great-grandfather, who "is reported to have been an African king" in Arrada, a former fort and settlement in what is now the Republic of Benin (p. 23). L'Ouverture's father, Gaou Guinou, is brought to Haiti from Arrada as a slave in the early eighteenth century, but Guinou enjoys "full liberty on the states of his proprietor" and is "allowed to employ five slaves to cultivate a portion of land" (p. 24). Guinou names his oldest son Toussaint and provides for his education; "a black esteemed for the purity and probity of his character" named Pierre Baptiste becomes "the godfather of Toussaint" and, "[c]ontinuing to speak his native African tongue, which was used in his family, Toussaint acquired from his godfather some acquaintance with the French" and "a smattering of Latin, as well as some notions of Geometry" (p. 25). These privileges notwithstanding, Guinou's son is still a slave and must work his way up from a shepherd to become "steward of the implements employed in sugar-making" (p. 28).

As a steward, Toussaint supports the plantation owners during a slave revolt in 1791: he prevents "the insurgents from setting the fields of sugar-cane on fire" and personally protects the white superintendent's white wife (p. 59). When the uprising becomes a political battle between French, English and Spanish interests in Haiti, however, he joins the slave army and eventually becomes a general. Toussaint fights brilliantly for the Spanish in 1793 but switches allegiances after the French Republic proclaims "the general freedom of the blacks," and beginning on May 4, 1794, he hoists "the French flag wherever he was in power" (pp. 125, 86).

To memorialize "the opening which Toussaint had made for himself in the ranks and the possessions of the enemy" and "to announce to his people that he was about to open the door to them of a better future" (p. 83), he adopts the surname L'Ouverture, French for the opening. L'Ouverture believes that he is "destined to great things" and that his rise to command is in fulfillment of prophecy: "A secret voice said to me, 'Since the blacks are free, they need a chief, and it is I who must be that chief, foretold by the Abbe Raynal'" (p. 125). Beard responds to L'Ouverture's claims by emphasizing his role as a type of Christ; L'Ouverture speaks "his ideas in parables" and "by the blacks he was regarded as a messenger of God" (p. 137).

L'Ouverture also acquires political power. After defeating the English in 1797, he is appointed "commander-in-chief of the army of Saint Domingo" and assumes control of the entire island in 1801. Beard explains that under L'Ouverture's rule, the island enters a golden age: "Distances were abridged; time was saved; the minds of the people were awakened from torpor; activity universally prevailed, and commerce and riches began to abound" (p. 132). According to Beard, "[e]ven the horses, under the influence of Toussaint's example, improved their pace" (p. 132).

But when L'Ouverture attempts to solidify his power by drafting a new constitution and sending it to the French legislature for ratification, Bonaparte responds by reinstituting slavery and sending an army to depose him. Despite the enemy's superior numbers, training and firepower, L'Ouverture fights Bonaparte's brother-in-law, the French General Leclerc, to a standstill, surrendering only when Leclerc agrees to re-abolish slavery. L'Ouverture retires in the Haitian countryside, but Bonaparte considers him a lingering threat and orchestrates L'Ouverture's arrest and imprisonment in Joux, where he dies.

Works Consulted

Bell, Madison Smartt, *Toussaint Louverture*, New York: Pantheon Books, 2007; Ruston, Alan, "Beard, John Relly," *The Dictionary of National Biography*, London: Oxford University Press, 1953.

Zachary Hutchins

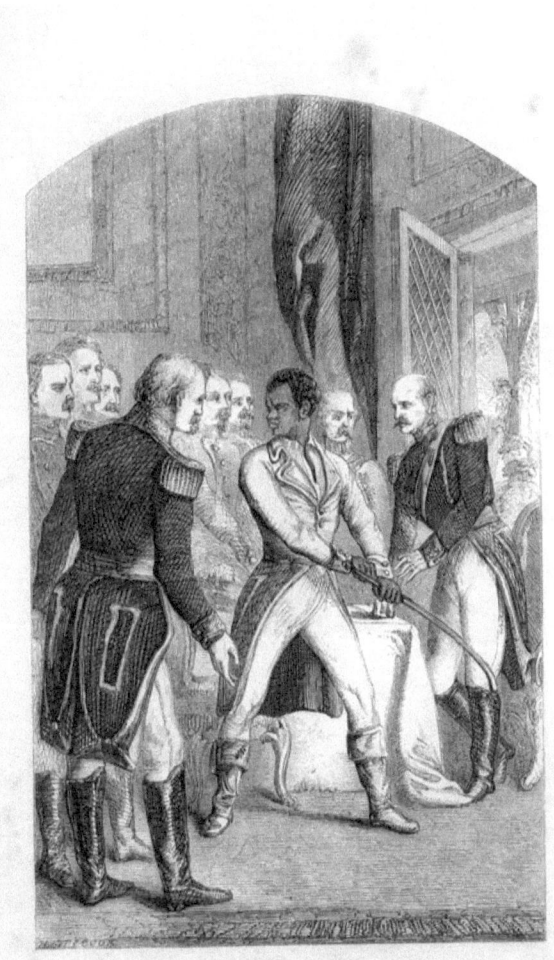

TOUSSAINT CAPTURED BY STRATAGEM.

TOUSSAINT CAPTURED BY STRATEGEM.

[Frontispiece Image]

THE LIFE
OF
TOUSSAINT L'OUVERTURE,
The Negro Patriot of Hayti.

By THE REV. JOHN R. BEARD, D.D.
MEMBER OF THE HISTORICO-THEOLOGICAL SOCIETY OF LEIPSIC, ETC.

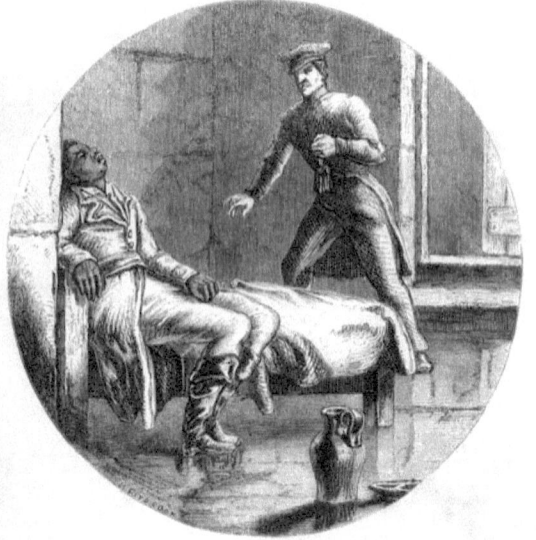

TOUSSAINT FOUND DEAD BY HIS GAOLER.

With numerous Engravings.

LONDON: INGRAM, COOKE, AND CO.;
And Sold by all Booksellers.
MDCCCLIII.

THE LIFE

OF

TOUSSAINT L'OUVERTURE,

The Negro Patriot of Hayti:

COMPRISING AN

ACCOUNT OF THE STRUGGLE FOR LIBERTY IN THE ISLAND,

AND

A SKETCH OF ITS HISTORY TO THE PRESENT PERIOD.

BY

THE REV. JOHN R. BEARD, D.D.

MEMBER OF THE HISTORICO-THEOLOGICAL SOCIETY OF LEIPSIC,
ETC.

With numerous Engravings.

LONDON:
INGRAM, COOKE, AND CO.
And Sold by all Booksellers.
MDCCCLIII.

PREFACE

THE life which is described in the following pages has both a permanent interest and a permanent value. But the efforts which are now made to effect the abolition of slavery in the United Sates of America, seem to render the present moment specially fit for the appearance of a memoir of TOUSSAINT L'OUVERTURE. A hope of affording some aid to the sacred cause of freedom, specially as involved in the extinction of slavery, and in the removal of prejudices on which servitude mainly depends, has induced the author to prepare the present work for the press. If apology for such a publication were required, it might be found in the fact that no detailed life of TOUISSAINT L'OVERTURE is accessible to the English reader, for the only memoir of him which exists in our language has long been out of print.

The sources of information on this subject are found chiefly in the French language. To several of these the author acknowledges deep obligation.

The tone taken on the subject of negro freedom in Hayti, by [Page vi] recent writers in two French reviews, is partial and unjust. Possibly this may be attributable to a mulatto pen. The blacks have no authors; their cause, consequently, has not yet been pleaded. In the authorities we possess on the subject, either French or mulatto interests, for the most part, predominate. Specially predominant are mulatto interests and prejudices, in the recently published *Life of Toussaint L'Ouverture,* by SAINT REMY, a mulatto: this writer obviously values his caste more than his country or his kind.

[Page vii] *CONTENTS*

BOOK THE FIRST.

FROM THE COMMENCEMENT OF THE STRUGGLE FOR LIBERTY IN HAYTI TO THE FULL ESTABLISHMENT OF TOUSSAINT L'OUVERTURE'S POWER.

CHAPTER I.
    Description of Hayti—its name, mountains, rivers, climate, productions, and chief cities and towns. p.1

CHAPTER II.
    Columbus discovers Hayti—Under his successors the Spanish colony extirpates the natives—The Buccaneers lay in the West the basis of a French colony—its growth and prosperity. 10

CHAPTER III.
    The diverse elements of the population of Hayti—The blacks, the whites, the mulattoes—Immorality and servitude. 16

CHAPTER IV.
    Family, birth, and education of Toussaint L'Ouverture—His promotions in servitude—His marriage—Reads Raynal, and begins to think himself the providentially appointed liberator of his brethren 23

CHAPTER V.
    Toussaint's presumed scriptural studies—The Mosaic code—Christian principles adverse to slavery—Christ, Paul, the Epistle to Philemon. 36

CHAPTER VI.
    Immediate causes of the rising of the blacks—Dissensions of the planters —Spread of anti-slavery opinions in Europe—The outbreak of the first French Revolution—Negro insurrection, Toussaint protects his master and mistress, and their property. 52

[Page viii]CHAPTER VII.

Continued collision of planter, the mulattoes, and the negroes— The planter willing to receive English aid—The negroes espouse the cause of Louis XVI.—The Arrival of Commissioners from France - Negotiations—Resumption of hostilities—Toussaint gains influence..... 60

CHAPTER VIII.

France equalizes mulattoes and negroes with whites—The decapitation of Louis XVI. throw the negroes into the arms of Spain— They are afraid of the Revolutionary Republicans—Strife of French political parties in Hayti—Conflagration of the Cape— Proclamation of liberty for the negroes produces little effect— Toussaint captures Dondon— Commemoration of the fall of the Bastille—Displeasure of the planters —Rigaud..... 69

CHAPTER IX.

Toussaint becomes master of a central post—Is not seduced by offers of negro emancipation, nor of bribes to himself—Repels the English, who invade the island—Adds the epithet L'Ouverture to his name—Abandons the Spaniards, and seeks freedom through French alliance..... 78

CHAPTER X.

Toussaint L'Ouverture defeats the Spanish partisans—By extraordinary exertions raises and disciplines troops, forms armies, lays out campaigns, executes the most daring exploits, and defeats the English, who evacuate the island—Toussaint is commander-in-chief..... 87

CHAPTER XI.

Toussaint L'Ouverture composes agitation and brings back prosperity— is opposed by the Commissioner Hedouville, who flies to France— Appeals in self-justification to the Directory in Paris.. ...97

CHAPTER XII.

Civil War in the south between Toussaint L'Ouverture and Riguad—Siege and capture of Jacmel..... 108

CHAPTER XIII.

Toussaint endeavours to suppress the slave trade in Saint Domingo, and thereby incurs the displeasure of Roume, the representative of France —He overcomes Riguad—Bonaparte, now first consul, sends commissioners to the island—End of the war in the south. . . . 118

[Page ix]CHAPTER XIV.

Toussaint L'Ouverture inaugurates a better future—Publishes a general amnesty—Declares his task accomplished in putting an end to civil strife and establishing peace on a sound basis—Takes possession of Spanish Hayti, and stops the slave trade—Welcomes back the old colonists—Restores agriculture—Recalls prosperity—Studies personal appearance on public occasions—Simplicity of his life and manners— His audiences and receptions—Is held in general respect. 123

CHAPTER XV.

Toussaint L'Ouverture takes measures for the perpetuation of the happy condition of Hayti, especially by publishing the draft of a constitution in which he is name governor for life, and the great doctrine of Free Trade is explicitly proclaimed. 126

BOOK THE SECOND.

FROM THE FITTING OUT OF THE EXPEDITION BY BONAPARTE AGAINST SAINT DOMINGO TO THE SUBMISSION OF TOUSSAINT L'OUVERTURE.

CHAPTER I.

Peace of Amiens—Bonaparte contemplates the restoration of Slavery in Saint Domingo—Excitement caused by reports to that effect in the Island—Views of Toussaint L'Ouverture on the point. 146

CHAPTER II.

Bonaparte cannot be turned from undertaking an expedition against Toussaint—Resolves on the enterprise chiefly to get rid of his republican associates in arms—Restores slavery and the slave-trade—Excepts Hayti from the decree—Misleads Toussaint's sons—Despatches an armament under Leclerc. 152

CHAPTER III.

Leclerc obtains possession of the chief positions in the Islan, and yet is not master therof—By arms and by treachery he establishes himself at the Cape, at Fort Dauphin, at Saint Domingo, and at

Port-au-Prince —Toussaint L'Ouverture depends on his mountain strongholds..... 160

CHAPTER IV.

General Leclerc opens a negotiation with Toussaint L'Ouverture by means of his two sons, Isaac and Placide—The negotiations ends in nothing —The French commander-in-chief outlaws Toussaint, and prepares for a campaign..... 170

[Page x]CHAPTER V.

General Leclerc advances against Toussaint with 25, 000 men, in three division, intending to overwhelm him near Gonaives—The plan is disconcerted by a check given by Toussaint to General Rochambeau, in the ravine Couleuvre.....p. 181

CHAPTER VI.

Toussaint L'Ouverture prepares Crête-à-Pierrot as a point of resistance against Leclerc, who, mustering his forces, besieges the redoubt, which, after the bravest defence, is evacuated by the blacks..... 188

CHAPTER VII.

Shattered condition of the French army—Dark prospects of Toussaint— Leclerc opens negotiations for peace; wins over Christophe and Dessalines —Offers to recognise Toussaint as governor-general—Receives his submission on condition of preserving universal freedom— L'Ouverture in the quiet of his home..... 198

BOOK THE THIRD

FROM THE RAVAGES OF YELLOW FEVER IN HAYTI UNTIL THE DEPOSITION AND DEATH OF ITS LIBERATOR.

CHAPTER I.

Leclerc's uneasy position in Saint Domingo from insufficiency of food, from the existence in his army of large bodies of blacks, and especially from a most destructive fever..... 213

CHAPTER II.

Bonaparte and Leclerc conspire to effect the arrest of Toussaint L'Ouverture, who is treacherously seized, sent to France, and confined in the Castle of Joux—Partial risings in consequence.. . . . 220

CHAPTER III.

Leclerc tries to rule by creating jealousy and divisions—Ill-treats the men of colour—Disarms the blacks—An insurrection ensues and gains head until it wrest from the hands of the general nearly all his possessions—Leclerc dies—Bonaparte resolves to send a new army to Saint Domingo. 237

CHAPTER IV.

Rochembeau assumes the command—His character, voluptuousness, tyranny, and cruelty—Receives large reinforcements—Institutes a system of terror—The insurrection becomes general and irresistible— the French are driven out of the island. 250

[Page xi]CHAPTER V.

Toussaint L'Ouverture in the Jura Mountains—Appeals in vain to the first consul, who brings about his death by starvation—Outline of his career and character. . . . . p. 267

BOOK THE FOURTH.

FROM THE EVACUATION OF HAYTI BY THE FRENCH TO THE PRESENT TIME.

CHAPTER I.

Dessalines promises safety to the whites, but bitterly persecutes them— Becomes Emperor of Hayti—Sanctions a wise constitution; yields to vice and folly; and is dethroned and slain. 284

CHAPTER II.

Feud between mulatto and negro blood, occasioning strife and political conflicts—Christophe president and sovereign in the north - Petion president in the south—The two districts are united under Boyer— Riche—Soulouque, the present emperor. 303

CHAPTER III.

Conclusion 317

NOTES AND ILLUSTRATIONS *321*

ILLUSTRATIONS

TOUSSAINT CAPTURED BY STRATAGEM.....*Frontispiece.*
TOUSSAINT FOUND DEAD BY HIS GAOLER.....*Vignette.*
MAP OF HAYTI OR ST. DOMINGO.....*page* 1
SLAVE TRADE ON THE COAST OF AFRICA.....17
TOUSSAINT READING THE ABBÉ RAYNAL'S WORK.....30
CAPE ST. FRANÇOIS.....53
TOUSSAINT PARTING FROM HIS WIFE AND CHILDREN.....231
REVENGE OF THE FRENCH ON THE BLACKS.....252

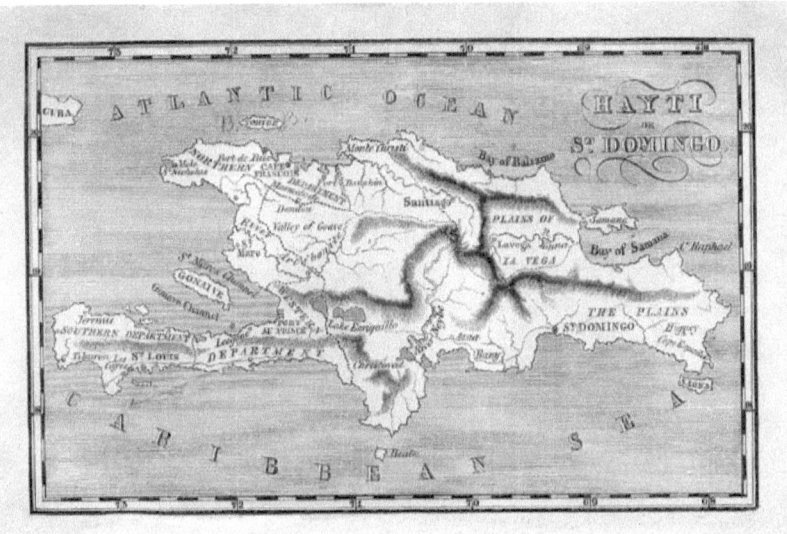

HAYTI

ORST. DOMINGO

THE LIFE of TOUSSAINT L'OUVERTURE.

BOOK I.

FROM THE COMMENCEMENT OF THE STRUGGLE FOR LIBERTY IN HAYTI TO THE FULL ESTABLISHMENT OF TOUSSAINT L'OUVERTURE'S POWER.

CHAPTER I.

Description of Hayti—its name, mountains, rivers climate, productions, and chief cities and towns.

I AM about to sketch the history and character of one of those extraordinary men, whom Providence, from time to time, raises up for the accomplishment of great, benign, and far-reaching results. I am about to supply the clearest evidence that there is no insuperable barrier between the light and the dark-coloured tribes of our common human species. I am about to exhibit, in a series of indisputable facts, a proof that the much misunderstood and downtrodden negro race are capable of the loftiest virtues, and the most heroic efforts. I am about to present a tacit parallel between white men and dark men, in which the latter will appear to no disadvantage. Neither eulogy, however, nor disparagement is my aim, but the simple love of justice. It is a history—not an argument—that I purpose to set forth. In prosecuting the narrative, I shall have to conduct the reader through scenes of aggression, resistance, outrage, revenge, bloodshed, and cruelty, that grieve and wound the hear, and exciting the deepest pity for the sufferers, raise irrepressible indignation against ambition, injustice and tyranny—the scourges of the world, and specially the sources of complicated and horrible calamities to the natives of Africa.

The western portion of the North Atlantic Ocean is separated from the Caribbean Sea on the south, and the Gulf of Mexico on the north, by a succession of islands which, under the name of the West India Isles, seem to unite in a broken and waving line, the two great peninsulas of South and North America. Of these islands, which, under the general title of the Antilles, are divided into several groups, the largest and the most important are, Porto Rico on the east, Cuba on the west, and St. Domingo between the two, with Jamaica laying on the western extremity of the latter. Situated between the seventeenth and twentieth degree of north latitude, Saint Domingo stretches from east to west about 390 miles, with and average breadth, form north to south, of 100 miles, and comprises about 29, 000 square miles, or 18, 816, 000 square acres;—being four times as large as Jamaica, and nearly equal in extent to Ireland. Its original name, and that by which it is now generally known, Hayti—which, in the Caribbean tongue, signifies *a land of mountains*—is truly descriptive of its surface and general appearance. From a ventral point, which near the middle of the island rises to the height of some 6, 000 feet above the level of the sea, branches, having parallel ranges on the north and on the south, run through the whole length of the island,—giving it somewhat the shape and aspect of a huge tortoise. The mountain ridges for the most part extend to the sea, above which they stand in lofty precipices, forming numerous headlands and promontories; or, retiring before the ocean, give place to ample and commodious bays. Of these bays and harbours, three deserve mention; not only for their extraordinary natural capabilities, but for the frequency with which two of them, at least, will appear in these pages. On the north-west of Hayti, is the Bay of Samana, with its deep recesses and curving shores, terminating in Cape Samana on the north, and Cape Raphail on the south. At the opposite end of the country, is the magnificent [Page 3] harbour called the Bay Port au Prince, enclosing the long and rocky isle Gonave—on the north of which is the channel St. Marc, and on the south the channel Gonave. Important as is the part which this harbour sustains in the history of the land, scarcely, if at all less important, is the bay which has Cape François for its western point, and Grange for its eastern, comprising on the latter side the minor, but well-sheltered Bay of Mancenille; and in the former, the large roadstead of Cape François.

The mountains running east and west break asunder, and sink down, so as to form three spacious valleys, which are watered by the three principal rivers. The River Youna, having its sources in Mount La Vega, in the north-east of the island, and receiving many tributaries from the north and the south, issues in the Bay of Samana. The Grand Yaque, rising on the western side of the Watershed—of which La Vega may be considered as the dividing line,—flows through the lengthened plain of St. Jago, until it reaches the sea in the Bay of Mancenille. The chief river is the Artibonite, on the west, which, having its ultimate springs in the central group of mountains, waters the valleys of St. Thomas, of Banica, of Goave; and turning suddenly to the north, along the western side of the mountains of Cahos, falls into the ocean a little south of the Bay of Gonaives, after a long and winding course. While these rivers run from east to west and west to east, innumerable streams flow in a northern and southern direction, proceeding at right angles from the branches of the great trunk. Hayti is a well-watered land; especially is it so in the west, where several lakes and tarns adorn and enrich the country. The more eastern districts are rugged as well as lofty, but the other parts are beautifully diversified with romantic glens, prolific vales, and rank savannahs. Though so mountainous, the surface is overspread with vegetation, the highest summits being crowned with forests. Placed with the tropics, Hayti has a hot yet humid climate, with a temperature of very great variations—so that while in the deep valleys the sun is almost intolerable, on the loftiest mountains of the interior, a [Page 4] fire is often necessary to comfort. The ardour of the sun is on the coast moderated by the sea and land breezes, which blow in succession. Heavy rains fall in the months of May and June. Hurricanes are less frequent in Hayti than the rest of the Antilles. The climate, however, is liable to great and sudden changes, which bringing storm, tempest, and sunshine, with the intensity of tropical lands, now alarm and now enervate the natives, and often prove very injurious to Europeans. On so rich a soil human life is easily supported, and the inducements to the labours of industry are neither numerous nor strong. Yet, in auspicious periods of its history, Hayti has been made abundantly productive.

At the time when the hero and patriot whose career we have to describe first appeared on the scene, the island was divided between two European powers; the east was possessed by the Spaniards, the west and south by the French. It is with the latter portion that this history is mostly concerned. Of the Spanish possessions, therefore, it may suffice to direct attention to two principal cities. The oldest European city is Santo Domingo, which had the honour of giving a name to the whole island. It was founded by Bartholomew, the brother of Columbus, who is said to have so called it in honour of his father, who bore that name. Santo Domingo stands in the south-eastern part of the island, at the north of the River Ozama. Santiago holds a fine position in the plain of that name, near the northern end of a line passing somewhere about the middle of the island. The French colony was divided into three provinces—that of the north, that of the west, and that of the south. At the beginning of the French Revolution of 1789, these provinces were transformed into three corresponding departments. The three provinces, or departments, were subdivided into twelve districts, each bearing the name of its chief city. The twelve districts were—in the north, the Cape, or Cap François, Fort Dauphin, Port-de-Paix, Môle Saint Nicholas; in the west, Port-au-Prince, Leogane, Saint Marc, Petit Goave; and in the south, Jérémie, Cape Tiburon, Cayes and St., Louis. The district of the Cape [Page 5] comprised the Cape, La Plaine-du-Nord, just above the Cape, Limonade, between the two; Acul, west of the Cape, and on the coast, Sainte Suzanne; with Morin, La Grande Rivière, Dondon, Marmelade, Limbé, Port Margot, Plaisance, and Borgne—thirteen parishes. The district Fort Dauphin, in the east of the northern department, comprised Fort Dauphin itself, Ouanaminthe, on the South of it, Vallière, Terrier Rouge, and Trou—five parishes. The district of the Port-de-Paix comprised, Port-de-Paix, Petit-Saint-Louis, Jean Rabel, and Gros Morne—four parishes. The district of the Mole Saint Nicholas comprised Saint Nicholas and Bombarde, two parishes. There were thus four-and-twenty parishes in the northern department. The district Port-au-Prince comprised, Port-au-Prince, Croix-des-Bosquets, on the north, Arcahaye on the north-west, and Mirebalais on the north-east—four parishes. The district of Léogane was identical with the parish of the same name. The district of Saint Marc comprised, Saint Marc, Petite Rivière, Gonaives—three parishes. The district of Petit-Goave comprised Petit Goave, Grand Goave, Baynet, Jacmel, and Cayes-Jacmel—five parishes. Fourteen parishes made up the western province. The district Jérémie comprised Jérémie and Cap Dame-Marie—two parishes. The district of Tiburon comprised Cape Tiburon and Coteaux—two parishes. The district of Cayes comprised Cayes and Torbeck—two parishes. The district of Saint Louis comprised, Saint Louis, Anse-Veau, Fond-Cavaillon and Acquin—five parishes. There were eleven parishes in the south.

Number of parishes in the north, ... 24
in the west, ... 14
in the south, ... 11
Total number of parishes, ... 49

The study of the map will show that these, the districts under the dominion of France, covered only the west of the island. As, however, they contained the chief centres of civilization, and the [Page 6] chief places which occur in this history, our end is answered by the geographical details now given.

The appearance of the island from the ocean is thus described by an eye-witness:—"The bold outlines of the mountains, which in many places approached to within twenty miles of the shore, and the numerous stupendous cliffs which beetled over it, casting their shadows to a great distance in the deep,—the dark retreating bays, particularly that of Samana, and extensive plains opening inland between the lofty cloud-covered hills, or running for uncounted leagues by the sea side, covered with trees and bushes, but affording no glimpse of a human habitation,—presented a picture of gloom and grandeur, calculated deeply to impress the mind; such a picture as dense solitude, unenlivened by a single trace of civilization, is ever apt to produce. Where, we inquire of ourselves, are the people of this country? Where its cultivation? Are the ancient Indian possessors of the soil all extinct, and their cruel conquerors and successors entombed with them in a common grave? For hundreds of miles, as we swept along its shores, we saw no living thing, but now and then a mariner in a solitary skiff, or birds of the land and ocean sailing in the air, as if to show us that nature had not wholly lost its animation, and sunk into the sleep of death."*

The interior of Hayti, however, lacks neither inhabitants nor natural beauty. The mountains rise in bold and varying outline against the brilliant skies, and in almost every part form a background of great and impressive effect. Broken by deep ravines, and appearing in bare and rugged precipices, they present a continued variety of imposing objects which sometimes rise into the sublime. The valleys and plains are rich at once in verdure and beauty, while from elevated spots you may enjoy the sight of the great centres of civilization, Cap-Français, Port-de-Paix, Saint-Marc,

---

*"Brief Notes on Hayti," by John Candler. London, 1842.

Port-au-Prince, &c., busy in the various pursuits of city and commercial life. Alas! that scenes so attractive should, at the time our narrative commences, have been disturbed and [Page 7] made repulsive by the forced labour of myriads of human beings occupied on the numerous plantations, which, but for greed, and oppression, and cruelty, would themselves have multiplied the natural charms of the island.

The wealth of Hayti comes from its soil. It is an essentially agricultural country. Cereal products are not cultivated; but maize or Indian corn grows there; and rice flourishes in the savannahs. The negro lives on manioc chiefly, and obtains other breadstuffs from the United States and from Canada. There are, however, other substances which supply him with food when corn fails—such as bananas, yams, and potatoes. Plantation tillage is the chief occupation. This culture embraces sugar, coffee, cotton, indigo, and cotton. In 1789, the French portion of the island contained 793 sugar plantations, 3, 117 coffee plantations, 789 cotton plantations, and 182 establishments for making rum, besides other minor factories and workshops. In 1791, very large capitals were employed in carrying on these cultivations; the capitals were sunk partly in slaves and partly in implements of husbandry; in the cultivation of sugar there was employed a capital of above fifty millions of livres;* forty-six millions in coffee, and twenty-one millions in cotton; and in 1776, there was employed a capital of sixty-three millions in the cultivation of indigo. The total value of the plantations was immense, as may be learnt from the fact, that the value of the products of the French portion was estimated,

In 1767 at 75, 000, 000 francs.
" 1774 " 82, 000, 000 "
" 1776 " 95, 148, 500"
" 1789 " 175, 990, 00 "

The last value is the highest. The sum represents the supreme pressure of servitude, and is consequently a measure of the injury done to the black dwellers in Saint Domingo. Already, in 1801, the value fell to 65, 352, 039—in other words, the slave-masters [Page 8] were, at the end of two years, punished for their injustice and tyranny by the immediate loss of nearly two-thirds of their property; so uncertain is the tenure of ill-gotten

---

*A LIVRE, OR FRANC, IS WORTH ABOUT TEN PENCE OF OUR MONEY.

gain. Among the territorial riches of Hayti, its beasts of burden and oxen must take a high position. In 1789, the soil supported 57, 782 horses; 48, 823 mules, and 247, 612 horned cattle.

Hayti possesses an abundant source of opulence in its numerous forests, which produce various kinds of precious wood employed in making and decorating furniture and articles of taste.

In 1791, goods exported from Hayti to France to the value of 133, 534, 423 francs—that is, above five millions sterling. The entire value of the territorial riches of the chief plantations, including slaves, amounted to no less a sum than 991, 893, 334 francs. Curious is it in the statistical table issued by authority, whence we learn these particulars, to see "negroes and animals employed in husbandry" put into the same class. Observe, too, the items. The value of the "negroes old and new, large and small" is set down at 758, 333, 334 francs, while the other *animals* are worth 5, 226, 667 francs. We thus learn, that three-fourths of the wealth of the planters consisted in their slaves. Such was the stake which was at issue in the struggle for freedom of which we are about to speak.

The population of Hayti was, in the year 1824, accounted to amount to 935, 335 individuals. This is not a large number for so fertile a land. But it has been questioned whether more than 700, 000 dwelt on the soil. Doubtless, the wars which have successively agitated the country for more than half a century, have greatly thinned the population. There has, however, been a constant immigration to Hayti from neighbouring islands, and even from the continent of America. Of the total number of inhabitants just given, there were, in 1824,

In the Kingdom of Henry I. (Christophe) 367, 721
In the Republic, under Pétion 506, 146
In the old Spanish District 61, 468
935, 335

[Page 9]This mass, viewed in regard to origin, was divided thus:—

Negroes 819, 000
Men of mixed blood 105, 000
Red Indians 1, 500
Whites 500

Foreigners 10, 000
936, 000

The small number of whites was occasioned by the strict enforcement of the law which declared "No white of any nation whatever shall set his foot on this territory, in the quality of a master or proprietor."

The language prevalent in the west and north is the French; that generally used in the East is the Spanish. Neither is spoken in purity. Not only has the French the ordinary grammatical faults which belong to the uneducated, but out of the peculiar relations in which they have stood in social and political life, as well as the nature of the climate and the products of the soil, a Haytian *patois* has been formed which can scarcely be understood by Frenchmen exclusively accustomed to their pure mother tongue. And while the educated classes speak and write what in courtesy may be called classic French, the few authors whom the island has produced do not appear capable of imitating, if they are capable of appreciating, the purity, ease, point, and flow which characterize the best French prose writers.

The religion of Hayti is the Roman Catholic. This form of religion is established by law. Under former governments other systems were tolerated. At present the spirit of exclusiveness predominates. The religion of Rome exists among the people in a corrupt state, nor are the highest functionaries free from a gross superstition, which takes much of its force from old African traditions and observances, as well as from the peculiar susceptibilities of the negro temperament. As soon as the native chiefs began to obtain political power in their struggle for freedom [Page 10] they practically recognised the importance of general education, well knowing that only by raising the slaves into men could they accomplish their task and perpetuate their power. Accordingly educational institutions have, from time to time, been set up in different parts of the island. These establishments have received favour and encouragement according to the spirit of the government of the day. At present they receive a support less liberal than that which is bestowed on the army.

The ensuing narrative will show the various forms of government which have established themselves in Hayti since the yoke of the planters and of France was broken. With a tendency to exaggeration, which is a marked feature in the negro character, the present ruler, not content with the title of president or with even that of king, enjoys the high-sounding dignity of emperor.

CHAPTER II.

Columbus discovers Hayti—under his successors, the Spanish colony extirpate the natives—The Buccaneers lay in the west the basis of the French colony—its growth and prosperity.

WE owe the discovery of Hayti to Columbus. When on his first voyage he had left the Leucayan islands, he, on the fifth of December, 1492, came in sight of Hayti, which at first he regarded as the Continent. Having, under the shelter of a bay, cast anchor at the western extremity of the island, and named the spot Saint Nicholas, in honour of the saint of the day, he sent men to explore the country. These, on their return, made to Columbus a report, which was the more attractive, because they had found in the new country resemblances to their native land. A similar impression having been made on Columbus, [Page 11] especially by the songs which he heard in the air, and by fishes which had been caught on the coast, he named the island Espagnola, (Hispaniola,) or *Little Spain*. Forthwith on his arrival, Columbus began to inquire for gold; the answers which he received, induced him to direct his course towards the south. On his way, he entered a port which he called Valparaiso, now Port-de-Paix; and in this and a second visit occupied and named other spots, taking possession of the country on behalf of his patrons Ferdinand and Isabella, sovereigns of Spain. The return of Columbus to Europe, after his first voyage, was accompanied by triumphs and marvels which directed the attention of the civilised world to the newly-discovered countries; and, exciting ambition and cupidity, originated the movement which precipitated Europeans on the American shores, and not only occasioned there oppression and cruelty, but introduced with African blood worse than African slavery, big with evils the most multiform and the most terrible.

At the time of its discovery, Hayti was occupied by—if we may trust the reports—a million of inhabitants, of the Caribbean race: they were dark in colour, short and small in person, and simple in their modes of life. Amid the abundance of nature, they easily gained a subsistence, and passed their many leisure hours either in unthinking repose, or in dances, enlivened by drums and varied with songs. Polygamy was not only practised but sanctioned. A petty sovereign is said to have had a harem of two-and-thirty wives. Standing but a few degrees above barbarism, the natives were under the dominion of five petty kings or chiefs, called Caciques, who possessed absolute power; and were subject to the yet more rigorous sway of priests or Butios, to whom superstition lent an influence which was the greater because it included the resources of the physician as well as those of the enchanter. Under a repulsive exterior, the Haytians, however, acknowledged a supreme power—the Author of all things, and entertained a dim idea of a future life, involving rewards and punishments correspondent to their low moral condition and gross conceptions.

[Page 12]On the arrival of Columbus, the natives, alarmed, withdrew into their dense forests. Gradually won back, they became familiarized with the new-comers, of whose ulterior designs they were utterly ignorant. With their assistance, Columbus erected, near Cap François, a small fortress which he designated Navidad, (nativity,) from the day of the nativity, (December 25th,) on which it was completed. In this, the first edifice built by Europeans on the Western Hemisphere, he placed a garrison of eight-and-thirty men. When (on the 27th of October, 1493) he returned, he found the settlement in ruins, and learned that his men, impelled by the thirst for gold, had made their way to the mountains of Cibao, reported to contain mineral treasures. He erected another stronghold on the east of Cape Monte Christo. There, under the name of Isabella, arose the first city founded by the Spaniards, who thence went forth in quest of the much coveted precious ore. Meanwhile the new colony had serious difficulties to struggle with. Barely were they saved from the devastations of a famine. Their acts of injustice drove the natives into open assault, which it required the skill and bravery of Columbus to overcome. His recall to Europe set all things in confusion. Restrained in some degree by his moderation and humanity, the natives on his departure rose against his brother and representative, Bartholomew; and receiving support from another of his officers, namely, Rolando Ximenes, they aspired to recover the dominion of the island. They failed in their undertaking, the rather that Bartholomew knew how to gain for himself the advantage of a judicious and benevolent course. The love of a young Spaniard, named Diaz, for the daughter of a native chief, led Bartholomew to the mouth of the river Ozama. Finding the locality very superior, he built a citadel and founded a city there, which, under the name of Santo Domingo, he made his head quarters, intending it to be the capital of the country. Meanwhile Ximenes, at Fort Isabella, carried on his opposition to the Government. Columbus's return to the island in 1498 did not bring back the traitor to his duty. Meanwhile, in Spain a storm had broken forth against Columbus, which occasioned [Page 13] his recall in 1499. The discoverer of the new world was put in chains and thrown into prison by his successor, Bovadillo. With the departure of Columbus, the spirit of the Spanish rule underwent a total change. The natives, whom he and his brother had treated as subjects, were by Bovadillo treated as slaves. Thousands of their best men were sent to extract gold from the mines, and when they rapidly perished in labours too severe for them, the loss was constantly made up by new supplies. In 1501, Bovadillo was recalled. His successor, Ovando, was equally unmerciful. On the death of Queen Isabella, and Columbus, the Haytians lost the only persons who cared to mitigate their lot. Then all consideration towards them disappeared. They were employed in the most exhausting toil, they were misused in every manner; torn from the bosom of their families, they were driven into the remotest parts of the island, unprovided with even the bare necessaries of life. In 1506, a royal decree consigned the remainder as slaves to the adventurers, and Ovando failed not to carry the unchristian and inhuman ordinance into full effect, especially in regard to those who were at work in the mines, four of which were very productive. A rising which took place in 1502, had no other result than to rivet the chains under which the natives groaned and perished. Another in 1503, brought Anacoana, a native queen, to the scaffold. In 1507, the number of the Haytians had by toil, hunger, and the sword, been reduced from a million down to sixty thousand persons. Of little service was it that about this time, Pedro d'Atenza introduced the sugar-cane from the Canaries, or that Gonzalez, having set up the first sugar-mill, gave an impulse to agriculture; there were no hands to carry on the work, for the master laboured not, and the slave, was beneath the sod. Ovando made an effort to procure labourers from the Leucayan isles. Forty thousand of these victims were transported to Hayti; they also sank under the labour. In 1511, there were only fourteen thousand red men left on the island; and they disappeared more and more in spite of the exertions for their preservation made by the noble Las Casas. In 1519, a young [Page 14] Cacique put himself at the head of the few remaining Haytians, and after a bloody war of thirteen years' duration, extorted for himself and followers a small territory on the north-east of Saint Domingo, where their descendants are said to remain to the present day.

Greatly did the island suffer by the loss of its native population; the working of the gold mines ceased, or was carried on to a small extent, and with inconsiderable results; agriculture proceeded only here and there, and with tardy steps; the colony declined constantly more and more on every side. The metropolis alone withstood the prevalent causes of decay, for it had become a commercial entrepôt between the old world and the new. Its prosperity, however, was, in 1586, seriously shaken by the English commander, Francis Blake, who, having seized the city, did not quit it until he had laid one half in ruins. A still greater calamity impended. The reputed riches of the new world, and the wide spaces of open sea which its discovery made known, invited thither maritime adventurers from the coasts of Europe. Men of degraded character and boundless daring, finding it difficult to procure a subsistence by piracy and contraband trade in their old eastern haunts, now, from the newly-awakened spirit of maritime enterprise, frequented, if not scoured by the vessels of England, Holland and France, hurried away with fresh hopes into the western ocean, and swarmed wherever plunder seemed likely to reward their reckless hardihood.

Of these, known in history as the buccaneers, a party took possession (1630) of the isle of Tortuga, which lies off the northwest of Hayti. With this, as a centre of operation, they carried on ceaseless depredations against Hayti, the coasts of which they disturbed and plundered, putting an end to its trade and occupying its capital. The court of Madrid, being roused in self-defence, sent a fleet to Tortuga, who, taking possession of the island, destroyed whatever of the buccaneers they could find; but the success only made the pirates more wary and more enterprising. When the fleet had quitted Tortuga, [Page 15] they again, in 1638, made themselves masters there, and after fortifying the island and establishing a sort of constitution, made it a centre of piratical resources and aggressions, whence they at their pleasure sallied forth to plunder and destroy ships of all nations, wreaking their vengeance chiefly on such as came from Spain. In time, however, these corsairs met with due punishment at the hands of civilised nations.

A remnant of the buccaneers, of French extraction, effected a settlement on the south-western shores of Hayti, the possession of which they successfully maintained against Spain, the then recognised mistress of the island. In their new possessions they applied to the tillage of the land; but becoming aware of the difficulty of maintaining their hold without assistance, they applied to France. Their claim was heard. In 1661, Dagaron was sent to Hayti, with authority to take its government into his hands, and accordingly effected there, in 1665, a regularly constituted settlement. At this time the Spanish colony, which was scattered over the east of the island, consisted only of fourteen thousand free men, white and black, with the same number of slaves: two thousand maroons, moreover, prowled about the interior, and were in constant hostility with the colonists.

As yet, the French colony in the west was very weak. Its chief centre was in Tortuga, It had other settlements at Port de Paix, Port Margot, and Léogane. When Dageron came to Hayti with the title of governor, the Spaniards became more attentive to what went on in the west of the island. They proceeded to attack the French settlements, but with results so unsatisfactory, that the new French governor, Pouancey, drove them from all their positions in the west. His successor, Cussy, who took the helm in 1685, was less successful. The Spaniards made head against him, and the French power was nearly annihilated. In 1691, France made another effort. The new governor, Ducasse, restored her dominion, and in the peace of Ryswick, Spain found itself obliged to cede to France the western half of Hayti. With characteristic enterprise and [Page 16] application, the French soon caused their colony to surpass the Spanish portion in the elements of social well-being; and in the long peace which followed the wars of the Spanish succession, Saint-Domingue, (so the French called their part of the island,) became the most important colony which France possessed in the West Indies. It suffered, indeed, from Law's swindling operations, and from other causes, but on the whole it made great and rapid progress until the outbreak of the first revolutionary troubles in the mother country.

Side by side with the advance of agriculture, opulence spread on all sides, and poured untold treasures into France, In a similar proportion the population expanded, so that in 1790, there were in the western half of the island 555, 825 inhabitants, of whom only 27, 717 were white men, and 21, 800 free men of colour, while the slaves amounted to 495, 528.

CHAPTER III.

The diverse elements of the population of Hayti—The blacks, the whites, the mulattoes; immorality and servitude.

The large black population of Hayti was of African origin. Having been stolen from their native land, they were transplanted in the island to become beasts of burden to their masters. The infamous slave-trade was then at its height. Nations and individuals who stood at the head of the civilised world, and prided themselves in the name of Christian, were not ashamed to traffic in the bodies and the souls of their fellow-men. Three hundred vessels, employed every year in that detestable traffic, spread robbery, conflagration, and carnage over the coasts and the lands of Africa. Eighty thousand men, women and children, torn from their homes, were loaded with chains, and thrown into the holds of the ships, a prey to desolation [Page 17] and despair. In vain had the laws and usages of Africa, less

SLAVE TRADE ON THE COAST OF AFRICA.

unjust and cruel than those of Christian countries, forbidden the sale of men born in slavery, permitting the outrage only in the case of persons taken in war, or such as had lost their liberty by debt or crime. Cupidity created an ever-growing demand; the price of human flesh rose in the market; the required supply followed. The African princes, smitten with the love of lucre, disregarded the established limitations, and for their own bad purposes multiplied the causes which entailed the loss of liberty. Proceeding from a less to a greater wrong, they undertook wars expressly for the purpose of gaining captives for the slave mart, and when still the demand went on increasing, they became wholesale robbers of men, and seized a village, or scoured a district. From the coasts the devastation spread into the interior. A regularly organised system came into operation, which constantly sent to the sea-shore thousands of innocent and unfortunate creatures to whom death would have been a happy lot. In the year 1778, not fewer than one hundred thousand of its black inhabitants were forcibly and cruelly carried away from Africa.

Driven on board the ships which waited their arrival, these poor wretches, who had been accustomed to live in freedom and roam at large, were thrust into a space scarcely large enough to receive their coffin. If a storm arose the ports were closed as a measure of safety. The precaution shut out light and air. Then who can say what torments the negroes underwent? Thousands perished by suffocation—happily, even at the cost of life, delivered from their frightful agonies. Death, however, brought loss to their masters, and therefore it was warded off when possible by inflections which, in stimulating the frame, kept the vital energy in action. And when it was found that grief and degradation proved almost as deadly as bad air and no air at all, the victims were forced to dance and were insulted with music. If on the ceasing of the tempest and the temporary disappearance of the plague, things resumed their ordinary course, lust and brutality outraged mothers and daughters unscrupulously, preferring as victims the young and the innocent. When [Page 18] any were overcome by incurable disease, they were thrown into the ocean while yet alive, as worthless and unassailable articles. In shipwreck, the living cargo of human beings were ruthlessly abandoned. Fifteen thousand, it has been calculated,—fifteen thousand corpses every year scattered in the ocean, the greater part of which were thrown on the shores of the two hemispheres, marked the bloody and deadly track of the hateful slave-trade.

Hayti every year opened its markets to twenty thousand slaves. A degradation awaited them on the threshold of servitude. With a burning iron they stamped on the breast of each slave, women as well as men, the name of their master, and that of the plantation where they were to toil. There the newcomer found everything strange,—the skies, the country, the language, the labour, the mode of life, the visage of his master,—all was strange. Taking their place among their companions in misfortune, they heard speak only of what they endured, and saw the marks of the punishments they had received. Among 'the old hands,' few had reached advanced years; and of the new ones, many died of grief. The high spirit of the men was bowed down. For the two first years the women were not seldom struck with sterility. In earlier times the proprietors had not wanted humanity, but riches had corrupted their hearts now; and giving themselves up to ease and voluptuousness, they thought of their slaves only as sources of income whence the utmost was to be drawn. It is not meant that the slaves of the French Haytian planters were worse treated than other slaves. Their condition, on the whole, was slightly better. But the inherent evils of slavery are very baneful and very numerous. Those evils prevailed in Hayti. The slave is helpless, ignorant, morally low, and almost morally dead—reduced as nearly as may be to a tool, a mere labouring machine, yet endued with strong emotions and burning passions. The master is all-powerful, self-willed, capricious, greedy of gain, and given to pleasure. In such a social condition vice and misery must abound; wherever such a social condition has existed, vice and misery have abounded.

[Page 19]The evils consequent on slavery are not lessened by the incoming of one or two stray rays of light. If the slave becomes conscious of his condition, and aware of the injustice under which he suffers, if he obtains but a faint idea of these things; and if the master learns that a desire for liberty has arisen in the slave's mind, or that free men are asserting anti-slavery doctrines, then a new element of evil is added to those which before were only too powerful. Hope on one side, and distrust and fear on the other, create uneasiness and disturbance, which may end in commotion, convulsion, cruelty, and blood. In the agitation of the public mind of the world, which preceded the first French Revolution, such feelings could not be excluded from any community on earth; they entered the plantations of Hayti, and they aided in preparing the terrific struggle, which, through alarm, agitation, and slaughter, issued in the independence of the island.

The white population was made up of diverse, and in a measure conflicting elements. There were first the colonists or planters. Of these, some lived in the colony, others lived in France; the former, either by themselves or by means of stewards, superintended the plantations, and consumed the produce in sensual gratifications; the latter, deriving immense revenues directly or indirectly from their colonial estates, squandered their princely fortunes in the pleasures and vices of the less moral society of Paris. Possessed of opulence, these men generally were agitated with ambition, and sought office and titles as the only good things on earth left them to pursue. If debarred from entering the ranks of the French nobility, they could aspire to official distinction in Hayti, and in reality held the government of the colony very much in their own hands, partly in virtue of their property, partly in virtue of their influence with the French court.

There were other men of European origin in the island. Some were servants of the government, others members of the army, both lived estranged from the population which they combined to oppress. Below these were *les petits blancs,* (the small whites,) men of inferior station, who conducted various kinds of business in the towns and who, despised by white men more elevated in [Page 20] station, repaid themselves by contemning the black population, on the sweat of whose brows they depended for a livelihood. Contempt is always most intense and baneful between classes that are nearest each other.

From the mixture of black blood and white blood arose a new class, designated *men of colour.* On the part of the planters, passion and lust were subject to no outward restraint, and rarely owned any strong inward control. African women sometimes possess seductive attractions. If in any case these were employed to mitigate the penalties of servitude, the blame must chiefly be imputed to the degraded condition in which the system held them; and if when they had obtained power over their paramours, they, in pride and jealousy, inflicted on them humiliating punishments, they did but serve as effectual ministers of well-merited retribution. Content to live in a state of concubinage, the proprietors could not expect the peaceful and refining satisfactions of a home; and alas! only too readily took the consequences of their licentious course in imperious mistresses, and illegitimate offspring. But vice is its own avenger. From the blood sprung from this mixed and impure source, came the chief cause of the troubles and ruin of the planters.

Some of the men of colour were proprietors of rich possessions; but neither their wealth, nor the virtues by which they had acquired it, could procure for them social estimation, Their prosperity excited the envy of the whites in the lower classes. Though emancipated by law from the domination of individuals, the free men of colour were considered as a sort of public property, and as such, were exposed to the caprices of all the whites. Even before the law they stood on unequal ground. At the age of thirty they were compelled to serve three years in a militia, instituted against the Maroon negroes; they were subject to a special impost for the reparation of the roads; they were expressly shut out from all public offices, and from the more honourable professions and pursuits of private life. When they arrived at the gate of a city, they were required to alight from their horse; they were disqualified for sitting at a white man's table, for frequenting the same school, for occupying the same [Page 21] place at church, for having the same name, for being interred in the same cemetery, for receiving the succession of his property. Thus the son was unable to take his food at his father's board, kneel beside his father in his devotions, bear his father's name, lie in his father's tomb, succeed to his father's property,—to such an extent were the rights and affections of nature reversed and confounded. The disqualification pursued its victims, until during six consecutive generations the white blood had become purified from its original stain.

Among the men of colour existed every various shade. Some had as fair a complexion as ordinary Europeans; with others, the hue was nearly as sable as that of the pure negro blood. The *mulatto*, offspring of a white man and a negress, formed the first degree of colour. The child of a white man by a mulatto woman, was called a *quarteroon*,—the second degree: from a white father and a quarteroon mother, was born the male *tierceroon*—the third degree: the union of a white man with a female tierceroon, produced the *metif*,—the fourth degree of colour. The remaining varieties, if named, are barely distinguishable.*

Lamentable is it to think that the troubles we are about to describe, and which might be designated *the war of the skin*, should have flowed from diversities so slight, variable, evanescent, and every way so inconsiderable. It would almost seem as if human passions only needed an excuse, and as

---

* SEE NOTE A AT THE END.

if the slightest excuse would serve as a pretext and a cover for their riotous excesses.

On their side, the men of colour, labouring under the sense of their personal and social injuries, tolerated, if they did not encourage in themselves, low and vindictive passions. Their pride of blood was the more intense, the less they possessed of the coveted and privileged colour. Haughty and disdainful towards the blacks, whom they despised, they were scornful toward the *petits blancs,* whom they hated, and jealous and turbulent toward the planters, whom they feared. With blood white enough to make them hopeful and aspiring, they possessed riches [Page 22] and social influence enough to make them formidable. By their alliance with their fathers they were tempted to seek for every thing which was denied them in consequence of the hue and condition of their mothers. The mulattoes, therefore, were a hot-bed of dissatisfaction, and a furnace of turbulence. Aware by their education of the new ideas which were fermenting in Europe and in the United States, they were also ever on the watch to seize opportunities to avenge their wrongs, and to turn every incident to account for improving their social condition. Unable to endure the dominion of their white parents, they were indignant at the bare thought of the ascendancy of the negroes; and while they plotted against the former, were the open, bitter, and irreconcileable foes of the latter. If the planters repelled the claims of the negroes' friends, least of all could emancipation be obtained by or with the aid of the mulattoes.

Such in general was the condition of society in Hayti, when the first movements of the great conflict began. On that land of servitude there were on all sides masters living in pleasure and luxury, women skilled in the arts of seduction, children abandoned by their fathers or becoming their cruelest enemies, slaves worn down by toil, sorrow and regrets, or lacerated and mangled by punishments. Suicide, abortion, poisoning, revolts and conflagration,—all the vices and crimes which slavery engenders, became more and more frequent. Thirty slaves freed themselves together from their wretchedness the same day, and the same hour; meanwhile thirty thousand whites, freemen, lived in the midst of twenty thousand emancipated men of colour, and five hundred thousand slaves. Thus the advantage of numbers and of physical strength was on the side of the oppressed.

[Page 23] CHAPTER IV.

Family, birth and education of Toussaint L'Ouverture—His promotions in servitude, his marriage; reads Raynal, and begins to think himself the providentially-appointed liberator of his oppressed brethren.

IN the midst of these conflicting passions and threatening disorders, there was a character quietly forming, which was to do more than all others, first to gain the mastery of them, and then to conduct them to issues of a favourable nature. This superior mind gathered its strength and matured its purposes in a class of Haytian society where least of all ordinary men would have looked for it. Who could suppose that the liberator of the slaves of Hayti, and the great type and pattern of negro excellence, existed and toiled in one of the despised gangs that pined away on the plantations of the island?

The appearance of a hero of negro blood was ardently to be wished, as affording the best proof of negro capability. By what other than a negro hand could it be expected that the blow would be struck which should show to the world that Africans could not only enjoy but gain personal and social freedom? To the more deep-sighted, the progress of events and the inevitable tendencies of society had darkly indicated the coming of a negro liberator. The presentiment found expression in the words of the philosophic Abbé Raynal, who, in some sort, predicted that a vindicator of negro wrongs would ere long arise out of the bosom of the negro race. That prediction had its fulfillment in Toussaint L'Ouverture.

Toussaint was a negro. We wish emphatically to mark the fact that he was wholly without white blood. Whatever he was, and whatever he did, he achieved all in virtue of qualities which in kind are common to the African race. Though of negro extraction, Toussaint, if we may believe family traditions, was not of common origin. His great grandfather is reported to have been an African king. Whatever position his ancestors [Page 24] held, certain it is that Toussaint had in his soul higher qualities than noble or royal descent can guarantee.

The Arradas were a powerful tribe of negroes, eminent for mental resources, and of an indomitable will, who occupied a part of Western Africa. In a plundering expedition undertaken by a neighbouring tribe, a son of the chief of the Arradas was made captive. His name was Gaou-Guinou. Sold to slave-dealers, he was conveyed to Hayti, and became the property of the Count de Breda, who owned a sugar manufactory some two miles from Cap François. More fortunate than most of his race in their servitude, he found among his fellow-slaves fellow countrymen by whom he was recognised, and from whom he received tokens of the respect which they judged due to his rank. The Count de Breda was a humane man ; as such he took care to entrust his slaves to none but humane superintendants. At the time the plantation of the Count de Breda was directed by M. Bayou de Libertas, a Frenchman of mild character, who, contrary to the general practice, studied his employer's interests without overloading his hands with immoderate labour.

Under him Gaou-Guinou was less unhappy than his companions in misfortune. It is not known that his master was aware of his superior position in his native country, but facts stated by Isaac, one of Toussaint L'Ouverture's sons, make the supposition not improbable. His grandfather, he reports, enjoyed full liberty on the states of his proprietor, He was also allowed to employ five slaves to cultivate a portion of land which had been assigned to him. He became a member of the Catholic Church, the religion of the rulers of Western Hayti, and married a woman who was not only virtuous but beautiful. The husband and the wife died nearly at the same time, leaving five male children and three female. The eldest of his sons was Toussaint-L'Ouverture.

These particulars illustrative of the superiority of Toussaint's family, are neither without interest nor without importance. If, strictly speaking, virtues are not transmissible, virtuous tendencies, and certainly intellectual aptitudes, may pass from [Page 25] parents to children. And the facts narrated may serve to show how it was that Toussaint was not sunk in that mental stagnation and moral depravity of which slavery is commonly the parent.

As might be expected, the exact day and year of Toussaint's birth are not known. It is said to have been the 20th of May, 1743. What is of more importance is that he lived fifty years of his life in slavery before he became prominent as the vindicator of his brethren's rights. In that long space he had full time to become acquainted with their sufferings as well as their capabilities, and to form such deliberate resolutions as, when the time for action came, should not be likely to fail of effect. Yet does it seem a late period in a man's life for so great an undertaking; nor could any one endowed with inferior powers have approached to the accomplishment of the task.

Throughout his arduous and perilous career, Toussaint L'Ouverture found great support himself, and exerted great influence over others, in virtue of his deep and pervading sense of religion. We might almost declare that from that source he derived more power than from all others. The foundation of his religious sentiments was laid in his childhood.

There lived in the neighbourhood of the Gaou-Guinou family a black esteemed for the purity and probity of his character, and who was not devoid of knowledge. His name was Pierre Baptiste. He was acquainted with French, and had a smattering of Latin, as well as some notions of Geometry. For his education he was indebted to the goodness of one of those missionaries who, in preaching the morality of a Divine religion, enlighten and enlarge the minds of their disciples. Pierre Baptiste became the godfather of Toussaint. Holding that relation to the child, he thought it his duty to communicate to him the instructions and impressions he had received from his own religious teacher. Continuing to speak his native African tongue, which was used in his family, Toussaint acquired from his godfather some acquaintance with the French, and aided by the services of the Catholic Church, made a few steps in the knowledge of the Latin. With a love of country which ancestral recollections [Page 26] and domestic intimacies cherished, he took pleasure in reverting to the traditional histories of the land of his sires. From these Pierre-Baptiste laboured to direct his young mind and heart to loftier and purer examples consecrated in the records of the Christian Church.

This course of instruction was of greater value than any skill in the outward processes which are too commonly identified with education. The young negro, however, seems to have made some progress in the arts of reading, writing and drawing. A scholar, in the higher sense of the term, he never became; and at an advanced period of life, when his knowledge was great and various, he regarded the instruction which he received in boyhood as very inconsiderable. Undoubtedly, in the pure and noble inspirations of his moral nature, Toussaint had instructors far more rich in knowledge and impulse than any pedagogue could have been. Yet in his youth were the foundations laid in external learning of value to the man, the general, and the legislator. It is true, that in the composition of his letters and addresses, he enjoyed the assistance of a cultivated secretary. Nevertheless, if the form was another's, the thought was his own; nor would he allow a document to pass from his hands, until, by repeated perusals and numerous corrections, he had brought the general tenour, and each particular expression, into conformity with his own thoughts and his own purpose. Nor is there required anything more than an attentive reading of his extant compositions, to be assured of the superior mental powers with which he was endowed.

In his mature years, and in the days of his great conflict, Toussaint possessed an iron frame and a stout arm. Capable of almost any amount of labour and endurance, he was terrible in battle, and rarely struck without deadly effect. Yet in his childhood he was weak and infirm to such a degree, that for a long time his parents doubted of being able to preserve his existence. So delicate was his constitution that he received the descriptive appellation of Fatrâs-Baton, which might be rendered in English by *Little Lath*. But with increase of years the stripling hardened and strengthened his frame by the severest labours [Page 27] and the most violent exercises. At the age of twelve he surpassed all his equals in the plantation in bodily feats. Who so swift in hunting? who so clever to swim across a foaming torrent? who so skilful to back a horse in full speed, and direct him at his will? The spirit of the man was already working in the boy.

The duty of the young slaves was definite and uniform. They were entrusted with the care of the flocks and herds. As a solitary and moral occupation, a shepherd's life gives time and opportunity for tranquil meditation. By nature Fatras-Bâton was given to thought. His reflective and taciturn disposition found appropriate nutriment on the rich uplands and under the brilliant skies of the land of his birth. Accustomed to think much more than he spoke, he acquired not only self-control, but also the power of concentrated reflection and concise speech, which, late in life, was one of his most marked and most serviceable characteristics.

Pastoral occupations are favourable to an acquaintance with vegetable products. Toussaint's father, like other Africans, was familiar with the healing virtues of many plants. These the old man explained to his son, whose knowledge expanded in the monotonous routine of his daily task. Thus did he obtain a rude familiarity with simples, of which he afterwards made a practical application. In this period, when the youth was passing into the man, and when, as with all thoughtful persons, the mind becomes sensitively alive to things to come as well as to things present, Toussaint may have formed the first dim conception of the misery of servitude, and the need of a liberator. At present he lived with his fellow-sufferers in those narrow, low, and foul huts where regard to decency was impossible; he heard the twang of the driver's whip, and saw the blood streaming from the negro's body; he witnessed the separation of parents and children, and was made aware, by too many proofs, that in slavery neither home nor religion could accomplish its purposes. Not impossibly, then, it was at this time that he first discerned the image of a distant duty rising before his mind's eye; and as the future liberator unquestionably lay in [Page 28] his soul, the latent thought may at times have started forth, and for a moment occupied his consciousness. The means, indeed, do not exist by which we may certainly ascertain when he conceived the idea of becoming the avenger of his people's wrongs; but several intimations point to an early period in his life. His good conduct in his pastoral engagements procured for him an advancement. Bayou de Libertas, convinced of his diligence and fidelity, made him his coachman. This was an office of importance in the eyes of the slaves; certainly it was one which brought some comfort and some means of self-improvement.

Though Toussaint became every day more and more aware that he was a slave, and experienced many of the evils of his condition, yet, with the aid of religion, he avoided a murmuring spirit, and wisely employed his opportunities to make the best of the position in which he had been born, without, however, yielding to the degrading notion that his hardships were irremediable. Sustained by a sense of duty which was even stronger than his hope of improving his condition, he performed his daily task in a composed if not a contented spirit, and so, constantly, won the confidence of the overseer. The result was his promotion to a place of trust. He was made steward of the implements employed in sugar-making.

Arrived at adult age, Toussaint began to think of marriage. His race at large he saw living in concubinage. As a religious man he was forbidden by his conscience to enter into such a relation. As a humane man he shrunk from the numerous evils which he knew concubinage entailed. Whom should he choose? Already had he risen above the silly preferences of form and feature. Reality he wanted, and the only real good in a wife, he was assured, lay in good sense, good feeling, and good manners. These qualities he found in a widow well skilled in husbandry, a house-slave in the plantation. The kind-hearted and industrious Suzan became his lawful wife according to "God's holy ordinance and the law of the land." By a man of colour Suzan had had a son, named Placide. Obeying the generous impulses of his heart, Toussaint adopted the youth, [Page 29] who ever retained the most lively sense of gratitude towards his benefactor.

Toussaint was now a happy man, considering his condition as a slave—the husband of a slave—a very happy man. His position gave him privileges, and he had a heart to enjoy them. His leisure hours he employed in cultivating a garden, which he was allowed to call his own. In those pleasing engagements he was not without a companion. "We went," he said to a traveler, "we went to labour in the fields, my wife and I, hand in hand. Scarcely were we conscious of the fatigues of the day. Heaven always blessed our toil. Not only we swam in abundance, but we had the pleasure of giving food to blacks who needed it. On the Sabbath and on festival days we went to church—my wife, my parents, and myself. Returning to our cottage, after a pleasant meal, we passed the remainder of the day as a family, and we closed it by prayer, in which all took part." Thus can religion convert a desert into a garden, and make a slave's cabin the abode of the purest happiness on earth.

Bent as Toussaint was on the improvement of his condition, he yet did not employ the personal property which ensued from his own and his wife's thrift, in purchasing his liberty, and elevating himself and family into the higher class of men of colour. His reasons for remaining a slave are not recorded. He may have felt no attractions towards a class whose superiority was more nominal than real. He may have resolved to remain in a class whose emancipation he hoped some day to achieve.

The virtues of his character procured for Toussaint universal respect. He was esteemed and loved even by the free blacks. The great planters held him in consideration. His intellectual faculties ripened under the effects of his intercourse with free and white men. As he grew in mind and became large of heart, he more and more was puzzled and distressed with the institution of slavery; he could in no way understand how the hue of the skin should put so great a social and personal distance between men whom God, he saw, had made essentially the same, and whom he knew to be useful if not indispensable to each [Page 30] other. Naturally he asked himself what others had thought and said of slavery. He had heard passages recited from Raynal.* He procured the work. And now he found how much is involved in the simple art of reading. Toussaint could read,— Toussaint did read. He read passages similar to what follows, and he became the vindicator of negro freedom:—"Scarcely had domestic liberty revived in Europe, when it was entombed in America. The Spaniard, whom the waves first threw on the shores of the New World, believed himself under no obligation to

---

* Histoire Philosophique et Politique des Etablissemens et du Commerce des Européens dans les Deux Indes, par G. T. Raynal. Geneva; 1780.

its inhabitants, for they had not his colour, or his customs, or his religion. He saw in them only his instruments, and he loaded them with chains. Those feeble men, unused to toil, soon perished from the vapours of the mines, and other occupations almost as baneful. Then arose a demand for slaves from Africa. Their numbers increased in proportion as cultivation extended. The Portuguese, the Dutch, the English, the French, the Danes—all nations, whether free or in serfdom, remorselessly sought an augmentation of fortune in the sweat, in the blood, in the despair of these poor wretches;—what a frightful system!

"Liberty is everyone's own property. There are three kinds of liberty—natural liberty, civil liberty, political liberty; that is to say, the liberty of the man, the liberty of the citizen, and the liberty of the community. Natural liberty is the right, which nature has given to every one to dispose of himself according. to his own will. Civil liberty is the right which society ought to guarantee to every citizen to do all that is not contrary to the laws. Political liberty is the condition of a people which has not alienated its own sovereignty, and which makes its own laws, or which is in part associated in its legislation.

"The first of these liberties is, next to reason, the distinctive characteristic of man. We subdue and enchain the brute, because it has no notion of justice or injustice—no idea of greatness and degradation. But in me liberty is the principle of my [Page 31] vices and my virtues. It is only the free man who can say, *I will*, or, *I will not*; and who can, consequently, be worthy of praise and blame. Without liberty, or the possession of one's own body and the enjoyment of one's own mind, there is neither husband, father, relation nor friend; we have no country, no fellow-citizen, no God. The slave, an instrument in the hands of wickedness, is below the dog which the Spaniard let loose against the American; for conscience, which the dog lacks, remains with the man. He who basely resigns his liberty, devotes himself to remorse and to the greatest misery that a sensible and thinking creature can experience. If there is no power under heaven that can change my organisation, and convert me into a brute, there is none that can dispose of my liberty. God is my Father and not my master. I am his child, not his slave. How, then, could I accord to political power that I which I refuse to Divine omnipotence?

"These are immovable and eternal truths—the foundation of all morality, the basis of all government will they be contested? Yes! and it will be a barbarous and sordid avarice which will commit the audacious homicide.

TOUSSAINT READING THE ABBÉ RAYNAL'S WORK.

TOUSSAINT READING THE ABBÉ RAYNAL'S WORK

Cast your eye on that ship-owner, who, bent over his desk, regulates, with pen in hand, the number of crimes which he may commit on the coast of Guinea; who, at his leisure, examines what number of muskets will be needed to obtain a negro, what number of chains to hold him bound on board his vessel, what number of whips to make him work: who coolly calculates how much will cost him each drop of the blood with which his slave will water his plantation who discusses whether the negress will give more or less to his estate by the labours of her feeble hands than by the dangers of child-birth. You shudder?—ah! if there existed a religion which tolerated, which authorized, if only by its silence, horrors like these; if, occupied with idle or contentious questions, it did not ceaselessly thunder against the authors or the instruments of this tyranny; if it made it a crime for the slave to break his chains; if it suffered in its bosom the unjust judge who condemned the fugitive to death;—if this religion existed, would it not be necessary that its altars should be broken down and left [Page 32] in ruins? Who are you who will dare to justify crimes against my independence, on the ground that you are the stronger? What! he who makes me a slave not guilty? He makes use of his rights? What, then, are those rights? Who has given them a character sacred enough to put my rights to silence? I hold from nature the right of self-defence; she has not given you the right to attack me. If you think yourself authorized to oppress me because you are stronger and more alert than I, do not complain when, after my hand becomes vigorous, it shall plant a dagger in your heart; do not complain when you shall feel in your veins that death which I shall have mingled with your food. Now I am the stronger and the more alert, it is your turn to be the victim; expiate the crime of having been an oppressor.

" 'But,' it is said, 'slavery has been generally established in all countries and in all ages.' True;—but what consequence is it what other nations have done in other ages? Ought the appeal to be to customs or to conscience? Is it interest, blindness, barbarity, or reason and justice, that we ought to listen to? If the universality of a practice proved its innocence, the apology of usurpations, conquests, and oppression of all kinds would irrefutably be completed.

" 'But the ancients,' you say, 'thought themselves masters of the lives of their slaves; we, having become more humane, dispose only of their liberty and their labour.' It is true, the progress of knowledge has on this important point given light to modern legislators. All codes, without an exception, have taken precautions to guard the life of even the man who pines away in servitude. They have put his existence under the protection of the magistrate. But has this, the most sacred of social institutions, ever had its due force? Is not America peopled with colonists who, usurping sovereign rights, inflict death on the unfortunate victims of their avarice? But suppose the law observed, would the slave materially gain thereby? Does not the master who employs my strength, dispose of my life, which depends on the voluntary and moderate use of my faculties? What is existence for him who has no property in it? I cannot kill my slave, but I may cause his blood to flow drop by drop under the drivers whip; I may overwhelm him with [Page 33] labours, privations, and pains; I may on all sides attack and slowly undermine the resources of his life; I may stifle by slow punishments the wretched embryo that a negress bears in her womb. It might be said that the laws protect the slave against a speedy death, only to leave to my cruelty the right of killing him in the course of time. In truth, the right of slavery is the right to commit crimes of all kinds.

" 'But the negroes are a sort of men born for slavery: they are of narrow minds, mischievous, deceitful; they themselves own the superiority of our intelligence, and almost recognise the justice of our dominion!'

"The negroes are of narrow minds because slavery destroys all the springs of the soul. They are mischievous,—not mischievous enough with you. They are deceitful, because they owe no fidelity to their tyrants. They acknowledge the superiority of our intelligence, because we have perpetuated their ignorance; the justice of our dominion, because we have abused their weakness. In the impossibility of maintaining our superiority by force, a criminal policy has had recourse to guile. You have almost got so far as to persuade them that they are an exceptional race, born for subjection and dependence, for labour and punishment. You have neglected nothing to degrade those unhappy creatures, and you reproach them with being vile.

"'But these negroes were born slaves.'—Whom will you cause to believe that a man can be the property of a sovereign? a son the property of a father? a woman the property of a husband? a domestic the property of a master? a negro the property of a planter? The contempt with which you treat them falls back upon yourself. You have no ground of self-respect but what is common to you with them. A common Father, an immortal soul, a future life—here is your true glory, and here is their glory.

" 'But the government itself authorizes the sale of slaves.'— Whence this right? However absolute the magistrate, is he the proprietor of the subjects of his empire? Has he any other authority than such as he derives from the citizens? And can any nation give the privilege of disposing of its liberty?

"'But the slave sold himself of his own accord.'—If he belongs [Page 34] to himself, he has the right to dispose of himself. If he is master of his life, why should he not be master of his liberty? Man has not the right to sell himself, because he has not the right to accede to whatever an unjust, violent, and depraved master may exact from him. He belongs to his first master—God, by whom he has never been emancipated. He who sells himself enters into an illusory agreement with his purchaser; for thereby he loses all his value. At the moment when he receives the price and the money become the property of the buyer. The very act of selling yourself, vitiates the bargain. He who sells himself is a fool, not a slave.

"'But those slaves were taken in war, and but for us would have been slaughtered.'

"'But for you would there have been fighting? Are not the dissensions of those tribes your work? Did you not carry to them murderous arms? Did you not give them the blind desire to employ them? And why did you not allow the conqueror to use his victory as he pleased? Why become his accomplice?

" 'But they were criminals condemned to death or slavery in their own country.' Are you, then, Africa's executioners. Besides, who were their judges? Do you not know that under a despotism there is only one criminal—the despot himself? The subject of a despot, like the slave, is in a condition contrary to nature. Whatever contributes to retain man in that condition, is a crime against his person. Every hand which binds man to the tyranny of a single person, is the hand of an enemy. Do you wish to know who are the authors and accomplices of this violence? Those who are around it. The tyrant can do nothing by himself.

" 'But they are happier in America than they were in Africa.' Why, then, do they continually sigh for their native land? Why do they resume their liberty as soon as they can? Why do they prefer deserts and the society of wild beasts, to a state which appears to you so agreeable? Why does their despair induce them to put an end to themselves, or to poison you? Why do their wives so often procure abortion? When you tell us of the happiness of your slaves, you lie to yourselves, and you deceive us. It is the height of extravagance to attempt to transform so barbarous an act into an act of humanity. [Page 35] " 'But in Europe as in America the people are slaves. The sole advantage which we have over the negroes is the power of breaking one chain to fall under another.' Too true. Most nations are oppressed. Scarcely is there a country in which a man can flatter himself with being master of his person, of disposing of his inheritance at his will, of enjoying peaceably the fruits of his industry. But as morality and wise polity shall make progress, men will recover their rights. Why, in waiting for the happy day, should there be miserable races to whom you refuse even the consoling and honourable name of *free men;* from whom you snatch even the hope of obtaining it, notwithstanding the changeableness of events? No, whatever may be said, the condition of those unfortunate beings is not the same as ours.

"The last argument employed to justify slavery says, that 'slavery is the only way of conducting the negroes to eternal blessedness by means of Christian baptism.'

"Mild and loving Jesus! could you have foreseen that your benign maxims would be employed to justify so much horror? If the Christian religion thus authorized avarice in governments, it would be necessary for ever to proscribe its dogmas. In order to overturn the edifice of slavery, to what tribunal shall we carry the cause of humanity? Kings, refuse the seal of your authority to the infamous traffic which converts men into beasts. But what do I say? Let us look somewhere else. If self-interest alone prevails with nations and their masters, there is another power. Nature speaks in louder tones than philosophy or self-interest. Already are there established two colonies of fugitive negroes, whom treaties and power protect from assault. Those lightnings announce the thunder. A courageous chief only is wanted. Where is he? that great man whom Nature owes to her vexed, oppressed, and tormented children. Where is he? He will appear, doubt it not; he will come forth, and raise the sacred standard of liberty. This venerable signal will gather around him the companions of his misfortune. More impetuous than the torrents, they will everywhere leave the indelible traces of their just resentment. Everywhere people will bless the name [Page 36] of the hero, who shall have re-established the rights of the human race; everywhere will they raise trophies in his honour."*

These eloquent words must have produced a deep and pervading impression on a mind so susceptible as that of Toussaint. Here reason and feeling were harmonized into one awful appeal. Here philosophy joined with common sense and common justice, to proclaim negro wrongs, and to call for a negro vindicator. That call Toussaint heard; he heard its voice in his inmost soul; he heard it there first in low reverberations; he heard it there at last in sounds of thunder. Dwelling on those principles, pondering those words, consulting his own heart, and reflecting on his own condition, he came in time to feel that *he* was the man here designated, and that

---

* Vol. III. p. 193-205. Some parts which breathe too much the spirit of revenge have been softened or omitted in the translation.

in the designation there was a call from Providence which he dared not disregard. But the time was not yet. Conviction must wait on opportunity. Besides, Toussaint was a religious man. Religion was his highest law. In one sense religion was his only law, for it comprehended every other form of law. What said religion? Read again, noble black; read with your own eyes; read the Bible for yourself and by yourself. Yes, if you will, consult the priest; but in retiring from the confessional, let Raynal's words echo in your ears, and fear lest you betray Christianity, even while striving to learn and obey its law.

CHAPTER V.

Toussaint's presumed scriptural studies—The Mosaic code—Christian principles adverse to slavery—Christ, Paul, the Epistle to Philemon.

IT is not to be supposed that Toussaint read the sacred Scriptures with a critical eye. Unversed in the science of Biblical interpretation, he could do no more than receive such impressions as certain great outstanding facts were fitted to produce. Nor, [Page 37] however valuable for its own purposes a scientific acquaintance with the Divine Word may be, did he need more than he and every other sensible person could gather from the general tenour and prominent aims of the Bible. There might even be particular passages which he was unable to comprehend in the harmony of scriptural truth, and a religious disputant might have found no great difficulty in presenting to his mind considerations wearing on the surface an appearance adverse to his general convictions. But those convictions would rest on such broad and deep foundations, and occupy in his mind so large a space; they would in themselves be so full, and so vivid, and so far-reaching, that as he reflected on them more and more, and they thus became an integral element in his mind, he could in no way doubt that slavery was disallowed by the Bible, and was adverse to the genius, the aims, and the operation of the Gospel.

Slavery, it is true, he found in the Scriptures. But how? Not as an institution of Divine origin. Moses found slavery in common practice; and unable to abolish it, did his best to mitigate its evils. And the system of servitude which he left rather than sanctioned, involved none of those atrocities which make American slavery so offensive and so baneful. The aim and tendency of slavery among the Hebrews, was the improvement of such as were under the yoke. Being of foreign extraction for the most part, slaves were permitted to enter 'the commonwealth of Israel,' by undergoing the distinctive rite of circumcision. (Gen. xvii. 23, 27.) Thus raised from a slave into a Hebrew, the slave had before him a brightening future, and could share in the privilege, and partake of the advantages, of worshipping the Creator of heaven and earth. Like England, Canaan was a land of refuge for slaves. The moment they touched that sacred soil they were free. Fugitive slaves could in no wise by delivered up to their masters, nor might they be reduced into bondage by Israelites. They chose their own residence, and followed their own pursuits. (Deut. xxiii. 16, *et seq.*) Expressly was it forbidden that a Hebrew should sell himself to a fellow-Hebrew as a bond-servant, and if one Hebrew hired himself to another Hebrew, he with his children obtained [Page 38] his liberty unconditionally at the end of six years at the furthest, or at the jubilee next ensuing after his service began. (Lev. xxv. 39, 40.) And he might be redeemed at an earlier day by either himself or a relative. (Lev. xxv. 48, 49.) Even thieves, who, when detected, were, in consequence of not being able to make compensation, put into servitude to Israelites, benefited by the laws regarding emancipation. As it was not permitted to send back or enslave a fugitive slave of foreign blood, so was it unlawful to sell a Hebrew to a foreign master. (Exod. xxi. 7—11)

These facts are the more striking, when we take into account the general practice of the slave trade in the ancient Eastern world. Egypt, which lay on the borders of Palestine, was a great slave mart. The long sea-board of Palestine afforded peculiar facilities for the detestable traffic. Streams of wealth would have poured into the land, had Israel encouraged the trade. The temptation was great. But religion was too strong for cupidity, and the people of God disallowed the commerce in human flesh generally, and modified their prescriptive usages so as to abate the evils and diminish the observance of slavery in their own territories.

Among the mitigations of their lot guaranteed to slaves by Moses were the following:—1. Entire rest from labour every seventh day. (Exod. xx. 10.) Noble recognition of man's religious nature and religious wants! 2. Immunity from deadly or cruel punishments. If a servant lost an eye or a tooth from a blow given by his master, he was thereon rendered free; if a slave died under a master's hand, the master underwent due retribution. (Exod. xxi. 20, *et seq.*) When advocates of slavery as it is in the United States cite in argument the Mosaic institutions, they would do well to give special attention to these merciful regulations. 3. Slaves were to join the Hebrew family in their rejoicings on occasions of religious festivity. (Deut. xii. 12, 18; xvi.

11, 14.) 4. Slaves recovered their freedom in the year of jubilee, and the bondman was not to go away with empty hands: "Thou shalt furnish him liberally our of thy flock, and out of thy flour, and out of thy winepress." The reason assigned is forcible; "Thou shalt remember that thou wast a bondman in [Page 39] the land of Egypt, and the Lord thy God redeemed thee. (Deut. xv. 13 *et seq.*; compare Exod. xxi. 2—4.) 5. A servant might not wish to leave his master's house; having been treated well, he had formed attachments and become one of the family: "If, therefore, he shall plainly say, I love my master, I will not go out free, then shall his master bring him unto the judges;" and his will being ascertained by a judicial investigation, he was permitted to remain in his own freely-chosen condition of domestic servitude. (Exod. xxi. 5, 6.) 6. A Hebrew bondsman was allowed to acquire and hold property, with which he might purchase his freedom. (Lev. xxxv. 49.) 7. If a master had no sons, a Hebrew slave might aspire to his daughter's hand. (I Chron. ii., 35.)*

On reviewing the features of the Mosaic slave code, could Toussaint for a moment identify its provisions with the *Code Noir* of Louis XIV., or with the system practised in Hayti? The contrast was too evident. Then did Toussaint see a slave, in some happy year of jubilee, going forth from bondage with a liberal supply from his master's flock, his master's barn, and his master's wine-cellar? Did he himself ever even think of asking for the hand, not of his master's daughter, but of his master's steward's daughter? Did he ever witness even a slave-driver punished for cruelly treating a slave? Could he point to a neighbouring land whose very air gave a slave his freedom the moment he breathed it? Did Spanish Hayti refuse to deliver up fugitive slaves to French Hayti, and did French Hayti refuse to deliver up fugitive slaves to Spanish Hayti?

But, it is objected, Christianity finding slavery in existence, did not proscribe it. Christianity did more than proscribe slavery—it undermined slavery; and wherever it prevailed in deed rather than profession, it brought slavery to the ground. The objection, if rightly stated, is this, and nothing more—namely, that the original promulgators of the Gospel did not commence an active and open crusade against slavery. The reason is, that they had an object before them higher than any immediate good. They waged

---

* Consult under the word bondage, "The People's Dictionary of the Bible," 2 vols. 8vo., third Edition, by the author.

no war against Roman despotism. They left, even on [Page 40] their native hills, the degenerate family of Herod in undisturbed possession of power. Their mission was not to remodel institutions, but to reform society. Their work was not to reap a premature and perishing harvest, but to sow the seed of quickening principles and imperishable sympathies. Disregarding thrones, principalities, and dominions, they went forth to preach the word of a new individual life, well aware that the acorn, in due time, would become an oak. Nor were their efforts nugatory. Within three centuries slavery was abolished in the Roman empire. And at this moment—such is the extensive and ever-living power of the Gospel—slavery, throughout the world, is tottering to its fall.

But chiefly, when he meditated on the words and the objects of the Saviour of the world, did Toussaint feel how incompatible slavery was with Christianity. Had he not, in those impressive words, "where the Spirit of the Lord is there is liberty." (2 Cor. iii. 17,) found the enunciation of a great Christian principle, and the announcement of a great Christian power, which must of necessity, as it was designed, break asunder every outward bond and emancipate every slave on earth? And in what terms did the Lord himself announce his mission? Toussaint, in thought, made one of his auditors in that small synagogue at Nazareth, where the Redeemer of men astounded his townsfolk and relatives by declaring, in words of the widest import, as he ushered in the grand spiritual jubilee, and so gave to all the subjects of His new kingdom liberty of body in giving them liberty of soul: "The Spirit of Jehovah is upon me, because He hath anointed me to preach glad tidings to the poor, He hath sent me to declare *deliverance to the captives,* and recovery of sight to the blind; to set at liberty those that are oppressed; to proclaim the acceptable year of Jehovah." "To-day is this Scripture fulfilled in your ears." (Luke iv. 18, *et seq.*) Unmistakable must Toussaint have found the import of these words. The great year of jubilee had come—the slave was free—slavery was abolished; not only that corporeal slavery which Moses tolerated, but the heavier slavery; which man, in consequence of sin, endured;— slavery of soul and, consequently, slavery of body was abrogated and destroyed. The blow [Page 41] was struck, and the dark edifice would inevitably fall. How could Toussaint hear from the lips of Christ himself that he came expressly to deliver the captive, and set the oppressed at liberty, without feeling that if he yielded to the grand thought which already swelled his breast, and became the liberator of the negro race, he would thereby be not a follower only, but a fellow-worker with "the Lord from heaven?" How could he learn, on infallible authority, that God, who had "made of one blood all nations," (Acts xvii. 26,) had, in his Son, opened and proclaimed the year of universal jubilee, and therefore, inaugurated the period of universal emancipation; and yet, with his convictions and sympathies, fail to conclude that on him too had, by the hand of Providence, been devolved a share in the truly religious task of liberating and upraising a cruelly oppressed and deeply injured tribe?

If from the Master, Toussaint turned to the greatest of his disciples, and asked Paul what, on this point, were the principles of the religion of Jesus, he learned that while the apostle urged no one in actual circumstances to hurry from the condition in which he was born, and judged that it was better to endure wrong than prematurely, and to the peril of the cause of Christ, disturb existing relations, and thereby convulse society already fearfully agitated, yet he recognised as equally members of the Christian church, and accessible to the same rights, immunities, and privileges, the bond and the free; (2 Cor. xii. 13;) and viewing the whole of human kind as divided into these two classes—in their high relations to God arid Christ and each other, declared that all outward distinctions had ceased, and must practically, in time, come to an end, for that there was no longer bond or free, any more than Barbarian or Scythian, but all were "one in Christ Jesus." (Gal. iii. 28; Col. iii. 11.) What! could the glowing terms in which the apostle—returning again and again to the subject, as if his soul was on fire with the thought—sets forth not only the equality of all the tribes of earth, but their essential unity;—could those terms be heard by the Roman slave in the primitive church, and not make his bosom swell and glow with the idea that he too was a man, that he too was free, that he too was comprehended [Page 42] in "the redemption which was in Christ Jesus?" And that idea once deep in his bosom, the rupture of his material bonds was merely an affair of time. Men, who know that they are *men*, cannot long be hold in bondage. Conscious children of God will not be slaves to selfish and brutal men. Those who feel that they have been purchased by Christ, the Son of God, may indeed "bide their time," but cannot be permanently held in the degrading and polluting condition of slavery. Yes, wisely for your own bad purposes, do ye, slave masters, keep the light of divine truth from your unhappy victims, or permit them to see it only through the discolouring medium of a ministration which stoops to make a gain of godliness; wisely for your own purposes do ye keep the Bible a scaled book on your plantations, or set hirelings to pervert its glorious and emancipating tidings; for otherwise your dominion would be shorter than in God's providence it is intended to be. But the day cometh; "the Lord is at hand."

You point me to the conduct of Paul? You tell me that Paul sent back Onesimus into slavery? You ask me if Toussaint in his scriptural studies comprised the Epistle to Philemon? and you triumphantly intimate that, by that example, his emancipating ardour ought to have been checked. I reply that the Epistle to Philemon is a plea against slavery; that if Toussaint comprehended what he read, he would thereby be greatly confirmed and built up in his righteous and most Christian purposes; and that if your own eyes were only free from the scales of prejudice and mistaken self-interest, they too would discern, in that letter, principles which are utterly inconsistent with the continuance of the abominable system of which you are the supporters.

The Epistle of Paul to Philemon is the most pregnant of compositions. Never was so much meaning compressed into so few words. And then, how weighty the topics. How much of doctrine is there in those few verses; how much of history. And the doctrine and the history are so presented, that while you cannot deny the history, you are encouraged to receive the doctrine. The letter is a series of implications;—implied facts, [Page 43] implied principles, implied duties, implied changes and triumphs, set forth in all the unconscious simplicity of a private and confidential communication, so as to conciliate attention and win belief. I hold this short Epistle to be of itself an antidote to scepticism and a confutation of slavery.

The letter, I have intimated, is a series of implications. It is also a group of pictures. First mark that fugitive slave hurrying from Colossæ, in Asia Minor, down to the shores of the Mediterranean sea. What a fell expression of countenance he has, as of one who, if well-endowed by nature, had been made bad by servitude, and who had had long and varied practice in misdoing. How stealthy are his steps, how clownish, yet how timid his manner! Ever and anon he casts back his anxious eyes as if he feared pursuit, and from the face of every one whom he encounters, he turns away, as if he dreaded to be recognised. At last, reaching the sea, he hastens on shipboard, and concealing himself in the most secret part of the vessel, effects his escape, and is carried to Rome,—that city which the greatest of ancient historians has described as the common sink of the world.*

Let a few years pass, and you may see the same person on his way back from Rome to Asia Minor and Colossæ. No longer do his movements betray fear. No longer does his countenance betoken ferocity. His steps are equable and firm. His manner discloses self-respect. He is returning with as much composure as determination, and on his way be receives and returns greetings with gentleness and confidence, as if he feared none, and wished to be friendly with all. And now that he is again on ship-board, mark how pure and refined is the expression of his face, how manly his whole bearing, as, no longer shunning the light, he walks up and down the deck, and has a good word for every one. Is this indeed the same person? It is Onesimus, the runaway slave. And he is going back to his master of his own accord. Yes, hundreds of miles does he travel on foot and [Page 44] by sea in order to return into bondage. Observe, he is unaccompanied. He is unmanacled; not by force, but by his own free will, is he led back to his proprietor Philemon in Colossæ.

Whence these changes? In order to understand them, you must form to yourselves another picture. There, in a small house in that narrow and secluded street of Rome, you behold an aged man, bound with a chain to that pretorian soldier, under whose custody he is night and day. That aged man is Paul the apostle of Jesus Christ; there, in that corrupt and guilty city, to answer, at the peril of his life, for daring to offer the Gospel to his countrymen in Jerusalem. Mean in person, and rude in speech, he has nevertheless preached Christ crucified with great success to the citizens. But he is oppressed with infirmities. His numerous sufferings, his long journeys, his ceaseless labours, have reduced him to that state of bodily endurance. And glad and thankful is he for humane attentions and ministries of Christian love. In that sacred work Onesimus has been engaged. Found by Paul,—and found, it may be, when the fugitive was in sickness,— he was taken to the apostle's own abode, and there cared for in mind as well as in body, until he came to possess both the ability and the will to make a return in kind to his apostolic benefactor. The reciprocation of kind offices begat mutual attachment. Learning to love the preacher, Onesimus

---

* TAC. ANN, XV. 44. QUO CUNCTA UNDIQUE ATROCIA AUT PUDENDA CONFLUUNT, CELEBRANTURQUE.

learned also to love and to espouse his doctrine. Now, therefore, is he a Christian,—a member of Christ's spiritual body, and a sharer with Paul himself in "the liberty wherewith Christ hath made him free." (Gal. v. 1.) So intimate do the two friends become, that the elder regards the younger as his "son," while the younger, loving and respecting the elder as his father, is as ready to obey as he is glad to serve him. But mark, as they sit there in that humble apartment, earnestly conversing with each other, mark the cloud that has fallen on the countenance of Onesimus. It is heavy and deep. In a moment it has disappeared. "You must return to Philemon." These are the words which darkened that face. "Return into chains? horrible." Shortly afterwards Onesimus is on the road.

They are great changes with which we have to do in this group of events. At the time of the publication of the Gospel, [Page 45] slavery was universal. Philemon, a prominent and zealous member of the church at Colossæ, held a slave by name Onesimus. Having served his master badly, Onesimus ran away. But now of his own free will he is going back into bondage. This is the first great change. Ah, how many a footstep must he set between Rome and Colossæ, and for every footstep there was an act of the will. Every act of the will said, "return to servitude." Yet the will never faltered, and the slave's own feet brought him into the house of Philemon. But what reception might he meet with there? There would be the jeers and jibes of fellow slaves to endure. There were past neglects and misdeeds to atone for. There was an injured and an offended master to encounter. Nevertheless, of his own accord, Onesimus returns. At the first appearance, this would appear the height of folly. Masters held the power of life and death over their slaves. Onesimus had everything to fear. On what does he rely? Has be no safeguard? He has a few lines written by a poor decrepid man hundreds of miles distant. Is that all? That is all. But it is enough; Onesimus knows that it is enough. What a wonder-working power is writing! We have read of charms, magical forms, and incantations; we have read of them, and of the powers they were said to possess. But even their fancied efficacy has in it nothing surpassing the efficacy of these few Greek characters written by Paul and borne by Onesimus. Guards, prisons, and chains—they are of less potency than words. Onesimus eluded the former, and goes back under the influence of the latter. These words, a token of the apostle's will, conduct Onesimus back and protect him from the natural consequences of Philemon's wrath. Such is the sovereignty of thought. A morsel— so to say—of Paul's mind, acts with supreme control beyond lands and seas.

But the return indicates another great change. If, now, Onesimus sets his face towards the east, it is because his heart is changed. In a change of the affections, is found the cause of that change of his will. This is, indeed, a great change—a fugitive slave willingly goes back to bondage. There is no compulsion: there can be no compulsion. No spies, no catchpoles are [Page 46] at work. No law in Rome compels the emperor to apprehend and restore to the Colossians any of their slaves that might seek shelter in the metropolis of the world. Though slavery then prevailed throughout society, legislation had not reached the height of wickedness which compels the freeman to be a police-officer to the slaveholder. In safety, and perhaps in prosperity, might Onesimus have remained in Rome. But no! a power stronger than the imperial power itself, sends him back. Go he must, go he will, and go he does. Why? he must put that right which he left wrong; he had injured his master, he must make him compensation. And though in the matter of right, Onesimus belonged to himself and not to Philemon, yet, as the law recognised the institution of slavery, and every Christian ought to avoid even the appearance of evil, so would Onesimus return to Philemon in order to adjust their relations one with another. Those relations had assumed a new aspect. The two persons who had known each other only as master and slave, were now in Christ "brothers beloved." And as Christians, they recognised a higher law than the world's—a law which rendered slavery impossible, but which also commanded each to do unto others as he would be done unto. Relying on the former, and acting on the latter, hoping to be set at liberty, yet believing it his duty to give Philemon an opportunity of declaring his emancipation, Onesimus has set his feet within his master's home. This, I repeat, is indeed a great change. The fugitive is the returning slave, because the slave has become a Christian. And the Christian so highly values moral obligations, that in the thought of his duties he almost forgets his rights, and at least is as regardful of the legal claims of his master, as he is of his own natural and indefeasible privileges.

Onesimus, I have intimated, regarded the legal claims of Philemon. There is no evidence that either Onesimus or Paul recognised any other claim. It was the general practice of the first disciples to pay obedience to the then existing civil laws.

This respect for existing institutions, however, was merely outward and temporary. Having its origin in prudential consideration, it came to an end as soon as duty could safely supersede [Page 47] expediency. Meanwhile, it implied at the bottom a disallowal of existing evils, and a determination to take the most effectual course for their abatement and removal. Tolerating slavery because it wished to take safe steps for rendering slavery impossible, it in reality hated the abomination of property in man's body and soul, and was ever silently at work to convert the slave into a man, and so to break the yoke and set the captive free. That this was the view under which Paul acted, is obvious from the language he employs in his Letter to Philemon:—

In that Letter there is first the distinct assertion of a right. It is the right of Paul to claim the freedom of Onesimus. On what was that right founded? On Christ. Paul, Philemon, and Onesimus were in Christ partners, they were sharers of a common Gospel, such is the meaning of the term "partner," employed by Paul in the 17th verse. As having, in common, "the redemption that was in Christ Jesus," they were alike free. Onesimus, as a Christian, was as free as Philemon, and both were equally free with Paul. Onesimus, in consequence, had a claim to be pronounced free. And that claim Paul was at full liberty to urge on Philemon.

I make this statement on the authority of the apostle's own words, as they are found in the 8th verse of the epistle; "though I might be much bold in Christ to enjoin thee that which is convenient." This, the English version, very imperfectly represents the original. "Convenient," is a most inadequate expression, at least in the sense in which it is now understood. Convenient with us signifies that which is easy and pleasant, rather than that which is obligatory; that which is suitable to the occasion, rather than conformable to the everlasting laws of right. The Greek word used by Paul, however, denotes that which is fit and proper, and in the third chapter of the Epistle to the Colossians, v. 18, it is rendered by the English term *fit*. "Wives, submit yourselves unto your own husbands, as *it is fit* in the Lord." That, in this injunction, the apostle spoke of duty, of Christian obligation, and not of any temporary expediency, is clear from the corresponding passage in his Letter to the Ephesians, v. 22, where he says, "Wives, submit yourselves unto your [Page 48] own husbands as unto the Lord." It is, then, an obligation, a Christian obligation, which Paul had the right to urge on Philemon. And this right he intimates he might freely urge. It was a manifest right; a right about which there could be no dispute between Christians; a right which the apostle was justified in urging boldly, nay, very boldly; for thus, when exactly translated, do his words run—"having much boldness in Christ, to enjoin on thee that which is proper." Observe the term "enjoin,"—it is duties that are enjoined, not expediency. The act as described in the Greek [epsilon, pi, iota, tau, alpha, sigma, sigma, epsilon, iota, upsilon] is the act of a superior—of a general who gives a command, of a governor who issues a decree. The imperial power of duty it was, which was in the writer's mind. As an inspired expounder of Christian rights and duties, Paul declares that he might, with full freedom of speech, require Philemon to declare Onesimus free. But he would take a milder— perhaps, for his purpose, a more effectual course; the assertion of rights sometimes revolts the wrong-doer. Certainly it would be more considerate, more kind, more Christian-like, to give Philemon the opportunity of doing what was right of his own accord, from his own sense of justice, from his own recognition of Christian principles; and therefore—to use Paul's own words— "yet for loves sake I rather beseech thee," (v, 9,) "for without thy mind would I do nothing; that thy benefit should not be as it were of necessity, but willingly." (v. 14.) "No; do you by your own act pronounce his freedom, not as if constrained by duty enforced by me, but as prompted by Christian principle and Christian love, abounding in your own heart."

Besides this unquestionable right which is not disallowed, but kindly thrown into the background, there is also in the Epistle the pleading of a claim grounded on the implication of a right. The claim is that of Onesimus who has a right to freedom. That claim and that right are now rather implied and intimated than declared. There is a sort of tacit appeal to principles recognised in common by the three persons concerned. Those principles are Christian principles. They are quietly put forth in the words, "Receive him for ever, not now as a servant, [Page 49] but above a servant,—a brother beloved." Observe here how adroitly Christian principles are insinuated. "Not now as a servant, but a brother." The original is yet more forcible—"no longer as a servant." No! no longer; the slave is a slave no more; in becoming a Christian, he has become a man; and your relation as well as his is changed; no more master as he is no more slave. So are both brothers. The same great fact is intimated in the words "for ever," "that thou shouldest receive him for ever." The bond which binds beloved brethren is not liable to be disturbed by quarrels or broken by flight; it is durable, it is everlasting, it is as permanent as life, as long as eternity. And those who are linked together by spiritual bonds are not masters and slaves, but citizens of the commonwealth of God, and joint-heirs with the saints in light. A higher relation has come and dissolved the lower, as the sun melts the snow on the mountains; "above a slave, a brother." And mark with what emphasis the apostle adds to this claim of brotherhood; "a brother beloved," "beloved specially to me," yea, "how much more unto thee?" What, this fugitive slave exceedingly loved by his injured master? Yes, "both in the flesh and in the Lord;"—in the flesh, because in the Lord, the slave loved because in becoming a Christian he had become a man, and because in his new relation, and in its moral consequences, Onesimus, slave by law as he still was, possessed the highest title to Philemon's regard. Surely these are views which dissolve slavery as with the breath of the mouth of the Lord. And with views such as these, Paul doubtless had the firmest confidence that Philemon would set Onesimus free. Free indeed Onesimus was in the court of conscience with both Paul and Philemon. It only remained for the latter to pronounce him free. How then has it come to pass that advocates for slavery have ventured to plead the example of the apostle Paul, saying, "Did not Paul send Onesimus back into slavery?" No! he sent him back to claim and to receive his freedom. It is true, however, that the apostle, like "a wise master builder," was careful to avoid giving offence to Philemon, and did his best by gentle and soothing words to conciliate his favour. Slavery advocates have mistaken this [Page 50] Christian consideration for the concession of a right. But in the consideration the right is virtually denied, what occasion for consideration was there if the right was admitted? We are considerate of the feelings of others when we impeach their claims, not when we concede them. In truth, Paul well knew that Philemon had the law on his side, and though Paul had a confidence that Philemon would not throw Onesimus back into chains, he could not be absolutely sure that the Christian would prevail over the slave-master, therefore he resolved to deal with the utmost delicacy with Philemon. He must avoid giving him pain. He must avoid arousing his prejudices. He must make the past calm, in order that the present might be bright; consequently, he puts that as an act of kindness on the part of Philemon which he might have required of him as a duty. "Onesimus," he in effect says, "Onesimus is free, for he is a Christian man; Onesimus is free, for he is beyond your reach, and desirous am I to retain his services, for of value are they to me; but without your mind I would do nothing; let his emancipation be your own good act: better were it so than that of necessity you should be compelled to forego his labour. I send him to you, therefore, in order that as a Christian you may perform your duty, and that as a man you may have the credit of declaring a fellow-man no longer a slave. Over past injuries throw the veil of Christian love. If you hesitate to forgive them, set them down to my account. I will assume the obligation. You are, you know, deeply in my debt, for your religion you owe to me; nay, your very self; what you are I have made you. Well, then, draw up a statement of debtor and creditor,—on the one side put what you owe me, on the other, put what Onesimus owes you. The totals shall balance each other, though your obligations are far greater than mine. And that the rather, because as being my son in Christ, you are bound to do more than repay me; you are bound to give me joy of you in the Lord, to let me have the pleasure of witnessing how Christian principles prevail in your life,—but I say no more, I need say no more. Having confidence in thy obedience, I have written unto thee, knowing also [Page 51] that thou wilt do more than I say." (21.) Yes, there is the ground on which Paul acted. He had confidence that Philemon would obey his injunction,—an injunction all the more imperative on a good man and a brother, because rather intimated than obtruded, and because surrounded with all the courtesy of that Christian charity which thinketh no evil, and hopeth all things. Whether duty was regarded by Philemon in its bare and severe aspect, or in the claims of brotherly love, or in the claims of that special love and gratitude which Philemon owed to Paul, alike in each case, and by the united force of all, Philemon, Paul was assured, would feel himself under the most sacred obligations to perform a formal act of emancipation on behalf of Onesimus.

Send Onesimus back into slavery? Paul sent him back into the warm embrace of a brother's love. He had confidence in that brother, because he was a brother. He believed that that brother would do even more than Christian duty required. Yes, he was of opinion that Philemon would not only emancipate Onesimus, but treat him as "a brother beloved." The example of Paul and Philemon? O yes! would that it were followed. Plead it, ye advocates of slavery; plead it, and do more than plead it, make it the model of your own conduct. To what is it that ye send back the slave? Not to a loving brother, but to a hard taskmaster; not to a happy home, but a dungeon and stripes; not to Christian freedom, but to heathen bondage and brutish toil, licentiousness, and degradation.

The epistle of Paul to Philemon, then, is a plea on behalf of emancipation, on behalf of human rights, on behalf of Christian, and as Christian, so civil and personal freedom. The gospel unbars prison doors, and strikes off the slave's chains. "The spirit of the Lord," swells the frame and bursts the bonds, as with Samson, when he threw off the Philistine cords, "and the Spirit of the Lord came mightily upon him, and the cords that were upon his arms became as flax that was burnt with fire, and his bands were melted from off his hands." (Judg, xv. 14.) With true Christianity, bondage is incompatible; the two cannot [Page 52] co-exist. The one destroys the other; the one displaces the other as much and as effectually as the light disperses the darkness and occupies its place.

If, then, the spirit of Christ is in our hearts, we are friends of liberty,—liberty of all kinds, and for "all orders and degrees of men;" liberty for the slave, liberty for the citizen, liberty for wife, children, and domestic. O the glorious liberty of the sons of God! O the divine citizenship of the kingdom of heaven! In the great spiritual commonwealth of Christ is the communion of saints instead of the interchange of injustice; the sweet harmonies of Christian love instead of the harsh wranglings of rival claims; the gentle ministries of mutual aid, instead of arbitrary requirements and grudging services. Oh! when shall that kingdom come? come everywhere?

This question Toussaint asked himself. The latter end of his life gives the reply of his heart. Satisfied by his religious studies that slavery was incompatible with the Gospel, he resolved to do what in him lay to annihilate slavery in his own vicinity. But the work was too important to be rashly undertaken, and Paul's prudence, and the prudence of the primitive church at large, taught him that patience and discretion were virtuous as well as desirable. He would therefore wait his opportunity. True, years passed away, and mature life threatened to wane. Yet, in so arduous and perilous a task, where one failure was irretrievable ruin, even long delay was preferable to precipitation.

CHAPTER VI.

Immediate causes of the rising of the blacks—Dissensions of the planters—Spread of anti-slavery opinions in Europe—The outbreak of the first French Revolution—Mulatto war—Negro insurrection—Toussaint protects his master and mistress, and their property.

WHILE Toussaint was pursuing a course of reading and meditation which was to conduct him in its issue to great achievements, the volcano of insurrection and mutual slaughter was preparing around [Page 53] him, the premonitions of which he was too sagacious not to discern. Hayti was prosperous. The masters daily grew more opulent on the produce of their plantations. The war of American independence made Hayti into a great commercial entrepôt, and largely augmented its wealth. Could the actual condition of the colony have been maintained, its riches would have

CAPE ST. FRANÇOIS.

continued to increase —and with its riches its voluptuousness. But already that very wealth had sown the seeds of disorder. The larger planters were too opulent and too powerful to be at peace with each other. There existed a rivalry between the two chief cities—the Cape and the Port-au-Prince. This rivalry was made more intense when, in 1787, the Superior Council of the Cape was suppressed, and its power transferred to the Council of Port-au-Prince, under the general designation of "the Superior Council of St. Domingo." Dissensions ensued, in which the west and the south soon took part. Appeal was made to France. The government listened, but gave no remedy. Recourse was had to indirect influence. Deputies were sent to Paris. Their activity called forth opposition on the part of the colonial proprietors who habitually resided in that metropolis; and they, carried away by the fashion of the hour, formed, for the furtherance of their views, a club called the Club Massaic—from the name of the hotel where the members assembled. Thus organized, they proceeded to withstand the deputies from Hayti—and specially strove to prevent their obtaining a hearing before the States General. The progress of events, however, creating a common alarm, the club united with the deputies in seeking the establishment of a Colonial Assembly. In this question, there was a new source of disagreement. What should be its constitution? Who should be its members? How should its members be elected? These debateable points occasioned long and disquieting discussions. The north and the west came again into collision, and the island was torn by discord. The great proprietors set the example of division and innovation. At no period could such an example have been more unseasonable. Throughout Europe there had spread and waxed strong a spirit of humanity, which denounced slavery and sought its abolition. In England and in [Page 54] France that generous spirit acquired immense social power. Then those philanthropists who acquired for themselves perpetual fame in proclaiming the rights of the slave, and procuring the abolition of the slave trade, Price, Priestly, Sharp, Clarkson, Wilberforce, began their generous and noble efforts. The society of "The Friends of the Blacks" was formed, and the stronghold of slavery was assailed in a manner which announced the certainty of its downfall.

Could the desire of these eminent men have prevailed, the contest would have been left exclusively to mental and moral resources. But the fermentation of the public mind in France, moved in its very depths by centuries of civil and ecclesiastical misrule and profligacy, provoked an appeal to the most violent of human passions and the most dreadful of human appliances. The oath of the Tennis Court and the taking of the Bastile commenced the battle of liberty against despotism. The announcement of these events in Hayti produced the greatest agitation. The existing discontents received fresh impulse. The planters hailed the revolution as a precursor of the independence of the colony. The officers of the government encouraged the dream of a counter-revolution. The *petits blancs,* intoxicated with enthusiastic sympathy, cheered and sustained the Parisian mobs, and hoped to pursue a similar course in the island. While the several classes of the whites were thus distracted, the mulattoes experienced the general excitement the more because they were watching their opportunity for self-liberation. As to the negroes, they in general pursued their wonted round of toil apparently, and for the most part really, indifferent to the social commotion. Certainly, among the agitated parties, no one thought of their emancipation. The factions were intent only on their several interests. The colonists wanted at least an increase of their power. The men of colour sought to raise themselves to an equality with the colonists. If these selfish views required a covering, the veil was found in the claim of sameness of privileges for all free men. The black was too much despised to be thought of by the colonial combatants.

[Page 55] The first marked effort was made by the mulattoes, and so the first contest was a contest for the attainment of mulatto interests. A deputation of men of colour was sent to Paris. Eager to promote the views of their caste, they presented six millions of francs for the service of the state, and offered the fifth of their property in mortgage of the national debt. They asked in return that they should in all things be put on a footing of equality with the whites, whom they alleged they equalled in number, and with whom they partook all the territorial and commercial wealth of the colony. The president of the Assembly replied, that "No part of the French nation should in vain claim rights at the hands of the representatives of the French people."

At the same time there took place in the Assembly a discussion respecting the servitude of the blacks. The entire nation seemed to have made the question its own; and a distinguished member of the legislature uttered these bold and disinterested words: "I am one of the greatest proprietors of St. Domingo; but I declare to you, that were I to loose all I possess there, I would make the sacrifice rather than disown the principles which justice and humanity have consecrated; I declare for both the admission into the administrative assemblies (of the colony) of men of colour, and the liberation of the blacks." This famous declaration made by Lameth produced an immense effect; it astounded the great planters, and filled them with distrust and hatred against the men of colour. That adverse feeling manifested itself in the execution at the Cape of the mulatto Lacombe, whose only crime was the affixing of his signature to a petition, in which he claimed the rights of man. The mulattoes of Petit Goave had addressed to the electoral assembly of the west of Hayti a petition in which they humbly requested, not equality of rights, but merely some improvements in their condition. Those who had put their names to the entreaty were all apprehended, and the person who drew it up, Ferrand de Baudière, though reputed a just and wise man, and though he had been high in office, was, with only the forms of a trial, hurried into the hands of the executioner, in spite of the efforts made to save him by [Page 56] the colonial government. While these and other displays of hope on the one side and jealousy and fear on the other, were taking place, a decree of the French Legislature (8th of March, 1790) arrived in the colony, which, founded on broad principles of justice, gave the men of colour the right to enter the colonial assemblies. The Haytian representatives, just constituted under the orders of Louis XVI., and assembled at Saint-Marc, with the title of "General Assembly," before they proceeded to any other business, formally declared that all the whites would die rather than share political rights with "a bastard and degenerate race." Moreover, they proclaimed themselves the sole legal and legitimate representatives of the colony, and disallowed the authority of the Governor-General, whose power emanated from the French government, merely consenting to submit their decrees for the royal sanction. By these and similar steps, the tendency of which was to concentrate all power in the hands of a portion of the resident planters, two authorities were set in operation, for the usurpations of the General Assembly compelled the Governor and the Superior Council of Port-au-Prince, in union with the Provincial Assembly of the North, to take measures of self-defence, and to maintain their position. A bitter contest ensued.

During the progress of these collisions, a new element of confusion intervened. Vincent Ogé, a man of colour, son of a wealthy butcher at the Cape, whom the mulattoes had sent to Paris, as one of their deputies, landed at Cap François, October 17th, 1790, under the name of Poissac, with the title of lieutenant-colonel, and the order of the Lion, which he had purchased of the prince of Limbourg; and having visited his mother, who lived in handsome style at Dondon, marched, in alliance with Chavanne, a man of his own caste, at the head of two hundred men to La Grande Rivière, in the department of the north. From the camp which he established there, he sent to the president of the Assembly of that department the following letter:—

[Page 57]"VINCENT OGÉ TO THE MEMBERS COMPOSING
THE PROVINCIAL ASSEMBLY OF THE CAPE.

"GENTLEMEN,
"A prejudice too long maintained, is about to fall. I am charged with a commission doubtless very honourable to myself. I require you to promulgate throughout the colony the instructions of the National Assembly of the 8th of March, which gives without distinction to all free citizens the right of admission to all offices and functions. My pretensions are just, and I hope you will pay due regard to them. I shall not call the plantations to rise; that means would be unworthy of me.

"Learn to appreciate the merit of a man whose intention is pure. When I solicited from the National Assembly a decree which I obtained in favour of the American colonists, formerly known under the injurious epithet of "men of mixed blood," I did not include in my claims the condition of the negroes who live in servitude. You and our adversaries have misrepresented my steps in order to bring me into discredit with honourable men. No, no, gentlemen! we have put forth a claim only on behalf of a class of freemen, who, for two centuries, have been under the yoke of oppression. We require the execution of the decree of the 8th of March. We insist on its promulgation, and we shall not cease to repeat to our friends that our adversaries are unjust, and that they know not how to make their interests compatible with ours. Before employing my means, I make use of mildness; but if, contrary to my expectation, you do not satisfy my demand, I am not answerable for the disorder into which my just vengeance may carry me."

Ogé was attacked by a force of six hundred men. The attack he repelled. The colonists sent another body of fifteen hundred men against him. Ogé was defeated and fled. He took refuge in the Spanish territories. His surrender was demanded from the Spanish authorities. Being delivered up, he was put on his trial. That trial, famous in the annals of Hayti, lasted two months. At last Ogé and his lieutenant, Chevanne, were condemned to be broken alive on the wheel, and their goods to be [Page 58] confiscated to the king. The sentence was immediately put into execution. Nevertheless the mulatto war was not brought to an end. On the contrary, the desire of ascendancy and the thirst for revenge became every day more and more intense.

Informed of the revolutionary proceedings of the Assembly of St. Marc, the authorities in the mother country declared what it had done null and void, divested its members of their authority, required a new election of deputies in their place, and sent two regiments of the line to carry their ordinances into execution. The mulattoes were enthusiastic with joy. The colonists repelled with indignation the thought of receiving men of colour as co-legislators with themselves. New risings took place, new conflicts ensued. The passions every day burned more fiercely, and while the mulattoes cherished boundless hopes, the whites, overflowing with indignation, put themselves in open revolt against the mother country, denying its prerogatives, and refusing the civic oath. In the midst of these thickening disorders, the planters resident in France were invited to return, and assist in vindicating the civil independence of the island. Then was it that the mulattoes appealed to the slaves. Terrible was the result. The slaves awoke as if from an ominous dream. Under one of their class, named Boukman, a man of Herculean strength, who knew not what danger was, the negroes on the night of August 21st, 1791, arose in the terrific power of brute force. Gaining immediate success, they rapidly increased in numbers, and grew hot with fury. They fell on the plantations, slaughtered their proprietors, and destroyed the property. Such progress did the insurrection make, that on the 26th, the third of the habitations of the Northern Department were in ashes. In a week from its commencement the storm had swept over the whole plain of the north, from east to west, and from the mountains to the sea. Those rich houses, those superb factories were in ruins. Conflagration raged everywhere. The mountains, covered with smoke and burning fragments, borne upwards by the wind, looked like volcanoes. The atmosphere, as if on fire, resembled a furnace. Everywhere were seen signs of devastation —demolished edifices, smouldering embers, scattered and [Page 59] broken furniture, plate, and other precious articles overlooked by the marauders; the soil running with blood, dead bodies heaped the one on the other, mangled and mutilated, a prey to voracious birds and beasts.* In proceedings so horrible, Toussaint could take no part. Faithful to his owner, he, during a whole month, protected the plantation, at the head of the negroes, whom he greatly contributed to keep in obedience, and prevented the insurgents from setting the fields of sugar-cane on fire. While all the whites were flying for their lives, and hurrying to find a shelter in the towns, Madame Bayou de Libertas, protected by Toussaint, remained in her own abode. The superintendent himself, who was in camp at Haut-du-Cap, not far from his plantation, safely ventured near every day, in order to keep up the vigilance of the slaves. His safety he owed to Toussaint, who, with inexpressible joy, saw Bayou among the negroes at a moment when a white skin insured instant death. Happy the slave-owner who, in such a crisis, has in his gang one who, like Toussaint, is a man and a Christian indeed. Having exerted every power to protect his mistress, assist his master, and defend the property, and seeing the insurrection becoming constantly more formidable, exhausted also by fatigue, Toussaint at length induced Madame de Bayou, whose life he knew was in danger, to quit Breda, and proceed to the Cape. In the absence of her husband he got the carriage ready, loaded it with articles of value, placed his mistress therein, and confided her to the care of his younger brother Paul. Nor was this the only service rendered to the family by their noble slave. One of the

---

* See Note B, at the end.

first uses which he made of the influence he acquired was to enable them to emigrate. While every white man and all he possessed were devoted to destruction, Bayou, with his family and a rich cargo, left Hayti and settled in the United States.[Page 60]

CHAPTER VII.

Continued collision of the planters, the mulattoes, and the negroes—The planters willing to receive English aid—The negroes espouse the cause of Louis XVI.—Arrival of Commissioners from France—Negotiations—Resumption of hostilities—Toussaint gains influence.

THE direful efficiency with which the negroes had devastated the country, indicated the presence among them of a skill superior to any they could possess. That skill was supplied by mulattoes, who organized the destroying bands and directed their movements. The "bastard and degenerate" race thus struck a deadly blow at their criminal parents.

During the progress of these furious excesses, a new general assembly of planters opened its sessions, under the title of "Colonial Assembly." Its first act was an act of rebellion. Refusing to apply to France for aid, and having taken measures of self-defence, it sought protection from England. These were the terms it employed in a letter addressed to the governor of Jamaica:—

Au Cap Français, August 24th, 1791.

"The General Assembly of the French part of St. Domingo, deeply affected by the calamities which desolate Saint Domingo, has resolved to send a deputation to your Excellency, in order to place before you a picture of the misfortunes which have fallen on this beautiful island; fire lays waste our possessions, the hands of our negroes in arms are already dyed with the blood of our brethren. Very prompt assistance is necessary to save the wreck of our fortunes—already half-destroyed; and confined within the towns, we look for your aid."

Without awaiting a reply, the General Assembly adopted the round English hat as the uniform of its troops, and substituted the black cockade for the French national colours.

[Page 61] The reply of the Governor, Lord Effingham, did not come up to the expectations of the planters; he merely sent five hundred muskets, with some ammunition, and commanded a vessel of fifty guns to cruise off the western coast.

Meanwhile the black insurgents, after augmenting their numbers by force as well as persuasion, placed themselves under the standard of royalty; they gave themselves the name of "The King's Own," and their leader, Jean-François, assumed the title of High-Admiral, while his second in command became Generalissimo of the conquered territories. Summoned to yield by Blanchelande, Governor of French Hayti, they replied,—

"SIR,—We have never thought of failing in the duty and respect which we owe to the representative of the person of the King, nor even to any of his servants whatever; we have proofs of the fact in our hands; but do you, who are a just man as well as a general, pay us a visit; behold this land which we have watered with our sweat—or rather, with our blood,—those edifices which we have raised, and that in the hope of a just reward! Have we obtained it? The King—the whole world—has bewailed our lot, and broken our chains; while, on our part, we, humble victims, were ready for anything, not wishing to abandon our masters. What do we say? We are mistaken; those who, next to God, should have proved our fathers, have been tyrants, monsters unworthy of the fruits of our labours: and do you, brave general, desire that as sheep we should throw ourselves into the jaws of the wolf? No! it is too late. God, who fights for the innocent, is our guide; he will never abandon us. Accordingly, this is our motto—*Death or Victory!* In order to prove to you, excellent sir, that we are not so cruel as you may think, we, with all our souls, wish for peace,—but on condition that all the whites, whether of the plain or of the mountains, shall quit the Cape without a single exception; let them carry with them their gold and their jewels, we seek only liberty,— dear and precious object! This, general, is our profession of faith; and this profession we will maintain to the last drop of [Page 62] our blood. We do not lack powder and cannons. Therefore, liberty or death! God grant that we may obtain freedom without the effusion of blood! Then all our desires will be accomplished; and believe it has cost our feelings very much to have taken this course. Victory or death for freedom!" This assumption of the part of Louis XVI. astounded and perplexed the planters. The fact, however, was only too plain. By means of the Spaniards of Hayti, the counter-revolutionary party in France gave secret support to the insurgents, if they did not also call them forth: and in order to impart feasibility and vigour to the movement, they gave out that the king's life had been put in danger by the whites, because he had resolved to emancipate the blacks. Strange reversals! While the colonists hoisted English colours, their slaves exhibited the white flag, with the words on one side *Long live the king;* and, on the other, *The ancient system of government.*

The insurrection proceeded; the negroes carried their arms from place to place, and subduing all the open country, reduced the colonists to the defensive. As the contest went on, horrors multiplied. The planters hung on trees and hedges the dead bodies of their black prisoners; the insurgents formed around their camp an enclosure, marked by the bleeding heads of those who fell under their hands. The fury of the negroes was stimulated by unworthy priests; but even religion was powerless when it endeavoured to place a barrier against tumultuous passion. A priest was hung on the spot for the crime of trying to protect innocent women from brutal violation.

The superior discipline at the command of the colonists, however, began to prevail. The negroes were checked, and driven back. Their bands were directed by three chiefs, Jean-François, Biassou, and Jeannot.

Jean-François belonged to a colonist of the name of Papillon. A young creole of good exterior, he had not been able to bear the yoke of slavery, though he had no special cause of complaint against his master; he had, long before the revolution, obtained his liberty. Flying from the plantation, he joined the maroons, [Page 63] or black fugitives, who wandered at large in the refuge of the mountains. He was naturally of a mild disposition, and inclined to clemency. If his career was stained by cruelties, the crime must be imputed to perfidious councils. Of no great courage, and little enterprise, he owed his command to his intellectual superiority.

Biassou belonged to the religious body designated "The Fathers of Charity." A contrast, in every respect, to Jean-François, he was fiery, rash, wrathful, and vindictive. Always in action, always on horseback, very suspicious, and very aspiring, he usurped the lead which the apathy of his principal almost let fall into his hands. Jean François loved luxury, fine clothes, and grand equipages; Biassou was given to women and drink.

Jeannot, a slave of the plantation of M. Bullet, was small and slender in person, and of boundless activity. Perfidious of soul, his aspect was frightful and revolting. Capable of the greatest crimes, he was inaccessible to regret and remorse. Having sworn implacable hatred against the whites, he thrilled with rage when he saw them; and his greatest pleasure was to bathe his hands in their blood. On his master's estate, the chief theatre of his crimes, he was sure, after committing a massacre, to gather up in his hands the blood which flowed on all sides, and carrying it to his mouth, was heard to exclaim—"Oh, my friends, how sweet—how good—this white blood! let us take full draughts; let us swear irreconcilable revenge against our oppressors; peace with them, never—so help me God!" Like cruel men in general, Jeannot was as cowardly as he was faithless. Yet was he daring in attack; and when danger pressed, his fear or his fury drove his troops to a resistance proof against attack, or compelled them to snatch a victory by cutting off every way of retreat.

Such were the men under whom Toussaint now found himself. No longer able to choose the moment for commencing his benevolent enterprise, he was hurried into the eddying torrent by the swelling streams of popular fanaticism. His fidelity to his proprietors making him an object of suspicion and a butt for negro attack, he was, even in self-defence, obliged to fall into the ranks of the raging insurgents. Generally known as much for his [Page 64] intelligence as his moderation, he was the less likely to be spared; but dragged into the rebellion against his better feelings and his judgment, he was regarded with distrust. Withheld, in consequence, from the military post for which his talents fitted him, he was commanded to employ his medical skill in taking care of the wounded. Quietly and usefully employed in an office which was agreeable to his feelings, he, at a distance from the conflict, turned his naturally reflective mind to the study of the personal qualities of his chiefs, and so acquired an acquaintance with their weaknesses, which greatly aided him in at length attaining supreme command. That post he reached without disgracing himself by blood or pillage, in a contest in which examples of both crowded on his sight. He was by nature retiring and given to seclusion, but in François Lafitte, whom he had long known, and whom he now found among the insurgents, he had one companion with whom similarity of ideas and feelings made intercourse both pleasant and profitable. It may well be supposed that these two men, united in the bonds of goodness and philanthropy, often deplored together the horrible excesses which they witnessed or of which they heard.

As, however, the insurrection passed on—and specially when defeat made its conduct difficult, the leaders found it imperative to bring forward all men of superior talent. No longer, therefore, was Toussaint permitted to pursue his medical occupations. Taken out of comparative privacy, he was made aide-de-camp to Biassou.

A grotesque spectacle did that negro army, or rather those negro bands, present. The slaves were ridiculously attired in the spoils of their masters. The cavalry were mounted on lumbering horses and mules, worn down by labour and fatigue. The horseman was armed with a musket almost as dangerous to himself as to his foe. The infantry were all but naked, and destitute of experience; their weapons were sticks pointed with iron, broken or blunted swords, pieces of iron hoop, and some wretched guns and pistols. Notwithstanding the alarm they inspired, the troops were almost without ammunition. Jean François, decorated with ribbons and orders which he had plundered in the sack of [Page 65] the abodes of the proprietors, gave himself out for a chevalier of the order of Saint Louis, besides taking to himself the titles of admiral and generalissimo. Biassou and Jeannot were brigadiers, a title which was fixed on Toussaint: the rest were marshals, commanders, generals, colonels, and some condescended to be captains. At a later period, Biassou, on having a disagreement with Jean François, assumed the pompous title of viceroy of the conquered countries. Only an iron discipline could maintain any order in such a body of men. The soldiers had sought liberty, and for the moment found the severest bondage. Disobedience was punished with severity, in the more flagrant instances with decapitation. Yet some regard was shown to the rights of property, for the stealer of cattle was hanged.

The leaders of the insurrection feared each other. Jeannot's cruelties were held in abomination by Toussaint. Jean François, by whom Jeannot was dreaded, resolved to disembarrass himself of the monster. Seizing his opportunity, he caused him to be apprehended. Tried by a summary process, Jeannot was sentenced to be shot. In this moment of peril, the wretch who had shed so much blood, and who had gloated over the sufferings of his victims, proved how cowardly a soul he had. He threw himself on his knees before Jean François, supplicated pardon, offered to purchase life by becoming his slave; and when the priest came up to offer him spiritual aid, he took him into his arms, pressing body to body, and was only by violence torn from him, to be dragged to execution.

The whites, although they had gained advantages in the war, were scarcely less than the blacks agitated with mutual dissensions. While they lost time and energy in discord, the men of colour assumed a formidable position under one of their caste, named Beauvais. The movement had an excuse in the cruelties which the colonists perpetrated at the Cape, where seventeen mulattoes had been put to death without even the forms of a trial, and where daily fugitive slaves, even the most faithful, were, on seeking an asylum in the city, forthwith hanged, after having escaped the dangers of being massacred on their road by some of the white scouts who scoured the neighbourhood.

[Page 66]On every side the grossest injustice prevailed; crime was repaid with crime; vengeance followed vengeance; the civilised master degraded himself no less than the neglected slave; between the two stood the mulatto, the enemy of both, and prepared to sacrifice either for his own aggrandisement.

The ease with which the mulatto betrayed the rights of the negro may be exemplified in the case of a number of men denominated *the Swiss*. In the ranks of the men of colour were three hundred slaves, who received the title of "the Swiss," from the resemblance which their service bore to that of the Swiss under the French monarchy. Used by the men of colour in their warfare against the whites, they were surrendered by the former at the demand of the latter the moment fortune began to frown on the mulatto cause. Consisting of men of colour as well as negroes, they were thrown on the coast of Jamaica. Driven thence, they either perished in the ocean or on the inhospitable shores of their birth, presenting in their sufferings and destruction a proof of the inhumanity of the whites and the perfidy of the mulattoes.

Disorder continued to increase. It would be a tedious as well as painful task to recount the misdeeds that were done on all sides, at the Cape by the colonists, at La Grande Rivière by the negroes, and in the west by the mulattoes. The leaders of the blacks began to feel that they had in hand a hopeless cause. The liberation of the negro population was not possible in the presence of two powerful enemies, the planters and their descendants. Consequently they were not disinclined to negotiate.

At this juncture, there arrived in Hayti, three commissioners, sent by the mother country on a mission of peace. These were Roume, Mirbeck, and St. Léger. Roume, a creole of Grenada, had been a councillor in that island, and afterwards a commissioner at Tobago. Under a simple and modest exterior, he possessed much knowledge; of a phlegmatic disposition, he would have been inaccessible to the attacks of the factions, had not his ordinary fickleness called forth their efforts. Mirbeck, a celebrated advocate in the council of state, where he had pleaded many causes for the colonists, was haughty and inflexible. St. [Page 67] Léger, had long lived as a physician in Tobago, where he possessed slaves. The first object of these three men, was to appease the civil war which wasted the west, and to stop the hurricane which covered the north with ruins. They wisely began by causing the gallows of the planters at the Cape to be demolished. The news of their arrival induced the masters of the slaves to open a negotiation. Raynal and Duplessy, the first a free mulatto, the second a free negro, being admitted to an audience by the Colonial Assembly, received for answer the following:—"Emissaries of the revolted negroes, the assembly established on the law and by the law, cannot correspond with people armed against the law—against all laws: the assembly might extend grace to guilty men if, being repentant, they had returned to their duty. Nothing would please its members better than to be in a condition to recognise those who, contrary to their will, have been hurried into guilt. We know how to measure out favours as well as justice. Withdraw!" "Withdraw" to men who came with the olive-branch in their hands! The deputies did withdraw—indignation burning in their hearts, and curses murmured from their lips. They made their way through the spectators with a haughty brow, and when that crowd tried to hoot them down, they hastened to register a new outrage in the book of vengeance.

On the arrival of the deputies at La Grande Rivière, the army of the population came together. Every one had fondly dreamt of union. What was the disappointment! When Raynal and Duplessy related the disdainful manner in which they had been treated, cries of vexation and rage rent the air. Biassou, unable to restrain his passion, ordered all the whites detained in the camp, to be put to death. The necessary preparations were made; when Toussaint—always humane—intervened, calmed his chief, and saved the lives of the intended victims. Such is the ascendancy of goodness. Such is the power of that rapid, animated, and picturesque eloquence which Toussaint possessed, and which, on very many other occasions, he employed for merciful results of a similar kind. We subjoin an instance. Biassou one day received from the Cape a proclamation intended to win [Page 68] back the slaves. The insurgent chief determined to publish it. Causing his soldiers to take their arms, he ordered the proclamation to be read aloud. Instantly there arose the awful cry of "Death to the whites." Toussaint shuddered, rushed forward, again read the proclamation, with a commentary of his own. The result was, that the desire for vengeance sank in those rude breasts, tears stole down their cheeks, and the prisoners were saved. Such a conquest is one of the highest achievements of humanity. A conference took place. There were present, the commissioners, and Bullet, a representative of the Colonial Assembly. Jean François, leaving Biassou at La Grande Rivière, hastened to La Petite Anse, in the vicinity of the Cape, to take part in the conference. He was followed by a considerable troop of cavalry. Full of confidence in the representatives of the king, he proceeded to alight from his horse, when Bullet, seizing the bridle, struck him with his riding-whip. Jean François might have taken instant revenge; he simply withdrew to his soldiers. Who was the greater? St. Léger saw the evil effects this brutal act might occasion, and, unattended, advanced towards Jean François. This act of confidence restored a friendly feeling. A peaceful arrangement was entered into, involving the emancipation of fifty persons, an exchange of prisoners, and the return of the slaves to their labours. Jean François required the liberation of his wife, who lay in the prisons of the Cape. There is no reason to believe that the request was complied with. But the insurgent, faithful to his word, the next day dismissed his prisoners, employing in the benevolent office the mild Toussaint, and his equally mild friend, Lafitte.

Peace seemed at hand. Alas! it was very distant. The colonists, displeased with the pacific tendencies of the commissioners, endeavoured to set aside their powers, and required their obedience. The mulattoes suffered disadvantages, but could not be put down. The negroes resumed their devastations. On every side was disorder, slaughter, and ruin. The pride and obstinacy of the planters rendered accommodation impossible; their weakness exposed the colony to carnage the most frightful, and depredations the most extensive. Meanwhile, Jean François [Page 69] and Biassou were each too powerful and too ambitious to act cordially together. They came to an open quarrel, and drew off their several forces into two camps. Toussaint, now the principal aide-de-camp of Biassou, brought on himself the enmity of his rival, Jean François, though hitherto he had succeeded in keeping on good terms with both. The hostile feeling seems to have been called forth by Toussaint's intellectual preeminence. However, Toussaint, disregarding the dissensions of the generals, quietly and efficiently discharged his duties, and gradually gaining the esteem of the army, laid the foundations of the great influence which he was one day to exert on behalf of negro independence. He alone wept when he saw the hope of peace vanish. e alone remained unsullied by crime, while Jean François and Biassou not only committed ravages and massacre, but even sold into slavery to the Spaniards many of the very men for whose liberty they pretended to be fighting, and who were their companions in arms.

CHAPTER VIII.

France makes the mulattoes and negroes equal to the whites—The decapitation of Louis XVI. throws the slaves into the arms of Spain—They are afraid of the revolutionary republicans—Strife of French political parties in Hayti—Conflagration of the Cape—Proclamation of liberty for the negroes produces little effect—Toussaint captures Dondon—Commemoration of the fall of the Bastille—Displeasure of the planters—Rigaud.

SUCH was the condition of affairs when there was brought to Hayti a decree of the Legislative Assembly which, among other things, declared that the men of colour and free negroes should be admitted to vote in all the parochial assemblies to be convened in order to elect a new general assembly and municipal corporations. The decree was supported by commissioners, of whom Sonthonax was at the head. It was, however, impossible to givs it immediate effect. The contest proceeded. The mulattoes [Page 70] overcome, joined the colonists against the blacks. The blacks defeated, took shelter in the mountains, and constantly renewed their predatory warfare. A fresh cause of complication added to the troubles of the island; Louis XVI. had been beheaded. Then the slaves gave up all thought of peace. Naturally inclined to a monarchy, they renounced the revolutionary government, and passed over into the service of Charles IV., king of Spain. Jean François received the title of Lieutenant-General in that monarch's army; Biassou became one of his brigadiers; and Toussaint was honoured with the same mark of confidence. A medal, bearing the effigy of Charles, was decreed to them. Under this powerful protection, the insurgents became more formidable than ever.

France, in the midst of her own troubles, did not cease to cast an eye, from time to time, on her distracted colony. She dispatched General Galbaud to take the command in Hayti. Disembarking at the Cape, (May 6, 1793,) he proceeded to assume the executive power. But the French commission already in the island, triumphant in the west and in the south, had everywhere established mulatto in place of white commanders. Returning on the 7th of June to the Cape with a detachment of freed men, commanded by Chanlatte, the commissioners directed Galbaud to re-embark. Unwillingly he obeyed. His brother, a man of ability, remained in the city, and agitated the minds of the people against the commissioners. The vessels in the harbour were loaded with prisoners sent thither by the Government. Breaking their chains, they, to the number of one thousand two hundred, effected a landing. Their bands increasing as they proceeded, they directed their course to the Government house, inhabited by the commissioners. The approaches to it were defended by men of colour. The National Guards and mounted volunteers joined the partizans of Galbaud. The troops of the line remained in their quarters, not knowing, in the strife of authorities, which was legitimate. Fighting took place in the streets, the fury of which was stopped only by night. The next day hostilities were resumed. At length the troops of the line declared for the commissioners. Nevertheless, their party seemed [Page 71] to lose ground. Then the prisons were thrown open, and the chains of the blacks were broken. Spreading themselves abroad, these captives showed themselves worthy of the liberty they had just received. Pierrot and Macaya, two black chiefs of the insurgent negroes on the hills of the Cape, being invited, came with their fierce associates to take part in the carnage. Galbaud was defeated. With a few of his followers he regained his ships. His brother remained in the hands of the commissioners. He himself, with more than ten thousand refugees of all hues, set sail for the United States. The city, "the Paris of the Antilles," as the colonist enthusiastically termed Cape Town, was in flames, and on every side presented the shocking tokens of pillage, slaughter, and conflagration. Truly did the flames of the French revolution set on fire the world. The strifes of political partizanship which raged in Paris, were transplanted to Hayti, where they raged with all the heat of a tropical climate and all the animosity of a civil war. As if to aid in wearing down the forces of the planters, white men, who should have healed grievances and restored tranquillity, came from the mother country only to call forth new enmities, and add new brands to the burning. These collisions among men of white blood, went far to remove and destroy the veil of *préstige* and fear with which, under centuries of domination, they were regarded by the blacks. It was now found that the planters were no more than men; very ordinary men; men of low passions; intensely selfish men; men who fell beneath the black man's sword; nay, men who could not keep their hands from each other; men who themselves destroyed the property which the negroes produced. These were pregnant and dangerous lessons. Yes, the blacks are on the road to freedom, and the whites are their guides and helpers.

    The commission retired from the burning city into the neighbouring highlands, where a camp was formed to protect the Cape from the irruption of the insurgents. Having no longer any confidence in the whites, all of whom they suspected of anti-revolutionary sympathies, and seeking new defenders of the cause of republicanism, they, on the 22nd of June, proclaimed the freedom of all slaves who should enrol themselves for the [Page 72] sacred cause of the republic. Pierrot, who commanded for Biassou, at Port François, not far from the Cape, was the first to respond to the proclamation; he, with his band, came to place himself at the disposal of the commission.

While yet the conflagration was not extinguished, pestilence and famine fell on the miserable inhabitants of Cape Town. A yet more dreadful enemy impended. The ferocity and ravages of the blacks alarmed the commissioners themselves. Perplexed as to the means of staying the fury of these dangerous allies, they put forth a proclamation, in which they said, "That those who had recently been set free could not be good citizens unless they were closely bound to their country by the touching ties of husband and father, and that, consequently, they were each invested with the right of bestowing liberty on their wives and their children." Admirable resolution! But has it come soon enough? Why will men delay justice until justice itself is of little or no avail? The blacks, degraded by life-long bondage, saw in these words only a recognition of their entire freedom; in other terms, only an authority to do what they pleased. But a small number of them responded to these efforts for their social improvement. The blame lay chiefly with white men, who caballed and plotted among the blacks in order to make them effective in maintaining the cause of royalty. Thus did the black chiefs, Jean François and Biassou, reply to the offer of the commission:—"We cannot conform to the will of the nation, because, from the beginning of the world, we have executed only the will of a king: we have lost the king of France, but we are esteemed by the king of Spain, who bestows on us rewards, and ceases not to give us succour; consequently we are unable to acknowledge you, the commissioners, before you have found a king." To this declaration of their intentions the negroes remained true. The expedient had failed. Hostilities became more bitter than ever.

In this refusal of the privileges tendered by the republican commissioners, Toussaint took his share of responsibility. Doubtless he partook of the monarchical prepossessions of his [Page 73] associates. Royalty he considered as the sole sufficient pledge of liberty. He both feared and distrusted republicans, of whose excesses in Europe he had read so much. He may have regarded the tardy concession of freedom as a subterfuge, and not unreasonably may he have suspected the danger that the negroes would be sacrificed in the collisions of the white factions. Uncertain too, was it, whether the commissioners would be able to maintain themselves in power, and should the planters gain the upper hand, they would easily deal with their slaves, then no longer enrolled and under discipline, but scattered over the land, indulging in the intoxication of recent freedom. Besides, he had taken a part; he was a soldier of the king of Spain, and had more to hope for from his interest in that quarter, than could be gained by rushing into the arms of the feeble commissioners.

Toussaint had already made his apprenticeship in warfare. With his superior knowledge and ability, and with his resolute yet silent will, he had readily fought his way into a foremost position, and won both confidence and distinction. The insurgents held strong places in the mountains which rise to the south of the Cape, in the neighbourhood of La Grande Riviére, Dondon, Marmelade, &c. Thither the commissioners directed their hostilities. The whole district was subject to the insurrection, except Marmelade. Thither Brandicourt, the government's commander, determined to retire. But there was in his councils a traitor, Pacot, who was in correspondence with the enemy. Under his influence it had been resolved that the retreat should take place during the day-time. Informed of the arrangement, Toussaint laid his ambuscades. Next morning, the army began its march. Planel, lieutenant of grenadiers, commanded the advanced guard. As he proceeded he was encountered with the cry, "Who goes there?" " France," was his reply. "Then let your general come and speak to ours—no harm shall befal him," answered one of Toussaint's officers, who, with a company of men, was posted there. Brandicourt, who was in the centre of his forces, on learning the confusion that had arisen, hastened [Page 74] to the spot, leaving the command to Pacot. Having reconnoitred the enemy, he ordered an attack. Forthwith, he was on all sides entreated to have an interview with Toussaint, whose humanity, it was urged, was well known. Besides, he had left behind a hundred invalids—how much better to recommend them to Toussaint's care. Brandicourt yielded to the representations, went forward, and was immediately seized. He and his officers were disarmed, bound and conducted to Toussaint's camp. The blacks are beginning to show that under an able leader they know how to make themselves respected. But the French general's soldiers yet stood in their ranks, armed, and ready for battle. "Write," said Toussaint to Brandicourt, "and command your forces to yield." Taking the pen, Brandicourt in tears wrote that, being a prisoner, he left Pacot to follow the course which prudence might seem to dictate. "No," added Toussaint, tearing the paper, "I must have from you an express order to Pacot, to lay down his arms." The order was sent. On receiving it, Pacot read the command to his officers, and added, "Do what you like; for myself, I surrender." The column yielded without delay. Brandicourt, being sent to Porto Rico, died there of grief and vexation. Yes, here is the man, and the hour is coming.

It is with difficulty that I bring myself to the utterance of commendation on merely warlike deeds. Having a deep aversion to war, I shrink from any approach to a eulogy of anything connected therewith. But if war is ever respectable, it is surely when it is employed as a means of liberating thousands of oppressed men from hopeless bondage. In the hands of Toussaint, arms were the instruments of freedom; the only instruments that could have been made use of. Nor was it an unimportant lesson which he had to teach, and did well teach, in proving to white men and to the world, that negro blood did not exclude its possessors from the highest renown which can attend military skill and achievements. In the victory which Toussaint had so easily gained over a French general of no mean repute, there appears great ability in military combinations, as well as extraordinary promptitude and determination. These [Page 75] are qualities which make a great soldier, and these qualities were in an eminent degree possessed by Toussaint.

By this achievement Dondon fell into the hands of the insurgents. Dondon was the centre of the country. Possessed of it, Toussaint had almost a free passage into the western department, while already the negro forces were triumphant in the north.

At this position of affairs, the commissioners at the Cape not unnaturally grew alarmed. Revolving the means at their disposal, they determined to celebrate the fourth anniversary of the capture of the Bastille, in order to revive the republican enthusiasm, and thereby gain power for renewed efforts against the insurgents.

Is the reader struck with the inconsistency of their conduct? Yes, these friends of liberty are seeking arms against liberty. Believing that the fall of the Bastille was the fall of tyranny in France, they deliberately turn the event to account in order to buttress up oppression in Hayti. Republicans ye may be, lovers of freedom ye are not, any more than those, your brothers and descendants, who recently put down liberty in Rome with republican bayonets, and under republican colours. Hypocrisy was added to inconsistency; the qualities are not unlike. Amid the festivities which were designed to aid in the subjugation of the revolted negroes, these words were spoken by the commissioner Polverel: "The oppressed were Africans whom kings and their satellites sent to purchase, at their own hearths, of kings who had not the right to sell them into perpetual slavery in America. The oppressed were descendants of the Africans who, even when they had recovered their liberty, were accounted unworthy of the rights of man. The oppressors are all the kings who traffic in the life and liberty of men of all countries and all colours. The oppressors are all the traitors and brigands who wish to restore royalty and slavery."

This effusion of indignation against "kings and their satellites" lacked one word. If "republicans" had been added, the description would have been more correct. The statement is illustrated by the fact that Sonthonax, another of the commissioners, in a speech delivered on the occasion, characterised the [Page 76] insurgents as "a mass of vagabonds and idlers who will neither cultivate the land nor defend the cultivators," and whom it was a primary duty to reduce and compel to resume their toils.

The treacherous favours offered to the blacks by the commission, had offended and alienated the skin aristocracy. At the town of Jéremie, in the extreme north-west of the southern department, the planters had even formed an encampment hostile to the civil authority. They had, moreover, driven from the towns of the district the men of colour who had taken refuge in Les Cayes on the southern side of the same tongue of land. Sonthonax having proclaimed liberty for all the slaves, sent Andrew Rigaud to carry his orders into execution, and to restore the mulattoes to their homes. Advancing from Petit Trou, (June l7th,) on reaching the plantation of Desrivaux, near Jéremie, Rigaud found himself stopped by an entrenchment defended by five hundred men and five pieces of cannon. Consulting only his ardour and the object of his mission, he hastened to attack the fortification. At the head of three columns he three times mounted to the assault; three times was he driven back. After fighting for four hours and losing several brave officers, he retreated, and at the head of fifty men protected himself in the midst of the greatest perils. Retiring to Petit Trou he received reinforcements and enrolled slaves. The last act made him a special object of hatred to the planters, who, disregarding the means, resolved to effect his destruction. Having crossed the country to Les Cayes, he took part in a repetition of the festivities which had been celebrated at the Cape. Whites, blacks, and mulattoes exchanged tokens of friendship and manifested a common joy. In the midst of scenes which promised lasting amity, he was fallen upon by Bandollet, commander of the white National Guard, and barely escaped through a shower of bullets, by extraordinary courage and activity. This disgraceful attempt at assassination excited general abhorrence, and added impulse and vigour to the negro cause.

Rigaud, who, next to Toussaint, was destined to play the chief part in this internecine conflict, was a mulatto in the true sense of the term; he was, that is to say, the son of a white man and [Page 77] a black woman. Educated at Bordeaux, where he had gone through a pretty good course of instruction, and learned the trade of a goldsmith, and having served in Savannah and Guadeloupe, he entered the militia in Les Cayes, his native place. While pursuing his business, which colonial prejudices regarded as too good for a mulatto, he was called into active service by the insurrection. Rigaud had in his soul the elements of a great man. In Hindostan he would have founded an empire. In Hayti he scarcely rose above a banditti chief; yet did he know how to make himself formidable. Of a martial aspect, his countenance was terrible in combat; yet after the excitement was over, it was mild and engaging. In the progress of the war of liberation he raised, organized, and commanded a legion, called "The Southern Legion of Equality," which proved the finest and the most effective of the troops formed in Hayti. Aware, in his own experience, of the value of knowledge, he took pains to have his soldiers instructed. "If"—to cite the words of a native of Hayti—"if in the south of the isle the traveller meets even now (1850) with aged Africans who possess the elements of classical instruction, he may salute them; they are Rigaud's legionaries. Admirable for good sense, they have a lofty spirit, above the prejudices of colour; with them, the white man, the mulatto, and the black man are sons of the same father. I thank Heaven that the epoch of my visit to the district allowed me to shake hands with these relies of the glory of my country, those old negroes whose excellence of heart and aptitude of mien Europe is ignorant of, and whose descendants lie under the obligation of justifying the hopes of the friends of equality."*

[Page 78] CHAPTER IX.

Toussaint becomes master of a central post—Is not seduced by offers of negro emancipation, nor of bribes to himself—Repels the English, who invade the

---

*Vie de Toussaint L'Ouverture, par Saint-Remy. Paris, 1850, p. 83.

island; adds L'Ouverture to his name, abandons the Spaniards, and seeks freedom through French alliance.

AFTER the conquest of Dondon, Toussaint rushed on Marmelade, which was commanded by Vernet, a mulatto of a feeble and distrustful mind, Having under his orders a legion composed of negroes recently liberated, as well disciplined as the battalions of Toussaint, he, in his timidity, importuned the commission to send him succours. On the 20th of July, 1795, Polverel wrote him these lines: "We do not think you a traitor, but you show not the courage of a republican; if you do not feel strength enough to die rather than yield, say so frankly; we can easily find citizens who make no account of death, when the honour of their country is at stake."

On the morning of the 27th, Toussaint having formed connexions in the place, made an attack on Marmelade. By the evening, opposition was overcome. Vernet, its commander, joined his fortunes with those of Toussaint, whose niece he afterwards married, and rising to the rank of general, died under the reign of the Haytian king Christophe. Meanwhile the Lieutenant-Colonel Desfournaux was advancing from Port-au-Prince against Saint Michel, in the hope of effecting a division in favour of the French civil authority. The republican troops suffered a complete defeat. Desfournaux himself received several wounds.

Encouraged by the victory, Toussaint advanced and captured Ennery. Thence he wrote to the inhabitants of Gonaïves, lying on the western shore, to induce them to surrender. A rising *en masse* was attempted, and failed. The heads of the population hastened to take flight by sea.

But Toussaint had not been able sufficiently to protect his [Page 79] rear. Hearing that Chanlatte was advancing from Plaisance against him, he judged it prudent to retreat. Driven back to Marmelade, he employed himself in efforts to abate the evils of the war. Recalling the planters who had taken refuge in the Spanish territories, he restored to them the possession of their estates, and so prevented the destitution which the conflict threatened to produce.

These varieties of success brought no settlement. If the commissioners gained an advantage here, a defeat there countervailed its effect. Once more would they try an appeal to the love of liberty. Accordingly Sonthonax proclaimed at the Cape universal freedom. Polverel repeated the proclamation at Port-au-Prince. Symbolic ceremonies were celebrated on these occasions, which were repeated in various places in which the authority of the commission still prevailed. The consequent enthusiasm was not without some effect. But Toussaint was not easy to be deceived. The destinies of the republic were, he knew, uncertain. The faith of its representatives in Hayti was worse than doubtful. The colonists would be neither gained nor overcome by an understanding with the civil commissioners. He had, therefore, no course before him, but to continue faithful to the king of Spain. His actual position was the only position he could hold consistently with his hope of ever achieving the independence of his caste. For the complications of the contest he was not answerable. If, therefore, he now had to defend the cause of the blacks against blacks themselves, he had no option but to submit to the painful necessity.

Never, perhaps, did a conflict present more heterogeneous combinations, or more regrettable collisions. The white republicans of France were arrayed against the white colonists of Hayti, whom they were sent to succour. The black man's hand was raised against his brother. The mulatto, enemy and friend of both, was by both distrusted and destroyed. Constituted authorities were in hostility. Bands of injured men seeking redress assailed each other. Spanish royalty fostered colonial insurrection. The forces of the country were exhausted in the mutual and ever-recurring strife. Without unity, and without result, [Page 80] the war raged on every side, uniform only in the universal ravages which it inflicted.

This ruinous complication was to be yet more complicated. Discord threw on the wasted shores of Hayti another brand.

We have already seen the planters make overtures to England. In their dissatisfaction with France, they renewed their application. The Court of St. James instructed Williamson, governor of Jamaica, to lend the required assistance. In this appeal, the proprietors of La Grande Anse sent to the governor a treaty, which was accepted. Among the points agreed on was that the island should pass into the hands of Britain, and that its representative should have full power to regulate and govern the island with a view to its restoration to tranquillity. From the tenour of this article, and from the express words of others, the object of the colonists was to turn the power of Great Britain to account, in order to effect that in which they themselves had failed—the humiliation of the mulattoes, and the subjugation of the blacks. With a view to the occupation of Hayti, Governor Williams, in September, 1793, sent an armed force under Colonel Whitelocke, which disembarked at Jéremie, on the 9th of the month, and on the 22nd, the harbour of Saint Nicholas was put into the possession of the English, who, in consequence, held two important positions in

Hayti, the latter at the extremity of the northern, the other near the extremity of the southern tongue of its western end. While the military chiefs of the mulattoes, stood aloof, many of the men of colour, not being soldiers, threw themselves into the arms of the British; and Saint Marc, Léogane, Le Grand Goave, and many towns of the south, adopted the conditions of La Grande Anse.

While little more than the Cape and Port-au-Prince remained in the power of the commissioners, an English fleet anchored in the harbour of the last-mentioned city, and demanded its surrender. This armament received an increase shortly afterwards. As usual, dissension and treason were at work among the forces of the authorities. With their aid, the English effected a landing, and took up a position. The commissioners fled to Jacmel. There they learned that a decree had been passed [Page 81] against them by the national convention in Paris. They submitted, and were received as prisoners on board L'Espérance. During the interval, Port-au-Prince became the scene of new horrors. The emigrant Bérenger, at the head of a legion, took possession of the town, and seizing Fort-Joseph, where the whites had taken refuge who could not find room on board the vessels in the harbour, he caused them to come forth one by one, and, as they appeared, he threw them headlong from the rampart into the fosse, saying, "Republican, leap down the Tarpeian rock." Thus perished two-and-thirty persons, and but for the orders of the English general, not one would have been spared.

England had not invaded the French part of Hayti without having an understanding with Spain. By the convention between the two parties, it was agreed on that England should establish its protection over the west and the south, and that Spain should extend its dominion from the east to the extremity of the north. Accordingly, while the English invaded the west and the south, the Spanish invited the creoles of the north, who had left the colony, to return and take possession of their properties. On the faith of the promises made to them, two hundred colonists quitted the United States, and entered their homes at Fort Dauphin. Shortly after, Jean François, at the head of a body of negroes, encamped under the walls of that place. Resistance was not offered, in the persuasion that they came only to second the operations of the Spaniards. The next day, after the celebration of mass, those blacks mingled with Spaniards, having formed themselves into bands, traversed the streets, and slaughtered every Frenchman they met with, as "enemies of the saints and of kings,"—to use the words by which they were encouraged to the butchery by the priests. The massacre was general; only fourteen persons escaped.

Meanwhile Rigaud, aided by Pétion and other mulatto chiefs, attacked the English, and, taking from them Léogane and Tiburon, blockaded them in La Grande Anse. Finding the enemy formidable, Whitelocke endeavoured to bribe Rigaud and Laveaux, then provisional governor of the colony, into acquiescence, if not submission. The former simply rejected the [Page 82] offer; the latter replied, "Your being my enemy does not give you the right to put on me a personal insult; as an individual I demand satisfaction for the injury you have done me." Laveaux, believing the Cape indefensible, took up his position at Port-de-Paix, which he fortified, and under its walls braved all the efforts of the English; while they, on their side, occupying the harbour of Saint Nicholas, commanded all the approaches to the city by sea.

The Spaniards, masters of nearly all the north, pressed Port-de-Paix by land, and cut off the supplies of provisions, so that the place underwent the privations of a siege. "For more than six months," wrote Laveaux, under date May 24th, "we have been reduced to six ounces of bread a day, officers as well as men; but from the 13th of this month, we have none whatever, the sick only excepted. If we had powder, we should have been consoled; our misery is truly great; officers and soldiers experience the greatest privations. We have in our magazines neither shoes, nor shirts, nor clothes, nor soap, nor tobacco. The majority of the soldiers mount guard barefooted, like the Africans. We have not even a flint to give the men. Notwithstanding, be assured that we will never surrender, if indeed, we shall ever capitulate; be assured, too, that after us the enemy will not find the slightest trace of Port-de-Paix. Sooner than be made prisoners, when the balls shall have destroyed everything here, and we have no longer anything to defend, we will retire, and flying from mountain to mountain, we will fight incessantly until aid comes from France."

Bravery and determination worthy of a better cause! The hope of aid from France proved chimerical, yet the notion helped to keep the soldiers in the line of duty. Relief, indeed, came to them, but it was from an unexpected quarter.

Miserably was this unfortunate island torn asunder by Spaniards, French, English, mulattoes, and the blacks; by monarchists, by republicans, by sceptics, by Romanists, by false friends and true friends of negro emancipation. A lamentable illustration of the diversity of these rival interests was presented at Saint Marc. The same day three flags balanced and negatived each other under [Page 83] the influence of political breezes. Four cockades symbolized four different sets of opinions: here were whites who wore the black cockade; there other whites who wore the white cockade; while the mulattoes wore the red cockade; and some soldiers wore the tri-coloured cockade.

About this time may be dated the final change which the name of Toussaint underwent by receiving the addition of L'Ouverture. L'Ouverture is a French word which signifies *the opening*. The surname is said to have been given as indicative of the opening which Toussaint had made for himself in the ranks and the possessions of the enemy. If this was its origin, the name is appropriate. Though not always successful, he rushed on his foes with an impetus which mowed down opposition. With poetic licence, Lamartine, in his drama, makes the designation—derived, according to him, from L'Aurore, *Day-break*—to have been given to Toussaint by a monk, who thus intimated to him that he was to be the morning-star of a new era in Hayti.

> Un jour, un capucin, un de ces pauvres pères,
> Colporteurs de la foi, dont les noirs sont les frères,
> En venant visiter l'atelier de Jacmel,
> S'arrêta devant moi comme un autre Samuël.
> Quel est ton nom? Toussaint. Pauvre mangeur d'igname,
> C'est le nom de ton corps; mais le nom de ton âme,
> C'est Aurore, dit-il. O mon père, et de quoi?
> Du jour que Dieu prepare et qui se leve en toi!
> Et les noirs ignorants, depuis cette aventure,
> En corrompant ce nom m'appellent L'Ouverture.*

A third explanation has been given. According to Pamphile de Lacroix,** Toussaint assumed the epithet, in order to announce to his people that he was about to open the door to them of a better future. In this view his name became a token of his object. That object he was too prudent to make known in the early period of his efforts. Now, however, might he make the announcement without serious risk. The event justified his conduct. That

---

*"Toussaint L'Ouverture," Poëm Dramatique, par A. De Lamartine. Act ii., scene 2.

** "Mémoires de Saint Dominique," vol. i. p. 303.

event would be aided forward by the name. *The*[Page 84]*opening* was before the negroes. Whenever they saw Toussaint, they were reminded of the opening; whenever they pronounced his name, they were encouraged to advance toward the opening. There was the door; they had only to be bold and enter in to the desired temple of freedom. Toussaint L'Ouverture had returned to his mountain stronghold, Marmalade, where he fixed his headquarters. From that place as a centre, he surveyed the whole island, which to a great extent he now held under his domination. Already the shepherd-boy had become a potentate. It was a time not only for repose, but for the endearments of home. From the time of his entering the service of Spain, he had removed his wife from the theatre of war. He himself conducted her to the mountain fastness of St. Miguel; and for seven months he had not been able to pay her a visit. Kind-hearted as he was, how must he have been moved, when now, after unexpected triumphs, he found his wife and children in safety. His entrance into the place was an ovation. The commander, in a truly Spanish fashion, ordered, among other tokens of rejoicing, bullfights, in honour of the victor. Toussaint L'Ouverture had gained the esteem as well as the confidence of his Spanish masters. Impressed with his respect for religion, as well as the general probity of his character, the Marquis Hermona, under whose orders he was, exclaimed, on seeing him take the communion: —"No, God cannot, in this lower world, visit a purer soul." Thus esteemed by the Spaniards, feared by the English, dreaded by the French, hated by the planters, and reverenced by the negroes, Toussaint L'Ouverture felt that a crisis had come in his public life, which required the calmest consideration and the soundest judgment. His achievements, his personal influence, and the condition of the conflicting parties, combined to show him the opening door, if only he had wisdom and strength to take the right path. What was that path? The colonists were all but deprived of power for harm. The mulattoes had no organization. The English held only a point or two of the country. From the colonists and the men of colour little, very little, was to be feared or hoped. The negroes had learnt the [Page 85] secret of their power. This result, if no other satisfactory result, had ensued from the conflict. On them might Toussaint L'Ouverture now place great reliance. If they were not already good soldiers, they had performed great things, and gave promise of soon being able both to deserve and achieve independence. But was their emancipation to be gained through Spain? Spain was powerful in Hayti; was its power likely to conduce to the opening? On the contrary, Spain was opposed to emancipation.

Her power, then, was power adverse to the great object of Toussaint L'Ouverture's life. What did fidelity to that object demand? Before the question could be answered, another element of thought had to be weighed. France in Hayti was in a miserable condition. Should she be crushed? If she was crushed, the alternative lay between the slave-dominion of England and the slave-dominion of Spain. But though France was depressed, could she be crushed? Her arms were triumphant in Europe, and a strong effort to rescue her favourite colony might reasonably be expected. The present depression was such as to call for gratitude towards any effectual helper. The possible continuance of the depression gave assurance of the probability that, even in opposition to France, still more in conjunction with France, the independence of the negroes—if not the independence of the island—might be achieved. Why, then, not seek "the opening" in union with France? The disposition implied in the question was confirmed by a recent decree of the French legislature (Feb. 4, 1794) which, declaring Hayti an integral part of France, confirmed and proclaimed the freedom of all the slaves. This was a very grave act; an act of the mother country, not a mere device of a local commissioner; this was a deliberate and solemn recognition of the very object of Toussaint's life, not a trick in war for the very purpose of frustrating that object. And this step was taken when, to some extent, the days of French republican weakness had given place to days of strength, and when the name of republican France had begun to become a terror in the world. Hence, many things pointed to a coalition with France—her weakness, her power, her liberality. Alliance, too, with her seemed the [Page 86] natural course. Independence by her, with her, and eventually —if it might be—without her, involved the introduction of no foreign element into the Haytian world; no new language, no strange customs and unacceptable manners. A French colony would still remain essentially French. Old usages would remain in honour; old observances would not be trampled on; old associations would not be disregarded or broken up. Especially would religion remain uninjured and unchanged. Hayti was a Catholic island, and France was a Catholic country. Toussaint L'Ouverture, too, was a sincere Catholic. Religious considerations, always powerful with him, seem to have received special attention, and had special weight in this juncture. The Abbé de la Haie was his adviser. The same clergyman went between him and Laveaux. At length, a distinct offer was made by the French commander. Toussaint L'Ouverture accepted *the opening.*

In this important step, he was doubtless influenced by a consideration derived from his actual position. He was surrounded by violent men. He was, in some sort, under the control of violent men. Certainly, he was intimately allied with men of colour by whom, or with whom, negro emancipation could not be wrought out. Of these facts he, about this time, was made painfully aware. His superior in command, Jean François, quarrelled with Biassou. Over the latter, Toussaint, as the former knew, possessed great influence. Choosing to implicate Toussaint in the quarrel, Jean François committed him to prison. By Biassou, he was delivered. The hazard had been great. He who could incarcerate might slay. A second peril of the kind was not to be thought of; therefore, the great, the final step must be taken. Having adopted precautions for the safety of his family, he made his military arrangements with skill, and carried them into effect with success. He then proclaimed universal liberty in all the districts under his influence. On the 4th of May, he pulled down the Spanish and hoisted the French flag wherever he was in power. Fright and confusion prevailed among the Spaniards. Joy agitated the bosoms of the negroes. Nearly all the north returned to their allegiance to France.

[Page 87] CHAPTER X.

Toussaint defeats the Spanish partizans—By extraordinary exertions raises and disciplines troops, forms armies, lays out campaigns, executes the most daring exploits, and defeats the English, who evacuate the island—Toussaint is Commander-in-chief.

TOUSSAINT L'OUVERTURE'S accession to the cause of France was followed by brilliant exploits. Rigaud suddenly fell on Léogane, which had been surrendered to the English, and with a very inconsiderable loss carried the place, though it had been strongly fortified. Among the booty were twenty thousand pounds of powder, eight of which he sent to Laveaux, who, with his fellow-combatants in Port-de-Paix, hailed the capture of Léogane with shouts of delight.

Toussaint now came into collision with Jean François, his former commander. He took from that Spanish ally all his posts, and drove him westward into La Montaigne Noire. Hastening into the valley of the Artibonite, Toussaint attacked the English, and, capturing several towns, fell on Saint Marc, the seat of the English power. Sitting down to besiege the city, he got possession of two important posts. In one of these, Morne-Diamant, he raised a battery which riddled the place. Then, while aiding the men to mount a gun, he crushed his left hand. He was compelled to resign the conduct of the attack to others. The consequence was injurious. Besides, his forces were insufficiently provided with ammunition. He was forced to retire. This partial failure occasioned perfidy in some of his forces, to which he himself nearly fell a victim. Thus, while he had to maintain an open warfare against Spain and England, he had also to guard against the treachery which those powers did not disdain to set in motion among his own adherents.

Retiring, as was his custom, to the mountain fastnesses, of which Marmelade may be considered as the centre, he collected [Page 88] forces, and on the 9th of October, 1794, quitted that place at the head of nearly five thousand men, and after some minor successes, carried San Miguel by storm.

This exploit raised him high in the estimation of the French commanders. Laveaux and Rigaud united in their eulogies of the skill and prowess he had manifested. An interview took place between Laveaux and Toussaint at Dondon. This was the first time they had seen each other. Toussaint presented to the general-in-chief his principal officers; Dessalines, commander of San Miguel, Duménil, commander of Plaisance, Desrouleaux, Clerveaux, Maurepas, &c., commanders of battalions.

Toussaint L'Ouverture had already become a great power. Very considerable influence did he exert in this conference of French authorities.

Raised to this eminence, and now seeing "the opening" in clear outline before him, Toussaint was indefatigable. Such was the rapidity of his movements, and at so many different places was he seen near the same moment, that he seemed, especially in the eyes of the ignorant negroes, as if he was superior to time and space. Specially was he found at every post of imminent danger. His energy and his prowess made him the idol of his troops. They also caused him to be dreaded by his enemies. He was no longer a leader of insurgents, but a commander of an army. He gave over marauding expeditions to lay out and conduct a campaign.

His immediate aim was to drive the English out of the island, and for that purpose, to make himself master of the port of Saint Marc. Coming down from the mountains with this view, he found that the English commander, Brisbane, had advanced into the interior of the valley of the Artibonite, and, taking Les Vérettes, had compelled his troops to retire. One small position alone held out against Brisbane. Toussaint determined to make one of those efforts which he so well knew how to direct, and by which he sometimes effected at a blow very great results. Starting forward in the night early in December, with a band of three hundred cavalry, he by ambuscade and sudden attack, drove the enemy back in disgrace.

[Page 89] As yet, however, he had not strength enough to hold the valley of the Artibonite, especially as Jean François, with his Spanish sympathies, was impending over it in order to assist the English. He withdrew towards the north. Before he left La Petite Rivière for Gonaïves, which is in that direction, he gave a proof of the humanity by which he was actuated. In the village of La Petite Rivière, there were children and women of different colours who were destitute of the means of subsistence. Two sisters of charity who had come hither from the quarters occupied by the English, ministered to others even in their own need. At the command of L'Ouverture bread was day by day supplied to these sufferers, and to the most wretched of them money also was distributed.

Returning with almost the speed of lightning to Marmelade, he set about organising a sufficient force to clear the district of La Grande Rivière and its heights, which lie above Saint Marc, of the bands of Jean François. Setting in movement four columns, he quitted Dondon in the centre of the forces on the 31st of December. In four days he took and destroyed twenty-eight positions. That of Barmby, situated on a frightful precipice, and defended by three pieces of cannon, besides fire-arms, was carried by the mere force of resolute bravery. Had his plan been carried into effect in all points, the insurrection would have been suppressed. It failed in one point; and so gave a passage to Jean François, who, passing through it with superior forces, surrounded Toussaint L'Ouverture. Disappointed, that brave man cut a way through his enemies, and after establishing a cordon of great extent, returned to his stronghold, Dondon, on the 7th of January, 1795.

The cordon of the west, which Ouverture commanded, had for its eastern extremity La Grande Riviére, in the centre of the department of the north, and for its western limit La Saline, in the plain of the Artibonite, in the department of the west, and extending above ninety leagues, comprised the following important posts: Saint Raphael, Saint Miguel, Dondon, Marmelade, and Gonaïves. This vast space of country Toussaint L'Ouverture defended for a long time against the English, the [Page 90] Spanish, and against French emigrants, with troops badly armed, badly disciplined, and little accustomed to military manœuvres. This single fact is evidence of his prodigious activity and surpassing talent. He had, indeed, under him officers of activity. But genius was demanded in his difficult and perilous position, and genius Toussaint himself alone possessed. Not only had he to survey and sustain the whole, but each particular part required his presence as well as his thoughts. At every threatened point must Toussaint himself be, and at every threatened point Toussaint was. Constantly in motion, he and his horse seemed almost one compound being. In the midst of active movements he had to satisfy the daily demands of a voluminous correspondence, which he always dictated with his own lips. Very needful too, was it that he should do his utmost to encourage the cultivation of the lands, lest provisions should fail his troops, or famine try the fidelity of the people. Nor was the maintenance of discipline in hands such as his an easy office or a slight labour. He accomplished the task, however, by a general course of consideration and mildness as well as by stern severity toward the disobedient.

Meanwhile the king of Spain ceded to France all his possessions and rights in Hayti. The cession inflamed the hopes of the English government, who, resolving to try a last effort, sent, under General Howe, an army of three thousand men, together with a fleet under Admiral Parker.

Laveaux had fallen into peril. Instigated by jealousy, Rigaud and Villate, another man of colour, arrested General Laveaux and threw him into prison. This attempt to set up a mulatto domination was overcome by Toussaint. Grateful for the service, Laveaux appointed Toussaint his second in the government of the island of Hayti, and in the proclamation which he thereupon issued, declared him to be that Spartacus, foretold by Raynal, whose destiny it was to avenge the outrages inflicted on all his race; and whom he set forth as the vindicator of the constituted authorities, adding that in future nothing should be attempted except in concert with him, and by his councils. This association of Toussaint in the government sensibly amended the [Page 91] disposition of the blacks, who now began to have some confidence in their white superiors, and in consequence were, in large numbers, prepared to obey.

Sonthonax having overcome his enemies in France, returned to Hayti, at the head of a commission of which Roume was the other important member. The commissioners found the colony in a condition approaching to prosperity. Instead of profiting by the favourable dispositions that prevailed, and the special good feeling with which he was received, Sonthonax preferred stirring men's passions afresh. He had formed the project of bringing the men of colour under subjection by the power of the law. In order to effect his purpose, he, ostensibly to reward Toussaint L'Ouverture for the conduct he had pursued in the recent troubles, appointed that distinguished man general of division. These measures irritated Rigaud, the champion of the mulattoes, who saw, with extreme jealousy, the black chief elevated to a rank superior to his own. Obeyed over almost all the south, Rigaud was deaf to overtures made to him on the part of the commissioners, and in discontent withdrew to Tiburon.

Toussaint L'Ouverture was not a man to lose time. Aware of the reinforcements the English had received, he hastened to the seat of war in the west, and having driven back Colonel Brisbane, who had invaded La Petite Rivière, he pushed forward to Saline, near Gonaïves, which the English had set on fire, and on the shore near which they had effected a landing. The English were on the point of advancing, when Toussaint appeared. Putting himself at the head of the cavalry, he fell on the English at Guildive, and directing the charge in his own person, he compelled them to re-embark in confusion, with the loss of their standards, their baggage, and their cannon. Toussaint received injuries in the conflict, but Brisbane was mortally wounded. The victorious soldiers, having their muskets crowned with laurels, were received in Gonaïves in the midst of the acclamations of the people.

The influence of Toussaint L'Ouverture grew every day. Almost at will, he drew the negroes round his banners, and [Page 92] reduced them into discipline. He also detached from the English colours bands which they had taken into their pay. Applying himself to matters connected with the general administration of the colony, he put on a firm footing the prosperity which had begun to appear. He applied his power specially to the restoration of the culture of the soil; wisely declaring, that the liberty of the blacks could be consolidated only by the prosperity of agriculture. This important averment, spreading among the black chiefs, awoke in them the desire to acquire and to conserve property.

While the English had great difficulty to struggle against the French arms in the west, they were vigorously pressed by Desfourneaux in the north. Four columns surrounded the heights of Vallière, where the enemy, with the aid of some detachments, kept up what they called "La Vendée of Saint Domingo." Henry Christophe, afterwards King of Hayti, powerfully contributed to the success of this expedition. In the south, Rigaud assumed the offensive. Having strongly fortified Les Cayes, be marched to attack Port-au-Prince. He met with a resistance so vigorous, so brave, and so well-conducted that any but a very superior man must have perished. In a sally made by Colonel Markham, at the head of a thousand men, his outposts were carried, and his head-quarters plundered. The rout was becoming general, when Rigaud, though urged to save his life by flight, leaped on his horse, and rallying fifty men, threw himself on the English occupied in pillage, and put many of them to the sword. The plunder was recovered, and Markham, forced to beat a retreat, fell pierced with balls.

L'Ouverture, not slow in sustaining the efforts of Rigaud, sat down before Saint Marc with ten thousand men. Thrice did he assail the town in vain. After prodigies of valour, he was compelled to retire.

Unwilling to derive no advantage from his exertions, Toussaint determined to rescue Mirebalais out of the hands of the Spaniards, by whom it was held. At his voice, the population rose in a mass, and, with his assistance, made him master of the district.

[Page 93]Mirebalais was a most important post. Lying in the mountains on the north-east corner of the western department, the district so called consisted of gorges, steeps, and narrow passes, which made almost every part of it a Thermopylæ. The village of Saint Louis, also called by the name of the district, commands an immense extent of level country. Favourable to animal life in general, the country abounds in superior horses. A skilful commander, possessed of Mirebalais, therefore, might almost defy attack, and at his pleasure sally forth to wage war in almost any part of the island.

The English, aware of the importance of this position, resolved to get it into their hands. They succeeded in the bold undertaking.

The loss was too heavy to be endured. L'Ouverture, as soon as other duties permitted, made arrangements for the recovery of Mirebalais. He was not in time, however, to prevent the occupants from covering it with fortifications. The command of the district had been entrusted to a French emigrant, the Count de Bruges, whose forces amounted to two thousand English troops of the line, besides a numerous militia. On the 24th of March, 1797, Toussaint L'Ouverture, by means of his lieutenant, Morney, intercepted the high road leading into the country, and encamping at Block-haus du Gros Figuier, repelled Montalembert, who was advancing into Mirebalais with seven hundred men and two pieces of artillery. The next day, Toussaint drove the English from all their possessions, and completing the investment of the village, ordered, on the south, the attack of the forts. With such unity of operation, and such impetuosity of assault was the attack made, that the whole was carried. Conflagration completed what the fire-arms left unsubdued. Toussaint L'Ouverture passed from eminence to eminence, and surveyed his troops victorious on all sides. A yet more pleasing sight to him was that which he had when he set at liberty two hundred prisoners of all hues who were suffering under a degrading punishment, and who every moment expected a horrible death from the flames which were approaching the place of their detention.

[Page 94]Pursuing his advantages, L'Ouverture, in a campaign of fourteen days, totally defeated the English, and brought under obedience the entire province. Among his spoils were eleven pieces of cannon, with their ammunition, and two hundred prisoners. As his recompence, Toussaint L'Ouverture received from Sonthonax the appointment of commander-in-chief of the army of Saint Domingo, vacant by the departure of Laveaux. The conquering hero was installed at the Cape in the presence of the garrison, composed of black troops, and the remains of the white troops. These are the words which he employed on the occasion: —"Citizen Commissioners, I accept the eminent rank to which you have just raised me, only in the hope of more surely succeeding in entirely extirpating the enemies of Saint Domingo, of contributing to its speedy restoration to prosperity, and of securing the happiness of its inhabitants. If to fulfil the difficult task which it imposes, it sufficed to wish the good of the island, and to effect it, in all that depends on me, I hope that, with the aid of the Divine Being, I shall succeed; the tyrants are cast down on the earth; they will no more defile the places where the standard of liberty and equality ought to float alone, and where the sacred rights of man ought to be recognised.

"Officers and soldiers, if there is a compensation in the severe labours which I am about to enter on, I shall find it in the satisfaction of commanding brave soldiers. Let the sacred fire of liberty animate us, and let us never take repose until we have prostrated the foe."

Lofty now was the position of Toussaint L'Ouverture. Glad was his heart. His joy did not arise from his own personal elevation. It is true that he had created an army which could beat European troops, and expel them from even the strongholds of Hayti. It is true that in his deeds and warlike achievements he had equalled the great captains of ancient and modern times. But he had not fought for his own aggrandisement; he had done all with a view to an ultimate object. And now that object seemed within his reach. The emancipation of his race was accomplished, therefore did Toussaint rejoice. "The opening" [Page 95] was made; what remained to be done was detail. Alas! such were the appearances, but the appearances proved delusions.

The achievement just set forth gave the final blow to the war. No longer could the English do more than maintain a desultory conflict with scarcely any hope of final success, whatever temporary advantages they might gain. When all but relieved from a foreign enemy, the French authorities began to disagree among themselves. The particulars are too tedious to be repeated. From the colony appeals were made to the legislature in Paris. The commissioner Sonthonax, fearing impeachment, requested to be sent home as a deputy from the colony. If at first sincere, he seems afterwards to have vacillated. Toussaint, however, convinced that his absence would be conducive to the restoration of harmony and the effective prosecution of hostilities, took measures that his request should not fail of effect. But Toussaint, victorious and powerful in the colony, had reason to fear the result of intrigues and plots against himself in the mother country. As a pledge of his honour and a token of confidence, he sent his two sons to France for their education. On their part the English, suffering greatly from the climate, and making no progress towards the subjugation of the island, employed the utmost of their power to seduce the hostile leaders. Having with little satisfaction to themselves attempted to secure the mulatto interest, they made the bold attempt of seducing Toussaint L'Ouverture himself. Little knowing the character of the man with whom they dealt, they offered as the price of his subserviency the title of King of Hayti. The incorruption of Toussaint on the occasion was the more remarkable and worthy, as General Hédouville, sent after the departure of Sonthonax as the representative of France, treated him with less consideration than was deserved by the man to whom that country owed the restoration of its colony. Toussaint had, indeed, become too powerful perhaps for France, certainly for its deputy Hédouville. In his anxiety to disembarrass himself of the black chief, that general, by means of his creatures, tried to induce him to embark for the mother country, in order to [Page 96] plead his cause and maintain his interests. Pointing with his hand to a sapling which grew near—"I will go," he said, "when that branch shall form a vessel of sufficient size to carry me thither."

During these unhappy divisions, the English had been losing ground. Worn down and dispirited, they at length began to take decided steps for the evacuation of the island. In the negotiations and measures which this involved, the polemics and distrusts of the French authorities displayed but too strongly their evil effects. Port-au-Prince, however, was surrendered by the English, who shortly afterwards found it prudent to place the Môle Saint-Nicholas in the hands of the French. Dissatisfied with the stipulations made by Hédouville, Toussaint repaired to Saint-Marc, and took into his own hands the settlement of the terms of capitulation. Not yet wholly without hope of winning over to English views their most formidable opponent, the English by their representative, General Maitland, rendered the highest honours to Toussaint L'Ouverture. The attempt met with deserved failure. Toussaint could see through the covered designs of his old foes. He had no faith that the freedom of his race would ensue from English domination; and he knew that their equality before the law had been recognised by France. Faithful to his great idea and final design, he remained superior to the blandishments of English wealth and adulation. After enduring so many fatigues and acquiring so much glory, L'Ouverture retired into the interior of the Artibonite, and took up his abode on the estate called Deschaux, which was situated in the mountains. There he flattered himself with the hope of some repose, and there, keeping an eye over the great centres of social movement, he could at any moment, like the eagle, descend to any part where his presence was required.

[Page 97] CHAPTER XI.

Toussaint L'Ouverture composes agitation, and brings back prosperity—Is opposed by the Commissioner, Hédouville, who flies to France—Appeals, in self-justification, to the Directory in Paris.

HAVING reached the commanding position which he held, Toussaint L'Ouverture, with a true patriotism and a wise benevolence, applied himself to the difficult task of healing the wounds of his country. The first task was to induce the planters to resume possession of their estates, and re-commence the tillage of the soil. This he effected in part by persuasion, in part by gentle compulsion; numerous detachments of infantry, traversing the cities, collected together the scattered owners and conducted them to the plantations. The conduct of the troops employed in the service was as worthy of notice as the obedience of the agriculturists; for, observing the strictest discipline, they showed the greatest respect to property, and conducted themselves towards all with becoming moderation and mildness. The control over these rude natures which this temperance implied, was the result of the discipline instituted by Toussaint, and of the love and the fear which his name inspired. Among his signal triumphs this was, perhaps, the most signal. Not by blacks only, but by whites, was this extraordinary man obeyed. Obedience secured Toussaint's protection. Regardless of the colour of the skin, he received with favour, and treated with confidence, and promoted with readiness, all whom he had valid reasons for believing sincerely bent on advancing the public good. Disdaining to govern by the rivalry of classes, he aimed to serve the whole, by the means and with the aid of each. Emigrant or creole, black or white, men were treated by him as men; being placed in the posts for which they were fitted, whether military or civil. If there was a difference in his conduct towards dependents, that difference was not in favour of white men. The injured, he rightly judged, had the first claim to his attention. [Page 98] Generally, however, his administration was impartial, severely impartial.

It scarcely need be added that he grew in universal estimation. Respected by men in general, his influence became immense, and even the fear or distrust which was secretly nourished against him by some, was an acknowledgment of his power. Under Toussaint's benign sway, parties began to melt away, and heart-burnings to cease. An unqualified amnesty, which he proclaimed, tranquillized men's minds, and reconciled them to the existing state of things.

Nor did the victorious general forget the All-powerful Arm to which he knew that he owed his triumph, and by whose aid only, he was equally assured, he could finish the work he had begun and so far accomplished.

But the governor disapproved of L'Ouverture's policy. Whether from a difference of view, or from suspecting Toussaint of ambitious designs, Hédouville, though a professed Republican, characterized his administration as "too mild and too full of results." Never having behaved towards the negro captain with cordiality, he now conveyed to Toussaint's ears words of open complaint and covert blame. Toussaint was not to be turned from a course which he had deliberately adopted, and found to be most beneficial. Afraid lest Hédouville's power would interrupt that course, or abate its good, he issued proclamations to his troops—his chief basis of reliance—in order to confirm them in their obedience by the strongest of ties, namely, the religious ties to which their susceptible and impulsive natures made them peculiarly sensible. "This," said he, "is the path which we must all follow, in order to draw down upon us the blessing of the Lord. I hope you will never depart from it, and that you will punctually execute what follows:—

"The heads of regiments are required to see that the troops join in prayer morning and evening, as far as the service will permit.

"At the earliest review, the Generals Commanding-in-chief, will cause high mass to be celebrated and a Te Deum to be sung in all the places of their several districts, as an expression [Page 99] of gratitude to Heaven for having vouchsafed to direct our last campaigns; for having caused the evacuation of the enemy to take place without effusion of blood; for having protected the return amongst us of many thousand men of every colour, who till then had been lost; and, finally, for having restored to the labours of agriculture more than twenty thousand hands. The *Te Deum* will be announced by a salvo of twenty-two pieces of cannon."

Under the effects of words so religious and so just, the credit of Hédouville was greatly lessened; in proportion as L'Ouverture gained ascendancy, he sank, until he retained among his supporters only those who were immediately around him, such as his officials, Frenchmen who were foreigners in the colony, and others who, from personal connexions with the mother country, desired to maintain its power in the hands of its agents.

The contrast was made greater by the diverse course pursued by the two in regard to the cultivators of the soil. While Hédouville unconditionally declared all the blacks free, Toussaint wisely prefixed to their actual freedom a kind of apprenticeship for five years, on condition of their receiving one-fourth of the produce, out of which the masters were to defray the cost of their subsistence. The plan of the governor, speciously designed to catch the popular breeze, would have issued in universal disorder. Instead of immediate emancipation, always pregnant with present and future disasters, Toussaint interposed a period of preparation, and in so doing, saved the property of the masters, as well as promoted the interests of the servants. So wise and moderate a use of his triumph and his power probably saved Hayti from the terrors of a universal convulsion, and certainly raised him to a high position in the respect of all impartial and judicious men.

Hédouville, aware to what an extent he had lost the public confidence, took measures for provoking a movement contrary to Toussaint among the men of colour. Rigaud he accordingly invited to the seat of government. As a cover, he invited Toussaint also to take part in the conference. But the negro chief was as wary as he was bold; and he may have heard that [Page 100] some time previously officers of Hédouville's staff had offered to seize his person, if only their master would put four brave soldiers at their disposal.

Remaining at Port-au-Prince, Toussaint was informed that Rigaud was on his way to the Cape. The commander of that place, and several black officers, advised Toussaint to intercept and apprehend Rigaud. "I could," he replied, "easily do so; but God forbid. I have need of Rigaud. He is violent. I want him for carrying on war; and that war is necessary to me. The mulatto caste is superior to my own. If I take Rigaud from them, they would perhaps find another superior to him. I know Rigaud; he gives up the bridle when he gallops; he shows his arm when he strikes. For me, I gallop also; but I know where to stop; and when I strike, I am felt, not seen. M. Rigaud can conduct insurrections only by blood and massacres; I know how to put the people in movement; but when I appear, all must be tranquil."

A general feeling of uneasiness spread abroad. Fear began to prevail. A counter-revolution seemed at hand. The blacks were uneasy, especially those who had compromised themselves in taking part with the English. The mulattoes were regarded with alarm. In Fort-Saint-Dauphin, a regiment ran to arms, declaring that the whites wished to restore slavery. A combat took place between the black troops and the white troops. The former being beaten, spread over the open country, which they raised on all sides. Then, once more, conflagration committed its ravages. Many unfortunate whites, taken by surprise on their estates, were slaughtered. The insurgents marched to the Cape. Toussaint hastened to the seat of the insurrection. The blacks were raging as in former days. Suddenly their chief appeared, and all was peaceful. Undertaking to be the exponent of their griefs, he led them to Cape City. The moment he arrived there, the alarm was given by the authorities, who seem to have desired a rencontre. The troops were assembled, but the effort proved nugatory. By little and little, the soldiers deserted their posts when they knew that Toussaint was at hand. Hédouville, failing in his *coup d'etat,* embarked to return [Page 101] to France. From on board the ship he published a proclamation, in which, being no longer able to profit by the prejudices of colour, he sought his account by appealing to national jealousies, and declared that Toussaint L'Ouverture was sold to the English.

The movement was at an end. The plotter was on his way back to France, and the regenerator of his country found himself in a freer field, and possessed of augmented resources. No less single than pure in his aims, Toussaint L'Ouverture rose in general regard and public confidence, even by the contrarieties which the Governor had thrown in his way. By the failure of the recent plot, too, the mulatto interest, considered as hostile to the interest of other classes, received a heavy blow.

As soon as General Hédouville had set sail, the blacks were not only tranquil, but obedient to the eye and the finger of their chief. Every one silently resumed his habitudes. The most perfect calm succeeded the most raging tempest. A *Te Deum* was chanted, and the name of Toussaint L'Ouverture was mingled with the Hallowed Name in the uttered gratitude of thousands. Toussaint was not insensible to the homage, and he desired the complete accomplishment of his mission. But he had seen the edifice he had so carefully and painfully raised, put in danger with only too much facility. The mulatto party, though weakened, were still powerful. At their head was Rigaud, who had not shown himself averse to the designs of his caste. Toussaint dreaded a collision. Possibly he himself was a hindrance to a peaceful and permanent settlement. Entertaining no merely personal objects, he gave utterance to a desire to be relieved of his weighty responsibilities. At a moment when, by a bold stroke, he might have set up a throne, and perhaps established a dynasty, he asked for his dismissal. The word called forth a universal remonstrance. The civil and the military authorities, the white, black, and brown inhabitants, the proprietors and the labourers, all combined in laying before him formal addresses, in which they entreated him to remain, to use their own terms, "their father and their benefactor."

But there was a court of appeal. Before that tribunal [Page 102] Hédouville would appear with singular advantage. Toussaint knew the disparity of his means for obtaining a fair hearing, but he resolved to employ such as were at his command. Accordingly, he sent Colonel Vincent, one of his secretaries, to explain and justify his conduct before the French Government, then in the hands of the Directory. Colonel Vincent was the bearer of a letter, of which the following contains the principal passages:—

"Toussaint L'Ouverture, General-in-Chief of the army of Saint Domingo, to the Directory of the Republic:

"CITIZEN DIRECTORS,—When in my last dispatches I determined to request my dismissal, I did so because, after having collected all the instances of opposition to the principles which the Constitution has established, which your wisdom has maintained, which your energy has defended,—all the instances of opposition, I say, manifested in conduct held by the agent Hédouville during the short space of time which he governed this colony,—foresaw the unhappy event which for an instant disturbed the public tranquillity I had had so much trouble to establish; and I did go after having calculated the consequences of the distance at which he held himself from me, and of which he gave public proofs on several occasions, fearing that my deposition, which he meditated, would be the reward of my long services, of my fidelity, and of my devotedness.

"The incident at Fort-Dauphin realized my apprehensions as to the convulsion for which preparations were made, and the proclamation which the agent put forth at the moment of his departure has justified my fears regarding the fate he intended for me.

"The most outrageous injury which can be done to a man of honour crowns the vexations which he has made me undergo. By this perfidious act he causes a vast number of Frenchmen to quit these lands who had congratulated themselves on their happiness here, and who, faithful to their country, were compelled to sacrifice their interests, rather than become accomplices in the crime of independence of which I was regarded as guilty; he carries with him, especially, the principal authorities, that (as he [Page 103] said on leaving) they may be the irrefragable proof of my duplicity, of my perfidy.

"Doubtless the first feeling of the Directory, whom I respect, on seeing them unanimously bear witness against me, will be to invoke vengeance on my head; that of the French people, whom I love, to devote me to execration; and that of the enemies of the blacks, whom I despise, to cry out for slavery; but when it shall be known that at the time which I was accused of wishing to sunder this island from France, my benefactress, I repeated the oath of fidelity to her, I take pleasure in believing that the government I own, and my fellow- citizens, will render me the justice I merit, and that the enemies of my brethren will be reduced to silence.

"The Agent, in reality, surrounded himself only with persons in the colony sunk in public opinion, ambitious and intriguing, who caress all the factions which have torn this unfortunate country. A band of young men, of no character and no principles, who came with him, then threw away the mask, and manifested a spirit both anti-national and insulting to me.

"The labourers who began to taste the sweets of repose in the midst of security, were surprised at the impure sounds which struck their ear, and wounded their heart. I became the depository of their griefs, and I composed their minds by assuring them of the good intentions of the agent of a benevolent government; but they soon accused me myself of partiality, having become certain that even at the table of the General Agent they were denounced as unworthy of the liberty they enjoy, and which they have derived from the equity of France.

"Often did the Agent reproach me with having received emigrants, with violating the constitution, with breaking the law. Whatever may have been the reasons of the continual blame which I received from him in regard to conduct in which I found nothing to reproach myself with, I could not ascertain them, and, persuaded that, from the moment that I lost his confidence, I could expect no more good, I asked of you my dismissal Happy would it have been if it had reached me prior to his departure! He would then have learnt that ambition never was [Page 104] my master, and especially he would not have done me the injury to publish that I desired to terminate my services to France by a crime towards which I was drawn by the men around me who were sold to the English.

"Whoever those may have been of whom I was obliged to make use to assist me in my important occupations, and without whom even with all the means given by education which I have not received, I could not have performed my functions, I will one day prove that no one less than myself merits the reproach laid at my door by my adversaries, namely, that I allowed myself to be governed.

"Could it be laid to my charge that I directed towards the public interests, that I employed for the advantage of the republic, activity, talents, and genius? And when my secretaries, whom bonds too sacred unite to their mother country to allow a moment's doubt of their attachment to her, are the sole depositaries of my secrets, the sole confidants of the projects which I could not confine within my own breast; why cast on men who will never influence me the blame of the ridiculous intentions imputed to me, and which never having entered my heart, again prove that I do not allow myself to be governed by the passions of others? If those passions had directed my steps, I should not have foreseen the event which has just taken place, and, walking like a blind man on my political course, I should have asked you for my dismissal.

"But that step which prudence forced me to take, the only one which could dissipate the storm with which I was threatened, was very far from restoring confidence in the minds of the people of Saint Domingo. The discontent of the labourers had increased by the compulsion of an engagement for three years. That seemed to them a step back to slavery. They called to mind the means proposed by Vaublanc to establish his system in this colony, and they were surprised that when the Directory had punished that conspirator, its Agent should propose the same measures, should prescribe them, should exact their prompt and full execution. This dissatisfaction which was fostered, was soon shared by the soldiers. By the discharge of more than three thousand men, effected after the evacuation of the west by [Page 105] the English, I had proved how necessary I thought it to cut down the armaments of the military. I was blamed in that operation, and I received the order not to cut down any troop. Nevertheless, on the departure of the English, it was declared that all the black forces ought to be disbanded in order to be sent back to agriculture, and that European soldiers only should be employed in the defence of the coasts. Then distrust entered the soldiers' hearts, and while previously a part of them had taken the hoe without a murmur, they showed aversion toward a measure which they regarded as an attack on liberty.

"Whatever were the grounds of distrust with which I was surrounded; however faithful the councils I received on all parts from the most sincere friends of the prosperity of Saint Domingo; whatever fears were infused into my mind by the crimes contemplated against my person; I did not hesitate to set out for the Cape, and even endeavoured to give a proof of my confidence in the highest authorities, by going unattended, except by an aide-de-camp and a cavalry officer; but having arrived on the Héricourt plantation, I was met by alarming rumours. I learned that at Fort-Dauphin, the fifth colonial regiment—which contributed so much to the restoration of order, to the purification of La Grande Rivière, (the Vendée of Saint Domingo,) to the expulsion of the English—had become the victim of the European troops, who formerly had delivered up to foreign powers the points of the colony which had been confided to their defence.

"Convinced, then, of the bad intentions of the Government in whose names all those horrors were committed; no longer seeing any security for any one who had acquired well-grounded claims to the national gratitude; fearing, with good reason, for my own life, I turned back and prepared to go and wait at Gonaïves official news of an event, the consequences of which I dreaded. I received a letter from the General Agent, which confirmed my fears, and in which he ordered me to repair to Fort-Dauphin to aid the citizen Manigat, whom he had invested with all civil and military power, in the re-establishment of order and public tranquillity. I then pressed on to Gonaïves, in order to take the escort, of which I had need. The [Page 106] crimes committed by Frenchmen against my brethren, forced me to this prudential measure. I left Gonaïves with the fourth regiment; but what was my grief, when, on arriving at the Héricourt plantation, I learned that the rising of the labourers had become general, that all the plain was in arms, and threatened Cape Town with an immediate irruption. Those who with that design had assembled on the Héricourt estate, surrounded me as soon as I arrived, reproaching me with having deceived them in answering for the good intentions of General Hédouville, and attributed to me the slaughter of their brethren at Fort-Dauphin, the arrest of some of them, and the dismissal of General Moyse; and then it was that I received information of all the details of that unfortunate event. Soon I learned that the evil was intruding into all the parishes, and that the people required that General Hédouville should be sent away, the restoration of General Moyse to his rights, and the liberation of the officers of the fifth regiment, made prisoners in the affair at Fort-Dauphin, &c.

"Whatever pain I felt at the excesses committed against a corps, respectable for its services, and against officers whom I knew always attached to their duties, against a chief who never failed in his attachment to France and to the principles of liberty— my own nephew—I regarded in so alarming an event only the imminent dangers to which the public interests were exposed. I sent on all sides faithful emissaries to calm the agitated minds of men; to announce to them my arrival, and to require of them to do nothing without my orders. I hastened to set myself in opposition to the enterprises of the more senseless, who had already taken possession of the heights of the Cape and of Fort Belair which commands the city. With difficulty could I make my way through the crowds; an immense influx of people, whom the blind desire for revenge had armed, covered all the roads which led to the Cape, and threatened that city with the greatest calamities. Frightened at the abyss, on the brink of which the city stood, I ran to draw it back. In my course, I learned that the General Agent had gone on board the fleet. Surprised at the news, I hastened to the Cape, which I reached [Page 107] with difficulty, after having, sometimes by prayers, sometimes by menaces, stopped the torrent with which it was threatened to be inundated. The astonishment caused by the departure of General Hédouville, was changed into grief when I learned that that Agent, alarmed, doubtless, at the dangers to which he had exposed the public weal, and despairing of any longer being able to conserve it, had resolved to go away, and that, to colour his pusillanimous flight, he had proclaimed that I was aiming at independence.

"The terror having augmented, more than eighteen hundred persons followed the Agent in his flight. He ordered the cannons to be spiked. The command was being executed, when there arose a cry 'To arms!' The troops drawn out in battle array were moved by the cry; they were pacified by their leaders; had a single musket been fired, the city would have perished.

"Strong in my conscience, I shall not remind you, citizen directors, of all I have done for the triumph of liberty, the prosperity of Saint Domingo, the glory of the French Republic; nor will I protest to you my attachment to our mother country, to my duties; my respect to the constitution, to the laws of the Republic, and my submission to the Government. I swear to you I am faithful, and my future conduct, more than all oaths, will prove to you that I shall always be faithful.

"If the defence of my cause, that of the freedom of my brethren, needed cunning and intrigue, and manly eloquence, in order to triumph over my enemies, I would give it up and weep over France; but as I am persuaded that it is sufficient to present the truth for it to be apprehended by the republican Government, I am satisfied with setting before you an exposition of my conduct, and of that of General Hédouville, and repose on your justice for the verdict which is to result.

"As soon as I had re-established the public tranquillity, I sent to the Commissioner Roume—your delegate in what was formerly the Spanish part of this island—to intreat him in the name of the public safety to come and take the reins of government thrown up by General Hédouville; persuaded that his determination will [Page 108] be conformed to the wishes of all good Frenchmen, I impatiently await his arrival, in order to aid him with all my power in the important functions of his new position."

The appeal of justice and rectitude prevailed. The Directory were satisfied with Toussaint's self-justification. More might have been expected; more ought to have been given. But suspicions began to prevail in France to the disadvantage of the negro emancipator. The purer his conduct, the more heroic his life, the greater was his crime, for his real crime was his power, and that power was the natural and inevitable consequence of his virtuous and high-minded career.

CHAPTER XII.

Civil war in the south between Toussaint L'Ouverture and Rigaud—Siege and capture of Jacmel.

IN quitting the shores of Hayti, Hédouville threw a torch of discord amidst the excitable population. Not only did he cause alarm by declaring that Toussaint was preparing to betray the colony to the English, but he called forth the slumbering passions of the men of colour, by intimating that with them lay the power and the duty of traversing his treacherous designs. He even addressed a letter to their leader, Rigaud, in which he formally set that mulatto general free from his obligations to Toussaint as Commander-in-chief, and requested him to assume the command of the southern department. This was nothing less than an invitation to civil strife. A correspondence took place between L'Ouverture and Rigaud. According to what he believed to be his duty, the former acquainted the latter with the departure of Hédouville, and exhorted him to pursue such a course as would promote the general weal. Rigaud, evading the real point at issue, brought into prominence the alleged partiality of Toussaint toward the emigrants, whom he requested him to drive away.

[Page 109]The request, of course, remained without effect, but it served as a pretext to the jealousies of Rigaud. Again did trouble take possession of the popular mind. The fear became the greater because Rigaud urged on Toussaint severity towards the proprietors, whereas the latter had determined to pursue his course of administering equal justice to men of all colours, so long as they proved themselves good citizens. In this state of excitement Toussaint L'Ouverture invited the Commissioner Roume to repair to the seat of government, in order to fill the post vacated by Hédouville. In this step he gave effect to a decree of the Directory. Roume appeared at the Cape on the 12th of January, 1799. Toussaint, though suffering from sickness, repaired thither to confer with him a few days afterwards. The two chief authorities in the island came to an amicable understanding after mutual explanations. Entering into the large and philanthropic views of L'Ouverture, Roume pronounced him "a philosopher, a legislator, a general, and a good citizen."

Anxious to scatter the clouds which overhung the horizon, Roume called together the chief captains of the island. In order to excite attention to the conference and commemorate the event, public festivities were celebrated. At the foot of the tree of liberty, planted in the great square, and surrounded by generals, Roume delivered a speech, in which he recommended peace, union, love of the republic, and self-sacrifice. He pronounced eulogies on the army, extolling the success of its arms against the enemies of France, and declared that the most perfect union existed between the generals, Toussaint L'Ouverture, Rigaud, Biassou, Laplume, and the other military chiefs. The following day business was entered into in earnest. The representative of the French Government requested Rigaud to cede certain portions of the territory which was under his control. The request looked like a concession to Toussaint L'Ouverture. Jealousy sprang into activity in Rigaud's mind. After a warm discussion, and some time for reflection, the mulatto chief gave in his resignation. Roume replied, urging its withdrawal. The request prevailed, and Rigaud set out for the south. On his way [Page 110] he evacuated Grand Goâve and Petit Goâve—a portion only of what had been required—which L'Ouverture caused his troops to occupy. The storm had receded; by no means had it passed away. The colonists rallied around L'Ouverture; for they had not forgotten that it was from the efforts of the free men of colour to gain equality of political rights, that the revolution had proceeded, which had changed the face of the island. They stirred up divisions among the blacks and the men of mingled blood. On their part the men of colour were displeased at seeing the supreme command settled in the hands of an African of pure blood, and flocked around the standard of Rigaud. The blacks, under the protection of the Government and Toussaint, beheld the gathering clouds not without excitement, yet in confidence; nor were they unwilling, after so many victories, to try a last fall with their special foe.

The contest began with extremes; free white men fought with black slaves. Its intervals have disappeared. The circle has narrowed. Those who are nearest each other are about to join in conflict. The black will fight with those who are a little less black than himself: therefore this will be the deadliest combat of all. The two parties stand and look at each other like inflamed beasts of prey. Which will make the first spring?

The mulatto, to the qualities of pride and meanness, adds singular strength of muscle and impulse of passion. Conscious of power, he also feels within him boiling emotions. If victory depended on a dash, he would be master wherever he dwells. But the very exuberance of his nature precludes caution and banishes prudence, and in the impetuosity of his rush he incurs as much peril as he occasions. Impatient of delay, he pays for momentary advantages by speedy and irretrievable defeat. Yet the same unbridled will which brings disaster nourishes vindictiveness; he is therefore ever prepared, if not panting, for revenge. The fight, consequently, is renewed, but without a change of result; and so life passes away in extravagant and disappointed efforts.

The mulattoes of Hayti could not restrain their wounded feelings. The opposition to the Government broke out at [Page 111] Corail, a small village in the southern department. The men of colour gaining the upper hand, threw into prison, at Jéremie, thirty of their prisoners, consisting of one colonist and nine-and-twenty blacks. Then was re-enacted the tragedy of the Black Hole in Calcutta. The prisoners perished from bad air. Premeditation was imputed to the mulattoes; of culpable inconsideration and blind passion they were guilty. "In all movements," remarked L'Ouverture, "the blacks are the victims." This dark event rendered the continuance of peace impossible. Both sides prepared for war. Toussaint, with a foresight becoming his position, looked calmly at the probable wants of the island in general. Hayti was indebted for the food of its inhabitants chiefly to importation. The condition of France gave small hope of sufficient supplies. War, too, would suspend the operations of agriculture in the island. He therefore negotiated a commercial treaty with the United States.

The conflict began with an attack by Rigaud's troops on Petit Goâve, the surrender of which had been obtained in the conference at the Cape. The place fell, and the colonists were all ruthlessly massacred. Profiting by the success, Rigaud advanced and took up a position against Grand Goâve. Hastening to Port-au-Prince, Toussaint justly accused Rigaud with having first drawn the sword, and made preparations for the campaign. Having called the mulattoes together into the Church, he ascended the pulpit and laid bare their bosoms, foretelling his own success and the ruin of their cause. "I see," he said to them, "I see to the bottom of your souls; you are ready to rise against me, but although all the troops are quitting the west, I leave behind my eye and my arm—my eye, which will watch you; my arm which, if necessary, will fall upon you."

A mulatto plot, which extended even to the north, had put the keys of Port-au-Prince into the hands of a traitor. L'Ouverture was a prisoner in a town which he thought his own. But his decision and courage were equal to all crises. He discovered the snare, punished the criminals, and then, with the fleetness and the force of the eagle, flew back over his own territories, and, forcing strongholds and capturing towns, went as far to the [Page 112] north-west as Saint-Nicholas, which he brought back to its duty. The men of colour were smitten with consternation, and many of them having been captured in the several collisions, suffered indignities the most humiliating. Suddenly Toussaint returned to the Cape. The guilty thought the hour of their doom was come. The high-minded victor invited the inhabitants to meet him at the church, and there, besides a concourse of people, all the civil and military authorities assembled. The garrison, which consisted of black troops, surrounded the place; and under the guard of a picket of soldiers in the church were the men of colour, almost naked, and in extreme dejection. Toussaint L'Ouverture ascended an elevation, pronounced a eulogium on the forgiveness of injuries as the duty of every Christian, and then proclaiming the pardon and the freedom of all the mulattoes, he distributed clothes and money to them severally, and gave strict injunctions that, on their way to join their families, they should be protected and treated as brothers. This unexpected generosity produced the most lively enthusiasm. As he left the church, benedictions were showered on his head.

While at the Cape, admiration at Toussaint's clemency was universal; the mulatto insurgents in the south only fought the more strenuously, in order to make up by military advantage that which L'Ouverture had gained by wise moderation. No wars are so bitter or so bloody as those of class, caste, and colour. The fact was illustrated in this terrible conflict. With such bitterness and ferocity did it rage, that Toussaint was compelled to employ all his influence to recruit his ranks. To the blacks he might look with confidence, as the war was specially for their benefit; but the blacks began to grow alarmed as the sanguinary struggle proceeded. The whites in the north and the west, who had hitherto been exempt from the service, were marshalled at the Cape, and sent into the south, to take part in a contest in which they had only a remote interest. A mute consternation prevailed. Scarcely was the conflict spoken of in the intercourse of private life, and the periodical press transcribed the reports of the several chiefs without permitting themselves to add any comments or reflections. Every one not actually engaged in the [Page 113] warfare feared to compromise himself, lest he should bring on his head the vengeance of the conqueror. Yet prudence did not prevent complications of all kinds, nor could Toussaint's mercy preclude horrors the most distressing. Rigaud, boundless in resources as he was brave and daring, put forth all his energy, and maintained his position at every cost. Toussaint, with a prowess not inferior to Rigaud's, was equally vigilant, and equally bold. Yet was he unable to guard against all stratagems. In the recesses of the mountains near Port-de-Paix, as he made his way with few attendants, he found that he had fallen into an ambuscade. A discharge of musketry rattled around his head, his physician fell dead at his feet. The plume of feathers which he wore was shot away, and he himself escaped as if by miracle. Saved from one, he shortly after was exposed to another ambuscade. The shots were directed at his carriage; the coachman was killed; he himself rode tranquilly on horseback a few paces distant. In the midst of perils, Toussaint L'Ouverture persevered. Yet he obtained only partial success. The troops of Rigaud, if fewer in number, were individually superior to the hasty levies of Toussaint, and collectively better disciplined. Many of them had long fought under their chief, and were conversant with all the resources and requirements of the war in which they were engaged. With the country in which the conflict was waged they were intimately acquainted, and of the character of their leader they knew enough to be aware that only defeat would bring discredit or occasion displeasure. Having to overcome such an enemy, Toussaint L'Ouverture found it necessary to put forth his utmost power, the rather as he had to hold possession of a wide extent of country, and that with troops of whom the bulk were of an inferior caste. Painful is it to read the alternations of defeat and victory in this terrible contest, especially as on both sides they were accompanied by acts of cruelty. The only relief that the mind can obtain in going through the now tedious, now revolting details, arises from the reflection that had such amount of effort and such patience of suffering as these events show man to possess, been employed, as happily one day they may be employed, in some cause of high [Page 114] benevolence, some undertaking to save and not to destroy men's lives, the results would have been no less satisfactory than glorious indeed. The terror inspired by Rigaud's successes and ferocity drove the labourers from the fields into the forts; from the forts they were driven into the towns; when one town was taken, they escaped into another. Then they assembled together to concert and make attacks. Thus the country was a desert, the cities overflowed. While agriculture was at a standstill, provisions were often destroyed, and while no supplies came from the country, the dense masses aggregated in the towns experienced want. The want arose to famine in Jacmel, lying on the southern side of the tongue of land which forms the southern department. Jacmel, on the seashore, formed the key of the district. It was under the power of Rigaud, commanded by Birot. Resolved to capture the place, which was capable of affording an obstinate resistance, Toussaint himself sat down before it. With the utmost difficulty were the preparations for the siege made. Women and children were employed to convey ammunition. Bands, amounting to six thousand labourers, drew huge pieces of cannon along frightful precipices, and down roads the most rugged, broken, and dangerous. At length, the troops were collected, and Jacmel was invested, so far as the sea would permit. Soon the harbour also was blockaded. Then the terrors of famine began to be experienced. So intense and various were the sufferings, that the officers at length determined to capitulate. The determination was opposed by the soldiers, who declared resistance still possible. The commander, with two of his staff, embarked in the night and escaped to Cayes. His post was assumed by Gauthier. The siege was pressed with vigour. Post after post was taken. Meanwhile, Rigaud neither came up to aid, nor operated a diversion. Then Petion, apprized of the critical position of the town, determined to assume the perilous command, and, with three vessels and some provisions, succeeded in making his way into the port, under the discharges of firearms from the enemy's posts. Entering into the duties he had voluntarily undertaken, he employed all his ability in the defence. But an enemy was at work over whom he had no [Page 115] power. The famine reached such a height, that the inhabitants were compelled to eat the horses belonging to the cavalry. Every green thing was torn up and devoured. Those thought themselves happy who, in their search for food, met with a rat or a lizard. In the public highways, famished men scarcely recognised each other. Frenzy and wailing filled every place. Mothers, worn down by want, fatigue, and woe, lay in the streets, with their dead infants on their exhausted breasts. At length Petion, seeing that further resistance was impossible, resolved to cut his way through the besiegers. In order to inspire his soldiers with his own courage, he tore the flags from the staffs, and commanded his men to bind strips of them round their bodies, so that if they perished, they might still be faithful to their colours. Jacmel fell, and its fall was a heavy blow to Rigaud. Having taken possession of Jacmel, Toussaint L'Ouverture addressed to the inhabitants of the southern department the following proclamation:—

"CITIZENS,

"By what fatality is it, that hitherto deaf to my voice, which invites you to order, you have listened only to the councils of Rigaud? How is it possible that the pride of a single person should be the source of your evils, and that to flatter his ambition, you are willing to destroy your families, ruin your property, and bring yourselves into disgrace in the eyes of the whole world.

"I repeat to you for the third and last time, that my quarrel is not with the citizens of the south, but solely with Rigaud, inasmuch as he is disobedient and insubordinate; whom I wish to bring back to his duties that he may submit to the authority of a chief whom he can no longer disown. You ought not to have supported in his misdeeds a proud soldier who evidently raised the standard of revolt. You ought to have left me free to act, since I had a right to reprimand and even to punish him. This Rigaud knew well, but, too haughty to bow before the organs of the law, he has employed every means to seduce you and to retain you as accomplices. Consult your conscience; [Page 116] put away all prejudices; you will then easily know that Rigaud has desired to drive into revolt all men of colour, in order to make them his partisans and co-operators. I need not remind you of the means he has taken for the purpose, and the resources he has employed to deceive you all. You know as well as I, perhaps better than I, his destructive projects, and all he has attempted to put them into execution; he pretended to command blacks and whites without being willing to be commanded by them. Yet the law is equal for all. Painful experience ought to have torn from your eyes the veil which hides the brink of the precipice. Give, then, close attention to what you are about to do, and the danger which you still run. Reflect on the perils and the calamities which threaten you, and hasten to prevent them. I am kind, I am humane, I open to you my fatherly arms. Come all of you, I will receive you all, no less those of the south than those of the west and of the north, who, gained over by Rigaud, have deserted your firesides, your wives, your children, to place yourselves at his side. And Rigaud himself, that ambitious man, if he had followed the advice which I gave him, to submit to his lawful superiors, would he not now be tranquil and peaceful in the bosom of his family? would he not be firm and untroubled in the command which was intrusted to him? But mastered by deadly passions, Rigaud has dug a gulf at your feet; he has laid snares which you could not avoid. He wished to have you as partisans in his revolt; and to succeed in his object, he has employed falsehood and seduction. If you carefully examine this artful but very impolitic conduct, you cannot but declare that Rigaud does not love his colour, and that he had rather sacrifice it to his pride and ambition than labour for its happiness by good example and wise councils. And in truth, citizens, the greater number of those whom he has misled, have perished either in battle or on the scaffold. Must not the others who persist in this revolt expect a similar fate, if they abjure not their culpable error? You may be well assured that if humanity did not direct the actions of a chief attached to his country as well as to his fellow-citizens, and more disposed to pardon than to punish, the calamity would be still greater; it [Page 117] belongs to you to prevent its augmentation. In consequence, I invite you, citizens, to open your eyes and to give serious attention to the future. Reflect on the disasters which may ensue from longer obstinacy. Submit to lawful authority, if you wish to preserve the south untouched. Save your families and your property.

"But if, contrary to my expectation, you continue to support the revolt raised and propagated by Rigaud, in vain will you reckon on the fortifications he has constructed. The army of Toussaint L'Ouverture, led by generals whose bravery you know, will assail you, and you will be conquered. Then, not without grief, and in spite of my efforts, shall I see that you have been the unhappy victims of the pride and ambition of a single man. I will say more; desiring to put an end to the evils which have already too long afflicted this unfortunate colony, and wishing to prove to the French nation that I have done everything for the safety and happiness of my fellow-citizens, if Rigaud —though the author of these troubles— presents himself in good faith, and without stratagem, and acknowledges his fault, I will still receive him. But if Rigaud persists, and if he refuses to profit by my offer—do you, fathers, mothers, families—do you all come; I will receive you with open arms. The father of the prodigal son received his child after he had repented."

This merciful invitation was not without effect on the population of the south. Rigaud himself, however, had gone too far to return. He was committed to the rebellion, and felt both compelled and disposed to abide the result. In order to counteract the loss of Jacmel, and the appeal of Toussaint, he made extraordinary exertions to raise in mass the population under his sway. On his side, L'Ouverture prepared to prosecute his advantages, and terminate the disastrous war.

[Page 118] CHAPTER XIII.

Toussaint endeavours to suppress the slave-trade in Santo-Domingo, and thereby incurs the displeasure of Roume, the representative of France—he overcomes Rigaud—Bonaparte, now First Consul, sends Commissioners to the island—End of the war in the south.

BUT Toussaint L'Ouverture found troubles and hindrances in an unexpected quarter. During the fratricidal war which deluged the south with blood, the horrible traffic of the slave-trade was revived on the east of the island. This commerce, originated by Jean François and Biassou, continued after their disappearance from the political scene, and went on constantly increasing. Young blacks, stolen in the north, were conveyed to the City of Saint Domingo, where they were shipped for Porto Rico and Havannah—there to bear the yoke of slavery. Many of the old officers of Jean François pursued this as their only means of subsistence.

Aware that representations had in vain been made against these barbarities at the court of Madrid, and indignant that slavery, when nearly extinguished in its old form, should be revived in a new, and even worse one, Toussaint wrote (Dec. 25, 1800) from the walls of Jacmel to the agent Roume, urging him, as the only effectual means of putting a stop to the evil, to take possession of the Spanish part of the island, conformably to treaty. Under the pretext that it was necessary to await the arrival of some European troops, Roume postponed the execution of the request. Toussaint was too versed in politics not to be aware that the ostensible postponement was, in reality, a refusal. He also became aware that Roume's adviser was one who owed no good will to himself. That person, being invited to give an account of his conduct, emigrated to Porto Rico—justifying the suspicion [Page 119] that he had interested motives for promoting the continuance of the infamous traffic.

This event, in which L'Ouverture appears to fresh advantage, and acted in agreement with the general tenour of his public life, occassioned an estrangement between him and Roume. The agent had conceived the plan of conquering the English possessions in the West Indies. On an enterprise of such a nature and magnitude, he ought to have consulted, and, if he were willing, employed, the commander-in-chief. But, either to show his independence of Toussaint L'Ouverture, or to put a public insult on him, he passed by that general, and confided to Marshall Bese the command of an expedition against Jamaica. In order to pave the way, he sent into the island two men of determined character, a white and a mulatto. Those emissaries were denounced, taken, and hanged. The event interfered with Toussaint's operations, for the English captured a flotilla which he intended for the blockade of Jacmel. From this time, there existed a rupture between Roume and Toussaint. Criminations were exchanged. Each threw impediments in the way of the other. Toussaint could not regard Roume as a sincere friend of his race. Roume affected to believe that Toussaint had sympathies in favour of the English, with whom France was at war. At last, Roume demanded a vessel to convey him to France.

As soon as Toussaint had become master of Jacmel, he proceeded to the Cape, and in an interview with the Agent, reproached him, in the presence of his staff, with being an enemy to the colony and to the liberty of the blacks. He further required him to give an order for the occupation of the east,— resolved to put down the slave-trade, of which that was the centre. Roume refused compliance. The consequence was, that he apprehended the Agent, and sent him to prison. The expedient prevailed. The order was given. Toussaint despatched General Agé to Santo Domingo, and returned to finish the war in the south. A regular campaign was begun. The rebels were defeated, and abandoned several posts the retention of which was [Page 120] indispensable to their safety. Rigaud saw his star grow pale. Most of his superior officers abandoned him. Desertion spread through the ranks. On the other side, Toussaint appeared amid his troops, radiant with victory. He brought with him pecuniary resources. With these, he distributed pay among the soldiers; and so, while supplying their wants, gained their confidence, and excited their enthusiasm.

The two armies sat down opposite each other. Skirmishing began. Then serious rencontres took place. At last, issue was joined, and the revolters suffered a signal defeat. After this trial of strength, Rigaud might be troublesome, but he could not be formidable. Driven to desperation by his failures, he ordered his men to lay waste the country, and, to use his own words, to take such steps that "the trees should have their roots in the air." His old hands, thinned by war, sickness, and age, became Rigaud's sole reliance. On every side his cause was abandoned by the citizens and the civic authorities. Thus was he reduced to a leader of banditti. He saw his position, and issued this proclamation,—it was his last word to the public:—

"Considering the crisis in which the department is, owing to the unjust and inhuman war carried on against it by the traitor Toussaint L'Ouverture, from whom no one must expect either safety or honour, I am obliged, in the position I hold, to take the only measures that remain to save the department: considering, moreover, that proposals for peace, or for suspension of arms, directly concern the executive power, and that, in all cases, it is to the chief of the armed force of the department that the right belongs of proposing peace or suspending arms, because he ought to seize the moment favourable for proposals of the kind, which, if made in critical junctures, and by those who have not the means of putting a stop to the evil, may imbolden the enemy, and cause calamities he would have avoided.

"For now a year this war has been going on; the popular bodies and the pretended friends of peace have taken no step [Page 121] to stop its course. At the present, when the enemy has had some success, and when terror has taken possession of feeble and timid minds, they fancy that a monster thirsting for human blood, an ungrateful wretch, a traitor towards the Republic, his benefactor, the devastator of Saint-Domingo, the executioner of the parish of Jacmel, the persecutor of all the French agents— finally, the slave of the English, that he only can grant a peace or a suspension of arms. Citizens of the southern department, undeceive yourselves, if you think that anything else than arms can save you, while you wait for the intervention of the French Government, to whom those differences between the south and the other departments have been referred. Be well assured, my fellow-citizens, that I have your tranquillity and your happiness too much at heart, not to seize all opportunities to procure for you peace or a suspension of arms; and if the enemy adhere not to the proposals which in proper time and place I shall think it my duty to make to him, I shall know how with the aid of my brave comrades, to make war on him even to extinction. Resume your courage. If he is powerful in numbers and in resources, your fellow-citizens, composing the southern army, possess courage and honour, and will find means to secure your safety.

"Under these circumstances, and employing the powers confided to me, I make these provisional arrangements, which are to be punctually executed; and accordingly ordain:—

"Article 1. The municipal government of the south shall for the future restrict themselves to the simple but useful functions of verifying births, marriages, and deaths; but all municipal deliberations, all assemblies, as well as deputations to the enemy, are interdicted. The municipalities shall only lay before me the wishes of their fellow-citizens, to which I will give replies.

"Article 2. Parochial assemblies may take place after permission has been obtained from the Commander of the southern department.

"Article 3. Before legal permission is given, if there are [Page 122] meetings, whether of individuals or of parishes, in the cities or in the country, martial law shall be forthwith proclaimed, and the chief of the armed force of the district is authorized to put his troops in movement to put down the said meetings; he shall begin with mild measures, and then employ severity, if he is forced to it.

"Article 4. The greatest vigilance shall be observed towards the disturbers of the public peace, and against secret disorganizers: the proprietors shall be protected, and their property shall be respected. The national armed police shall be in permanent activity in the interior, and those who shall be denounced for any crime against order and safety, shall be apprehended and tried by a council of war, and punished according to the laws."

This manifesto, the spirit of which is even worse than its logic and its grammar, served only to show how undone Rigaud was, and how necessary that all who had any regard to themselves or the public good should abandon the desperate gladiator. His bands, however, were unwilling to yield. Blood, therefore, flowed in streams. The old men of the South are said still to shudder when they think of that conflict, which they designate "the war of the knife," thus showing to what extreme means the combatants resorted in their deadly hatred and murderous strife. The proclamation was scarcely anything more than the half-articulate words of a man who was staggering to his fall. Two more serious conflicts tried, and lost, and Rigaud's star went down below the horizon.

While, during the weeks and months of a long year, these frightful scenes of mutual carnage had been covering one of the finest parts of Hayti with corpses and ruins, the Directory in the mother country, too much occupied with its own divisions and party interests, gave no attention to the distracted colony. A change was at hand. Bonaparte, hastening from Egypt, overturned the Directory, and snatched the reins of power. Having taken his seat, he called around him (Dec. 2, 1799) those who were thought to be conversant with the condition of the colony, in order to discuss the means of restoring peace [Page 123] within its borders. The representatives of Toussaint and of Rigaud were alike heard. Shortly after, a decree was issued, by which Vincent, Raymond, and Michel, were deputed to Hayti, in order to carry thither the Consular Constitution, and a proclamation addressed to the inhabitants. Rigaud was recalled to France. Toussaint L'Ouverture was confirmed in his post as General-in-chief.

The proclamation was far from inspiring confidence or promoting tranquillity among the blacks, since it postponed and deferred to another legislative act the promulgation of the laws which were to govern Hayti. Michel, dissatisfied with the bravery of Toussaint L'Ouverture, returned into France. Raymond, whose mulatto's skin made him an object of suspicion, was ordered to remain at the Cape. Vincent alone was received with confidence. He presented to the Commander-in-chief the new Constitution, a letter written from the Minister of Marine, and the proclamation of the Consuls. In the proclamation were these words:—"Brave blacks, remember that the French Republic has given you liberty, and that it only can cause that liberty to be respected." These words, it was ordered, should be inscribed in letters of gold on all the flags of the colonial national guard. Toussaint manifested no haste either to publish the proclamation or embroider the sentence on the colours. How could he promulgate a known falsehood? The Republic had not given freedom to the blacks. The blacks, under their able leader, had extorted freedom from the hands of their masters. Toussaint, who was well informed of the views and intrigues regarding the colony which were nourished in Paris, knew that his ruin had been resolved on before the self-elevation of Bonaparte to the Consulship. Had the ill-feeling passed away? Why, then, had not the First Consul written to him under his own signature? Distrust and disquietude prevailed in the relations of L'Ouverture and the representatives of the new government in France. It is true that Rigaud was disowned, but Toussaint was not cordially embraced; nor were the rights of the blacks frankly recognised and legally settled.

As soon as he had given audience to Vincent, Toussaint [Page 124] L'Ouverture set off for the seat of the not yet wholly terminated war. After a few days, he sent for Vincent, in order that the chief civil and military powers should be on the spot. In the hope of bringing the business to an amicable termination, the General induced Vincent, accompanied by a black man and a man of colour, to go on a deputation to the revolters, who yet stood out. He put into the hands of the deputies an act of amnesty in favour of all who had taken part in the war, not even Rigaud excepted. The deputies reached Cayes, where Rigaud held his head-quarters. That city, exhausted by so long and so disastrous a conflict, heard with pleasure of the object of their mission. Rigaud was quickly informed of the arrival of the deputies. On reading the despatch he flew into the most violent passion. The outburst was so violent as to endanger Vincent's life. That agent, however, was the bearer of a letter from Rigaud's son, to whom he had shown the kindest attentions, and who declared to his father the gratitude he felt in return. The mulatto chief eagerly threw his eyes over the lines. All at once his wrath ceased. But the warrior soon overcame the father. Vexation took the place of vengeance. He would not live; he could not endure to live. Again and again he tried to kill himself. At length he was calmed down, and ere many days he quitted Saint Domingo for the shores of France. Thither he was accompanied by Petion and some of his principal officers. The other mulatto chiefs emigrated to various parts of the archipelago of the Antilles.

Thus terminated the war in the South. With that war every obstacle to the freedom of the blacks disappeared. One after the other had hindrances and opposition been swept out of the way by the strong hand of Toussaint L'Ouverture, the negro-champion of the negro race. Against the colonists, against the Spaniards, against the English, against the mulattoes, against the French representatives, and in a measure against blacks themselves, had he, by prudence, perseverance, and prowess, by singleness of aim, by unity of purpose, by personal efforts the most astounding, and a union of skill, caution, and daring [Page 125] rarely equalled, vindicated the freedom of the Africans, in Hayti. There was yet a stronger power. Religion, in its relation to the grand work he had undertaken, rose in his breast to enthusiasm. In some sense he was, he believed, God's envoy and God's agent in the fierce and sanguinary struggle. In that conviction he found light and strength which had, to him, the vividness and the authority of what, in a qualified sense, may be called inspiration. Here was the grand secret of his success. He has himself given an outline of his career, which may appropriately find insertion in this place. "At the beginning of the troubles of Saint Domingo, I felt that I was destined to great things. When I received this Divine intimation I was four and fifty years of age; I could neither read nor write; I had some Portuguese coins; I gave them to a subaltern of the regiment of the Cape, and, thanks to him, in a few months I could sign my name and read with ease. The revolution of Saint Domingo was taking its course. I saw that the whites could not endure, because they were divided and because they were overpowered by numbers; I congratulated myself that I was a black man. A necessity was laid on me to commence my career. I went over to the Spanish side, where the first troops of my colour had found an asylum and protection. That asylum and protection ended in nothing. I was delighted to see Jean François make himself a Spaniard when the powerful French Republic proclaimed the general freedom of the blacks. A secret voice said to me, 'Since the blacks are free, they need a chief, and it is I who must be that chief, foretold by the Abbé Raynal.' Under this feeling I joyously returned to the service of France. France and the voice of God have not deceived me." These words are reported from memory.

As depending on the ear and the tongue, they must be received only in their general tenour. Our narrative, which rests on satisfactory vouchers, shows that, long prior to the age of fifty-four, Toussaint could at least read. If taken as indicating the defectiveness of his scholarship even at the time when he began his task, they are, doubtless, substantially correct; and their testimony goes to confirm the [Page 126] unquestionable fact, that not by ordinary human appliances and aids did this extraordinary genius accomplish his meritorious and noble work.*

CHAPTER XIV.

Toussaint L'Ouverture inaugurates a better future—Publishes a general amnesty —Declares his task accomplished in putting an end to civil strife, and establishing peace on a sound basis—Takes possession of Spanish Hayti, and stops the slave-trade—Welcomes back the old colonists—Restores agriculture —Recalls prosperity—Studies personal appearance on public occasions— Simplicity of his life and manners—His audiences and receptions—Is held in general respect.

ON the first of August, 1800, L'Ouverture made his triumphal entrance into Cayes. All official honours were rendered to him. Hearts on every side beat with enthusiastic gratitude towards the general benefactor. He ascended the pulpit and proclaimed the oblivion of wrongs. He complained only of

---

* THE INSTRUCTION WHICH TOUSSAINT RECEIVED IN BOYHOOD IS TESTIFIED BY HIS SON ISAAC, IN HIS INTERESTING NOTES TO THE MEMOIRS HE WROTE, "SUR l'EXPÉDITION DES FRANÇAIS SOUS LE CONSULAT DE BONAPARTE," APPENDED TO METRAL'S HISTOIRE DE l'EXPÉDITION DES FRANÇAIS À SAINT DOMINGUE," PARIS, 1825. ACCORDING TO ISAAC'S TESTIMONY, TOUSSAINT WHEN A BOY LEARNT SOMETHING OF LATIN AND GEOMETRY (P.326). WHILE YET HE WAS IN THE SERVICE OF SPAIN, ISAAC SAYS OF HIM:—"WITHOUT HAVING TOPOGRAPHICAL MAPS OF THOSE COUNTRIES, AFTER THE EXAMPLE OF CAPTAINS OF THE ANCIENT WORLD, LUCULLUS, POMPEY, CÆSAR, TOUSSAINT MADE ONE; HE LAID DOWN ON PAPER, ACCORDING TO INFORMATION GIVEN HIM BY PEOPLE WHO KNEW THE DISTRICTS, THEIR EXTENT, THEIR RESPECTIVE DISTANCES, THE DIRECTION OF THE MOUNTAINS, AND OF THE RIVERS, AND EVERYTHING REMARKABLE, SUCH AS DEFILES, &C.,&C." (P. 329). THE SKILL TO FORM SUCH A MAP, BESIDES INVOLVING READING AND WRITING, GIVES COUNTENANCE TO THE INTIMATION OF ISAAC TOUSSAINT, THAT HIS FATHER HAD SOME ACQUAINTANCE WITH GEOMETRY AS WELL AS DRAWING. DOUBTLESS, THE FATHER'S SCHOLARSHIP WAS ALWAYS QUITE RUDIMENTAL.

the absence of the mulattoes. The sense of their discomfiture was too recent. Two of their chiefs, however, went to meet him afterwards, and he received them in a cordial manner. His aim [Page 127] was to direct men's minds from the dark past to the bright future. On the 17th of the month he put forth his proclamation.

"Citizens,—All the events which have taken place at Saint Domingo during the civil war occasioned by Rigaud are of a nature to merit public attention.

"Now that they are no longer likely to be renewed, it is of importance to the prosperity of the colony, and to the happiness of the inhabitants, to draw the curtain on the past, in order that we may be occupied exclusively in repairing the evils which, of necessity, have resulted from the intestine war brought forth by the pride and ambition of an individual.

"A part of the citizens of Saint Domingo have been deceived, because, too credulous, they did not sufficiently suspect the snares which had been laid to draw them into their criminal designs. Others have acted in these circumstances according to the impulsion of their hearts. Moved by the same principles as the chief of the revolt, they considered it beneath them to be commanded by a black man. Him they judged it necessary to get rid of, at whatever cost, and they spared nothing to succeed in their object. The ambition of their chief led him to make the country his own. His satellites had at heart nothing so much as to give him aid. For their reward he assigned to them aforehand the offices they were to occupy. They are disappointed in their expectation; and in my quality as the victor, wishing and very ardently desiring to promote the happiness of my native land, penetrated by what is set forth in the Lord's Prayer, 'Forgive us our transgressions as we forgive those who transgress against us,' I have published a proclamation by which I grant a general amnesty. That proclamation is known to you. It has produced the happy result which I promised myself. The southern department has returned to its obedience to the laws. Let us forget that bad men had led it away from duty to gratify their criminal passions, and let us now consider only as brothers those who, through their easy faith, dared to turn their arms against the flag of the Republic, and against their lawful chief. I have ordered all citizens to return to their several parishes to enjoy the benefits of this amnesty. Citizens, not less generous [Page 128] than myself, let your most precious moments be employed in causing the past to be forgotten; let all my fellow-citizens swear never to recall the past, let them receive their misled brethren with open arms; and let them in future be on their guard against the traps of bad men.

"Civil and military authorities, my task is accomplished. It now belongs to you to see that harmony is no more troubled. Do not allow the least reproach on the part of any one against those who went astray but have returned to their duty. Notwithstanding my proclamation, keep an eye on the bad and do not spare them. The man is unjust, he is inclined to evil rather than good. Firmly put down his perverse designs, and never close your eyes on his conduct and his proceedings. Honour should guide you all. The interests of our country require it; its prosperity needs peace, true and confiding peace. Such a peace must be your work. On you solely now depends public tranquillity in Saint Domingo. Take no rest until you have secured it. I expect this from your courage and from your devotion to the French Republic."

The spirit of moderation, the spirit of mercy itself dictated these words. Reference to the late troubles was prescribed by a rigid sense of duty. The reference made in no way exceeds what the occasion demanded, and falls very short of what the evil inflicted by the revolt would have justified. It was of absolute necessity to characterize Rigaud. But how different the tone of Toussaint L'Ouverture compared with the injurious epithets lavished in his proclamation by that mulatto leader against his lawful chief! But even for the bad L'Ouverture had forgiveness. How terrible a punishment might he now have inflicted on the men of colour! Had he been open to the prejudices of caste and skin, he would have let loose on them the desire of retribution and the thirst for revenge. One word of his, and the race would have been nearly extirpated. Not by their forbearance was he kept from uttering that word; nor by their softened feelings towards the negroes; nor by a confidence that they would no more attempt disturbance; but solely by a [Page 129] regard to his religious duty, and a manly confidence in the right and the merciful.

"My task is accomplished." And yet he had obtained nothing for himself. The military position he held, as it was won by the sword, so was it necessary to the work he had performed. It was a burden rather than a recompence—a duty and an obligation instead of an honour. Not for himself, but for his country, did he hold the command of the armies of Saint Domingo. "My task is accomplished." It *is*, noble black: it *is* accomplished, and accomplished well, if only thou lookest to the weal of Hayti. But hast thou no object of thine own? Opposition can no longer hold up its head.

Thy foes are prostrate. Every eye is turned to thee. Every heart is fixed on thee. Hast thou nothing to ask for thyself? The crown and sceptre of Hayti? Nay, frown not. Other successful warriors have taken regal titles as their due. Nor need thou fear opposition. The Agent is weak and disesteemed. Bonaparte is reaping laurels in Italy. England will be prompt to aid thee. Then consider how much thy race needs elevation. What could so much raise them from the dust? Yes, thou must, as thou canst, be King of Hayti; and thy name, glorious for its military deeds, will be more glorious still as the first of a long line of illustrious sovereigns of negro blood.

Instead of troubling himself and others in arrangements for placing on his head the bauble of a crown, Toussaint L'Ouverture turned his attention to the condition of the country. Hayti was not yet wholly in the power of France. Though formally ceded to the French, the eastern part of the isle remained under Spanish rule. Not sincere in his wishes to take possession of Spanish Hayti, Roume had sent forces so inconsiderable, that they were easily defeated. On their return, he revoked his order for its occupation. On learning the fact, L'Ouverture was indignant. Was slavery, then, in its worst form, to be established and acknowledged in Hayti? Was the Government to be an assenting, if not a concurring, party? And were all his own labours and sacrifices to be thus frustrated? Frustrated by low self-interest and base intrigues? [Page 130] Could he, who had conquered freedom for the negroes, allow their children to be kidnapped and transported to strange countries and foreign lands, there to be degraded and rained? Impossible! Yet such was the alternative, if Roume retained possession of the civil government: for he had tried what could be done in this matter with Roume by argument and moral influence. The effort had failed, and now Roume had availed himself of his absence, and his absorption in military duties, to reverse a policy in which they had in council come to an understanding. Besides, he had proved himself unfaithful to France, by virtually surrendering a portion of his rightful possessions. In such hands, power could not be safely trusted. And, doubtless, the home government would thank him if Toussaint vindicated its rights and secured its territory.

Actuated by those considerations, Toussaint L'Ouverture arrested Roume, and sent him to Dondon. On the occasion, he issued this address:—

"Toussaint L'Ouverture, General-in-Chief of his fellow-citizens.

"The duties of the office held by Citizen Roume were, in his quality of representative of the French Government, to consecrate his moral and physical faculties to the happiness of Saint Domingo and to its prosperity. Very far from doing so, he took council only of the intriguers by whom he was surrounded, to sow discord amongst us, and to foment the troubles which have not ceased to agitate society. However, in spite of the calumnies which he has continually thrown out against myself in his letters to France and Santo Domingo, he shall be protected from every penalty. But my respect for his character must not prevent me from taking the proper steps in order to deprive him of the power of again plotting against the tranquillity which, after so many revolutionary concussions, I have just had the happiness to establish. In consequence, and in order to isolate him from the intriguers who have kept him in their shackles, and to respond to the complaints made in respect to him by all the parishes, the brigadier-general Moyse will [Page 131] supply the said Citizen Roume with two carriages and a sure escort, which, with all respect due to his character, will conduct him to the village of Dondon, where he will remain until the French Government shall recall him to render an account of his administration.

"At Cap Français, 5 Frimaire (26 Nov.), the ninth year (1800) of the French Republic, one and indivisible,

"The General-in-Chief, TOUSSAINT L'OUVERTURE."

Roume remained a prisoner at Dondon for several months, and then was permitted by L'Ouverture to return to France by way of the United States.

As soon as he had removed the impediment, Toussaint L'Ouverture took effectual steps for putting down the slave-trade, and occupying the east of the island. After a few shots, he entered Santo Domingo on the 2nd of January, 1801, at the head of 10, 000 men, and hoisted the flag of the French Republic on its ramparts to the salvo of two-and-twenty cannon. He was received at the mansion-house by the chief authorities, who wished him to take, in the name of the Holy Trinity, an oath to govern with wisdom. "Such a course would be proper," he replied, "in an officer appointed by the court of Madrid; but I am the servant of the Republic. Therefore, I am unable to do what you ask; but I swear solemnly before God, who hears the oath, that I forget the past, and that my watchings and my cares shall have no other object than to render the Spaniards, now become Frenchmen, contented and happy." On the utterance of these words, Don Garcia, the governor, handed him the keys of the city. "I accept them," said Toussaint, "in the name of the French Republic;" and then turning towards the assembly, he added, with an humble voice, "let us go and thank the Author of all things for having crowned with the greatest success our enterprise, prescribed by treaties and the laws of the Republic." Followed by the governor and all the Spanish authorities, he went to the cathedral, where a *Te Deum* was chanted in token of gratitude to God.

Thus, from Cape Samana in the east, to Cape Tiburon in the [Page 132] west, the power of Toussaint L'Ouverture was everywhere established and acknowledged. Knowing the favourable effects produced on the popular mind by the progress of distinguished personages in the parts under their administration, Toussaint L'Ouverture traversed the Spanish territory, and visited the principal places. He was everywhere received with the acclamations of the people, the merry peal of bells, and the thunders of cannon. The clergy, bare-footed, came on all sides to give him welcome. He treated them with profound respect. Within a few days he was master of the obedience of the Spaniards as much as of the confidence of the blacks.

The union of the Spanish to the French part of Hayti procured reciprocal advantages, the effects of which soon became apparent. The French gained facility in acquiring horses and mules for the cultivation of the soil, and the Spaniards found enormous gain in the exportation of its animals, flocks, and horned cattle. The black regiments, restrained by Toussaint's powerful hand, had done but little damage in the invasion; and those who were left in garrison put large sums of money in circulation. The elements of French administration which followed the troops bestowed on the country new principles and sources of industry and wealth. Magnificent roads were formed. Carriages were then for the first time introduced. Even the horses, under the influence of Toussaint's example, improved their pace. Distances were abridged; time was saved; the minds of the people were awakened from torpor; activity universally prevailed, and commerce and riches began to abound. Amid the general excitement, prosperity, and hope, the enthusiasm towards its cause became greater every day, and Toussaint's name was pronounced with blessings by all tongues.

Having given the command of Santo Domingo to his brother Paul, who had risen by merit to the rank of brigadier-general, Toussaint L'Ouverture returned to the French part of Hayti, and forthwith applied his mind to the condition and wants of the island.

He was thoroughly acquainted with the theatre on which he had to act, and the character of the people subject to his [Page 133] power. He took the wisest measures to develope the powers of the former, and to gain the confidence of the latter. Aware that he had a mass of prejudices to overcome, and the most tangled web of interests to set in order, he mingled discretion with zeal; and while aiming at the general weal, forgot not the deference that might conciliate, nor failed in the bland and courteous manners that might win. The old colonists he welcomed to his presence without familiarity, and showed respect even to their prejudices, so far as the public good would permit. The steward of the plantation on which he had himself been a slave, vegetated in the United States. L'Ouverture being informed of the fact, wrote him an invitation to return to Hayti, to put himself "at the head of the interests of their good old masters." The letter, conceived in a friendly and urgent tone, brought back the steward. Toussaint gave him an interview, and among other things said to him, "Return to the plantation; be just and inflexible; see that the blacks do their duty in order to add, by your prosperity, to the prosperity of the land."

The discontinuance of the war led to the resumption of agriculture. The change from the musket to the hoe was of course gradual; but such was the influence and such the determination of the great black, that ere long the rich cultivable districts began to put on a smiling aspect, promising riches as well as abundance. Had the peace continued, the promise would have been realized in the fullest degree. Forthwith, however, did the culture of the soil, besides providing for the wants of the inhabitants, furnish the public treasury with sufficient resources. Intelligence of the returning prosperity reached foreign lands. The colonists who were scattered up and down in those lands saw a ray of hope, and, notwithstanding what they had undergone in Saint Domingo, notwithstanding their dislike of the predominance of the blacks, they invited and gladly accepted permission to return home and resume possession of their estates. Their letters coming from various countries, and unanimously expressing confidence in the integrity and the power of the General-in-Chief, as well as in the justice and excellence [Page 134] of his administration, greatly contributed to strengthen his hands and confirm his authority. Scarcely could a more satisfactory or a more striking proof be given of the claim of Toussaint to our respect and admiration than is found in the readiness with which this class of men embarked their all in the vessel which he commanded.

The political evils and civil wars that had afflicted Saint Domingo, in causing the expatriation of proprietors, had in many cases occasioned the loss of traces to the succession. Under Toussaint's orders, the property so circumstanced was secured to military chiefs, and was thus restored to cultivation and productiveness. At the same time, regulations were issued by which the labourers on the estates became a sort of co-proprietors. He had, aforetime, thrown his protection over emigrants, and thereby had brought on himself difficulty and suspicion. He now took into his service subaltern officers of emigrant regiments, and offered protection to those who were unwilling to join his forces. Disregarding colour and position in his appointments, he sought in his servants and fellow-labourers for those who were most fitted for the duties of the several offices. If his favour was less marked toward any, it was toward those of his own blood; not because he loved them less, but because, having their confidence, he could employ in relation to them a freedom of word and action which might have been misunderstood by others. With his strong and vivid religious sentiments, he was naturally prompted to pay special regard to the priests, and to the interests of religion in general. Nor, environed as he was by men whose senses were the avenues to their affections, did he neglect personal appearance. Studious in his attire, he surrounded himself with a numerous guard, in which were names distinguished in the olden time. When he went forth in public he was accompanied by a splendid retinue which fixed and dazzled all eyes. Surrounded by a guard of from fifteen to eighteen hundred men, brilliantly clad, and having for his own personal use a stud containing hundreds of horses, he appeared before the eyes of the people in the exterior of a prince. But, beneath this imposing show, he himself studied the utmost [Page 135] simplicity. Always temperate, he often carried moderation to abstinence. His iron frame received strength chiefly from the deep and full resources of his vigorous mind. Master of his soul, he had no difficulty in mastering his body. While partaking of none but the most frugal diet, with water for his drink, and vegetable preparations for his meat, he rarely slept more than two hours. The whole energy of his life was absorbed and consumed in the great task which he had undertaken, and which, in truth, demanded more vital power than even he had to bestow. Though advanced in life, he was incessantly in movement, and travelled with a rapidity which defied calculation and excited amazement. Seeing everything with his own eyes, he had little need to rely on the reports of others, and he at once promoted his independence and augmented his power by deriving his policy and his plans from his own knowledge, and his own meditations. Little should we expect to see such a person addicted to the labours of the cabinet. Yet in replying, by means of several secretaries, to two or three hundred letters daily, he seemed to experience a pleasure as lively as that enjoyed by other men in the satisfaction of the senses.

As the governor of the land, Toussaint L'Ouverture felt it necessary to keep up some kind of state. Like other chief magistrates, he had his receptions of ceremony, as well as his less formal audiences. The union of French vanity and negro love of parade in the foremost people, made him feel the importance of requiring due attention to appearances and etiquette. Hence he instituted what bears the name of "circles," at which all who were invited were expected to be present. These circles were of two kinds, the greater and the less. To the greater, formal invitations were given. Toussaint himself appeared in the assemblies in the undress uniform of a general officer. His simple attire, in the midst of surrounding brilliancy, contrasted favourably with the dignified tone which he knew how to maintain. When he presented himself, all the company, females as well as males, arose from their seats. Attentive even to the proprieties, he showed his disapproval of any exposure of the person in female dress. On one occasion, he was seen to throw [Page 136] his handkerchief over the bare bosom of a lady, saying—"Modesty is the best charm of the sex." After having made the tour of the hall, and spoken to everybody, he withdrew by the door at which he entered, bowing right and left to the company. The less circles were public audiences, which took place every evening. At these, Toussaint L'Ouverture appeared clad like the ancient proprietors when on their plantations. All the citizens entered the grand saloon, and were, irrespectively of rank and position, addressed by the governor as convenience served. After having gone round the room, he retired, and took with him into a small apartment in front of his bedchamber, which he used as a study, the persons with whom he wished to converse more freely and more at length. The greater number of these were the chief whites of the colony. There seating himself, he requested all others to be seated. Then he proceeded to talk with them of France, of his children, of religion, of his old masters, and of God's grace in giving him liberty and granting him means for discharging the duties of the post in which he had been placed by the mother country. He also conversed of the progress of agriculture, of commerce, and never of political concerns: he questioned each respecting his own private affairs, and of his family, and appeared to take an interest in the several matters. With mothers, he spoke of their children, and inquired whether they attended to their religious education; and the young he would sometimes briefly examine in their catechism. When he wished to put an end to the audience, he arose, and bowed. The company then retired, being attended by him to the door. As they left, he appointed times for special interviews with those who made the request. Then he shut himself up with his private secretaries, and commonly continued his labours far into the night.

In this practical regard to show and parade, L'Ouverture may have been influenced by his own personal defects. Small in person, he was of a repulsive aspect, and having a difficult utterance, he spoke with as little elegance as grammar. Yet, his were words of power, for they came from a strong soul, and were the heralds of a resolute will. A man of few words, and [Page 137] powerful imagination, he sometimes uttered his ideas in parables —the rather that in such a form he could the more effectually imprint them on the minds of the rude natures with which he had to deal. On more occasions than one, he took a glass vase, and, having filled it with grains of black maize, he put therein some grains of white maize, and said—"You are the black maize; the whites, who would enslave you, are the white maize." He then shook the glass, and, placing it before their eyes, he cried, as if inspired, "See the white ones only here and there."

The army, Toussaint L'Ouverture kept under the most vigorous discipline. Every breach of duty was severely punished. Even during the civil wars, plunder was restricted as much as possible. He was, however, adored by his soldiers.

Scarcely less was the veneration paid him by other members of Haytian life. He won and enjoyed the esteem of the colonists; he was valued highly by the ministers of religion; by the blacks he was regarded as a messenger of God. Even the mulattoes began to look to him with hope and respect.

The confidence which Toussaint inspired, soon produced good effects in the colony. The lands once more cultivated, and cultivated under judicious regulations, became productive, and, as of old, poured forth abundance and wealth. With the spread of industry and the increase of riches, population, which had been greatly diminished in the wars, recovered its impulse and augmented its numbers. A large and prosperous people restored the churches, which had been burnt or allowed to become dilapidated, decorated the cities with fine buildings, enriched the public treasury, cultivated the arts, and, ere long, indulged in luxury. The general intelligence was raised, and manners were refined. Human nature vindicated itself against its calumniators: for in a short time, after a period of frightful wasting, the black state of Hayti could endure a comparison with the higher forms of white and European civilization. There was at the Cape, under the name of the Hôtel de la République, an inn, the exterior and interior splendour of which scarcely yielded to the richest establishments of the kind in any part of the world. It was frequented by the principal blacks and by the Americans [Page 138] of the continent. There mere etiquette was unknown; the most perfect equality prevailed. At the same table sat private individuals and the heads of the state, officers of every rank, men of all conditions. It was frequently visited by L'Ouverture, who took his place, without preference, in any vacant seat: for he often said that distinction of rank ought to exist only in the moment of public service.

Travellers who visited the island at the beginning of the present century, warriors who played a part in the events of that epoch, agree in declaring that in the society of Saint Domingo the men were polite and the women easy and elegant; that the relations between the sexes lacked neither attraction nor dignity, and that the prejudices of colour seemed to have lost their former power. The theatre came into vogue; the greater number of the new actors were blacks, and some of them gave proof of talent in comedy and in pantomime. A taste for music became general; the guitar was specially cultivated. Men of negro and mulatto blood not only formed the bulk of the population, but occupied the higher positions. Even the most important duties of the administration were in their hands. Yet life went forward with ease and efficiency. Religion was honoured. Morals were at least not inferior to what they are in white society. The arts were cultivated. The elegances of life were not unknown. Among men and women who had but recently quitted the brutalizing condition of servitude, an ability and a refinement were observed, which you sometimes look for in vain among men who have the reputation of being highly cultivated.

[Page 139] CHAPTER XV.

Toussaint L'Ouverture takes measures for the perpetuation of the happy condition of Hayti, specially by publishing the draft of a Constitution in which he is named governor for life, and the great doctrine of Free-trade is explicitly proclaimed.

THIS happy condition had no guarantee of permanence. True, all was tranquil within the borders of Hayti. One after another had Toussaint L'Ouverture removed hindrances out of the way, until he had succeeded in establishing a universal accord. But would the harmony endure? Its continuance was essential to the full developement of the resources of the colony; and, to all appearance, that continuance was the sole prerequisite. As yet, however, there had been no general recognition of the established order. If all were to work for the general good, all must concur in the formation and acknowledgment of a constitution by which the established order might be perpetuated.

In bringing that constitution into existence, and giving it the force of law, three powers must concur. These three powers were the inhabitants of Hayti, France, and Toussaint himself. Self-government was a recognised right of the colony. The concurrence of France was equally an admitted fact in the colonial government, and L'Ouverture held, under the authority of the mother country, the highest functions in the island. When the question of a constitution assumed a practical shape, it became important to determine with which of these three authorities the initiative should lie. Was the colony to look to France? That question involved another,—was France sincere in her acknowledgment of negro freedom? France appeared unworthy of trust. The last despatches on the matter of a code of laws for Hayti wore a suspicious aspect, and were generally disliked. And if France wished to give the colony a good code of laws, had she the power? How could the requisite knowledge be possessed by a legislature which sat thousands of miles distant [Page 140] from those who were to obey the laws? Metropolitan government for colonial dependencies is full of evils, arising not only from ignorance and incompetence, but intrigue and corruption. Beside, Bonaparte was now the sole legislative and the sole ruling power in France. The position which Louis XIV. had fancied himself to possess, when he declared himself to be the state—"L'état, c'est moi,"—the Corsican adventurer had fully realized. The ruling passion of Bonaparte was ambition; his means, resort to force. What had the colony to expect but a *coup d'état* similar to that which had just suppressed the Directory and concentrated all power in the hands of the first consul? The thought is said to have disturbed the short hours of Toussaint's repose. The probability was, that the conqueror of Italy only waited the moment of necessary leisure, and that moment, as the event afterwards showed, might shortly arrive. Undesirable was it, therefore, to leave the initiative with France. The colony itself must act. Indeed, the colony only could act with wisdom and effect. "But in so doing the colony was setting up for independence." To take the first step in drawing up a constitution cannot be justly so characterized. A draft of a constitution was only a species of petition. Until sanctioned by legislation, it amounted to nothing more than a bill of rights. It did no more than say, "Here is a formal statement of what will suit us, what will consolidate and augment our existing weal, what we entreat you to send back with the seal of your solemn sanction." And were such a step a step towards independence, who can blame it? If the colony had acquired strength enough to run alone, why should it remain in leading-strings? Nay, the desire for independence, if cherished, was a worthy feeling. Such a desire showed that black men could appreciate liberty, and well deserved the degree of freedom they had already gained. The rather was a cautious approach to independence praiseworthy, because tokens were not wanting that Bonaparte, in his ambitious passions, had grown impatient of the ascendancy of the great negro Haytian. Resolved to be master of the world, he could not endure a rival power, and watched his opportunity to establish his supremacy in the island. [Page 141] The rather was he desirous of establishing the exclusive rule of France there, because Hayti, he felt, could be made a bulwark for hostile operations against the English power in the West Indies.

Yet was the colony passively and quietly to await the blow? What was this but to invite the blow? Whereas, to propound a constitution while it ought to give no offence, would prove that the Haytians were sensible alike of their rights and of their power. In the great issue, Toussaint had himself a problem to solve. If, as he had reason to fear, Bonaparte intended his overthrow, was he to submit without an effort? Was he not, as a prudent man and a wise legislator, to enter on such a course, as seemed most likely to ward off the blow, and strengthen his own position? As to the necessity of his continuing to hold that position, he could not for a moment doubt. The retention of the position was indispensable to the continuance of the peace in the island. As all mountains had become plains before his energy and determination, so would all be undone, if he were removed from the head of affairs; once more the smouldering fires of passion and prejudice would burst into a flame, and a war arise not less bloody and terrific than that which he had so recently brought to a happy conclusion. Yes; there, at the helm, had he been placed by the resistless stream of events, or what to him, nor without reason, seemed the hand of Providence; and there duty, in the clearest and loudest tones, called upon him to remain. This is, in substance, the feeling to which at this time he gave utterance in these terms: "I have taken my flight in the region of eagles; I must be prudent in alighting on the earth: I can be placed only on a rock; and that rock must be a constitutional government, which will secure me power so long as I shall be among men." Yes, if in any case, certainly in Toussaint L'Ouverture's was a constitutional dictatorship of indispensable necessity. Rightly did he interpret his position, and well did he understand his duties. This new Moses had brought his people out of Egyptian bondage, and must now give them a code of laws, over the execution of which, for the few remaining years of his life, it is his most solemn duty to watch. Such [Page 142] conduct asks no defence, and admits no excuse. It is positively and highly virtuous, and any other course would have been a betrayal of a sacred duty, a breach of a momentous trust.

Again the hour of temptation has come. The victorious general who commands universal obedience and enjoys universal respect may become a president or a sovereign. The good principle conquers; Satan is dismissed with a rebuke; the crown is refused, the presidency is deliberately chosen.

Does the reader think of Washington, who, when he might possibly have become a king, became a private citizen? We are not sure that Washington's means for establishing a throne in the midst of the high-minded republicans of the Anglo-Saxon race were equal to those which Toussaint possessed among the uncultured and recently liberated Haytians, whom nature made fond of parade, and custom had habituated to royalty. The greater the opportunity, the greater the temptation; nor can he be accounted the inferior man who overcame in the severer trial. Nor must it be forgotten, that while Washington could, with confidence and safety, leave his associates to their own well-tried and well-matured powers of self-government, L'Ouverture had, in comparison, but children to deal with and provide for. Would it have been either prudent or benevolent to retire from the oversight of those children at the very moment when they had ceased to do evil and were learning to do well? Clearly, duty, in the most solemn and emphatic tones, demanded the continuance of that fatherly care which had rescued those babes in intellect from impending ruin, and so far led them toward the attainment of individual strength and social excellence. Yes, Toussaint L'Ouverture, an eagle thou hast proved thyself to be; an eagle's eye shows thee distant but coming realities; may thine eagle's pinion bear thee above danger, and place thee, where thou longest to be, "on a rock,"—the rock of a wisely constituted and well governed commonwealth! Then, like thy Hebrew prototype, when at last thou descriest the promised land, and while thou contemplatest its fertility and loveliness, thou mayest depart from "among men," falling to sleep in thy lofty eyrie, and [Page 143] buried on the mountain, which shall be at once thy sepulchre and thy monument.

We do not possess the materials to determine whether the idea of drawing up a constitution for Hayti originated with Toussaint L'Ouverture himself, or was presented to him as the proper course by his colonial advisers. The determination of the question is of the less consequence since, beyond a doubt, unanimity prevailed to a very great extent between the general-in-chief and the principal authorities and persons in the island. One party, and but one, evinced repugnance to the measure. The small number who represented the views of Bonaparte in the colony were naturally adverse to the constitution. At their head was Brigadier-General Vincent, who employed the influence which excellence of character justly gave him with L'Ouverture to turn him aside from the project. The effort proved nugatory.

Resolved to persevere in a course which his judgment approved, and his position required, Toussaint L'Ouverture, as possessing the highest authority in the island, called together a council to take into consideration the propriety of drawing up a constitution, and to determine what its provisions should be. The council consisted of nine members. The composition of this deliberative assembly displays the integrity of the general-in-chief. He might have formed it out of his officers. He might have given predominance in it to negro blood. These things, doubtless, he would have done, had he sought his own aggrandizement. But he chose its members among the men of property and intelligence. Of the nine members, eight were white proprietors, and one a mulatto; not a single black had a seat at the council-board. Even the purest patriotism might have required him to place himself at the head of the council. Its president was the white colonist Borgella, who had held the office of mayor of Port-au-Prince. The constitution, carefully prepared by this council, was presented to Toussaint L'Ouverture, who, having approved it (May 19th, 1800), sent a copy by the hands of General Vincent to Europe. The draft was accompanied by the following letter, addressed to "Citizen Bonaparte, First Consul of the French Republic (16th July)."

[Page 144] "CITIZEN CONSUL,—

The Minister of Marine, in the account which he has rendered to you of the political situation of this colony, which I have taken care to acquaint him with in the despatches which I addressed to him, sent by the corvette *L'Enfant Prodigue,* will have submitted to you my proclamation, convening a central assembly, which, at the moment when the junction of the Spanish part to the French part had made of Saint Domingo one single country, subject to the same government, should fix its destinies by wise laws, framed with special reference to the localities and the characters of the inhabitants. I have now the satisfaction to announce to you, that the last hand has been put to that work, and that the result is a constitution which promises happiness to the inhabitants of this colony, which has so long been unfortunate. I hasten to lay it before you for your approbation, and for the sanction of the government I serve. With this view, I send to you citizen Vincent, general director of fortifications at Saint Domingo, to whom I have confided this precious deposit. The central assembly, in the absence of laws, and considering the necessity which exists of substituting the rule of law for anarchy, having demanded that I should provisionally put it into execution, as promising to conduct the colony more rapidly towards prosperity, I have yielded to its desires; and this constitution has been welcomed by all classes of citizens with transports of joy, which will not fail to be manifested afresh, when it shall be sent back invested with the sanction of the government. With salutations and profound respect.

TOUSSAINT L'OUVERTURE."

This constitution, which had been made public and accepted amid solemn formalities and universal joy, was worthy of the cause in which L'Ouverture had risked his life and employed the utmost of his strength. Proceeding on the basis that slavery was abolished and could never more exist in Saint Domingo, and that all men there born were free citizens of the French Republic, it provided that every one, whatever his colour, was admissible to all employments, on the special ground that among the citizens there was no other distinction than the distinction [Page 145] of virtue and of ability. Establishing Roman Catholicism as the sole religion to be professed and protected, it recognised the sanctity of marriage by abolishing divorce. It required that agriculture should receive special encouragement, for which purpose measures were to be taken for the increase of the number of labourers. The reins of government it entrusted to one governor, to be appointed for the period of five years, with authority to prolong the term as a recompence of good conduct; and that "in consideration of the important services which General Toussaint L'Ouverture has rendered to the colony, he is named Governor for life, with power to choose his successor."

One provision we have advisedly omitted in order to bring it into full relief. In a very short sentence the constitution declares *commerce free*. Thus free trade was first proclaimed by the negro chief of Hayti. Is any other proof necessary that Toussaint was more than a successful warrior? more than a social liberator? more than a disinterested patriot? His economical views were large and liberal. They were in advance of their age; how much in advance let the fact declare, that nearly half a century had to elapse before even England obtained the boon which Hayti not only claimed but decreed. Yet what was there in Toussaint L'Ouverture which may not be found in other negroes? His sole external advantage was that he received some rudimental instruction in the simple arts of reading and writing. Give that advantage to the myriads of blacks that now vegetate and pine in slavery in the United States, and other practical philosophers will appear among them to vindicate the race by wise laws as well as philanthropy and heroism. But "oh, it is not safe." Safe? yes, much more safe than is the present course, which does but concentrate the lava of the volcano, which, at no distant day, will burst forth, unless precautionary measures are taken, and due preparations be made for lifting slaves into a condition fit for freedom. Surely this lesson is taught in the tenor of the preceding narrative.

BOOK II.

FROM THE FITTING OUT OF THE EXPEDITION BY BONAPARTE AGAINST SAINT DOMINGO TO THE SUBMISSION OF TOUSSAINT L'OUVERTURE.

CHAPTER I.

Peace of Amiens—Bonaparte contemplates the subjugation of Saint Domingo, and the restoration of slavery—Excitement caused by report to that effect in the island—Views of Toussaint L'Ouverture on the point.

THE year 1801 did not close without seeing the peace of Amiens definitively concluded. By the treaty then signed, France found herself confirmed in the possessions she had captured during the war, and at liberty to prosecute any enterprise which she might judge required by her position, or likely to conduce to the confirmation of her power. Her destinies were in the hands of Napoleon Bonaparte, who, under the modest title of Consul, concealed designs which already looked to an imperial throne, and ruled the nation and its dependencies with a sceptre more powerful and more despotic than the sway of any contemporaneous legitimate monarch. Born with the qualities which give and ensure command, Bonaparte, to a boundless ambition, added a restless activity which constantly prompted new efforts, a thirst for dominion, which as constantly demanded new acquisitions, and a jealousy of power which made rival greatness intolerable. With an evil eye, therefore, did he regard the high position obtained by Toussaint L'Ouverture through his wise and generous efforts in the French colony of

Saint Domingo. The brilliancy of his own fame seemed dimmed in his eyes by the glory achieved by a negro chieftain who had been a slave.

[Page 147]The termination of the war had left unoccupied in France a large body of soldiers, who might be dangerous at home, and whose leaders, in the repose of peace, might trouble his actual position, or prove impediments to his ambitious designs. Dissatisfied with seeing themselves outstripped by a soldier of fortune, they were ready for political intrigue rather than civil obedience, and would be most safely employed in a distant expedition in which success would increase the number of his own laurels, and failure issue in their permanent removal out of his path. That the climate in which he thought of employing them was destructive to Europeans, was a consideration which could not deter him, and only added another reason why, on his part, he should decide in favour of the attempt.

Yet if he left Hayti in the hands of Toussaint L'Ouverture, he would possess, in an army of thirty thousand black troops obedient to their actual commander, the means of countervailing the power of Great Britain in the West Indies, and of controlling its descendants in the United States. The employment, however, of such an ally seemed scarcely compatible with the dignity which he affected; nor was it impossible, if the ruler of Saint Domingo were left undisturbed in his authority, that he might assist the absolute independence of the colony, and either by augmenting his own power or joining the English, inflict a heavy blow on the supremacy of France. Then the question of colonial slavery presented itself for consideration. Should he recognise or nullify the freedom which existed in Saint Domingo? The recognition would bring him no advantage, for Toussaint his associates considered their work as accomplished. To nullify it would secure on his side the sympathies and co-operation of the colonists who had lost their estates, and who, regretting their past opulence, and believing its recovery impossible in the present state of the island, besieged the cabinet of the Tuilleries with importunities for the restoration of slavery. The wise and just held a different language. Even as a matter of policy an expedition to Hayti, they urged, was to be deprecated, for the risk would be very great, and failure would end in disgrace. Those who now held power in the island, were men of [Page 148] valour and of great military skill. As administrators of the colony they enjoyed general sympathy and support, and had proved their ability by the prosperity they had called into being. And while it did not become France, who had gained her own liberty, to suppress freedom in one of her own colonies, it was contrary to the laws of everlasting right to tear from men that freedom which they had purchased with their blood, and, by their moderation, proved they well deserved. These diverse views occupied the minds and dwelt on the tongues of men in Paris, according as position, character, or personal interests swayed their bosoms. The consul heard them all, and kept shrouded in his own dark breast the design which he meditated and was maturing. At the moment Vincent arrived from Saint Domingo, he presented the constitution to the consul. Here was the spark which that sombre genius desired. "He is a revolted slave whom we must punish; the honour of France is outraged." In vain was it pleaded before Bonaparte that the adoption or rejection of the constitution lay with himself, and that it contained only the expression of the wishes of Toussaint and his fellow-labourers. Bonaparte was too adroit not to seize, and too skilful not to make the most of the opportunity. His words, which we have just reported, circulated through Paris, and excited a feeling in favour of war. An expedition was decided on. And the popular fervour was increased when the consul declared in the senate that Toussaint was a brigand chief whom it was necessary to bring to justice. One voice was raised against the undertaking—a voice in the high places of authority. The minister Forfait, a man of high character, attempted to dissuade Bonaparte by setting before him a picture of the inevitable calamities of such an enterprise. He was silenced by the answer, "There are sixty thousand men that I want to send to a distance."

And so, from the most unworthy considerations, an armament against a peaceful and flourishing state is to be speedily fitted out. Yet the adventurers call themselves Christians. What but robbery on a large scale is such conduct? And who can [Page 149] believe that the man who decreed that robbery, had in his heart any genuine love of liberty?

Once more, Toussaint L'Ouverture, must you take the buckler and draw the sword. The hero of Europe, panting for conquests in another world, comes against you. Once more must the broad rich plains of your native land resound with the clash of hostile armies, and run with human blood. A cloud is on your countenance. Yet let it pass away. Take courage, noble heart! The coming struggle is only another step in the path of freedom. Necessary is the step, or you would not have to take it. And if the effort is painful, and the prospect dark, weigh well the magnitude of the issues. On the fields of Hayti the battle of your race will be fought out. It is before the eye, not of a few islanders, but of the world, that you are about to try your strength with the Gallic gladiator, and settle the question once for all, whether Africans are men or brutes, worthy of freedom, or doomed to servitude. Success? No, the settlement of the question depends not on success. You will perish in the combat, yet will you win; your cause will triumph even over your grave. Be just, and fear not.

Meanwhile, rumours and intelligence brought to Hayti produced sinister impressions, and disturbed the public mind. It appeared probable that slavery would be maintained in the French colonies of Martinique and Cayenne, and that at Saint Domingo France would make an effort for its restoration. Fears began to prevail, disturbances were threatened. Every eye turned to Toussaint L'Ouverture. On his part, he was not without forebodings, which recently had grown into apprehensions. He had written to the consul, and received no reply. He felt himself humiliated. At times tears stole from his eyes when he thought of the possibility that Bonaparte meant to undo all that he had done; foreseeing the long train of calamities which would ensue from such an attempt, he was now and then for an instant unmanned, and spoke hasty words. "Bonaparte," he said, "is wrong not to write to me; he must have listened to my enemies, otherwise would he refuse me proofs of his satisfaction? [Page 150] Me, I say, who have rendered greater services to France than any other general? The English and Spanish governments treat with more regard the generals who have signalized themselves by services of the first order." His fears and his vexation became greater, and affected his demeanour in a more marked manner, when he heard that preliminaries of peace between England and France had been signed at London. Peace in Europe he saw foreboded war to Hayti.

What now should be his course? Should he anticipate the blow, and prepare for it by proclaiming the independence of the colony? By rousing its inhabitants to resistance, and marshalling his forces with his own ability and vigour, he might repel even the attack of France when at peace with the world. And right would such a policy have been. Not impossibly it would have proved successful. But L'Ouverture was not prepared to adopt it. Equal to the demands on his courage and energy which a determination of the kind would make, he was not equal to the requisite demands on his sense of justice. Hayti was a French colony;—as a French colony it had gained its freedom. A free republic would not sanction its subjugation; and should Bonaparte attempt to wrest "the rod of empire" out of his own hands, he had better lose his power than forfeit his self-respect. Anyway, the duty of the moment was clear; he must calm men's minds. For that purpose, he issued a proclamation (18th Dec. 1801), which, among other things, declared that it was necessary to receive the orders and the envoys of the mother country with respect and filial regard. Yet, while he encouraged obedience, he could not be insensible to the possibility that resistance might be his duty. He was, therefore, under an obligation to foster the means of resistance, and not only to appear confident himself, but to keep up the spirits of his soldiers. This twofold state of mind is seen in words which he uttered from time to time, as in these:—"A well-educated child owns submission and obedience to his mother; but if that mother becomes so unnatural as to seek the ruin of her child, the child must look for justice with Him to whom vengeance [Page 151] belongs. If I must die, I will die as a brave soldier, as a man of honour. I fear no one."

It did not escape the eye of those who, having access to the president, narrowly watched him, that the agitation of his mind increased, and had risen to a great height. Catching alarm from these symptoms, some began to take measures for quitting the island. One of the most distinguished Creoles of Port-au-Prince, and who afterwards settled in France, was of the number. He one day asked Toussaint in private for a passport, in order to proceed to the mother country. The unexpected request disturbed the president. Hastening to the door, to ascertain if he could reckon on their not being disturbed, he speedily returned and asked, looking his companion fixedly in the face, "Why do you wish to go away? You, whom I esteem and love?" "Because I am white, and because, notwithstanding the good feelings you have for me, I see that you are on the eve of being the irritated chief of the blacks, and that within these few days you are no longer the protector of the whites, since you have just sent out of the island several for having expressed joy that the Europeans were about to come to Saint Domingo." "Yes," replied Toussaint, with warmth, "they have had the imprudence and folly to rejoice at such news, as if the expedition was not destined to destroy me—to destroy the whites— to destroy the colony. In France I am represented as an independent power, and therefore they are arming against me. —Against me, who refused General Maitland to establish my independence under the protection of England, and who always rejected the proposals which Sonthonax made on the subject. Since, however, you wish to set out for France, I consent to it; but, at least, let your voyage be useful to the colony. I will send by you letters to the first consul, and I will entreat him to listen to you. Make him acquainted with me; make him acquainted with the prosperous state of the agriculture and the commerce of the colony; in a word, let him know what I have done.

It is according to all that I have done here that I ought, and that I wish to be judged. Twenty times have I written to Bonaparte, to ask him to send civil commissioners, [Page 152] to tell him to despatch hither the old colonists, whites instructed in administering public affairs, good machinists, good workmen; he has never replied. Suddenly he avails himself of the peace (of which he has not deigned to inform me, and which I learn only through the English) in order to direct against me a formidable expedition, in the ranks of which I see my personal enemies, and people injurious to the colony, whom I sent away. Come to me within four-and-twenty hours. Very ardently do I wish that you and my letters may arrive in time to make the first consul change his determination, and to make him sensible that in ruining me he ruins the blacks—he ruins not only Saint Domingo, but also all the western colonies. If Bonaparte is the first man in France, Toussaint is the first man in the Archipelago of the Antilles." After a moment of reflection, he added, in a firm tone, "I was going to treat with the Americans and the English to procure me twenty thousand blacks from the coast, but I had no other object than to make soldiers of them for France. I know the perfidy of the English. I am under no obligation to them for the information they give me as to the expedition coming to Saint Domingo. No! never will I arm for them! I took up arms for the freedom of my colour, which France alone proclaimed, but which she has no right to nullify. Our liberty is no longer in her hands; it is our own! We will defend it or perish."

CHAPTER II.

Bonaparte cannot be turned from undertaking an expedition against Toussaint— Resolves on the enterprise in order chiefly to get rid of his republican associates in arms—Restores slavery and the slave-trade—Excepts Hayti from the decree—Misleads Toussaint's sons—Despatches an armament under Leclerc.

IN vain was it that Vincent, who had attempted to dissuade Toussaint against the adventure of a constitution, now employed his honest and prudent arguments to turn aside Bonaparte from [Page 153] the intended expedition against Saint Domingo. Disregardful of the effect which his advice might have on himself, he urged on the consul that the victorious warriors of Europe would lose their energy, together with their strength, under the climate of the Antilles; that such a climate would annihilate the army, even if the ascendancy of Toussaint L'Ouverture over the inhabitants did not succeed in destroying it by arms; he added the consideration of the probability that the English would openly or secretly endeavour to traverse his object, and frustrate his attempt. To the last remark Bonaparte answered—"The cabinet of St. James's has been disposed to set itself in opposition to my sending a squadron to Saint Domino; I have notified to it, that if it did not consent, I would send to Toussaint unlimited powers, and acknowledge him as independent. It has said no more to me on the point." If this is correct, England, it may be presumed, was influenced by fear for the effects of such a recognition on her neighbouring slave colony of Jamaica. Thus does wrong support wrong. Having effected nothing in conversation, Vincent addressed to the consul a written document, in which, after setting forth the means of defence which the colony possessed, he said—"At the head of so many resources is a man the most active and indefatigable that can possibly be imagined. It may be strictly said, that he is everywhere; and especially at the spot where sound judgment and danger would say that his presence is most essential; his great moderation, his power, peculiar to himself, of never needing rest—the advantage he has of being able to resume the labours of the cabinet after laborious journeys; of replying to a hundred letters every day, and of habitually fatiguing five secretaries; more still, the skill of amusing and deceiving everybody, carried even to deceit, make him a man so superior to all around him, that respect and submission go to the extent of fanaticism in a very great number of persons; it may be affirmed, that no man of the present day has acquired over an ignorant mass, the boundless power obtained by General Toussaint over his brethren in Saint Domingo; he is the absolute master of the island; and nothing can counteract his wishes, whatever they are, although some distinguished men, of whom, [Page 154] however, the number among the blacks is very small, know and fear the extent to which his views proceed." Bonaparte was displeased at the frankness of these representations, and banished Vincent, their author, to the island of Elba, whither, at a later period he was himself to be banished.

Resolved to disembarrass himself of the veterans in union with whom he had gained his renown, but who now from their strong republican sympathies blocked up his way to the imperial throne, he called a council to deliberate on the most effectual means to be taken in order to bring Toussaint under his yoke. The members of the council were, of course, Bonaparte's creatures. Their desire to please the real sovereign of the land was stronger than their professed attachment to liberty. The councillors recommended the employment of force in order to re-establish slavery; a large number proposed, that for the sake of terror, those whom they characterized as "the guilty" should be decimated. The bishop of Blois, Gregory, that immortal friend of the cause of the blacks, had not given his opinion. "What do you think on the matter?" asked the consul. "I think," he replied, "that the hearing of such speeches suffices to show that they are uttered by whites; if these gentlemen were this moment to change colour, they would talk differently." The restoration of slavery was resolved in the legislative body by a vote of two hundred-and-twelve against sixty-five. Such was the love of Frenchmen for liberty, for the rights of man, for the rights of their fellow-citizens, for the freedom of the black population of Hayti. The determination of itself justifies the course pursued by Toussaint L'Ouverture. His constitution may prove an ineffectual guarantee of the hardly-earned liberties of his colour, but clearly it afforded the only feasible chance of perpetuating the good he had wrought out.

On the 20th of May, 1801, Bonaparte published the infamous decree which replaced the French colonies in the state in which they were before the year 1789, and which, authorizing the slave trade, abrogated all laws to the contrary. This execrable measure marks the real character of the Corsican adventurer, and hands his name down to posterity covered with disgrace. Soon, [Page 155] however, did he find that in an evil hour he had overstepped the limits of prudence; and therefore he put forth another decree which hypocritically excepted Saint Domingo and Guadaloupe, "because these islands are free, not only by right, but in fact— whilst the other colonies are actually in slavery, and it would be dangerous to put an end to that state of things."

The preparation of the public mind for the unjust and wicked attempt to put down liberty in Saint Domingo, was aided by the less obvious but powerful efforts, not only of the colonists in general, but by the mulattoes who dwelt at Paris, of whom Rigaud may be considered as the head. Overcome and exiled by Toussaint, Rigaud panted for revenge. In that vindictive sentiment, he well represented his race, who could not forgive the black president for having extorted the freedom of his colour out of their hands.

There were in Paris two young men who looked on the arrangements for the expedition which they saw everywhere proceeding, with anxiety and alarm. These were Isaac and Placide L'Ouverture, sons of the liberator of Hayti, whom, as a testimony of his confidence, and a pledge of his fidelity, their father had sent to Paris for their education. They both resided in the College La Marche, of which Coasnon was the principal. The consul judged it politic to throw a veil over their eyes. Intending to destroy the father, he had no scruples of conscience about deluding the sons. Coasnon, their teacher, being gained over, assured the young men that the French government had none but pacific views. A few days afterwards, he received a letter from the Minister of Marine, apprising him that the consul wished to see and converse with his pupils before their departure. Repairing to the minister's residence, they received in the presence of Coasnon a confirmation of his statement that the intentions of the government were of a friendly nature. They were then conducted to Bonaparte, who, the better to conceal his real purposes, received them in a flattering manner. Having ascertained which of the two was Toussaint's own son, he said to him:— "Your father is a great man; he has rendered eminent services to France. You will [Page 156] tell him that I, the first magistrate of the French people, promise him protection, glory, and honour. Do not think that France intends to carry war to Saint Domingo; the army which it sends thither is destined not to attack the troops of the country, but to augment their numbers. Here is General Leclerc, my brother-in-law, whom I have appointed Captain-General, and who will command that armament. Orders have been given for you to arrive at Saint Domingo a fortnight before the fleet, to announce to your father the coming of the expedition." On the next day, the delusion was carried still farther, for the Minister of Marine, as a kind of practical assurance how well Toussaint and his children stood with the highest authorities, entertained the young men at a magnificent repast; and shortly after, in order to complete the farce by an appeal to negro vanity, he, in the name of his government, presented to them a superb suit of armour, and a rich and brilliant military costume.

It scarcely needs be stated that the promise that the youths should have time to assure their father of the pacific intentions of France, was not observed. Having answered its momentary purpose, it was openly and deliberately violated. The real design of all this collusion was that, misled by the reports of his sons in Paris, Toussaint L'Ouverture might be taken off his guard. Alas! that in the crisis of his fate, he should have given credit to men who blushed not to deal in falsehood.

It has already appeared from the consul's own words, that he had chosen Leclerc, who was the husband of his sister Pauline, to be at the head of the expedition. Bonaparte was well pleased to have the opportunity of separating himself from Leclerc, whom he regarded as a relative little worthy of his present and his future greatness. The obscure birth of Leclerc in the small town of Pontoise, disquieted his pride. Every day there came to Paris persons of low condition who gave themselves out as relatives of the consul's sister. That sister possessed so rare a beauty, that Canova reproduced her features in his statue of Venus Victrix, *Victorious Venus*. To personal charms she added subtlety and grace of mind. Her looks [Page 157] awakened desires in the most indifferent hearts. She gathered around her all the artifices of voluptuousness. In her furniture she was luxurious; elegant in her personal decorations, and choice in the persons attached to her suite. She was attended by painters, musicians, and buffoons. Pauline accompanied her husband in the expedition. Leclerc was small in stature, but he had vivacity of mind and grace of manner. In countenance he was thought to bear some resemblance to the consul. Though he had showed some courage and perseverance in the campaigns of the Alps and the Rhine, he was little else than the blind instrument of his brother-in-law, whom he imitated in war as well as in peace, with a closeness which betokened a contracted intellect. From such a man was expected the final settlement of the long quarrel of colour in Saint Domingo.

The preparations for the armament were made in different ports. No expense was spared. Holland, then under the domination of France and Spain, kept in alliance with it by fear, furnished ships. The fleet, when collected, was composed of twenty-one frigates, and thirty-five vessels of war. It had on board all the best sailors of France, and was commanded by Villaret Joyeuse. In December, 1801, portions of it left the ports of Brest, Rochefort and Lorient. The rest were to sail from other points. The ocean was covered with ships in order to punish a contumacious slave! The magnitude of the equipment is a measure of Toussaint's power. This fleet bore to Hayti one of the most valiant of armies. The Alps, Italy, the Rhine, and the Nile resounded with the exploits of the veterans who formed its strength. They now left lands which boasted of their civilization, to carry chains to a people who, uncultured though they were, had vindicated their freedom, and used that freedom wisely.

As soon as the fleet had anchored off Cape Samana, at the eastern end of Saint Domingo, Leclerc numbered his sea and land forces, including others which he expected. They amounted to sixty ships and more than thirty thousand men, commanded by generals and captains of experience and renown. Among them were men of colour, who had become illustrious in [Page 158] the sanguinary struggle for emancipation. There was found

Rigaud, whose valour had disputed the laurel with Toussaint himself There was found Pétion, who under a mild physiognomy bore a lofty spirit; he was destined to found and govern a republic in the island he took part in invading. There was found Boyer, his illustrious successor, who by a treaty with the king of France was one day to secure the permanent independence of his native land. All these mulatto chiefs had consented to second the expedition with their council, their courage, and their example. On the other side, the forces of Toussaint consisted at most of sixteen thousand men; five in the north, four in the west, four in the south, and three in what was formerly the Spanish territory. These troops thus scattered, were, however, commanded by captains well trained to mountain warfare; all were animated by the love of freedom, which they cherished the more because they had acquired it at the cost of labour, peril, and bloodshed. Everywhere the Haytian army would find auxiliaries; soldiers, women, children, citizens, had all lived in the camps of the civil wars. Full of recollections of their former servitude, they were ready to perish sooner than submit.

The gathering of the fleet at Samana took several weeks. The effect of a sudden descent was lost. On hearing that a fleet was approaching the island, Toussaint L'Ouverture threw the bridle over his horse's neck, and galloped to Cape Samana to reconnoitre the squadrons. Unversed in marine affairs, he at first took the manœuvring for hesitation. But as the vessels anchored in their several places, having never seen so large a fleet before, he was struck with astonishment, and feeling for a moment discouraged, he exclaimed to his officers, "We must perish; all France is coming to Saint Domingo; it has been deceived, it comes to take revenge and enslave the blacks."

Convinced as he was of the hostile designs of the armament, Toussaint could not deny that its heralds had announced friendship. As little did he possess the right of making war against the forces of the country to which he professed allegiance. Had he already proclaimed the independence of Hayti, he would have been relieved from the perplexity of a dubious position. Even [Page 159] had he at this last moment proclaimed independence, he would have been saved from the evils of vacillation. But being neither at peace nor at war with his assailants, he laboured under a great disadvantage. However, he made such arrangements as his unhappy position permitted. To act on the defensive was compulsory on him in the circumstances, and probably such a policy was every way the best. Should the armament prove really hostile; should it attack the island, then resistance must be made; and if defeat ensued, there were the mountains for a retreat, and a succession of strong holds where an almost unlimited defence might be maintained.

At length the fleet put itself in movement. After having detached Kerverseau to go and take possession of the city of Saint Domingo, Leclerc directed the armament in three divisions against three principal points; Fort Dauphin, and the city of the Cape in the north, and Port-au-Prince in the west. The island was thus invested. No declaration of war was made, no negotiations were opened. The squadrons sailed to the several points as if they approached a friendly shore, and as a matter of course entered friendly harbours. Nor could they be challenged. Toussaint possessed no vessels, and if he had had vessels, was he not a French subject, and were these not French ships and French commanders?

It was not possible for Isaac and Placide L'Ouverture any longer to doubt the nature of the errand on which the armament had been sent. They drew up in writing remonstrances which they presented to Leclerc, who doubtless smiled in his thoughts at their easy faith.

[Page 160] CHAPTER III.

Leclerc obtains possession of the chief positions in the island, and yet is not master thereof—By arms and by treachery he establishes himself at the Cape, at Fort Dauphin, at Saint Domingo, and at Port-au-Prince—Toussaint L'Ouverture depends on his mountain strongholds.

THE main squadron, under the immediate direction of Leclerc, proceeded to act against Cape City. Sent on an errand of duplicity, the commander meant war, yet was obliged to feign peace. His aim was, if possible, to obtain possession of the Cape, under the cover of friendship. Surely, admission into a French port could not be denied to French forces. In order to effect his purpose, he sent Lebrun, aide-de-camp of the admiral Villaret Joyeuse, on shore, to announce his intention of landing his troops. Lebrun was conducted to General Christophe, who held the place on behalf of the insular authorities. As Lebrun passed along, he, as if by accident, let fall a number of proclamations, intended to serve the cause of Bonaparte by stirring up the inhabitants. Having put his papers into the hands of Christophe, he received for answer, "Without the orders of the Governor-General Toussaint L'Ouverture, who at present is in the Spanish part, I cannot receive the squadron and the troops which are on board." Lebrun whispered in the ear of Christophe, that General Leclerc was the bearer of splendid tokens of the favour of the government toward him. "No, sir," was the prompt and decided reply, "I cannot listen to any proposition without the orders of the governor. The proclamations you bring breathe despotism and tyranny. I shall go and administer to my soldiers an oath to maintain our liberty at the peril of their lives." The proclamation covertly published by Lebrun, was not wholly without effect. A deputation of citizens waited on Christophe to impress on him the responsibility he took on himself in withstanding the orders of the mother country. He replied that he was a soldier; that he acknowledged as his supreme chief only Toussaint [Page 161] L'Ouverture; that nothing proved to him that a squadron over which they saw foreign banners float, had been sent by the mother country; that France would have taken other means to cause its commands to be acknowledged, and that it would have sent them by an envoy, and not by foreign squadrons. He ended by declaring, that if Leclerc, who called himself Captain-general, persisted in his resolution to enter the Cape, he would set the whole in flames rather than the ships should anchor in the harbour. However, he permitted a deputation of the city to go on board Leclerc's ship, and entreat a delay of two days, in order that Toussaint might be consulted. The general assured the deputies, that France, full of affection for the colony, had made every arrangement for its happiness; he set forth in a few words the great and benevolent projects which the mother country had for Toussaint L'Ouverture, whose sons it sent back after having educated them with the greatest care; he announced that he brought General Christophe proofs of the public gratitude, and remarked how monstrous would be the ingratitude of which those two chiefs seemed disposed to render themselves guilty. He added, that the conduct of General Christophe having caused him to fear that he would employ the delay asked for in order, by drawing together his forces, to secure the success of the meditated resistance, he could not postpone the entrance of the squadron, and that he should make his arrangements in the space of half-an-hour—time sufficient to enable General Christophe to repair the disgrace of his revolt by prompt submission. Christophe remained unmoved by the allurements and the threats of the French commander, though supported by the following letter:—

"I learn with indignation, citizen general, that you refuse to receive the French squadron and army which I command, under the pretext that you have not any order from the governor general.

"France has made peace with England, and its government sends to Saint Domingo forces able to subdue rebels, if rebels are to be found in Saint Domingo. As to you, citizen general, [Page 162] I avow that it would give me pain to reckon you among rebels. I warn you that if this very day you do not put into my possession the forts Picolet, Belair, and all the batteries of the coast, to-morrow at dawn fifteen thousand men shall be disembarked. Four thousand at this moment are landing at Fort Liberté, eight thousand at Port Republican; you will find my proclamation joined to this communication; it expresses the intentions of the French government; but, remember, whatever esteem your conduct in the colony has inspired me with, I hold you responsible for whatever may take place.

"The general-in-chief of the army of Saint Domingo, and captain-general of the colony. (Signed) "LECLERC."

The letter, and the tone of the captain-general served only to inflame the spirit of resistance, which had time to gather strength, because the squadron, not being able to procure pilots, was obliged to gain the open sea without being able to land the troops. Christophe mustered the soldiers of the line and made them swear to conquer or die, conformably to the proclamation of Toussaint L'Ouverture, dated the 18th of December, 1801. The proclamation of Leclerc, intended to win over the civil authorities and the inhabitants, assumed a more pacific character, and promised to all the soldiers and functionaries of the colony, whatever their colour, the confirmation of their rank and their offices. Smitten with fear, some of the civil authorities endeavoured to prevail with Christophe, but he was not a man to be easily overcome.

That chief, born in the island of Grenada, first an emancipated slave, then an innkeeper, a tradesman, and a cattle dealer, ended by becoming a king. To the advantage of great height, he added that of a majestic carriage, and an eye fall of fire. He had a strong soul, adorned with civic, domestic, and military virtues. His prudence led him to trust little to fortune. He was active, patient, and temperate. Without having been instructed in the schools, he spoke with ease and grace: he took peculiar pleasure in diverting his guests by the recital of adventures or his valorous [Page 163] exploits. He was moreover liable to contrasts of temper which indicated the fiery impulses of his character. Some of his excellencies he lost when seated on a throne. When the messenger Of Leclerc urged him to surrender the city, he replied with hauteur, "Go and tell your general that the French shall march here only over ashes, and that the ground shall burn beneath their feet." He afterwards wrote his determination in these terms—"The decision of arms can admit you only into a city in ashes, and even on these ashes I will fight still!" Inexorable to the entreaties of treacherous natives, he was assailed by the following proclamation from Bonaparte, which they received from the hands of Leclerc, and put into circulation.

"THE FIRST CONSUL TO THE INHABITANTS OF SAINT DOMINGO.

"Whatever your origin and your colour, you are all Frenchmen; you are all free and all equal before God and before men.

"France, like Saint Domingo, has been a prey to factions, and has been torn by civil war and by foreign war; but all is changed; all nations have embraced the French, and have sworn peace and friendship towards them: all Frenchmen likewise have embraced each other, and have sworn to be friends and brothers; do you embrace the French, and rejoice at again beholding your brethren and your friends from Europe. The Government sends to you the Captain-General Leclerc; he brings with him large forces to protect you against your enemies and against the enemies of the Republic. If you are told, 'Those forces are destined to rob you of liberty,' reply, 'The Republic will not allow that liberty shall be taken from us.'

"Rally round the Captain-General, he brings you abundance and peace; rally round him. Whoever shall dare to separate himself from the Captain-General, will be an enemy to his country, and the wrath of the Republic will devour him as the fire devours your dried sugar-canes.

[Page 164]"Given at Paris, at the Government Palace, the 17th Brumaire, in the tenth year of the French Republic (8 Nov., 1801).

"The First Consul, (Signed)   "BONAPARTE."

This proclamation was not of a nature to inspire confidence in men whom servitude had made habitually distrustful. The words of the Consul appeared those of a master who alternately employs promises and threats. The people of the Cape had no need of being assured of a liberty which they actually enjoyed; and that wrath presented under the image of the conflagration of their harvests, looked, in their eyes, like a token of slavery. All declared that they would rather perish than return to servitude. While time was thus spent in useless words, the war had begun without any negotiation with Toussaint, whether an order to that effect had been given by the Consul, that he might strike terror into the inhabitants, or whether Leclerc considered that promptitude was the best means of commanding obedience. Rochambeau, who had been sent against Fort Dauphin, attacked the place by land and by sea. Everything soon yielded to French valour. The blacks fled, but in flying set the city on fire. At the sight of the flames, Rochambeau slaughtered all the prisoners, whom he treated as revolters. The bay of Mancenille was stained with the blood of many unarmed blacks, whose crime was that they had shouted "No whites! no slavery!"

Afraid lest Christophe should carry his threat into execution and set Cape City on fire, Leclerc resolved to take the enemy in the rear by landing his forces in the Bay of Acul. But the movement of the vessels and the noise of the cannon spread on all sides tumult and alarm. Burning plantations announced that flames would soon rise from the town. Christophe, threatened by sea and by land by two bodies of foes, determined to set fire to the Cape. After distributing torches to his soldiers, and to all who were devoted to so sacred a cause, he called the Almighty Protector of liberty to witness that he was driven to extremity, and commenced the conflagration with his own residence, [Page 165] decorated in a costly manner by the arts of luxury. An ocean of flames rose in the air; roofs fell in all on fire; and in those flames the black man saw the preservation of his liberty. The appearance of the fleet, the blood of blacks and whites flowing on two parts of the coast, terror, confusion, the loss of so much wealth, awoke in all hearts the former furies of freedom and slavery. At the sight of the flames, which changed night into day, those passions painted themselves on white as well as black countenances. But no cries, no complaints were heard. Only fingers were pointed to the high lands above the Cape where freedom might find an asylum. The flight took place in silence, as if vengeance was deferred in order to be more terrible. An explosion of a powder magazine crowned that work of courage and despair. The flames of the conflagration were seen nearly at the same time by the French fleet and by Toussaint L'Ouverture, who arrived in the neighbourhood from Santo Domingo, and who then regretted that he had not lost his life, in the plains of the Artibonite when he fought for France and for his country, so great was his grief. He showed compassion to a multitude of old men, women and children, who were scattered on all the roads, and who were flying through the mountains. How embarrassing his Position; the Cape and Fort Dauphin had been treated as hostile cities.

Christophe, who had set on fire his own house and the city, manifested a generosity too rare in war; fearing lest, in the confusion and the tumult of the conflagration, some two thousand whites with their wives and children might become victims of his men, he conducted them into a place of safety. After abandoning the Cape, Christophe joined Toussaint, and conjointly they raised fire and flames everywhere. At the request of his chief, Christophe took up a position at La Grande Rivière, while Toussaint himself went towards the plain of the north. Both were thus immediately above the invading forces. The latter in proceeding to his post found himself face to face with the advanced guard of Leclerc, and passed through a most terrible fire. His cloak was riddled with balls, and his horse was wounded. Reaching Mornay, he received a letter from [Page 166] Rochambeau, who sought to set off his glory by affectations of pity. "I did not expect," he said, "that my soldiers in arriving here would have to dye their bayonets in the blood of their brothers and their friends." Toussaint L'Ouverture found it desirable to quit Mornay, and passing through Ennery, where was his wife with apart of his family, made his way toward Gonaïves in the west. While Leclerc and Rochambeau were conquering in the north towns which were in ashes, their co-operator, General Boudet, in the west, was seeking by stratagem as much as by force to take possession of Port-au-Prince. That city, built of wood, was the rival of the Cape. Agé, who was entrusted with its defence, had not a soul proof against treachery. But along side of him there served a captain worthy of "the good old times." Lamartinière possessed an heroic soul; his firmness, his courage, and his patience could not be surpassed. With a handful of soldiers, he was capable of resisting the efforts of an army. When the surrender of the city was demanded, the reply was the same as that which had been given at the Cape, only the threat of carnage was subjoined to the threat of conflagration. "If," replied the blacks, "if the French disembark before we can be informed of the resolution of Toussaint, three cannon shot, repeated from mountain top to mountain top, shall be the signal for the conflagration of our homes, and for the death of those who may endeavour to make us slaves."

Not without disgust nor without fear, did Boudet, who had gained renown in the Antilles by wresting Guadaloupe from the hands of the English, land near Lamentin, distant about a league to the west of Port-au-Prince. At the appointed signal, flames arose on all sides. Frightful disorder prevailed in the town. The blacks, dreading slavery, pursued the whites through the streets, and even searched for them in hiding-places. At the recollection of the evils of their past servitude, marks of which many of them still bore in their mutilated bodies, they saw in the whites only pitiless masters, and slew them unsparingly, or carried them away as hostages into the mountains. A large number of women, children, and old men sought in a church an asylum against the rage of their former slaves, who, in spite o[Page 167] the sanctity of the place, were on the point of sacrificing them as victims to their liberty; but a priest appeared, and called out for mercy; presenting the sacred utensils of the altar, and assuaging the wrath of the assailants, he saved the lives of the trembling and helpless crowd; but the raging men hastened away to find, in less hallowed places, whites on whom they might effectually wreak their terrible vengeance. Boudet, unused to the terrors that arose on every hand, exhorted his soldiers to mercy. "My comrades," he said, "you must regard these people as fellow-citizens; this is no foreign land, it is your country. Do not make use of your arms; uncover your breasts to them, in order that those who follow us may have the right to avenge us." By the treachery of its defenders, he obtained possession of Fort Bizoton, by which his progress might have been long stopped. Agé was thinking of surrendering the city itself, but Lamartinière, indignant at a second instance of perfidy, called into action, for its defence, all his resolution. At the council-board, he blew out the brains of a captain of artillery who refused the keys of the arsenal. So daring a stroke put an end to indecision and enkindled courage; he drew after him four thousand men to the gate of Leogane, where a redoubt, armed with six pieces of artillery, defended the town. Death was spread in the ranks of the French, who advanced slowly, uncertain of the use they should make of their arms. Soon their ardour burned up; they rushed across the moat, threw themselves into the city, and preserved it from the threatened conflagration.

Lamartinière, less afflicted at his defeat than at not having reduced Port-au-Prince into ashes, hastened to intrench himself in Croix-des-Bouquets, a little to the north; a position surrounded by moats cut in a very hard soil. There he was waited for by Dessalines, who had come up too late to defend the city. That chief, who had the west under his command, was of a bold, turbulent, and ferocious spirit; now from revenge, now from ambition, he imbrued his hands in the blood of both white men and black men. Hunger, thirst, fatigue, and loss of sleep he seemed made to endure as if by a peculiarity of constitution. His air was fierce, his step oblique, his look sanguinary. His face [Page 168] furrowed with incisions, indicated the coast of Africa as his birthplace. Under that terrible aspect he concealed an impenetrable dissimulation. His barbarous eloquence lay in expressive signs rather than in words. What is strange in his destiny, is that he was a savage, a slave, a soldier, a general, and died when an emperor, under the dagger of a Brutus. When he learnt that Port-au-Prince had escaped from conflagration, he turned pale, scolded, and roared with wrath.

Boudet, intending to follow up his victory, flew to Croix-des-Bouquets, where he was awaited by those two formidable chiefs. But Dessalines understood his business too well to encounter the French general in set battle array. Knowing how by bold and rapid movements to deceive as well as escape from an enemy, he outflanked Boudet, and getting in his rear, set on fire Leogane, a charming city built on a promontory, before the invaders could arrive in the vicinity. The flames which destroyed that city rejoiced the soul of the barbarian, but did not console him for the escape of Port-au-Prince; he meditated fresh conflagrations.

While the north and the west were theatres of fire and carnage, the east and the south submitted without the endurance of calamity. General Kerverseau, on presenting himself before Santo Domingo, found the inhabitants the more disposed to receive him, because in perilous missions in Santo Domingo, he had acquired a reputation for prudence and honour. Kerverseau was not a great general, but a good man, modest and mild; respected by parties, he enjoyed much popularity. Paul L'Ouverture, who commanded the city, refused to yield without instructions from Toussaint, his brother. Negotiations, nevertheless, were opened, but they came to a stop when the news arrived that all was in flames in other parts. Then Kerverseau invested Santo Domingo by sea and land. Paul, meanwhile, had written for instructions to his distinguished brother. Toussaint sent a despatch commanding him to destroy the city if he was unable to hold it against his adversary. But fearing the message might fall into the hands of Kerverseau, he sent another, which recommended conciliation. These communications, intercepted by Spaniards who had taken sides with [Page 169] the

French, fell into the hands of the besieging general. Kerverseau conveyed to Paul the message which bore a friendly character. Paul, importuned by the townsmen, admitted his assailant, and joined his ranks. Thus fell Santo Domingo, and with it there passed under the power of France a portion of Toussaint's forces.

The southern province, inhabited chiefly by mulattoes, and being the scene of Rigaud's revolt, was not likely to offer a stern resistance. Its commander, Laplume, no sooner heard that the French were masters of the Cape and Port-au-Prince, than he resolved to submit to the authority of the mother country. His troops, mostly of his own blood, cherished no friendly recollections toward Toussaint, by whom they had been subdued, and were easily induced by their leader, who painted to them vividly the evils of civil war, and read the proclamation of the Consul, whose power, genius, and glory he extolled, to join him in taking place side by side with the assailants of the constitutional rights of the island. Thus, the strong points of Hayti were in the hands of Leclerc.

At the Cape and at Fort-Dauphin in the north, at Santo Domingo in the east, at Cayes in the south, and at Port-au-Prince in the west, the French invader had succeeded in taking up strong positions. In vain had Toussaint L'Ouverture organised the best resistance in his power. The enemy were on the island. True, some of the places they held were only heaps of ruins. Nevertheless, they had effected a landing. The island, however, was not in their possession. Neither arms nor treachery had subdued the natives. Toussaint well knew that the sea-ports could not withstand so formidable an assault. But he knew also that a country which is full of mountains is inexpugnable. For the desultory warfare of the mountains he prepared himself, and, backed by the population at large, men of his own blood, he defied defeat, and felt confident that time and the climate would unstring the arm, and lay waste the spirits as well as the frames of his assailants. Even one advantage he had gained; for whereas at the first, the islanders knew not whether they had to expect peace or war, their leader, consequently, could fully [Page 170] prepare for neither; now at length the cloak was stripped off, and to all eyes it was clear that the only alternative was victory or servitude.

On his part, Leclerc, though victorious, did not deceive himself with the notion of having accomplished his work. On the contrary, in view of the facts to which we have just adverted, he was aware that he had everything but the first step to accomplish. The Spartacus of Hayti was on his own mountains, supported by a whole people able and ready to resist to the utmost. How was Leclerc to succeed? How could a desultory warfare in ravines and on precipices, in recesses and in mountain fastnesses, be either carried on or brought to a desirable issue against what was not in name but literally a *levy en masse?* A different method must be tried. So long as Toussaint L'Ouverture was at the head of those predatory bands, the consequences of victory would be only a little less beneficial than those of defeat. But treachery has power, and treachery of the basest kind was put into action.

CHAPTER IV.

General Leclerc opens a negotiation with Toussaint L'Ouverture by means of his two sons, Isaac and Placide—the negotiation ends in nothing—the French commander-in-chief outlaws Toussaint, and prepares for a campaign.

BEFORE he was yet informed of the success of the expedition in the east, the south, and the west, Leclerc, well aware that in Toussaint L'Ouverture he had to do with an enemy not easy to overcome, resolved, when now he had himself taken up a firm position in the north, to put into play a method of operation from which he expected a decisive and immediate result. Vincent, who foresaw the terrible wasting that the European troops would have to endure under the tropics, advised the Consul to send back, partly as hostages, and partly as mediators, the [Page 171] sons of Toussaint—and so take a means for bringing the colony into subjection, both more sure and less costly than the appeal to arms. This advice he urged specially on the ground that as Toussaint had strong domestic feelings, he would not be able to stand out against the influence which the return of the young men, after a long absence, would exert on their father in favour of the Consul's designs. Accordingly, the Captain-General having sent for the youths, who had remained on board the fleet, spoke to them of the calamities which had befallen the island, urged the necessity of a speedy accommodation, and reminded them of the letter written to their father by the First Consul. "I have," he added,"the greatest hope of coming to a good understanding with your father; he was absent; he could not command the resistance. You must carry to him the First Consul's letter; let him know my intentions, and the high opinion I entertain of him." It was somewhat late to set on foot a friendly negotiation. But the hour was well-timed, since the delay had given Leclerc a footing in the island, if it had not also served, as intended, to show Toussaint L'Ouverture the inutility of opposition to the will of Bonaparte, The young men felt that their mission of peace should have preceded hostilities; but they felt, also, a very strong desire to see their parents and their home; nor were they wholly without a hope that even yet a pacific arrangement might be made. They therefore gladly accepted the embassy, and set out for Ennery, their father's dwelling-place, accompanied by their tutor, M. Coasnon. Behind them they left a horrible image of civil war—old men, women, children, flying from fire and sword; everywhere alarm and consternation. Soon they came into view of peaceful scenes, the work of their father's genius—cultivated fields, abundant crops, happy families. There was a land of desolation—here a land of prosperity. On their route they saw many inhabitants, but not one soldier. As soon as it was known who they were, crowds came out to greet them with acclamations; they were surrounded, welcomed, embraced, and questioned. Their object? It was to convey friendly assurances to their father. The news was gladly heard. Nevertheless, doubt soon resumed the ascendancy. Those were indeed the sons of [Page 172] their venerated chief; they had been sent back unhurt; it was a token for good; yet, why announce peace by cannon balls? Why land on a friendly shore with a charge of bayonets? Along the whole route, the same eagerness to see and welcome the youths was displayed. Delight for a moment took the place of terror. The family had been warned of the approach of the young men. At last, about nine o'clock in the evening of the second day after the departure from the Cape, their mother, accompanied by a few friends, came with the aid of torch-light to receive them in the midst of an immense crowd. It is more easy to conceive than describe the tender scenes which passed that evening in the home of Toussaint L'Ouverture. After the mother had for the moment indulged all her emotions in regard to her sons, she turned to their preceptor, whose care and trouble she acknowledged in the fullest and warmest terms. All the family, for a short hour, forgetting the common miseries of their country, gave way to the sweetest and most joyous sentiments. Duty had prevented Toussaint himself from taking his place in this affecting interview. But, at eleven o'clock in the evening of the next day, the sound of a trumpet and the rattling of horses' feet announced his arrival. On his entrance, Isaac and Placide threw themselves passionately on his neck. Their father long held them pressed closely to his heart, while tears streamed down his hardy cheeks. M. Coasnon was sent for, to whom L'Ouverture expressed the high sense of his obligation for the attentions he had bestowed on the young men; thanking him for having accompanied them into the bosom of their family—though he was sorry that their arrival took place in the midst of war, the cause of which, he said, was unknown to him, and which he had in no way expected. Then M. Coasnon presented to him the Consul's letter, to which was suspended by a silk cord the state seal—the whole enclosed in a golden casket. The epistle was as follows:—

"TO CITIZEN TOUSSAINT, GENERAL IN CHIEF OF THE ARMY OF SAINT DOMINGO.

"CITIZEN GENERAL,

"The peace with England, and all the Powers of Europe, which has just placed the Republic on the summit of [Page 173] power and greatness, gives the Government the opportunity of occupying itself with the colony of Saint Domingo. We send thither citizen General Leclerc, our brother-in-law, as Captain-General, as First Magistrate of the colony. He is accompanied by forces sufficient to cause the sovereignty of the French people to be respected. In these circumstances, we have pleasure in hoping that you will prove to us and to all France the sincerity of the sentiments you have constantly expressed in the different letters that you have written to us.

"We have conceived an esteem for you, and we take pleasure in recognising and proclaiming the services which you have rendered to the French people. If its banner floats over Saint Domingo, it is to you and the brave blacks that we owe it.

"Called by your talents, and the force of circumstances to the highest post, you have destroyed civil war, put reins on the persecution carried on by ferocious men, restored to honour religion and the worship of God—from whom all things proceed.

"The constitution yon have formed, while containing many good things, contains some which are contrary to the dignity and the sovereignty of the French nation, of which Saint Domingo forms a portion.

"The circumstances in which you found yourself, surrounded by enemies, while the mother country could not succour you, nor send you provisions, rendered legitimate articles of that constitution which otherwise could not be legitimate; but now, when circumstances are so happily changed, you will be the first to pay homage to the sovereignty of the nation which counts you in the number of her most illustrious citizens, both for the services which you have rendered, and for the talents and force of character with which nature has endowed you. Conduct contrary to this would be irreconcileable with the idea which we have formed of you. It would cause you to forfeit the numerous rights you have to the gratitude of the Republic, and would dig before your feet a precipice which, in causing your own ruin, might contribute to the ruin of those brave blacks whose courage we love, and whose rebellion we should be sorry to find ourselves compelled to punish. [Page 174] "We have made known to your children and their preceptor the sentiments which animate us, and we send them back to you.

"Assist the Captain-General with your counsels, your influence, and your talents. What can you desire? The freedom of the blacks! You know that in all the countries where we have been, we have given freedom to the nations who did not possess it. Respect, honours, fortune? After the services which you have rendered, and which in this juncture you may render, with the special sentiment we entertain toward you, how can you be uncertain as to the respect, the fortune, and the homage which await you?

"Let the people of Saint Domingo know that the solicitude which France has always felt for their happiness has often been powerless through the imperious circumstances of war; that men come from the continent to agitate the island and support factions, were the products of the factions which distracted the mother country; that henceforth peace, and the strength of the Government, will secure the prosperity and the freedom of the colony. Tell them, that if to them liberty is the first of blessings, they cannot enjoy it except as French citizens, and that every act contrary to the interests of the mother country, to the obedience which they owe to the Government, and to the captain general which is its delegate, would be a crime against the national sovereignty, which would eclipse their services, and render Saint Domingo the theatre of a destructive war in which parents and children would slay each other.

"And you, General, reflect, that if you are the first of your colour that has reached such a height of power, and that has gained distinction by bravery and military talents, you are also, before God and us, the person who is responsible for the conduct of the inhabitants of the colony.

"If there are evil-disposed persons who tell the individuals that have played the principal parts in the troubles of Saint Domingo that we have come to investigate what they have done during the times of anarchy, assure them that we shall inquire only as to their conduct in this last circumstance; that we shall search into the past only to discover the deeds which have made [Page 175] them distinguished in the war against the Spaniards and the English, who were our enemies.

"Reckon unreservedly on our esteem, and conduct yourself as he ought who is one of the principal citizens of the greatest nation in the world.

"The First Consul,

(Signed) "BONAPARTE"

Toussaint L'Ouverture, after running his eyes rapidly over this compound of cajolery and menace, was about to reply, when his sons and M. Coasnon spoke to him of the handsome reception they had had from the Consul, and the magnificent promises he had made them; they also did justice in setting forth the assurance given them by Bonaparte, that the army commanded by Leclerc was not sent to Saint Domingo with hostile views; adding, that it was the desire of that general to enter into an accommodation with Toussaint L'Ouverture. Then the liberator of Hayti said in reply: "You, M. Coasnon, you, whom I consider as the preceptor of my sons, and the envoy of France, must confess that the words and the letter of the First Consul are altogether in opposition to the conduct of General Leclerc; those announce peace—he makes war on me.

"General Leclerc, in falling on Saint Domingo as a clap of thunder, has announced his mission to me only by the burning of the capital, which he might have avoided; by the capture of Fort Dauphin, and the landing on the coast of Limbé effected by main force.

"I have just been informed that General Maurepas has been attacked by a French division, which he has repulsed; that the commander of Saint Marc has forced two French vessels which cannonaded that city to put to sea. In the midst of so many disasters and acts of violence, I must not forget that I wear a sword. But, for what reason is so unjust, so impolitic a war declared against me? Is it because I have delivered my country from the plague of foreign and civil conflict; that with all my power I have laboured for her prosperity and her splendour; that I have established order and justice here? Since these actions are [Page 176] regarded as a crime, why are my children sent to me, in such a juncture, to share that crime?

"As for the rest, if, as you tell me, General Leclerc frankly desires peace, let him stop the march of his troops. He will preserve Saint Domingo from total subversion, and will tranquillize minds exasperated by his system of aggression and invasion. I will, M. Coasnon, write him a letter having this tenour, which you, my two children, and M. Granville, the tutor of my younger son, shall put into his hands."

The conversation was prolonged far into the night. Toussaint remarked on the inconsistency of recognising him as Commander-in-chief of Saint Domingo, at the very time that he was assailed by an overpowering force. He could not suppress the indignation which he felt at the thought that his children were offered to him as the price of his surrender. He bade M. Coasnon take them back to General Leclerc, because, at every hazard he owed the sacrifice of his life to the freedom of his fellow-citizens. The father struggled with the liberator, and brought a flood of tears from his eyes. The liberator overpowered even the father, and exacted the sternest regard to public duty.

In two days the letter was ready. On the night of February 11th, 1802, the appointed messengers were despatched with the communication. As they travelled toward the Cape, M. Granville acquainted M. Coasnon with the irritation that prevailed among the blacks. The life of the unfortunate whites hung by a thread, and at any moment a word would be sufficient to sunder the slender tie. In his reply, Toussaint reproached Leclerc with having come to displace him by means of cannon shot; with not having delivered to him the letter of the First Consul, until three months after its date; and with having by hostile acts rendered doubtful the rights and the services of his colour. He declared that those rights imposed upon him duties that were superior to those of nature; that he was prepared to sacrifice his children to his colour, and that he sent them back that it might not be supposed they were bound by his presence. He ended by saying, that being more distrustful than ever, he [Page 177] required time in order to decide the course which remained for him to take.

Leclerc hastened to send back the young men with a reply, in which he invited Toussaint to come and concert with him means for putting a stop to the public disorders, giving him his word that the past should be sunk in oblivion, that he, Toussaint, should be treated with the greatest distinction, and that if he complied with the request, he should that moment be proclaimed the first lieutenant of the Captain-general of the colony. Leclerc finished his epistle by stating that though he had precise instructions not to discontinue warlike operations, if he found it necessary to commence them; yet in the hope of a good understanding, he would condescend to an armistice of four days, but, that delay over, he would, by a proclamation, declare Toussaint an enemy of the French nation, and put him beyond the pale of the law.

The allurement was too weak: the threat was impotent. Duty with Toussaint was superior to every other consideration. He could be neither bought nor intimidated. Irritated by this ultimatum he resolved to employ all his energies for the maintenance of the liberties he had achieved. Yet had he no wish to involve his sons in the issue. He therefore, after announcing to them his final resolution, declared that he left them free to choose between France and their father; that he did not blame their attachment to the mother country; but that his colour stood between him and France; that he could not compromise the destinies of his colour by placing himself at the mercy of an expedition, in which figured several white generals, as well as Rigaud, Petion, Boyer, Chanlatte and others, all his personal enemies; that the order not to cease from fighting to negotiate, showed that France had more confidence in its arms than in its rights; that a confidence of such a nature indicated the despotism of mere force, and that if no practical regard was paid to the rights of the blacks, while they had some power, what would their condition be when he and his should be powerless?

His sons threw themselves into his arms, imploring him to yield. Their tears and their caresses failed to move him. [Page 178] Remaining inflexible, he merely repeated, "My children, make your choice; whatever it is, I shall always love you." At length his own son Isaac, detaching himself from his father's arms, exclaimed, "Well, behold in me a faithful servant of France, who can never resolve to bear arms against her." Placide, Isaac's uterine brother, manifested indecision. Toussaint, petrified, gave his paternal benediction to Isaac, whom he gently put away from him, Meanwhile Placide, overpowered, threw himself on his father's neck, and sobbing said, "I am yours, father; I fear the future, I fear slavery; I am ready to fight against it; I renounce France." Immediately L'Ouverture invested him with the command of a battalion of his guard, whom a few days after he led against the invaders. With all Toussaint's affection for his own son, Isaac, he was unable to bring himself to offer the least opposition to his joining the French. A mother's tenderness, however, knows no claims but those of natural affection, and impelled by that powerful sentiment, Toussaint's wife succeeded in causing Isaac to change his determination. The young man wrote that he was prevented from returning to the Cape by his mother's urgent entreaties.

This scene, which was reported to Leclerc, sufficed to prove to him the failure of the device by which the parents were to be enslaved through their attachment to their children. Most unworthy purpose! What a terrible thing is war! How blind is ambition! A thirst for self-aggrandisement, when supported by power and sustained by position, confounds right and wrong, desecrates the holy, disowns moral obligation, and spreads wasting and woe through families, cities and nations.

Further attempts at accommodation were made. Toussaint offered to prevent resistance, if Leclerc would communicate to him the instructions he had received from the First Consul, and stop the advance of the French troops. Toussaint added, that should Leclerc continue to press forward, he would repel him by force of arms. A deputation of the natives waited on the French commander. To their solicitations, Leclerc insolently replied, that he was the brother-in-law of the First Consul, that he had the bayonets on his side, and that he would take Toussaint [Page 179] before he had his boots off. Full of himself, and fancying that he was about to become the Bonaparte of America, he issued to the inhabitants of Saint Domingo the following proclamation!—

Head Quarters of the Cape, le 28 Pluviose, an 10. (17th February, 1802.)

"INHABITANTS OF SAINT DOMINGO,
"I have come hither in the name of the French Government, to bring you peace and happiness; I feared I should encounter obstacles in the ambitious views of the chiefs of the colony; I was not in error.

"Those chiefs who announced their devotion to France in their proclamations, had no intention of being Frenchmen; if they sometimes spoke of France, the reason is that they did not think themselves able to disown it openly. At present their perfidious intentions are unmasked. General Toussaint sent me back his sons with a letter in which he assured me that he desired nothing so much as the happiness of the colony, and that he was ready to obey all the orders that I should give him.

"I ordered him to come to me; I gave him an assurance that I would employ him as my Lieutenant-general: he replied to that order by mere words; he only seeks to gain time.

"I have been commanded by the French Government to establish here prosperity and abundance promptly; if I allow myself to be amused by cunning and perfidious circumlocutions, the colony will be the theatre of a long civil war.

"I commence my campaign, and I will teach that rebel what is the force of the French Government.

"From this moment he must be regarded by all good Frenchmen residing in Saint Domingo only as an insensate monster.

"I have promised liberty to the inhabitants of Saint Domingo; I will see that they enjoy it. I will cause persons and property to be respected.

"I ordain what follows:—

"Article 1.—General Toussaint and General Christophe are outlawed; every good citizen is commanded to seize them, and to treat them as rebels to the French Republic.

[Page 180] "Article 2.—From the day when the French army shall have taken up quarters, every officer, whether civil or military, who shall obey other orders than those of the Generals of the army of the French Republic, which I command, shall be treated as a rebel.

"Article 3.—The agricultural labourers who have been led into error, and who, deceived by the perfidious insinuations of the rebel Generals, may have taken up arms, shall be treated as wandering children, and shall be sent back to tillage, provided they have not endeavoured to incite insurrection.

"Article 4.—The soldiers of the demi-brigades who shall abandon the army of Toussaint, shall form part of the French army.

Article 5.—General Augustin Clervaux, who commands the department of the Cibao, having acknowledged the French government, and the authority of the Captain-General, is maintained in his rank and in his command.

"Article 6.—*The General-in-chief of the Staff will cause this proclamation to be printed and published.*

"The Captain-General commanding the army of Saint Domingo,

(Signed) "LECLERC."

This is plain language, Leclerc could speak so as to be understood, when it suited his purpose.

Toussaint L'Ouverture, on his part, was not dismayed by the threatening storm. The greater the danger the loftier was his spirit; he reviewed his guard, and acquainted them with General Leclerc's imperious determination. "General," they shouted with one voice, "we will all die with you."

[Page 181] CHAPTER V.

General Leclerc advances against Toussaint with 25, 000 men in three divisions, intending to overwhelm him near Gonaïves—the plan is disconcerted by a check given by Toussaint to General Rochambeau in the ravine Couleuvre.

THE Captain-general of the French army, having mustered all his disposable forces in the north, and received a reinforcement of seven thousand men, commenced operations in three divisions, amounting in all to five-and-twenty thousand men. One division, commanded by General Rochambeau, set out from Fort Dauphin to march to Saint Michel; the second, led by Desfourneaux, advanced from Limbé to occupy Plaisance; and the third, under General Hardy, marching to the centre, went to take possession of Marmelade. These three divisions were, together with Boudet, who was to proceed from Port-au-Prince, to effect a junction at Gonaïves, in order to surprise Toussaint in his head quarters there, and put a speedy termination to the war. In proportion as the French army forced its way into the interior of the country, which was broken by mountains, gorges, and defiles, the conflict became more and more difficult. The soldiers were vexed and harassed at having to do with a flying enemy, who, constantly fighting in ambush, inflicted wounds or death as if from an invisible cause, with perfect impunity to themselves, whether from the speed with which they fled into well-known retreats, or from the height of the mountains, on which the sun burnt with a heat intolerable to Europeans. In these marches, which were rather difficult than long, the soldiers suffered from hunger, thirst, and extreme lassitude; and after the perils and penalties of the ocean, they found on the land, instead of repose or glory, a warfare in which victory brought no honour, and defeat entailed deep disgrace; and in which victory was purchased by intolerable endurance, and defeat was made afflicting by contempt for the foe, and disastrous by the revenge which that foe could on his own soil so easily take. In quitting Fort [Page 182] Dauphin,

Rochambeau traversed the country called Ouanaminthe, passed round the north of La Grande Rivière, climbed the black mountain of Gonaïves, and descended towards the savannahs of La Desolée.

The division commanded by Desfourneaux took possession of the district of Plaisance, which was treacherously delivered to him by its commander without striking a blow.

The division under Hardy scaled and captured the formidable position at Boispin, and carried at the point of the bayonet Marmelade, which was defended by Christophe.

The theatre of the war lay accordingly on the chain of the mountains which separates the north from the west, and which overtop the heights of Dondon, Vallière, and the black mountain of Gonaïves. In those places Toussaint had concentrated his inferior army in order to prevent the French, who had landed on three points of the coast, from concerting their operations, and from surrounding his own troops, overwhelming him at once with all their sea and land forces.

The situation of Toussaint had become perilous, environed as he was on all sides by advancing foes. The peril, however, was neither unexpected nor unprovided for. Rochambeau was near Lacroix, lying in the mountains in a line between Esther and Gonaïves. In order to descend into the plains he must pass through the ravine Couleuvre. This ravine was a narrow gorge flanked by precipitous mountains, covered with wood, and which swarmed with aimed black labourers.

Rochambeau, by a movement in this direction, seemed likely to effect great results. He might render himself master of the person of Madame Toussaint, of her sister and her two nieces, who had just arrived at Lacroix. He might also cut off Toussaint's connexion with Dessalines and Belair, and so bring the contest to an end by one blow. It was then necessary for Toussaint to prevent the advance of Rochambeau, unless he was willing to be the next morning attacked by all Leclerc's army, in a semicircle, of which the coast, off which lay vessels of war, would have been the diameter. Leaving General Vernet, therefore, in command of his troops at Gonaïves, he put himself [Page 183] at the head of a squadron and of the grenadier battalion of his guard, and marched to his habitation at Lacroix. Not finding his wife and family on his arrival, he inquired where they were, and at what distance Rochambeau might be. He could learn nothing more exact than that at the news of the enemy's approach, the ladies had sought shelter in the forest. Toussaint having surveyed the district, made his arrangements for attack. To stop or retard the foe, he closed the defile with trees that were felled and thrown across the narrow path. In the flanks of the two mountains he placed ambuscades, that were to fall on the French on their sides and in their rear, at the same time that he would assail them in front, thus surrounding them every way. For fear of being discovered he lighted no fire during the night. Accompanied by one of his aide-de-camps and two labourers, he went forward to reconnoitre. One of his guides having pushed on venturously, fell into the midst of an outpost belonging to Rochambeau. Captured, he was put to death without being able even by a cry to warn Toussaint of the proximity of his foes. Having learned all he could, that general rejoined his band, gave orders for battle, and addressed to the soldiers the following speech:—

"You are going to fight against enemies who have neither faith, law, nor religion. They promise you liberty, they intend your servitude. Why have so many ships traversed the ocean, if not to throw you again into chains? They disdain to recognise in you submissive children, and if you are not their slaves, you are rebels. The mother country, misled by the Consul, is no longer anything for you but a step-mother. Was there ever a defence more just than yours? Uncover your breasts, you will see them branded by the iron of slavery. During ten years, what did you not undertake for liberty? Your masters slain or put to flight; the English humiliated by defeat; discord extinguished; a land of slavery purified by fire, and reviving more beautiful than ever under liberty; these are your labours, and these the fruits of your labours; and the foe wishes to snatch both out of your hands. Already have you left traces of your despair; but for a traitor, Port-au-Prince would be only [Page 184] heap of ruins; but Léogane, Fort-Dauphin, the Cape, that opulent capital of the Antilles, exist no longer; you have carried everywhere consuming fires, the flambeaux of our liberty. The steps of our enemies have trodden only on ashes, their eyes have encountered nothing but smoking ruins, which you have watered with their blood. This is the road by which they have come to us. What do they hope for? Have we not all the presages of victory? Not for their country, not for liberty do they fight, but to serve the hatred and the ambition of the Consul, my enemy, mine because he is yours; their bodies are not mutilated by the punishments of servitude, their wives and their children are not near their camps, and the graves of their fathers are beyond the ocean. This sky, these mountains, these lands, all are strange to them? What do I say? As soon as they breathe the same air as we, their bravery sinks, their courage departs. Fortune seems to have delivered them as victims into our hands. Those whom the sword spares, will be struck dead by an avenging climate. Their bones will be scattered among these mountains and rocks, and tossed about by the waves of our sea. Never more will they behold their native land; never more will they receive the tender embraces of their wives, their sisters, and their mothers; and liberty will reign over their tomb."

On his side, Rochambeau, too much accustomed to treat the Africans with pride and contempt, nevertheless thought it prudent to encourage his men by telling them that this day would raise their glory to the highest pitch, since there would be no part of the world which would not be a witness of their triumph; that the Tiber, the Nile, and the Rhine, where they had conquered very formidable adversaries, resounded with the echoes of their exploits; that now they had to combat slaves, who, not daring to look them in the face, were flying on all hands; and that they had not come thousands of miles from home to be overcome by a rebellious slave.

As soon as the day broke, Toussaint's advanced guard, in passing a river, encountered the advanced guard of Rochambeau, which was on its march. Then the action began. The impetuosity of the attack was checked by the bravery of the resistance.[Page 185] The troops in ambush pressed forward on the flanks and in the rear of the French, who everywhere presented a bold front to the assailants. The retrenchment having been opened, the conflict became bloody and obstinate. Now the victory inclined to this side, now to that. The uncertainty did but inflame the courage of both. Toussaint was then seen to brave a thousand perils. Some of his grenadiers yielding a little before the French impetuosity, a young officer called back their powers by these words, "What! you desert your general!" That moment he put himself at the head of a platoon of grenadiers, and ascending an eminence which commanded Rochambeau's right wing, annoyed him with a destructive fire. At this moment an officer of dragoons having informed Toussaint that his wife and family were behind a mountain not far from the place of action; he replied, "Do you see that they take the road to Esther; I must here perform my duty." His duty he did perform. Regardless of himself, he encouraged his men when they vacillated, and ever again led them into the fight. With such fury did the conflict rage that arms were thrown aside, and combatants, seizing each other, struggled for life and death. The field of battle was covered with the slain. A decisive effort was necessary. Putting himself at the head of his grenadiers, Toussaint rushed to the attack, and drove Rochambeau over the river, where, in the morning, the fight had begun. He then returned, and took up a position on his side of the stream.

The issue remained undecided, but Toussaint had rescued his family and stopped the impetuous career of Rochambeau. He had also gained time, while Christophe, by a vigorous defence, retarded the advance of Desfourneaux and of Hardy. Thus had he saved himself from being surrounded on the plain of Gonaïves. Like a man of genius, he had chosen the place and the time of the combat, and in a crisis obtained great advantages.

Retiring toward his centre, Toussaint pitched his camp on the banks of the Esther. There, surrounded by his soldiers and his family, and covered with a cloak, he had only a plank on which to sit and to sleep. He passed the greater part of the night in despatching orders written with his own hand, and in going [Page 186] from post to post. The next day he sent his wife and family to the mountain known by the name of Grand Cahos, which runs in a line with the Artibonite. His visit to Esther, however, was only for a temporary purpose. He was too good a soldier to meet the concentrated forces of the enemy in a level country, where, with all his valour, he would not have been able to prevent his comparatively diminutive army from being crushed. His ability to offer any effectual resistance had arisen from the judgment he had employed in making the mountains the seat of the warfare. Justified in this policy by the success which he had gained, he determined to evacuate Esther, and to collect troops in another mountainous stronghold, still more favourable than that in which he had defeated Rochambeau.

A review of the operations of Toussaint L'Ouverture, from the point at which our narrative has arrived, shows that the method of his warfare consisted in passive or active resistance, which, after spreading fire and devastation before the enemy's march, withdrew from the coast and made the mountains its centre and its bulwark. That this plan was carefully weighed and well laid out, may be presumed from a knowledge of Toussaint's character. It was also carried into effect as thoroughly as circumstances permitted. If in any respect it failed, the failure was owing to no remissness on the part of the great chief. The following letters written by him at the beginning of the campaign, may serve to illustrate and confirm these observations, and may conduce to the reader's acquaintance with the character of our hero.

"Liberty. "Equality. "The Governor-General to General Dessalines, Commander-in-chief of the army of the West.

Head Quarters, Gonaïves, Feb. 8, 1802.

"There is no reason for despair, Citizen-General, if you can succeed in removing from the troops that have landed the resources offered to them by Port Republican. Endeavour, by all the means of force and address, to set that place on fire; it is [Page 187] constructed entirely of wood; you have only to send into it some faithful emissaries. Are there none under your orders devoted enough for this service? Ah! my dear General, what a misfortune that there was a traitor in that city, and that your orders and mine were not put into execution.

"Watch the moment when the garrison shall be weak in consequence of expeditions into the plains, and then try to surprise and carry that city, falling on it in the rear.

"Do not forget, while waiting for the rainy season which will rid us of our foes, that we have no other resource than destruction and flames. Bear in mind that the soil bathed with our sweat must not furnish our enemies with the smallest aliment. Tear up the roads with shot; throw corpses and horses into all the fountains; burn and annihilate everything in order that those who have come to reduce us to slavery may have before their eyes the image of that hell which they deserve.

"Salutation and Friendship,

(Signed) "TOUSSAINT L'OUVERTURE."

"Toussaint L'Ouverture, Governor of Saint Domingo, to citizen Domage, Brigadier-General, commanding the district of Jéremie

"Head Quarters, Saint Marc, the 9th of Feb. 1802.

"I send to you, my dear General, my aide-de-camp, Chancy. He conveys to you the present communication, and will tell you from me what I have charged him to make known to you.

"The whites of France and of the Colony, united together, wish to take away our liberty. Many vessels and troops have arrived, which have seized the Cape, Port Republican, and Fort Liberté.

"The Cape, after a vigorous resistance, has fallen; but the enemy found only a city and country of ashes; the forts were blown up, and everything has been burnt.

"The town of Port Republican was surrendered to them by the traitor Agé, as well as Fort Bizoton, which yielded without striking a blow, through the cowardice and the treachery of [Page 188] Bardet. The General of division, Dessalines, at this moment maintains a cordon at Croix des Bouquets; and all our other places are on the defensive.

"As Jéremie is very strong through its natural advantages, you will maintain yourself in it, and defend it with the courage which I know you possess. Raise the labourers in a mass, and infuse into them this truth, namely, that they must distrust those who have received proclamations from the whites of France, and who secretly circulate them in order to seduce the friends of liberty.

"I have ordered Laplume, Brigadier-general, to set on fire the city of Cayes, the other towns, and all the plains, in case he is unable to withstand the enemy's force, and then all the troops of the different garrisons, and all the labourers, should go to Jéremie to augment your band; you will take measures with General Laplume, for the due execution of these things; you will employ the women engaged in agriculture in making depôts of provisions in great abundance.

"Endeavour as much as you can to send me news of your position. I reckon entirely on you, and leave you absolutely master, to do everything in order to save us from the most frightful yoke.

"Wishing you health, "Salutation and Friendship,

(Signed) TOUSSAINT L'OUVERTURE."

CHAPTER VI.

Toussaint L'Ouverture prepares Crête-à-Pierrot as a point of resistance against Leclerc; who, mustering his forces, besieges the redoubt, which, after the bravest defence, is evacuated by the blacks.

THE district into which Toussaint L'Ouverture had sent his family was that to which he meant to transfer his resistance. The mountain range which he resolved to occupy and entrench, [Page 189] bears the name of Artibonite, and is divided into two districts, the one called the Grand Cahos, the other the Petit Cahos. These mountains, over which he spread his army, are intersected with deep ravines and precipitous outlets, at every one of which a handful of brave men could arrest an army. The principal entrance was defended by Crête-à-Pierrot, a redoubt which blocked up the pass, and which the English had constructed when they invaded the west.

In passing toward the new seat of war, where he was joined by his chief generals, Toussaint was suddenly attacked with a burning fever. His mind, however, so far mastered his body, that he scarcely abated his activity, and formed designs of the greatest daring, in making arrangements for attacking the enemy in the rear. Ill as he was, he set out to survey the district, and arrived in time to prevent the demolition of Crête-à-Pierrot, which had been abandoned, and which Dessalines had ordered to be rased. He then proceeded to add to its strength. He supplied it with water and food, as precautions against a siege. He placed in it a garrison, and gave the command to Dessalines. Having called the officers together, he harangued them thus:—"Children, yes, you are all my children—from Lamartinière, who is white as a white, but who knows that he has negro blood in his veins, to Monpoint, whose skin is the same as mine:—I entrust to you this post; take measures for its defence." The officers declared that he might rely on them, living or dead.

To more destructive hands than those of Dessalines, this important post could not have been confided. In his retreat, that ferocious monster had dragged away from their homes all the whites he could seize, whom the sword and the musket had spared. These were conducted to Verettes, Mirebalais, and Petite Rivière, towns lying along the banks of the Artibonite. There were renewed the frightful scenes of the first insurrection. At the sight of the conflagration which reduced into ashes the villages and the fields, at the foot of Mount Cahos, where Toussaint had entrenched himself, a vast carnage was made of the whites. Four hundred men were massacred at Mirebalais [Page 190] and Petite Rivière. In no place was the slaughter so terrible as at the village of Verettes. At the nod of Dessalines, men who had been slaves, and who dreaded the new servitude with which they were threatened, slew seven hundred of the poor wretches that Dessalines had dragged after him. The daughter breathed her last on the bosom of her expiring mother. The father was unable to save the son; the son was unable to save the father. There a sister died in the arms of a brother; here a nurse tried to make her body a means of defence for her infant; her milk and her blood flowed in one stream. Farther on, old men in vain implored pity from their former slaves, whom they called on by name, to bring back the remembrance of past acts of kindness. Whole families were thus bathed in blood. More frightful and more atrocious still was the sight when sons slew their fathers, thus revenging themselves for the black blood of their mothers, and the neglect and disavowal of their fathers. So great was the fury of the blacks and mulattoes, that they even wreaked their rage on domestic animals which belonged to the planters. Thus the banks of the Artibonite were covered with fire and blood. Before the arrival of the French expedition all there was peaceful, prosperous and happy.

The French felt deep compassion when on coming up they beheld at Verettes so many victims who still remained unburied, and who retained the attitudes in which they perished, as if to paint an awful picture of the evils of slavery. They there saw the arm of one victim locked in that of another, hand grasped in hand, faces fixed on the same object; father, mother, children grouped together, a family even in death; young women who in the last moments forgot not they were women; bodies which had served as useless ramparts to friendship, and to filial and paternal love: the scenes were horrible. Nor was their horror abated by the fact that ravages scarcely less atrocious had been committed by the white invaders. A little before, the bay of Mancenille had smoked with innocent blood. And on more than one occasion had prisoners been slain in bands, in order to strike alarm into the defenders of their native soil. All the blacks, however, were not barbarians. Many, moved by pity or [Page 191] gratitude, saved the lives of unfortunate colonists; some concealed them in the mountains, and supported them by what they took in hunting; others led them through bye paths, into districts occupied by the French. There were blacks who, to prevent suspicion on the part of pursuers, covered their white friends with leaves and branches, and counterfeited drunkenness when they thought there was special danger of discovery. Calamities public and private so numerous and so terrible were more than human strength could endure, and under their pressure some persons lost their reason and others committed suicide. What a complication of sorrows, all caused by slavery!

Having provided for the defence of the country of the Artibonite, and directed Belair to occupy the mountains of Verettes, Toussaint proceeded to execute his daring plan of taking Leclerc in the rear in order to operate a diversion in favour of the Artibonite lines, and to reanimate the courage of the north. With a small but resolute force Toussaint ascended the defiles, and the chain of mountains which separate the Artibonite from the district of Saint Michel. In vain was General Hardy detached in pursuit of him by Leclerc, whose army was in movement to attack Crête-à-Pierrot. Toussaint appeared at Ennery, and the French garrison which Leclerc had left there fled at his approach to Gonaïves. He presented himself before Gonaïves, and might have captured it had he chosen. He was satisfied with alarming the garrison, which was on the point of embarking on board a frigate that was in the roads. Having attained his end he returned to Ennery where he organized battalions of militia, who were employed to guard and defend the country. This work finished, he betook himself to Marmelade. There he sent an order to Christophe, who was at Petite-Rivière, to return promptly into the north, where, in the forest of Grande-Rivière, there had, without the French being aware of it, been formed a considerable depôt of arms and ammunition. From Marmelade Toussaint went to Plaisance. On his arrival he proceeded to reconnoitre a fort situated on a height. A few hours after, he placed himself at the head of two companies of grenadiers and captured it. The following day he divided his troops into two [Page 192] bodies. Taking the command of the right wing, he marched to meet Desfourneaux, who was coming up to attack him. He bore up against the impetuosity of the French troops, who were much more numerous than his own, and at length succeeded in putting them to flight. Sending in the moment of action an aide-de-camp to learn how things went on in the left wing, he was led to believe that Desfourneaux was manœuvring so as to circumvent him. Thereupon he left the right to the care of Colonel Gabarre, and with a few men hurried to the point of danger. Among the European troops he recognised the uniform of the ninth Saint Domingo regiment. Advancing quite alone to within five or six paces of the regiment, which easily recognised their proper commander, he said, "Soldiers of the ninth, will you dare fire on your general and on your brethren?" The words fell like a thunder-clap on the soldiers; who forthwith were on their knees, and, but for the European troops, who began to fire, they would have joined Toussaint. Seeing the peril of their general, Toussaint's forces defended him against the Europeans. He escaped through the thick of a fire which was very destructive. A young officer, bearing a letter from Dessalines to the Governor of the island, received a mortal blow at the moment that he delivered it, and expired in Toussaint's arms. From that letter the General-in-chief learned that his aid was urgently required at Crête-à-Pierrot; thither therefore he repaired.

The French had been drawing their strength under the foot of the mountains of Cahos. As they made their way they beheld the ravages committed by the enemy. Traces of fire and death appeared everywhere. Here and there they met a great number of colonists wandering in the woods and hanging on the sides of the rocks, with their wives and children, having escaped from death only by chance or flight. The soldiers restored to them hope, and promised them revenge. The sight of these unhappy people, whose clothes were in rags, their cries, their moanings, the horror with which they were stricken, inflamed the minds of their rescuers, and prepared them for any atrocities. Without scruple and without pity they massacred the herds of blacks whom the fate of war had thrown into their hands; two hundred they [Page 193] immolated at the fort of Mount Nolo; a little further on, six hundred fell beneath their murderous hands. Thus carnage was added to carnage, and black blood flowed to avenge white blood. The savage and torn sides of Mount Cahos, the odorous banks of the Artibonite, offered the spectacle of barbarity opposed to barbarity, and war was only prolonged assassination. These are the horrible devastations of slavery.

No graves were dug, no mounds were raised for sepulture. Dessalines had prohibited interment, in order that the eyes of his assailants might see his vengeance even in the repulsive remains of carnage. It is said that the monster slew a mother for having buried her son. The French, carried away by the movements of the war, gave no attention to the religious duty of burial, so that the dead bodies became food for dogs, vultures and crocodiles; and their bones, partly calcined by the sun, remained scattered about, as if to mark the mournful fury of servitude and lust of power.

Fortune seemed to smile on Leclerc. He lost no time in announcing to his brother-in-law his success, which he failed not to exaggerate—entire battalions that had joined his ranks, the two provinces of the South and the East subdued, all the maritime cities in his power,—such were the heads of his triumphant report. He described Toussaint L'Ouverture as a party-chief, sullen, violent, fanatical, hateful, breathing only fire and slaughter; he called him a barbarian, an unnatural father, sacrificing his children to his passion for revolt, a mere fugitive slave, devoured by remorse, abandoned and pursued. This news, which gave the consul joy, delighted the colonists who had remained in France, and revived the cupidity of the slave-dealers whose vessels had for six years remained in harbour unproductive.

When however Bonaparte began seriously to reflect on all that had taken place, his satisfaction was not a little diminished. It was true that he held under his domination, the South rich in manufactures, and the East fertile in pasturage. But what had he conquered? Lands in ashes. Port-au-Prince had miraculously escaped from the incendiary torch. But what a sight in other parts! Those barbarians do not place the keys of their cities at [Page 194] the feet of their conquerors. Toussaint, designated a bandit, is a formidable general in his mountains. The consul applies himself to study that remarkable man. He is the soul of the war, and him he must reach, seize, and put in chains. That accomplished, what then? He must attach to himself the men of mixed blood, who are already partly his. Then discord must be disseminated. The black in revolt will be overcome by the subjugated black. This was the consul's policy. These were his means for bringing the island into subjection. To this purpose, and for these results, he wrote to Leclerc. But suddenly the war took a new aspect.

Twelve thousand men, the bravest soldiers of the republic, are assembled near Petite-Rivière to put down a revolted slave! Rochambeau, Hardy, Debelle, generals of great skill and high powers, are stopped in a ravine by a handful of revolted slaves! their passage is barred, their valour rendered nugatory by a few men whom they despise! officers and soldiers who have gained victory and renown against the first troops of Europe, perish in huge numbers under the blows of half-civilized blacks. So much do the issues of war depend on opportunity; so dear is freedom; so odious is servitude.

The first division which came up to the attack of Crête-à-Peirrot was that of Debelle. As soon as the French troops were seen in the redoubt, Dessalines opened the gates. "The gates have been opened," he said, "for those who do not feel themselves courageous enough to die; while there is yet time, let the friends of the French depart; they have nothing but death to look for here." After having sent away all whom sickness or fear made desirous of going, he spread a train of gunpowder as far as the first gate, and seizing a torch, exclaimed, "Now for the first fire: I will blow up the fort, if you do not defend it." During these things the French were advancing, preceded by a herald (4th March 1802). The herald held a letter in his hand. Dessalines ordered his men to fire. The herald fell dead. Firing began on both sides in real earnest. For several hours it continued without an interval. The French rushed forward with their usual bravery and enthusiasm, but it was only to meet death. The [Page 195] moment they were within reach, the batteries were opened and the ground was strewed with dead. The general-in-chief Debelle was grievously wounded, as well as Brigadier-general Devaux. The division was compelled to fall back with the loss of four hundred men.

This defeat deeply affected the mind of Leclerc, who was then at Port-au-Prince. Was his victorious career, then, to be delayed by a single stronghold? Not without apprehension he hastened to the scene of action. He brought with him the division of Boudet. While the troops were assembling, a scout of Toussaint's, in his zeal to ascertain all he could, entered their camp, pretending to be a deserter. In the midst of his guard, General Boudet questioned the man. When the former asked him how many whites he had put to death, the latter, with well feigned fear, appeared overwhelmed. In the twinkling of an eye, having learnt the condition of the French, he leapt from his horse. Boudet, the first to observe the movement, attempted to seize him, and had his thumb nearly bitten off. The man got away, slipped beneath the horse's legs, overthrew the soldiers who attempted to stop him, ran toward the Artibonite, plunged into the stream, and escaped amid a shower of balls. Arrived on the opposite bank, he appeared to have been struck, for he fell as if his thigh were broken. The presence on the other side of the river of a reconnoitring party of the foe prevented pursuit. The black scout, who had the rank of captain, appears to have been carried off by his friends.

Among the troops which now advanced to the attack, there were Rigaud and Pétion. True to his instructions, Leclerc added to the skill of his white soldiers the fury and the animosity of mulatto blood.

In the interval which had elapsed since the first attack, Dessalines had erected a new fort on an eminence which commanded that on which stood the famous Crête-à-Pierrot. The new redoubt, though hastily constructed, was to witness the defeat of the consul's boastful brother-in-law.

The French in advancing surprised a camp of blacks who were asleep. They fell on them; the blacks ran toward the fort [Page 196] and the French pursued them. Those who could not enter the fort threw themselves into the moat. Immediately the fort opened its fire and mowed down the assailants. General Boudet received a wound. At the moment when his division was on the point of perishing that of Dugua came up. Forthwith that general was struck. Only one general officer kept the field. Then the blacks rushed to the charge. The French retreated. In the retreat, Leclerc himself, who came up with reinforcements, received a serious contusion. This second attack cost the captain-general eight hundred men.

In their retrograde movement the Europeans had opportunities of ascertaining how entirely the population was in enmity against them. On the plantations they saw the labourers watching their movements. Those labourers exchanged shots with the soldiers who flanked the column. If a party of scouts were detached, they fled; as soon as the scouts retired, they re-appeared. The French army inspired only terror.

A third attack was to be made. The stronghold was regularly invested. Fresh troops had come up. All that ability, experience, labour and prowess could contribute was set in vigorous action.

While the operations for the blockade were proceeding, the French soldiers heard from the strongholds the words of the very songs to which they had themselves marched against the enemies of liberty in Europe. The effect was singular and deep. "What! those black men the injured, and we the injurers! those black men the oppressed, and we the oppressors! Are we then no longer the servants and patrons of liberty? The republic gives freedom; we are fighting for servitude." Such impressions were little likely to increase the efficiency of republican soldiers. Their duty they would continue to do, but services higher than a mere sense of duty can command were now required.

By degrees, the works were completed and brought into play against the redoubt. Partial successes were obtained. Encouraged by these, Rochambeau thought himself able to carry a battery, which he had for a moment silenced, by one blow. [Page 197] He lost three hundred men in the useless attempt. Then a constant cannonade was commenced. From the 22nd to the 24th of March, it was carried on with great activity. The redoubt was in the greatest peril.

At this time a black man and a black woman were captured. Suspected to be spies, they were subjected to the severest punishment. The man said he was blind; nothing but the whites of his eyes were to be seen. Only in leaning on the aged negress, his companion, did he appear able to walk. She affected to be deaf. Scarcely any thing but groans and sobs could the cruellest treatment extort from them. At length, compassion prevailed. They were bid go about their business. They had dreadfully suffered, and seemed unable to move. Not before they were threatened to be shot, did they attempt to walk. They were conducted beyond the outlying sentinels. When fairly out of the reach of their enemies, they began to dance; and instantly darted off for the fort, where they were received. They conveyed to its commander intelligence of the approach of Toussaint L'Ouverture.

That very night (March 24) an attack was made on the French lines which was repulsed only with difficulty and loss. That attack was led by Toussaint himself, who had conceived a project worthy of his own genius. Having reason to think the north could for some time give him no more trouble, and afraid lest Crête-à-Pierrot might be carried by storm, he hastened to the Artibonite, intending with a few trusty soldiers to penetrate to Leclerc's head quarters, make him prisoner and ship him off to France. To aid him in his daring plan, a feint was made in the attack of which we have just spoken. And the captured fugitives were sent to encourage the garrison to hold out.

The stratagem was too late. Lamartinière, who had taken the command, with his accustomed bravery had done and endured everything that man can do and endure. With his soldiers he patiently bore hunger, thirst, sickness, exhaustion, and the prospect of death at any moment. With their aid, he performed prodigies of heroism. But stone-walls are not proof against cannon balls and bombs. The forts were defended against [Page 198] thousands of brave Frenchmen, even when falling into ruins. But the hour at length came. Then, when resistance was vain, the commander resolved to cut himself a passage through the ranks of his enemies. He escaped from the hands of 12, 000 men, not having lost half his garrison, and leaving to his assailants only the dead and the wounded amid a heap of ruins.

CHAPTER VII.

Shattered condition of the French army—Dark prospects of Toussaint—Leclerc opens negotiations for peace—wins over Christophe and Dessalines—offers to recognise Toussaint as Governor-General—receives his submission on condition of preserving universal freedom—L'Ouverture in the quiet of his home.

DEARLY had the reduction of Crête-à-Pierrot been bought by the French. The loss deeply afflicted the captain-general, who induced his subordinates to make it appear as slight as possible, remembering the contemptuous terms in which he had spoken of Toussaint and his forces, and well dreading the moral effect on the inhabitants of the island.

After the capture of this stronghold, Leclerc took measures for re-establishing his communications. He ordered Rochambeau's division to open them by forming a junction at Gonaïves with Desfourneaux; and directed Hardy with his forces to make for the Cape. The latter division were compelled to form for themselves a road with their arms in their hands. Under the impression that the invaders had suffered a total defeat, Hardy had with him only bands of fugitives who hastened to the Cape in order to fly by sea from the island, while on the whole line of his march, he encountered opposition from regular troops or armed labourers. But for the courage of the soldiers who were kept under discipline, and the judgment and energy of the [Page 199] commanders, the whole division would have perished. From four to five hundred men were lost on the route.

While the divisions of Rochambeau and Hardy proceeded toward the north, that of Boudet, under the command of General Lacroix, was commanded to return to Saint Marc, in order to attack Belair, who up to that time had remained in observation on the heights of Matheux, which stand to the south-east of that post, between it and Mount Cahos. We give a report of the undertaking in the words of its leader.

"We climbed the heights by the sources of Mount Ronis. I had often heard speak of a 'carabined road;' but I was, I avow, far from forming an idea of the obstacles which I had to overcome in order to open the carabined road of Matheux. Yet was I expert in work of the kind, having a year before opened the passage of Splugen. In the memorable campaign of the army of reserve, I had also traced round fort Bard, routes on peaked mountains declared impassable. I had conveyed cannon by those roads, thus executing an enterprise till then regarded as impossible. That path round fort Bard threw down the barrier which stood against the fortune of the first consul; by that road the army of reserve gained the plains of Piedmont and reconquered Italy on the field of Marengo. Precipices and road accidents are every where the same; but in the Alps the bush-wood is at least accessible, and the trees are of a determinate height, while in America the former are fine mountains and the latter colossal masses which you can scarcely take in in one view, and which you can displace only by strength of arm and length of time. I doubt whether I could have been able to gain the plateau of Matheux, if Belair had added the efforts of his resistance to the obstacles of the locality in which he was.

"After the most fatiguing march, I at last arrived at Matheux. Belair had quitted the plain the previous evening to join Dessalines on Mount Cahos.

"I wrote to him, suggesting that he should imitate the examples of Generals Clervaux, Paul L'Ouverture, and Maurepas, and announcing that I was authorized by the captain-general to guarantee to him and to his officers their military rank. He [Page 200] answered that he blindly followed the authority of Toussaint L'Ouverture, recognised governor for life, by the constitution of the colony, and by his numberless services, which France seemed disposed to disown.

"The lofty position of Matheux presented to us the aspect of the champaign lands of France; we there found its atmosphere; the lungs of our soldiers dilated; we were agile; on the contrary, the blacks, whom we had as auxiliaries, wore a shrunk appearance. In the different gorges of the mountain, we delivered from five to six hundred persons who had fled thither from Saint Marc and the neighbouring lands. Hardy and Rochambeau had set at large a thousand fugitives in Mount Cahos.

"I collected on Matheux a large number of horses, mules, and horned cattle, which Belair had got together. Two days after, I began to march toward Port-au-Prince. A letter was brought me from General Boudet, who, directing me to conduct his division to that city, requested that I would make a processional entrance into it, and that in so doing, I should make the troops appear as numerous as possible, in order to efface from the minds of the men of colour in the West the impressions they had received as to the extent of our loss. I put the troops into two ranks; our sections marched at great distances; all our officers were on horseback; artillery ready for the field was sent to meet me; I distributed it in the column with the baggage; and our entrance produced the moral effect which we expected."*

Nothing can more clearly show the valorous resistance made by Toussaint L'Ouverture than the frank confessions made by this respectable writer of the disorganized and weakened condition of the French troops after the capture of Crête-à-Pierrot. Scarcely able to keep the field or effect a retrograde movement, the decimated and shattered armies of Leclerc could not be allowed, except when tricked out in this fashion, to return to the capital of the island. What impudence, then, was that which described the great African leader as a mere chief of banditti! [Page 201] and what did that leader want but the support of some European power, friendly to human freedom, in order to establish on a permanent basis

---

* "MÉMOIRES POUR SERVIR À L'HISTOIRE DE LA RÉVOLUTION," &c., VOL. II. P. 172, SEQ.

that constitution which had been so wisely constructed, and that liberty which had been purchased at so large a price, and of which the Haytian negroes had proved themselves so worthy? Alas! such a friendly power did not exist. England and the United States were both committed to the support of slavery; and the great war of the African world had to be fought out by Toussaint alone. Well was the conflict sustained, and though the immediate result was adverse, the strife, we trust, will not have to be renewed. If the plains, the mountains, and the ravines of Saint Domingo say nothing effectually on behalf of negro rights, surely they cry with so loud a voice, declaring the horrors of a war of "bloods," that even fear will suffice to break the bonds of the slave!

From the ruins and carnage of Crête-à-Pierrot, L'Ouverture hastened to the recesses of Mount Cahos, whither he had ordered the brave defenders of that post to follow him. They, as well as he, needed a few days' repose. And there, where he had for some time formerly dwelt, he met his wife and family, and in their society enjoyed a short tranquillity. Of this brief leisure, he availed himself to write to Bonaparte, in order to explain to him the conduct of General Leclerc and to ask him to send another to take his place, into whose hands he might resign the command of the island.

This was an hour for calm reflection Toussaint L'Ouverture did not let slip. Thoughtful by nature, he now by the force of circumstances was drawn to the consideration of his past career and his present position. He had effected much. At one time, he thought he had achieved the permanent freedom of' his colour. But alas! the constitution had not been ratified. In defence of that solemn national act, he had not only again and again risked his life and nearly forfeited all he possessed, but he had given many a severe lesson to its assailants, and taught them to respect and fear a man whom they disgracefully attempted to enslave. Yet amid these triumphs, the final success of his undertaking seemed now to recede into distant [Page 202] mists. The present was dark and gloomy. Leclerc, with shattered forces, was still strong, and should the army now under his command be annihilated, it could easily be replaced by the inexhaustible resources of France. Yet, so long as he himself lived, he was bound to labour in the sacred cause he had undertaken. With the past full in his view, he could not despair. Any way it is for man to deserve, as it is for God to give, success.

Instead of sinking beneath his sense of the great loss suffered by the destruction of Crête-a-Pierrot, Toussaint, after a brief interval, resumed hostile operations with an active energy not surpassed even in his days of triumph. He had indeed disappeared from the view of his foes, but it was only to deceive them by false and rapid marches, to prepare ambuscades, to harass them on their flanks and in the rear; to make them sink under the fatigue, hunger, thirst, and want of sleep he compelled them to undergo. Now he covered his flight by deserts and by flames, to make their victory more baneful than ordinary defeat; now he waited for his prey in a defile, always doing much, by the force of his genius, to carry the warfare beyond all acknowledged rules. Christophe in the north, Dessalines in the west, supported his adroit and rapid movements. At the sound of the church bells, he sent forth from the pulpit a manly and magical eloquence, which painted to the eye and impressed on the heart the horrors of servitude and the delights of liberty, and preached a religion which, acknowledging all men as brothers, disclaimed and condemned slavery, and made his soldiers feel that in fighting for freedom they fought on the side of God and Christ. His sermon over, he resumed the soldier and the general, disappeared, flew, re-appeared, and seemed almost as if he possessed a species of omnipresence. All the time he had an army at his command, though where they were, or what the number and resources of his troops, was hidden to all but himself and a chosen few; while, by means as sure as they were hidden, he learnt all thatt ook place among his assailants. Moved by his authority, his spies and scouts, now in appearance blind, deaf, lame, and now beggars or fugitives, made light of toil, peril, and torture [Page 203] in a service which religion, as well as civil obedience, seemed to them to exact.

The different bodies of the French army, who believed Toussaint ruined, if not dead, felt his blows on every side; as they returned to the Cape, or to Port-au-Prince, he disturbed them, beat them, worried them, alike in their communications, in their attacks, in their marches, in their retreat. Everywhere, he carried alarm and dread. When the soldiers entered the Cape, Toussaint appeared in its suburbs. The city required both walls and defenders. The blacks, if they appeared to be friends, proved to be enemies in reality. With all despatch, Leclerc raised anew the fortifications of a town in which, more than ever, the party of servitude and the party of liberty disputed and contended. In that war, no man knew his neighbour; you lived side by side with your enemy; you slept under the same roof, you ate at the same table with him, and yet you knew him not; for there were blacks on the side of the consul, and there were whites on the side of Toussaint. At length, arms were taken up, the ships supplied cannon, and the sailor was brought on shore to fight. Only the more vigour did Toussaint put forth, and the city was about to become his prey when fresh troops arrived from France, and the black hero thought it prudent to retire.

The position of Leclerc had become one of extreme difficulty. By painful experience, he had learnt with what singular enemies he had to contend. Of what use was it to continue a war in which victories cost so much and were so readily effaced by reverses? Already had he lost five thousand men in battle; a like number, sick or wounded, were in the hospitals. Besides, the war offered no reward; what glory was there even in totally subjugating semi-barbarian blacks? Conquest, instead of enriching the soldier, only carried him into burning towns or desert mountains. The army murmured; the climate was intolerable; the work they had to perform was repulsive. "The consul," they said, "has sent us here to perish, companions though we are of his achievements and sharers in his glory."

These, and similar complaints, which reached the ears of the [Page 204] captain of the expedition, occasioned him lively disquietude, the rather because his army was attacked by a malady which, bad as it was, threatened to become more deadly; and although he expected fresh troops, scarcely would all suffice to keep the population in order, to say nothing of the exigencies of war. He had, it is true, many blacks under his banners, but could he count on their fidelity? Did he not know, that their chiefs who showed the most zeal and devotion, were wrapped in impenetrable dissimulation, and that he kept them obedient only by reiterated promises of liberty.

The people of colour appeared to him more devoted, but had they not, in preceding wars, passed now into the party of the whites, and now into that of the blacks, as much from inconstancy as for the sake of liberty? The barbarous chiefs, however, who were his enemies, gave him most concern; Christophe, filled with prowess and intrepidity; Dessalines, that savage Achilles, of unequalled courage and fury; Toussaint, who by his prolific genius was capable of everything, who escaped only to reappear, who everywhere caused foes to spring up under the feet of his army, as if they were born of the mountains.

Reflecting on these things—counting his losses, surveying his disappointments, measuring his enemies, calculating his difficulties, and forecasting his prospects—Leclerc came to the determination that he should act wisely, if he tried what could be done in the way of negotiation. Should the attempt fail, he would have gained time; should it succeed, he would have put an end to a doubtful and disastrous war.

Among the heads of the hostile army, Christophe had shown the least aversion to accommodation. With him, Leclerc commenced his negotiations; he intimated to Christophe that, as the mother country would unquestionably give legal confirmation to the abolition of servitude, the war was useless and without an object, and that the sole obstacle to peace being the ambition of Toussaint, he would arrange with him in order to arrest that chief in the most secret manner possible. Instead of becoming the instrument of that perfidy, Christophe replied in language and tones of virtue, saying that to arrest his friend, [Page 205] his companion, his chief, would be to betray at once friendship and honour, as well as his country; and that a treason so disgraceful could not for a moment be entertained by him. He ended his letter with these words: "Show us the laws which guarantee our liberty, then Toussaint, my brethren, myself—all of us—will with joy throw ourselves into the arms of our mother country. How could we believe the consul's words, brought to us, as they were, amid demonstrations of war? Excuse," he added, "the fears and the alarm of a people which has suffered so much in slavery: give it grounds of confidence, if you desire to terminate the calamities of Saint Domingo; then, forgetting the past, we shall in security enjoy the present and the future."

Struck with the wisdom and energy of this reply, Leclerc felt that it was more than ever necessary to put away all idea of slavery, which could be restored only in very different circumstances. With this view, he dealt freely in protestations. The consul, he urged, could not have proposed laws for a country with which he was not acquainted, but in the name of the Supreme Being, the avenger of falsehood, he affirmed that the liberty of the blacks was the basis of the laws which would be passed.

An interview ensued, and, in reliance on the protestations and the oath of Leclerc, Christophe went over to the French with twelve hundred men, surrendering the mountains of Limbé, Port-Français, and Grande Rivière, with an immense amount of warlike stores.

Christophe immediately sought an interview with Toussaint, and among other things, remarked that Leclerc appeared very sorry at having undertaken the war, that he had done so in the persuasion that he could soon bring it to a successful termination, and that, being now disabused of that error, was desirous of concluding a peace; adding that, at the express request of the captain-general, he wished to converse with Toussaint on the subject.

On his part, Toussaint complained that Christophe had listened to overtures from the enemy, contrary to military [Page 206] discipline, since he had no authority from his superior officer. Before leaving, Christophe put into the hands of Toussaint a letter from Leclerc. Prevented at the moment from reading the communication, Toussaint did not learn till after Christophe's departure, that he had gone over to the French. The regret which he felt gave place to astonishment, and astonishment was succeeded by indignation. He sent for Adjutant-General Fontaine, the chief of his staff, and to him alone communicated the contents of the letter, directing him to go to Christophe, and command him to repair to the head-quarters at Marmelade, in order to explain his conduct. The traitor affected compliance. Many of his officers, on hearing of the mission of General Fontaine, declared that they had been misled. On his return, that officer reported the surrender of Port-Français and other places. Toussaint L'Ouverture assembled his chief officers, and announced to them the extraordinary event. Christophe's conduct appeared to them no less incomprehensible than blameworthy. The news having spread among the people and the soldiers, they burst forth in reproaches against him, and by a spontaneous -movement, assembled around Toussaint's dwelling, to assure him of their fidelity and devotedness.

In this conjuncture, the hope of an approaching peace, which for a moment even Toussaint had indulged, vanished wholly. The warlike spirit became universal, together with indignation at the treachery. All swore to die for their chief, because in so doing they would die for liberty. Toussaint's orders flew on all sides in order to prevent or abate the consequences of the perfidy. He still had, in the west and in the north, faithful battalions and devoted districts; the less his resources became, the more grand did his character appear. Had fortune, then, abandoned him? Could he no longer look to the Highest of all Powers, whose work he had undertaken, and by whose hand he had been guided and protected? Was his country, after all, to fall under the dishonourable yoke of servitude? Adversity crushes only ordinary men; Toussaint took courage even from despair.

Shortly, he learned that Dessalines had imitated Christophe [Page 207] and joined the ranks of the enemy. This was the second heavy blow. Toussaint did not so much regard the individual loss of these two leaders, nor the loss of the troops they carried with them, nor the loss of the lands they commanded, as the loss of his own influence which must ensue, and the perplexity in which he found himself as to who was and who was not trustworthy. His best captains—Christophe, Dessalines, Laplume, Clervaux, his two brothers, his nephew, were in the camp of his foes. Where could he be sure to find men worthy of his confidence?

Under these circumstances it was that Leclerc put every means into action in order to induce Toussaint to come to an accommodation. The captain-general was the more desirous of such a result because, though he knew that Toussaint's power was broken, he knew also that the population at large were wholly alienated from his own government, and might at any moment be roused to a resistance more determined and more sanguinary than what they had made already. With a view to appease the hardly suppressed ill-humour, Leclerc had sent Rigaud out of the island, hoping thereby to gain some favour with the blacks. The effect on the whole was inconsiderable. Even after their treachery, the negro chiefs were idols, while Frenchmen were objects of indifference or detestation. This contrasted feeling was observed, and is spoken of by an eyewitness thus:—

"On arriving at the Cape, I had occasion to make very serious reflections. I saw many of our general officers in full uniform pass by; the inhabitants, no matter what their colour, showed no sign of exterior deference. Suddenly I heard a noise—it was General Dessalines; he came for the first time to pay his respects to the Captain-General Leclerc. The population of both sexes and of all colours rushed to meet him: they fell down at his approach. I was saddened rather than revolted. Dark and painful ideas accompanied me to the mansion of the general-in-chief. In the ante-chamber I found General Dessalines. The horror he inspired me with kept me at a distance from him. He asked who I was, and came to me, and without looking me in the face, said, in a rough voice,'I am General [Page 208] Dessalines; in bad times, General, I have heard you much spoken of.' His bearing and his manners were savage; I was surprised at his words, which announced assurance rather than remorse. The barbarian must have felt himself powerful, or he would not have dared to take that attitude."*

Once before had Leclerc made an attempt to bring Toussaint to treat. The attempt failed. A second effort had a different result. To Leclerc's overture, Toussaint in substance replied, "I am powerful enough to burn and ravage, as well as to sell dearly a life which has not been useless to the mother country." But with bootless destruction such a mind as Toussaint's

---

* MÉMOIRES, &C., PAR LACROIX, II. 191, 2.

could not be satisfied. For a great object he had taken up arms: if that object could be secured by peaceful means, his duty was clear. This view, on which his own mind had for some time been dwelling, was enforced by the representations and advice of persons around him, whose fidelity and courage gave them a right to be heard. Toussaint became less indisposed to listen to terms of accommodation. Leclerc proposed, as the principal conditions of peace, to leave in Toussaint's hands the government of Saint Domingo, to hold by his side the office of delegate from France, and to employ Toussaint's officers according to their rank. "I swear," he said, "before the face of the Supreme Being, to respect the liberty of the people of Saint Domingo."

Toussaint L'Ouverture replied, "I accept everything which is favourable for the people and for the army; and, for myself, I wish to live in retirement."

Noble resolution! resolution worthy of all thy previous conduct, thou noble-hearted man! All for others, nothing for thyself! Yet had he now the option of retaining supreme power in the island, sanctioned and guaranteed by French authority. And out of that supreme power, were he ambitious, he might have carved a crown. But didst thou think that thy frank disinterestedness might be turned to thy own ruin? The possibility could hardly have escaped thy sagacious and foreseeing mind. Nevertheless, rather wilt thou incur any personal risk than prolong the horrors of this war, which every day becomes more fratricidal and more disastrous!

[Page 209]As a consequence of this accommodation an interview between Toussaint and Leclerc was agreed on. It was proposed that they should meet on a spot in the mountains of Mornay. Learning that the place had given rise to suspicions, Toussaint magnanimously resolved to repair to the Cape. His journey was a triumph. Everywhere crowds pressed and prostrated themselves before the hero. They hailed him as their friend; they hailed him as their liberator; for in their acclaim they bore in mind that the liberty for which he had fought, was sanctioned and secured by the captain-general's solemn oath. His arrival at the Cape was announced by salvos from both the sea and the land forces. The multitude surrounded him with demonstrations of love and veneration; the mother pointed him out to her child, and girls strewed his path with flowers. Leclerc received him in his mansion, situated near the sea. During the interview four hundred horsemen, who had accompanied Toussaint, stood near, drawn up in order and with bare sabres. To the captain-general Toussaint was no longer a fanatical slave in revolt, and condemned to death, nor was he an unnatural father. The consul's brother-in-law took pains to laud his good faith and his magnanimity. He dwelt with emphasis on the reconciliation thus ratified, which would restore prosperity to the colony. He repeated his oath in presence of the chiefs of the two armies: "General," he said, "one cannot but praise you and admire you when one has, as you have done, borne the burden of the government of Saint Domingo. Your presence in this city is a proof of your magnanimity and your good faith. Our reconciliation will make this island, of which you are the restorer, bloom again; and will consolidate its new institutions, which are the fundamental basis of the liberty and the happiness of all."

"When the people of Saint Domingo," replied L'Ouverture, "triumphed in a war foreign both in relation to France and to themselves, they never thought that they should ever have to resist their natural protector. If explanations had preceded your arrival in this island, the cannon would not have been fired, except to welcome the envoy of a great power, and you would, on reaching these shores, have seen no other lights than *feux de*[Page 210]*joie*. You knew for certainty that I was at Santo Domingo. There was still time to send me news of your mission. When you were before the Cape, General Christophe begged you to grant him delay sufficient to acquaint me with the fact that a French squadron was on our shores; you might reasonably have acceded to his request, instead of reducing the people to despair by your threats, and exposing your army on the crater of a volcano."

Leclerc admitted that pilots, whom he had taken near the bay of Samana, had assured him that Toussaint L'Ouverture was at Santo Domingo. "But I am the brother-in-law of the first consul; I am commander-in-chief of a French army, and consequently in position and rank superior to General Christophe, and I did not think it consistent with my dignity to stop before a brigadier-general, and to listen to all his allegations."

"Nevertheless," rejoined Toussaint, "you waited for four days, and you will agree that some days more would not have done an injury to your honour, since, according to the words and the letter of your brother-in-law, you are intrusted with only a pacific mission. It seems to me that by patience you would have served equally France and Saint Domingo."

"It is true; but I was not master of myself. Let us retain no recollection of the past; all shall be repaired. Let us, General, rejoice at our union. Your sons, the officers who have accompanied you, as well as the generals and officers of my army, who are here, must be witnesses of our common gladness." At these words the door of the hall opened, and at Leclerc's invitation all the persons who were in the next apartment entered and took their places. In their presence the captain-general renewed his oaths. During this exchange of words Leclerc, pressing Toussaint as to the reduced condition of his resources, asked him where he could have obtained arms to continue the war. In a truly Lacedemonian manner the hero replied, "I would have taken yours."

Presently there entered a fine boy, who leapt on the neck of Toussaint L'Ouverture—it was his youngest son. During the war he had been lost by his father, and carried off by the French. [Page 211] Taken to the Cape, he was consigned to the care of his tutor; and now, as a touching pledge of friendship, he had been restored to his father, who was deeply affected by thus recovering his beloved child.

In returning from this conference, in the details of which we learn on how insignificant causes depend peace and war with all their mighty issues, Toussaint L'Ouverture passed through the posts of the French army, in the midst of the acclamations of the soldiers, the militia, and the people, who crowded around him; and under salvos of artillery entered Marmelade, where the commander received him at the head of his own troops. The day following he addressed the grenadiers and the dragoons of his guard. Having spoken to them of the peace, and shown them that it could not be violated except by perjury, he praised their courage, and thanked them for the love and devotedness they had displayed toward himself, and solemnly declared that the recollection of their deeds would for ever remain engraven on his mind. In order to testify to them his satisfaction, and at the same time take his farewell, he embraced all their officers. Those brave and hardy veterans could not restrain their tears, and the soldiers were sad and inconsolable. Toussaint then took the road for Ennery, which he had chosen for his residence. When near it, he was surrounded by crowds of people, who shouted out, "General, have you abandoned us?"

"No, my children," he answered, "all your brethren are under arms, and the officers of all ranks retain their posts."

When Toussaint L'Ouverture had fixed himself in the fertile and delightful valley of Ennery, to enjoy the repose of private and domestic life, he found occupation a necessity, and employed his energy in repairing and improving the dwellings of the inhabitants, and dispensing around him other benefits. Though retired from the world he was not forgotten.

Generals and other officers of the French army, and strangers from distant lands, came to visit him, and were welcomed with an affability which was a part of his nature. Exempt from fear and disquietude, he lived in the bosom of his family as if he had been [Page 212] guarded by an army. He rode over the country, and was everywhere greeted with tokens of respect.

With the cessation of hostilities, bands of black troops descended from the mountains, and the two armies mingled together as brothers. Freedom rendered friends those whom slavery had made deadly enemies. The population laid down their arms to engage in the labours of the field. The dwellings, which the fear of servitude had burned down, rose again under the reign of liberty. With a view to confirm the peace, the captain of the expedition put into the hands of Christophe the police of the north, and into those of Dessalines the police of the west. The cities which had been consumed were rebuilt. Vessels soon filled the ports. Commerce began once more to flourish. Everything promised a smiling future. Songs were heard and dances were seen in the villages. The whole country offered a proof how happy this world would be but for the disturbances occasioned by human passions.

[Page 213] BOOK III.

FROM THE RAVAGES OF THE YELLOW FEVER IN HAYTI UNTIL
THE DEPORTATION AND DEATH OF ITS LIBERATOR.

CHAPTER I.

Leclerc's uneasy position in Saint Domingo from insufficiency of food, from the existence in his army of large bodies of blacks, and especially from a most destructive fever.

ERE long, the natural consequences of the ravages which had been carried over the country, and of the abstraction from agriculture of a large portion of the population, were felt in scarcity of provisions, the rather that Saint Domingo did not abound in articles of human food of a superior kind. This scarcity was augmented by the necessity of supporting out of the public magazines a large number of soldiers, for though the European part of the army was much reduced, a large number of blacks and men of colour had been thrown on the government stores. Shortness of food and the high prices which ensue, are specially trying to a government of force. Complaints began to spread among the native population, and not without difficulty were the servants of the state supplied with the necessaries of life.

Application for aid was made to the governors of foreign possessions in the neighbourhood. The Spaniards furnished supplies with chivalrous generosity; but those supplies were very far from being sufficient. The English, who had not anticipated the success of the French arms, and saw that success with uneasiness, refused to give succour. From Americans a similar answer was received. The conduct of their agents disclosed the [Page 214] regret which their governments felt in not finding at Saint Domingo, under the French sway, the commercial advantages which they enjoyed while it was ruled by Toussaint L'Ouverture. The state of the island, combined with the native politeness of the French character, caused attentions to be paid to foreign ships and visitors, which were interpreted into tokens of a sense of civil and political weakness. This adverse impression found its way into the minds of the blacks, so that the spirit of the colonial army became increasingly difficult to manage. Thus what at first was the captain-general's power, proved a source of weakness and embarrassment. To provide a remedy, he attempted to incorporate the colonial troops with the reinforcements that came from France, but the prejudices of Europeans rendered the plan all but nugatory. Yet, if it was dangerous to have entire large bodies of blacks, it was not less dangerous to discharge and dismiss them at once. Leclerc had no resource but time, and sought to govern by dividing. Accordingly, he took care to employ black soldiers only in small detachments, and regarded even desertion with satisfaction. He could not, however, feel at ease unless he knew that the blacks were resuming their agricultural labours, and though in sending them back to the plantations, he received assistance from some of their chiefs, he was made sensible of the want of such an influence as that which Toussaint L'Ouverture had exerted before the war, and effected his purpose only on a limited scale.

These difficulties, however, though in themselves not small, were inconsiderable compared with those which sprang from a terrible malady with which the island, and especially its European inhabitants, was now visited. The yellow fever, which had already proved destructive, broke out with great violence at the same time at Port-au-Prince and at the Cape. It appeared there in a form unusually repulsive and deadly. It seized persons who were in good health, without any premonition. Sometimes death was the immediate consequence. Happy those who were immediately carried off! Ordinarily it was slow in its progress as well as frightful in its inflictions. The disorder began in the brain, by an oppressive pain accompanied or followed by fever. The [Page 215] patient was devoured with burning thirst. The stomach, distracted by pains, in vain sought relief by efforts to disburden itself. Fiery veins streaked the eye; the face was inflamed, and dyed of a dark dull red colour; the ears from time to time rang painfully. Now mucous secretions surcharged the tongue, and took away the power of speech; now the sick man spoke, but in speaking had a foresight of death. When the violence of the disorder approached the heart, the gums were blackened. The sleep, broken, or troubled by convulsions or by frightful visions, was worse than the waking hours, and when the reason sank under a delirium which had its seat in the brain, repose utterly forsook the patient's couch. The progress of the fire within was marked by yellowish spots, which spread over the surface of the body. If, then, a happy crisis came not, all hope was gone. Soon the breath infected the air with a fetid odour, the lips glazed, despair painted itself in the eyes, and sobs, with long intervals of silence, formed the only language. From each side of the mouth spread foam, tinged with black and burnt blood. Blue streaks mingled with the yellow over all the frame. Death came on the thirteenth day, though more commonly it tarried till the seventeenth. All remedies were useless. Rarely did the victims escape.

The malady produced a general melancholy. Its depressing effects were visible in the troops who had not yet been stricken with the fever. You saw the men regard each other with furtive glances, and in deep yet ominous silence: their arms looked tarnished; their steps were heavy and slow. Unconquerable in the field, they already felt themselves the victims of destiny. When undergoing review, the men, scarcely expecting to see each other again, affected a foolish gaiety, the real character of which was betrayed by a bitter smile, or took leave of each other sadly, as pilgrims, through suffering, to the dark shores of the eternal world.

The city of the Cape then presented one of those sights which are rare in the history of human calamities. Scarcely had a part of the buildings destroyed by the conflagration been hastily reconstructed, when the town and the hospitals were filled with [Page 216] the sick and the dying. The chief hospital, situated on a height which overhangs the city, having been burnt down, consisted now only of large sheds covered with sugar canes. Therein the patients were for the most part laid in straw, unprovided with necessary appliances, exposed now to the fury of storms, now to torrents of rain, and now to the burning rays of the sun. Those remaining in the city were better protected and cared for, but breathing an impurer air, and deprived of breezes by the mountains, they suffered scarcely less, and died as certainly.

Military discipline disappeared: the common soldier had the same authority as the general, and each general acknowledged no authority except his own. Men spoke no more of combats, of exploits, of glory. The heart of the soldier sank within him. Even the funeral knell ceased its mournful sounds; the common calamity crushed the sense of religious observance. In the midst of disorder and confusion death heaped victims on victims. Friend followed friend in quick succession; the sick were avoided from the fear of contagion, and for the same reason the dead were left without burial. Despair alone remained in activity— fierce despair, for the dying man could cast his eye on neither friend nor nurse, and had to suffer and expire in terrific solitude or more terrific companionship. The country, the mountains, the sea, afforded no place of refuge. The troops that were removed to a distance from the towns were not the less attacked. Their camp was transformed into an hospital. Soldiers died under trees laden with fruit and under plants breathing perfumes. The ships of war and merchant vessels lost their crews. Eight and forty passengers from Bordeaux expired in disembarking at the Cape. Terrified at the destruction, some, on nearing the island, went on board vessels that were quitting its infected shores, yet perished, smitten by the poisoned air. Four thousand men who came in Dutch vessels perished, Fear multiplied the victims.

When the malady was in all its force, human passions manifested their guilty excesses. Virtue was disregarded when it no longer offered an earthly reward. Some sought distraction and relief to their wretchedness in gambling and in voluptuousness; [Page 217] violence and adultery became common. Others endeavoured to drown their torments in reckless intoxication; others, again, attired in military costume, which at such a moment was simply ridiculous, threw insult at the disease, and braved death, either in satirical gaiety or in buffooneries, or in roars of silly laughter. The words "Ah! the funny fellow," became a derisive phrase to indicate a poor wretch that was trying to laugh or trick away his calamity. Others, again, deep sunk in guilt, sought to deceive death in the arms of a mistress or in perfumed baths. While all around was perishing, songs were heard from the sea. They were the attempts of men who thus tried to cheat themselves into momentary joy. The nearer men were to eternity, the more greedy they were of the pleasures of earth.

Pauline, the wife of Leclerc and the sister of the consul, did not renounce her voluptuous habits in the midst of so terrible a plague. In the hope of breathing a less infected air, she had gone to a country house, on the declivity of a pleasant hill which overhung the sea. Here she passed her hours in pleasure and luxury. She saw die around her officers whose incense she had welcomed, but for whose sufferings she showed no concern— intent only on putting away all unpleasant objects, and seizing with avidity on sources of gratification. Now she caused herself, like a queen, to be borne in a palanquin through the most beautiful scenes of nature; there would she, for hours together, dwell in contemplating the ocean and its delightful shores, loaded with the luxuries of tropical vegetation: now she plunged into the depths of odoriferous forests, and surrendered herself to the captivating reveries of love; and now she sailed on the sea, accompanied by courtiers, musicians, and buffoons, as if she would sustain the character of Venus rising from the waves.

What is still more remarkable is that she took pains to defy the malady by festivities, in which she gathered around her dancing, music, pleasure, and voluptuousness: there she drew on herself admiration by her wit, her graces, her beauty, and the ravishing tenderness of her looks. But around and in those festivities, Death bore his funeral torches. The balls which she ceased not to give took place on the brink of [Page 218] the grave. The dancers of to-night were dead on the morrow. But the more joyous did she affect to appear. "These," she said, "are our last moments; let us pass them in pleasure."

As the disorder raged in other places as well as in the cities of the Cape and Port-au-Prince, there died every day, on land and on sea, not less than from three to four hundred persons. More and more irregular in its symptoms and its course, the fever baffled and defied the skill of the physicians, who died together with their patients.

The little attention which at first was paid to funeral rites, became less and less, and soon was wholly discontinued. The dead bodies were put on the outside of the doors and carried off by night. If anything could excite compassion, it was to see on some of those livid frames the scars of wounds received in the battles of Europe, where he had gained his fame who sent those warriors and heroes to die on a distant foreign and deadly shore. As it was necessary to remove the dead as soon as they had breathed their last, some were carried off while yet alive; groans were heard in the heaps of abandoned corpses, and from the putrid mass some rose and returned to take their place among the living. As very many bodies were tossed into the sea, the waves bore them up and down the harbour, or left them on the shore, painful mementoes to spectators, and food for birds and beasts of prey, while they added to the foul infection with which the atmosphere was burdened.

During the prevalence of these accumulated disasters, the black population, proof against the pest, remained faithful to the peace which had been forced on them and their venerated chief. Had they chosen to rise, the whole expedition would have perished. Their virtue was more than abstinence from self-avengement. With characteristic hospitality they received sick persons into their homes, and gave them unlooked-for aid: they did more; they gave them tears and sympathy, seeing in them not Frenchmen and assailants, but sufferers. There were other benefactors. Sisters of charity, truly worthy of the name, went from street to street, and from bed to bed, ministering with tenderness and skill to the sick, the despairing, and the [Page 219] departing. Womanly love was almost the only virtue that maintained itself erect. When all other remedies had proved vain, that noble affection showed itself fertile in resources, nor was it the less respectable because in the extremity it resorted to fetish practices which had their origin in Africa. More simple and even more touching was that manifestation of it which compelled young women to follow their lovers to their graves,

Amid the faithless only faithful found.

It is terrible to think that some of these worthy women may afterwards have been repaid with slavery.

At length, when the summer heats had reached their height, the malady redoubled its fury, and broke down alike benevolence and virtue. Then was the harvest of death. According to authentic tables, there died fifteen hundred officers, twenty thousand soldiers, nine thousand sailors, and three thousand persons who loosely hung about the skirts of the army in quest of employment or fortune. Not fewer than fourteen generals lost their lives in the plague. Of that number was Debelle, whose virtues made him regretted alike by foes and friends; Dugua, an intrepid and joyous old man, whose hairs had grown grey on the borders of the Nile; Hardy, who had displayed rare courage in the victories and the reverses of the expedition. Almost incredible is it that there died seven hundred medical men, worthy, for the most, of high praise, such was their courage, their patience, their devotedness.

The malady changed the character of the army. Those who survived, experiencing a long and difficult convalescence, became habitually depressed, morose, or exasperated. Some had their memory weakened; some remained broken down or crippled for life. Discipline was restored with difficulty. Even news from home brought little pleasure, and gave only a transient relief; and communications with France were intercepted, in order, so far as possible, to conceal from the mother country the awful loss which she had endured.

Such was the terrible punishment which fell on the predatory [Page 220] expedition sent by the Corsican adventurer against the hero and patriot of St. Domingo.

And can there be a more decisive proof of anything than we have here of the honour of Toussaint L'Ouverture? The necessity of the French was his opportunity. With what ease now might he have mustered those blacks which were in Leclerc's way, and extorted from his enfeebled hands the sovereignty of the island. That Toussaint remained quiet at Ennery disproves the base insinuations which were fabricated expressly for his ruin.

CHAPTER II.

Bonaparte and Leclerc conspire to effect the arrest of Toussaint L'Ouverture, who is treacherously seized, sent to France, and confined in the castle of Joux; partial risings in consequence.

IF the establishment in Saint Domingo of the authority of France had been the object of the expedition, the present settlement of its affairs would have been left to unfold its resources, and the blessings of the existing peace would have been permanent. All opposition had been put down. Mutual explanations had been given. With one exception the leaders of the blacks held rank and power in the French army. Toussaint L'Ouverture, the only exception, was engaged in rural pursuits and acts of beneficence. Leclerc was sole master in the island. Hayti was now at least a colonial dependency of France. And if there were evils or obstacles which he could not at the moment put away, they were nothing more than such as promised to disappear before good government, aided by the healing and reformatory hand of time. Even through the tempest of the plague, tokens of coming serenity were readily discerned. But the occupation of the island was only the first act in the drama.

The intelligence of the ravages of the fever in St. Domingo shocked the mind of Bonaparte, though he had foreseen and [Page 221] even premeditated the calamity. One obstacle which lay in his way to the imperial throne had been removed. So far the expedition had not proved nugatory. There were two other obstacles. One was the freedom of the blacks. Such freedom, in the consul's eyes, was licentiousness. It was, moreover, incompatible with his designs. If Saint Domingo remained free, the other French colonies must and would be free. In their emancipation, the colonial system would be endangered, nay, would soon be lost; for freedom was the precursor of independence: and if the colonies became independent, what strongholds would France possess in the West Indies to check the growing power of England; and where would be its outposts to keep the United States in good behaviour? Even more important were those dependencies when considered as pastures for the powerful and the aspiring around the consul's person. Let the colonies be reduced into servitude; then would they naturally enter as constituent parts in an empire under governors with more than the power of ordinary princes, who, with Bonaparte at their head, would form a regular and august political hierarchy, and so lay the basis of a dominion which might extend widely over both hemispheres, if not in time comprehend the civilized world. To the ambitious Corsican the prospect was enchanting. The herds of Haytian negroes must be sent back into slavery.

This resolution, he knew, could not be carried into effect so long as Toussaint L'Ouverture lived on the island. His existence there was the second great impediment. That impediment, too, the consul determined to remove. The determination was the more readily formed because the world had come to regard Toussaint as a sort of rival to Bonaparte. The phrase became current which designated the one "the first of the blacks," and the other "the first of the whites." Comparisons were made between the two which the First Consul always found offensive, and which were not always to the First Consul's advantage. Was his bright star to pale before the fiery meteor of a slave? Besides, that slave had not been easily subdued; he had all but overcome and destroyed the soldiers of Egypt and Italy. When peace was concluded, it was difficult to say whether the [Page 222] assailant or the assailed was in the worse condition. This manly and effective resistance Bonaparte could not forgive. It would have been less intolerable had it been made by Europeans; but to come from negro slaves—it was an unpardonable offence. Yes, Bonaparte hated Toussaint, and resolved to effect his destruction. His arrest was the first point to be gained. With Toussaint in his hands, everything else he judged would be easy.

The First Consul was not deterred by the consideration that such a step could not be taken without dissimulation and perfidy. The end covered, if it did not justify, the means, in his eyes. In Leclerc he had a ready and passive instrument. Nor was the captain-general without his own reasons for the contemplated apprehension. The hatred borne by the master had taken possession of the servant's soul. Little satisfaction did he feel in a peace which a hard fate had induced him to seek and conclude. The popularity of the negro chief caused him to be an object of fear with Leclerc. In the war, the chief glory had been gained by his foe, and now that foe, having become his rival, eclipsed Leclerc in the estimation of the natives of nearly all classes and all opinions. He had, moreover—and he knew he had—injured, deeply injured Toussaint L'Ouverture, and injury invariably begets a hatred in proportion to its own intensity. Besides, the original plan, which so far had been successful, remained to be completed. Leclerc, in consequence, was well disposed to execute the consul's will.

Without waiting for express directions in a matter on which he well knew the mind of Bonaparte, the captain-general began to prepare the way for the final act. For this purpose he spoke of Toussaint, not as an independent power who had of his own accord laid down arms, and declined the highest post in the colony, but as a revolter who had been outlawed and condemned to death, but pardoned by an act of grace on his own part. Consulting him as to the disposition of the troops, so as to prevent suspicion, he sought occasions which, in extorting complaints from him, might form the grounds of a disagreement, and so afford pretexts for his seizure. Two frigates anchored off [Page 223] Gonaïves. The soldiers no longer paid Toussaint military honours. The plot was dimly seen by friends, who advised the black hero to be on his guard. Some went so far as to recommend him to take measures for his personal security. He replied, "For one to expose one's life for one's country when in peril is a sacred duty; but to arouse one's country in order to save one's life, is inglorious."

In order to give some colour to the contemplated arrest, Leclerc complained that Toussaint's body-guard had not been wholly disarmed. Toussaint replied that he had given orders for its disbandment, and advised the captain-general to proceed mildly in bringing that result about. Impatient of contradiction, Leclerc employed force, and with difficulty succeeded. In this opposition an excuse was found for filling the district of Ennery with European troops. The inhabitants complained. Toussaint L'Ouverture became the medium for making those complaints known. "This was exactly what was wanted," says one who knew Leclerc's designs.

On the 7th of June, General Brunet wrote to Toussaint L'Ouverture the following letter:—

Head Quarters at the Plantation of Georges, 18 Prairial, An. X.

BRUNET, GENERAL OF DIVISION, TO THE GENERAL OF DIVISION, TOUSSAINT L'OUVERTURE.

"The moment, citizen-general, has come to make known to General Leclerc, in an incontestable manner, those who may deceive him in regard to yourself: they are calumniators, since your sentiments tend only to bring back order in the district which you inhabit. It is necessary to render me aid in order to restore the communication with the Cape, which was yesterday interrupted, since three persons have been murdered by a band of fifty brigands, between Ennery and Coupe-à-Pintade. Send toward those places faithful men, whom you will pay well; I will be accountable for the outlay. There are, my dear general, [Page 224] arrangements which we ought to make in concert, which it is impossible to treat of by letter, but which an hour's conference would terminate. Had I not to-day been overwhelmed with business, I would myself have brought the answer to your letter. Occupied as I am, I must beg you to come to my residence. You will not find there all the pleasures which I would wish to welcome you with, but you will find the frankness of an honourable man, who desires nothing but the happiness of the colony and your own happiness. If Madame Toussaint, whom I shall have the greatest pleasure to become acquainted with, could accompany you, I should be gratified; if she has occasion for horses, I will send her mine. Never, general, will you find a more sincere friend than myself. With confidence in the captain-general, and friendship toward all under him, you will enjoy tranquillity.

"I cordially salute you,

"BRUNET."

Now here is a piece of consummate villany. This man, who signs himself Brunet, who calls himself a man of honour, and who would have run any one through who should have thrown on that honour the slightest doubt—this man, who probably went to church, and heard mass and professed Christianity, or who, at any rate, did not in private pick pockets or cut throats, this man deliberately sits down and employs his ingenuity in fabricating a tissue of lies in order to ensnare to his ruin an innocent patriot, the liberator of his country. Every word in this diabolical composition is selected with a view to deceive. By implication, inuendo, and direct averment, the tissue of falsehoods goes forward to its end. "You are, you know, alleged to be less quick than might be wished. False, doubtless. Now you may prove how false by acting in concert with me. Come hither, and so convict your calumniators; let the captain-general see how earnest you are for the furtherance of public tranquillity." This is a dexterous movement. To remind Toussaint that he was suspected was to prepare him for the offered means of exculpation. An innocent man, from a consciousness of his [Page 225] innocence, and a guilty man, in order to affect and display such consciousness, would alike be inclined to accept the expedient. Then for this honourable man, who does not invent, but merely employs groundless suspicions, he himself is quite confident that his victim is calumniated. "No, in coming to me, you come to a friend who knows the real facts, and so is fully aware of what you have done and are doing to tranquillize the country. But, notwithstanding your efforts, disturbances exist. These must be put a stop to. I have said I have confidence in you: I now show it, for I ask you to take the requisite measures." Excellent Jesuit! Yes, the way to beget confidence is, you well know, to show confidence. But how show confidence so much as by employing a man to put down the very evils he is accused of causing? Surely this, if anything would make him feel that he is trusted, or at any rate show him how desirable, even for his own bad purposes, if he has bad purposes, it is that he should act as if he felt that he is trusted.

"Then as to the cost of these efforts, we will settle that when we meet." Yes, it is a small affair of business between two generals of division—nothing more—some brigands to exterminate, some expense to be incurred,—all to be amicably talked of when the two friends are taking a glass of wine together, and to be ended by an order for payment on the public purse. What more simple, what more natural, what more straightforward? None but one deeply versed in deceit could have thought of treachery.

But the tricks are not exhausted. "We must have an interview. For that purpose I intended to come and see you. I had ordered my horse and an escort; but really I cannot leave; I am nailed to the spot. I must throw myself on your goodness; pray come; I will do all I can to make you comfortable, and bring your wife with you on this little excursion—a mere party of pleasure. Shall I send my own horses to convey her and her domestics? What! do you hesitate? still hesitate? Ah! take care you fail not to confide in the Captain-general. Distrust on your part may justify distrust on his part. Insinuations are best repelled by confidingness. And, you know, trust [Page 226] in Leclerc involves friendship towards me. Yes, you must come; you will come."

In this wily epistle there is only one mistake, but it is a serious one. Brunet declares that he is an honourable man. Over this declaration, you, Toussaint, surely paused. Here the cunning hand displays its cunning. Yet thy guileless nature will not entertain a distrust. In general, the epistle has a fair seeming. You will accept the invitation. Suspicion of treachery is dishonourable to him who entertains it. And had not Toussaint, when the clouds were really dark, gone to the Cape? And did not a friendly arrangement ensue? The oath of Leclerc remained in force. And here was an opportunity not only to benefit his neighbours, but to purge himself from any suspicions which weak men, or designing men, had raised. As to the rumours of peril to himself, the timid always abound in illusions of their own fabrication. A brave man never fears danger, and a wise man is not very careful to shun danger. Besides, the civilities of hospitality have their claims. Clearly, on the whole, there was no valid reason against going, and many valid reasons for going. Toussaint had intended to go to Gonaïves before he received Brunet's letter. He was on his way thither: he turned not back when the invitation was put into his hands.

Proceeding on his journey, he met Brunet on the plantation called Georges, where the general was waiting for him. For some time they conversed together. Then Brunet begged to be excused, and left the room. The next moment there entered from eighteen to twenty officers, with drawn swords and pistols in their hands. Toussaint L'Ouverture took them for assassins, and arose. He drew his sabre, resolved to sell his life dearly. Then the colonel, who was at the head of the band, seeing that he waited for them with intrepidity, advanced toward him with his sword lowered, and said, "General, we have not come here to attempt your life. We have merely the order to secure your person." At these words, Toussaint put his sword back into the scabbard, saying, "The justice of Heaven will avenge my cause."

[Page 227]Those prophetic words have had accomplishment; those prophetic words will have accomplishment: nor ever will they be fulfilled until slavery is blotted out of America, and is known no more in the world.

From the plantation, where he was arrested, to Gonaïves, troops had been placed from distance to distance along the road. At midnight, the prisoner was taken on board a French frigate, called the 'Creole.' The officer who commanded the ship was touched, even to tears, at the lot of that victim of the basest treachery. They sailed for the Cape, where Toussaint was transferred to the Hero, which waited for them off the port. "Adieu, Captain," said the captive, on leaving the Creole, "I shall remember you, till my last sigh." When he reached the Hero, he found in his arms, St. Jean L'Ouverture, the very son, who, on a brighter day, had been restored to him by Leclerc. Placide L'Ouverture was arrested next day. Isaac was at Ennery. Ignorant that his father had been seized, he was tranquilly reading about seven o'clock in the morning, when he was startled by a brisk firing, followed by alarming cries. Hastening from the room, he beheld labourers, women, and children, running hither and thither in terror, and from three to four hundred French soldiers firing on them in pursuit. A servant urged him to fly. He feared that evil had befallen his father, but remained. Forthwith he was arrested. The officer told him that his father had been embarked, and that he had orders from General Brunet to apprehend him and all the family; adding that he should not have fired on the people, had they not attempted to bar his passage. The money and the papers belonging to Toussaint L'Ouverture were taken possession of. The house was rifled; insolence was added to robbery. Madame Toussaint and her niece were carried off. "Only a heart of stone," says Isaac L'Ouverture,* who has described the whole scene, "could fail to be softened by the tears and the lamentations of the men, the women, and the children who were present, and who deplored her (Madame Toussaint's) lot, when she was for ever [Page 228] quitting her country, a part of her family, and her abode, which was the abode of beneficence and hospitality. Those men, those women, and those children, in the excess of their grief, expressed their fears and their regrets with deep sensibility. "Madame," cried they, "are you leaving us? shall we never see each other again?" then addressing the commanding officer, they added, "Ah! at least, Sir, don't kill her, don't kill her children;"—they all believed that Toussaint L'Ouverture himself was dead. That woman, who was worthy of those marks of attachment and love, quitted her home without taking anything with her. Madame Toussaint and her son Isaac, and her niece, were conducted to the Cape, and put on board the Hero; the vessel forthwith set sail for France. It is related that, in fixing, for the last time, his straining eyes on the mountains made memorable by his

---

*"Mémoires d'Isaac, fils de Toussaint L'Ouverture," &c., p. 309.

exploits, Toussaint L'Ouverture exclaimed, "They have only felled the trunk of the tree (of the freedom of the blacks); branches will sprout, for the roots are numerous and deep."

And in that confidence, thou large-hearted man, dost thou, sail over that waste of waters; saddened, but not overwhelmed. Thou carriest the cause of thy colour in thy soul, and, with a mind replete with Christian principles and affections, thou neither doubtest nor despondest. Twenty-five days hast thou to live on the sea, uncertain of thy own fate; but with such knowledge of thy oppressors as must have occasioned dark forecastings. To thy own view, however, thy past is bright. Not for thyself, but for others hast thou toiled and bled: and those others are the outcast, the ignorant, the injured, and the lost. True disciple of thy Galilean Master, bear up in the recollection of His load and His persecutions—yet heavier than thine. And now, in the hour of darkness, find and acknowledge thy glory, in that which heathen France accounts thy shame. Not on man's judgment dost thou rely. Not by a local tribunal wilt thou be judged. The wide earth will take cognizance of what thou didst attempt and achieve, and pronounce thee a benefactor, not of thy colour only, but of thy kind. Regret not the president's chair, left vacant in thy beloved mother country, nor let men's ingratitude and perfidy sour thy feelings. From high motives [Page 229] thou wroughtest for a high purpose; and that purpose, though not in thine own way, will be attained. Be greater by patience, in the day of thy weakness, than thou wast in the day of thy power by thy valour; and thy name will pass down to posterity, encircled with undying fame. Listen to that solemn voice in thy own heart, which tells thee that Hayti will be free.

On the voyage, Toussaint was denied all intercourse with his family; he was confined constantly to his cabin, and the door was guarded by soldiers with fixed bayonets. Uncertain as to his fate, yet apprehensive of a very dark future, he determined to make a solemn appeal to Bonaparte, and prepared the following epistle:—

"On board the Hero, 1 Thermidor, an X. (12th July, 1802).

"GENERAL TOUSSAINT L'OUVERTURE, TO GENERAL BONAPARTE, FIRST CONSUL OF THE FRENCH REPUBLIC. "CITIZEN FIRST CONSUL—

"I will not conceal my faults from you. I have committed some. What man is exempt? I am quite ready to avow them. After the word of honour of the

Captain-general who represents the French Government, after a proclamation addressed to the colony, in which he promised to throw the veil of oblivion over the events which have taken place in Saint Domingo, I, as you did on the 18th Brumaire, withdrew into the bosom of my family. Scarcely had a month passed away, when evil-disposed persons, by means of intrigues, effected my ruin with the General-in-chief, by filling his mind with distrust against me. I received a letter from him which ordered me to act in conjunction with General Brunet. I obeyed. Accompanied by two persons I went to Gonaïves, where I was arrested. They sent me on board the frigate Creole, I know not for what reason, without any other clothes than those I had on. The next day my house was exposed to pillage; my wife and my children were arrested; they had nothing, not even the means to cover themselves.

"Citizen First Consul—a mother fifty years of age, may deserve the indulgence and the kindness of a generous and liberal [Page 230] nation; she has no account to render; I alone ought to be responsible for my conduct to the Government I have served. I have too high an idea of the greatness and the justice of the First Magistrate of the French people, to doubt a moment of its impartiality. I indulge the feeling that the balance in its hands, will not incline to one side more than to another. I claim its generosity.

"Salutations and respect,

"TOUSSAINT L'OUVERTURE."

When he wrote this high-spirited letter, in which the writer characteristically shows his concern for others more than for himself,—and the tone of which contrasts favourably with that which his oppressor, when fallen, and on the point of quitting Europe for St. Helena, addressed in true French melodramatic style to the English people,—Toussaint obviously had no idea of the extent of the perfidy to which he was about to fall a victim. He had been seized and carried off, but only, as he thought, that he might be confronted with his maligners, and have a fair trial in France. All he requested, therefore, was an impartial hearing, assured that the even hand of Justice would repair the injuries he had suffered. Little did he then foresee the dreadful end to which he had been destined by the Consul's blind ambition.

While on board the Hero, Toussaint wrote also to Admiral Décrès, Minister of Marine and of the Colonies:—

"CITIZEN MINISTER,—
"I was, with all my family, arrested by the order of the Captain-general, who nevertheless had given me his word of honour, and who had promised me the protection of the French Government. I venture to claim both its justice and its goodwill. If I have committed faults, I only ought to suffer the punishment of them.

"I beg you, Citizen Minister, to employ your interest with the First Consul, on behalf of my family and myself.

"Salutation and respect,

(Signed) "TOUSSAINT L'OUVERTURE."

This simple and dignified letter is reported to have drawn tears from the eyes of the minister. That minister felt the [Page 231] contrast between the dark designs of the Government and the unsuspicious tone of the communication. "Justice!" As well ask mercy from tigers; as well seek grapes on a bramble-bush.

As soon as the vessel arrived at Brest, the First Consul, glad to have so formidable an enemy in his hands, gave free course to his resentment. Without paying any respect to Toussaint's character, fame, services, or former position, he, consulting only his fears and selfish interests, tore him from his family, and began the persecution which was to end in a most painful death. Toussaint was immediately hurried on shore. On the 13th of August, the maritime provost of Brest, at five in the morning, sent an officer of police and four men to transfer the negro chief from the vessel. On the deck only was he permitted to have an interview with his wife and children, whom he was to meet no more in this life. Only his servant was he allowed to take with him. When in the boat, he bade a last adieu to Madame Toussaint, to Isaac, to Saint-Jean, who then remained on board the Hero, and extended his hand to Placide, whom a cruel policy at the same moment was tearing from the arms of his mother, and was conveying on board the corvette La Naïade to Belle-Isle en Mer. In the evening, Placide learnt of the removal of his father from the Hero. Previously, he had sent the following letter to him, which was found under Toussaint's pillow:—

"Brest Roads, 24 Thermidor.

TOUSSAINT PARTING FROM HIS WIFE AND CHILDREN.

"MY DEAR FATHER AND MOTHER,
"I am on board the brig La Naïade. As yet, I am ignorant of my lot. Perhaps I shall never see you again. In that, I do not accuse my destiny. No matter where I am, I entreat you to take courage, and sometimes to think of me. I I will send you news of myself, if I am not dead; give me news of yourselves, if you have an opportunity. I am very well situated; I am with persons who are very good to me, and who promise to continue so. Isaac and Saint-Jean, do not forget your brother! I shall always love you. Many kind thoughts to you all; embrace my cousins for me. I embrace you, as I love you.

"Your son,

(Signed) "PLACIDE L'OUVERTURE."

[Page 232]When he thus rudely broke up this amiable and interesting family, the First Consul did not foresee that one day he would be torn away from his wife and son. Curious coincidence in the destiny of the oppressed and that of the oppressor! Bonaparte was repaid in his own coin, nor in this instance merely—others have presented themselves in our narrative. But what a "superfluity of naughtiness" have we here! why are all the members of the L'Ouverture family involved in their father's ruin? And if stern policy required their deportation from Hayti, why are wife and children separated from their natural head, and why should the aged captive be denied the companionship of her who was the choice of his youth, became the comfort of his adult age, and might still have supported his overladen heart to bear his troubles? Was she severed from him expressly to exasperate his feelings, and augment his woes, making his load heavier, the more surely and the more speedily to put an end to his existence? Oh the depth of wickedness with which what is called policy is chargeable! Reader, be not hoodwinked by general terms. Policy would be nothing without politicians, and when statesmen lose their manhood in state-craft, and perpetrate, in their public capacity, wherein they have power, deeds which they dare not attempt in their individual capacity, wherein they are weak, then do they contract a criminality which should make them abhorred by all good men, and which is a virtual forfeiture of the tenure by which they hold their high position. Office does not change the character of realities. What is the painful reality here? It is nothing less than theft. Toussaint L'Ouverture was stolen. The First Consul was a man-stealer. He was more, he was a burglar:

he broke into Toussaint's house, and having ransacked and plundered it, he stole the family, after having perfidiously carried off its head. And having stolen father, mother, and children, he not only separated them one from the other, but murdered, at least, the father. This is plain speaking. At least, it is intended to be so. Crime does not appear crime in men's eyes, unless it is branded as crime. Therefore do I declare and proclaim, that Bonaparte and his accomplices were, and for ever remain, guilty [Page 233] of man-stealing, robbery, and murder, in their treacherous, violent, and most wicked conduct towards this virtuous household.

Madame Toussaint and her children were conveyed to Bayonne, where they were placed under the supervision of General Ducos. L'Ouverture, with his servant, Mars Plaisir, was put on shore at Landerneau, where they were taken in charge by two companies of cavalry. Compelled to quit immediately, Toussaint in one carriage and Mars in another, set out for Paris under a strong guard. At Guingamp, some officers of the eighty-second, who had served under Toussaint L'Ouverture's orders, prevailed on the commander to stop the cavalcade, that they might enjoy the opportunity of saluting their old general. The permission was accorded. This was the only solace that the captive enjoyed on the French soil. He reached Paris on the 17th of August, and was immediately imprisoned in the Temple. Thence, without any interview with Bonaparte or his ministers, and without the slightest explanation he was hurried away into the department of Jura, and consigned to the dungeons of the castle of Joux. Singular caprice of what is called history, at that very hour the same prison held in chains Rigaud, the rival and the foe of Toussaint. Separated in the busy hours of public life, Toussaint and Rigaud were united by misfortune. And yet the union was little more than nominal, for they were too powerful, even in a dungeon, to be allowed to confer together. Suffering deserves compassion even when it cannot command respect. Therefore, I leave Rigaud to his endurance, without commenting on his guilt in joining Leclerc's marauding enterprise. Rigaud and Toussaint, the first a man of colour, the second a negro, but for your skin, or rather but for European prejudice against your skin, you would not have come to your present unhappy condition. You are dark in hue, therefore are you persecuted. Distinguished representatives of your respective races, there are still men who deal in the like of you as they deal in pigs, in poultry, in flocks, and in herds, and there are others who justify this traffic in human flesh on the ground that your [Page 234] epidermis contains a colouring matter of a somewhat deeper shade than their own. Yes, to this issue the question comes at last. How long, O reason, shall so patent and flimsy a pretext prevail? A brown complexion, commonly called white, ensures and justifies personal immunity and personal freedom; a rather deeper brown, and a complexion of a somewhat sable tinge, ensures and justifies the loss of personal liberty, and therein the loss of all the rights, privileges, and possibilities of manhood. Nay more, the former may buy and sell, oppress, maim, mutilate, brand, scourge, imprison, and even kill the latter; and that, too, not only with perfect impunity, but with all the high bearing of unquestionable right. The relation of master and slave, when reduced to its last link, is the relation of simply more or less in the hues of the skin, of which the varieties are so very numerous, and which extend from the fair Circassian to the raven-black negro. Where, in this minutely graduated scale, is the point at which liberty ends, and slavery begins? And who has fixed that point? And on what authority? In truth, slavery in its origin and in its essence is simply man-stealing, is robbery of the very worst kind; it is the strong preying on the weak; it is the law of the bludgeon, the bayonet, the fetter, the prison, the ship, the gallows. Bonaparte, in carrying off Toussaint L'Ouverture, did no more than his African prototypes in power did before him, and, alas! continue to do to the present hour. One and all, he as well as they, and they not more than he, are robbers and plunderers. What then are those who purchase the stolen goods? And what they who grow rich and fatten on the system? Let men, then, renounce the Christian name, or change from the top to the bottom a "domestic institution," which, having piracy and theft for its basis, and violence for its support, stands in flagrant contradiction to the clearest precepts, the simplest doctrines, and the fundamental principles of the Gospel.

As soon as the carrying off of L'Ouverture was known in St. Domingo, General Belair, in the mountains of Saint Marc; Colonel Sans-Souci, at Valière; the chief of the battalion of Noel, at Dondon, took up arms as by one accord, and set in [Page 235] movement the population of those districts. The latter made his way as far as Ennery, overcoming all opposition in his route, and augmenting his troops at every step. A multitude of men and women who followed him, at the sight of the French garrison, made the hills of Ennery resound with their cries of woe, indignation, and vengeance. Sans-Souci had no sooner drawn his sword than he was arrested, as well as General Baradat, by Christophe, sent to the Cape, and embarked for France. Belair was at the head of considerable forces, when

Dessalines, who was despatched from the Cape against him, came into the mountains of Saint Marc, and requested a colloquy; Belair, hoping that the interview might bring a similarity of sentiments to light, acceded to the request. He thus fell into the snare laid against him by Dessalines. He was arrested; and, with his wife, conveyed to the Cape, where they were both shot. Thus perished General Charles Belair, the victim of his devotion to Toussaint, and of his confidence in Dessalines. A model of friendship, with bravery, and military talents, he united the qualities which make a good and amiable man. Toussaint, well pleased with his conduct when he was his aide-de-camp, once said to him, "Charles, you have acted to-day like Labienus." "General," he replied, "I hope I shall be more faithful to you than Labienus at last proved to Cæsar." The hope became a reality. Other less distinguished, but worthy and faithful friends of Toussaint L'Ouverture, impelled to espouse his cause, suffered death in ways which soldiers account disgraceful.

Society exacts from bad men an account of their deeds, and bad men, unable to give a satisfactory account, feel it necessary to put forth at any cost colourable pretexts. Leclerc could not endure the voice of public opinion, even as it existed in Saint Domingo. He had treacherously seized, and hastily sent from the island, one who had been both its hero and its pacificator. The evil work given him to perform by his brother-in-law, he had fully executed. Yet did he fear men's tongues. As a palliation of the misdeed, he set abroad a statement that Toussaint was plotting against the peace of the island. What [Page 236] was the evidence? A fabrication. Two letters, said to be written by Toussaint, and intercepted, were put into circulation. The fraud has come down to these days; it is so clumsy as to bear its own condemnation on its front. If the authenticity of these letters were ascertained, they prove nothing to Toussaint's disadvantage. Even the most tortuous interpretation could not extract from them a valid suspicion. But their broken and scattered words only show to what extremities their fabricators were driven, in the fear of detection. And so far as their sense can be made out, neither the ideas nor the style corresponds with the warm, energetic, rapid, and figurative manner of Toussaint L'Ouverture. The fabricator was some poor mean creature, who was utterly unable to give to his wretched composition the most superficial mark of that genius which appears in all that we possess of Toussaint's writing or dictation. However, the fragments in some way served their purpose, in turning attention from Leclerc's perfidy to the allegation of evil designs on the part of his victim. Even if the evidence were less worthless than it is, the presumption would be against the Captain-general, who shunned a public investigation, and condemned unheard a man to whom he had solemnly pledged his honour.

The blacks, guided by a simple sense of right and justice, gave no credence to the alleged conspiracy, and saw the blood of innocent men and women shed with alarm and indignation. At the same time, they lost all trust in Leclerc, for had they not seen their Liberator seized and sent away, contrary to the obligations of an oath, the claims of a solemn compact, and the sacred rights of hospitality?

[Page 237] CHAPTER III.

Leclerc tries to rule by creating jealousy and division—Ill-treats the men of colour—Disarms the blacks—An insurrection ensues, and gains head, until it wrests from the violent hands of the general nearly all his possessions—Leclerc dies—Bonaparte resolves to send a new army to Saint Domingo.

As the news of the deportation of Toussaint L'Ouverture spread abroad, secret and deep discontent began to prevail, which threatened disturbance, if not disaster. In vain Leclerc tried to prevent these consequences of his own misdeeds, by a slow concealed tyranny. He created division among the black chiefs by insinuating into their violent natures rivalry, jealousy, and hatred; he set the ambition of one in opposition to the moderation of another; now he brought into contrast this man's fidelity with that man's want of fidelity; mingling adroitly together praises and enticements, favours and disgrace, encouraging and rewarding mutual accusations. Special pains did he take to revive the old animosities between the blacks and the men of colour; animosities which in reality were only a consequence of the difference in the servitude to which they were in common subject. As a result of this Machiavellian policy, many officers of black and of mixed blood were persecuted, imprisoned, or banished to a distance. Of this number was Rigaud, next to Toussaint the most renowned of all. He was arrested in the port of Saint Marc, whither he had been sent as if to take a command. In his indignation, he threw his sword into the sea, to prevent its being sullied by traitors. He was sent to France, and curiously enough, was, as we have seen, cast into the prison which held Toussaint L'Ouverture. Lamartinière, who had displayed the virtues of a champion of liberty behind the walls of Crête-a-Pierrot, was massacred in an ambuscade. Thus was manifested the hatred of the colonists against men whom they could not endure to see in the enjoyment of freedom. That hatred was fostered by the Consul, and by his representative Leclerc. Of special consequence did the Captain-general consider the disarming of the blacks; but the [Page 238] step was one of extreme difficulty. Men, whose passions are excited, and whose future is uncertain, do not easily surrender their arms. Cajolery and mutual distrust were put into action; the result was, that thirty thousand muskets were collected and laid up in the common armoury. But in the midst of the operation, discontent was displayed, menaces were uttered, sedition was fostered, risings took place; the Government was compelled to employ vigour as well as adroitness. Troops were set in movement, blacks who were in subjection were employed against others who were ripe for revolt; some sullenly gave up their arms, others hid them, waiting their opportunity. Ferocious bands were formed, who practised all kinds of atrocities. The disarming succeeded best in the south; in the west it was very partial; the coloured population, distrustful and disquieted, especially since the deportation of Rigaud, betook themselves to the mountains; then most unjust and injudicious severities were exercised; suspicions sufficed for the infliction of death; the scaffolds were loaded with victims of both sexes, and of all ages. Several of the wives of the officers of the seventh colonial brigade were publicly executed. After capturing Belair, Dessalines slaughtered three hundred blacks and men of colour in the vale of the Artibonite, to avenge the death of some European soldiers, massacred within the country under his command. Meanwhile, an impression had been obtaining prevalence that the disarming and other offensive measures were parts of a system intended to issue in the restoration of slavery. Some imprudent colonists, whom experience of evil had not taught anything but revenge, uttered in one of their assemblies the old maxim—"No slavery, no colony." The alarm caused thereby was augmented by news that slavery had been restored in other French dependencies, and that even the slave-trade was resumed. Under the growing fears and distrust, some applied to purchase their freedom. The request was refused by their former owners. "We are then," said mothers of families, with tears in their eyes, "we are then about to fall back into slavery." To prevent the calamity, the blacks made such preparation as they could. Circumstances were in their favour; a malady which had gone far to destroy [Page 239] the army and the fleet; the rainy season, which was at hand, not less baneful to the whites than favourable to the blacks; the asylum of the mountains, where their foes would pursue them almost in vain. Full of fear yet full of courage, they spoke to each other words of exhortation: "Do they expect to find slaves in us? why did they not leave us at large in our forests? Was Africa, our native land, weary of us? Have our rivers been dried up? Did not our flocks, our fields, did not hunting and fishing suffice for our wants? We learnt no other wants but at the price of our liberty; they have deceived us in our simplicity by poisoned gifts. Were not our feet accustomed, unshod, to walk over burning sands; and did not our uncovered heads brave the fires of the torrid zone? Our skin, given by nature to enable us to live near the sun, performed the office of garments fabricated by luxury. Was not the limpid wave of our fountains preferable to the liquors which cause brutal fury? To enjoy the sweet manifestations of friendship, the guileless smile of our children, the caresses of a mother who, during three years, nurtured us with her milk; to trouble neither our own lot nor the lot of others; to pass our life without fear and without desires, as a river of a tranquil and uniform flow—such were the precious advantages of which we have been robbed by our enemies." While thus they inflamed each other by fancy pictures of their ancestral mode of life, they drew a too true and a very painful contrast in adverting to their actual condition. Here a man held forth his arm, mutilated by a barbarous monster; there another pointed to his leg, eaten into by the links of an iron chain; others drew attention to the scars left by the driver's thong; women uncovered their breasts, which showed traces of the branding-iron,—the breasts which had suckled their masters' children. And then, with what pride did they turn to the blessings of freedom! "Heaven, in its pity, has given us a new country in this land of exile, of grief, and of shame shall it be torn from us?"

Soon the standard of revolt was raised. At first the banner was unfurled by obscure men who occasioned little solicitude. But civil wars are pregnant with great leaders. In the [Page 240] mountains of Saint Domingo there were always tribes of untamed Africans, who had thrown off the yoke of slavery. At the head of one of these tribes was Lamour de Rance, an adroit, stern, savage man, half-naked, with epaulettes tied by a cord, for his only token of authority. At home in the mountains, he passed from one to the other with something of the ease of one of their own birds. Toussaint himself had in vain pursued him in those retreats, whose proper inhabitants are wild beasts; that chief acknowledged no other authority than that which nature gave, in no way thinking or caring about monarchy or republicanism. His tender of obedience to the Government had been a matter of mere form. His dress, his manners, his character, his mode of fighting, at the Cape, where he just showed himself, were objects of curiosity and amusement with the French army. A greater insult could not be given than to ask this savage warrior for his arms. Were they not the protectors of his life? He avenged the insult by carrying fire and sword over the Highlands in the vicinity of Port-au-Prince. In the plain of Léogane he reduced to ashes more than a hundred plantations; he carried off the labourers, and inflicted barbarous cruelties on the whites.

The revolt extended. In the north, as well as in the south and the west, it broke out and spread devastation. As reports of these insurrections got abroad at the Cape and Port-au-Prince, consternation increased. News was eagerly sought after, though almost always the source of fresh anxiety. Some reported that they had seen on fire the mountains which overhang Port-au-Prince; others that Lamour de Rance had reduced to ashes the plantations of Léogane. This day brought intelligence that Sans-Souci was in arms at Vallière; the next that Noël had seized Dondon and Sylla Plaisance. "You have heard that Macaya raises the country around Port-de-Paix?" "No; but a band of insurgents is spreading terror in the island of Tortue." More lamentable still were the narratives which some had to give how their brothers, their wives, their children, had been massacred with an incredible refinement of cruelty.

The general alarm was exaggerated by the colonists, who, forgetful of the share they had had in causing it, and that but [Page 241] for them there would have been no conquest of the island, no violation of oaths, no intention of restoring slavery, accused (as is the custom of such men) their destiny, the Government, Heaven, every object but themselves, the real sources of all these evils. "Heaven, then," they said, "has not ceased to persecute us; have we not suffered enough during ten years of exile and misery? Shall we always be driven into flight, or be massacred by our ferocious slaves? Was there ever a similar succession of reverses and misfortunes? Are we not the most unfortunate of men? Our slaves are before our eyes kindling incendiary torches, and twice have we seen our plantations and our towns burned to the ground. Why does not the Government act with decision? Why leave us to certain and speedy destruction?" Then they invoked the aid of the black chiefs who remained attached to their party, and who replied to them only by a fierce silence or by dissimulation. But always allowing themselves to be borne away by vengeance, they surrounded the Captain-general with their pernicious counsels, and he, instead of employing clemency and mildness, made use only of arms and punishments. In the cities scaffolds were raised, which were bathed in the blood of the blacks. They even executed women and children, whose only crime was that they had brothers, fathers, or husbands, among the revolters; they were accused of corresponding with them—the penalty of such intercourse was death. Port-au-Prince, in consternation at the ravages of Lamour de Rance, became the special theatre of executions. All suffered death with intrepidity, calmness, and resignation. The more numerous the executions, the more extensive were the desertions. Instead of terrifying they exasperated; they fed the insurrection, though they intended to suppress it.

While the scaffolds were crowded with victims, Leclerc applied to Dessalines for assistance. He went to the Cape, and renewed his protestations of fidelity and devotedness. Cruel as false, the monster declared that he thirsted for the blood of the revolters. In a moment when his indignation had gained the mastery, and the agitation of his members manifested more rage than even his words, the General-in-chief said to him in transport, "The [Page 242] troops which I expect from France will give me the power of striking a terrible blow." "There shall be," shouted Dessalines, in fury, "a general earthquake!" A Government that stimulates and employs such wretches condemns itself and forfeits its authority. Instead of carrying on the war honourably, Dessalines pretended to entertain feelings in favour of the revolt. By this means it was that he entrapped General Belair.

While Dessalines was subduing mounts Cahos, Leclerc ordered Rochambeau to punish Lamour de Rance; but the troops who went in pursuit of him, saw only vast fields of fire which covered his flight. When circumstances suggested, the barbarians sheltered themselves in the heart of precipitous mountains, which were to them fortifications stronger than any which the art of man ever constructed. All that could be done was to oppose some limit to the ravages of the foe in the west and the south, the frontiers of which two provinces he had laid waste.

At the same time the captain of the expedition, seconded by Christophe and Maurepas, employed all his efforts both to put down the sedition in the Isle of Tortue, and to arrest the progress of the revolt in the north. But Sans-Souci was an African not less agile than Lamour do Rance. He also covered his flight with deserts and flames; he did not, however, fear to try actual combat. Twice he defeated the troops sent against him.

Meanwhile the black generals still attached to the French preserved only a suspected fidelity, and barely concealed their disquietude. Christophe, afraid of being arrested like Toussaint, did not accept Leclerc's invitation to a banquet, until he had directed his troops to be in readiness for a sudden blow. An officer who sat next him at table, took pleasure in filling his glass. Christophe, suspecting an evil design, turned to him in rage, and said, "Dost thou know, thou little white thing, that if I had drunk the wine which thou pouredst out for me, I should have desired to drink thy blood and that of thy general?" These words caused great agitation among the guests. Leclerc reproached Christophe with what he called Toussaint's treason, and commanded the officers of his guard to run to arms. "Vain is it to call your soldiers," the chief replied; "mine are under [Page 243] arms, and with a single word I can make you a prisoner; but, as to my betraying you, learn to know me, I remain subject to you as I was to Toussaint; had he said to me, 'Hurl this island into the sea,' I would have done my best. This is the way I obey or command. The faith of oaths and treaties— security of person—sacred rights of hospitality—has not all been violated by your cruel policy? Prison, banishment, death, are the rewards of those whose blood flows for our liberty. No longer are you around me, friends, soldiers, heroes of our mountains! And thou, Toussaint, the pride of our race, the terror of our enemies—thou whose genius led us from slavery to liberty— thou whose hand adorned peace with lovely virtues— thou whose glory fills the world, they have put thee in irons like the vilest criminal! But what is there in common between you, Captain-general, and Toussaint? Your name came amongst us only as his who turned parricidal arms against the representatives of your country. It is this crime, doubtless, that the Consul wished to reward in giving you the government of Saint Domingo." These were bold words to be spoken at the Governor's table. The guests looked astounded. Leclerc, alarmed in his inmost soul, affected composure.

In truth, the condition of the colony was lamentable. The fever continued its wasting career. The Government every day lost power, while its enemies increased. Suspicion and alarm opened on every hand. This state of things finds a good description in the words of an eyewitness. Thus does General Pamphile de Lacroix speak: "I was invited to the heights of the Cape by General Boudet, whom the General-in-chief was sending to France to acquaint the Government with the true condition of the island. At the house of General Boudet I found Generals Clervaux and Christophe. I asked them the cause of the progress of the insurrection. The latter replied, 'You are a European, and you are young; you have fought merely in the armies of the mother country; you, consequently, cannot have any prejudices regarding slavery. I will therefore speak to you with frankness.

The revolt grows because distrust is at its height. If you had our skin, you would not, perhaps, be so confiding as [Page 244] myself, who am intrusting my only son, Ferdinand, to General Boudet that he may be educated in France. I make no account of the brigands who have given the signal for the insurrection. The danger lies not there; the danger is in the general opinion of the blacks; those of Saint Domingo are frightened because they know the decree of the 30th Floréal, which maintains slavery and the slave-trade in the colonies restored to France by the treaty of Amiens. They are alarmed at seeing the First Consul re-establish the old system in those colonies. They are afraid lest the indiscreet talk that is heard here on all sides should find its way to France, and suggest to the Government the idea of depriving the blacks of Saint Domingo of their liberty.' In order to pique his self-love, I asked him how it was that he, who had so much influence in the south, should not have found troops sufficiently devoted to put Sans-Souci into his hands? His reply struck me: 'If Sans-Souci was a soldier, I might get hold of him; but he is a mean and cruel brigand, who has no scruple to kill whomsoever he suspects; he knows when to fly, and he knows how to cover his flight with the deserts which he leaves behind him. He goes about the affair better than we did at the time of your disembarcation. If, then, instead of fighting, our system of resistance had consisted in flight, and in well alarming the blacks, you would never have been able to overtake us. So said old Toussaint: no one believed him. We possessed arms; the pride of making use of them was our ruin. These new insurgents follow the system of Toussaint; if they persist in it, we shall have difficulty to reduce them.'

"General Christophe urged me not to return that evening to Fort Dauphin; saying, that the revolters having attacked his posts in the plain, were probably informed of my journey. I thanked him; but urging that the danger would be greater to-morrow, I said that I should return as soon as I had seen the General- in-chief. General Leclerc acquainted me with his melancholy situation, congratulating himself in seeing none but bandits among the new chiefs of the insurrection, and added, that in the feeble state of the forces of the mother country, he was [Page 245] glad to find the generals of colour still faithful to France. On my way to Saint Michel, I stopped at General Christophe's, who hearing discharges of fire-arms in the mountains, repeated his request that I would not that evening press on to Fort Dauphin. I persisted in my intention. He then ordered six of his guides to accompany me. 'Bear in mind,' he said to them repeatedly, 'that you are escorting a general whom I esteem and love.'

"We set out. Of a sudden the guides, who led the way with torches, stopped before a detachment of thirty blacks, who had concealed themselves in a ditch. Forthwith one heard the words, 'Halt! stop! halt!' Shots succeeded. The commanding officer meanwhile recognised in Don Diego Polanco, who was with me, an old friend. We were saved. But I had seen reason to believe that the chiefs of the colonial troops and the coloured generals had communications with the insurgents.

"Too frequently did the Europeans speak of the reinforcements captured from France for the blacks not to perceive the need in which we stood of them."

The news of the events which had taken place at Guadaloupe, the maintenance of slavery at Martinique, indiscreet talk, and insinuations from foreigners, fomented distrust in the minds of the black chiefs. The words which the First Consul had addressed to the Abbé Grégoire, at an officeal presentation at the Institute, were repeated in the colony: "From what is taking place in Saint Domingo, I wish the friends of the blacks throughout Europe had their heads covered with mourning crape." The words struck men's imaginations. The minds of the blacks and of the men of colour were at the height of disquietude when the frigate, Cocarde, entered the roads, having on board blacks sent from Guadaloupe; many of them in the night jumped into the sea, swam to shore, and by their reports made the alarm still greater. At the same time, some men of colour, also from Guadaloupe, brought to Saint Domingo information that the slave-trade in that island comprehended their caste. Here were dark presages of what might be expected in Saint Domingo, The fidelity of the chiefs of the Colonial troops was from that hour irrevocably shaken.

[Page 246]General Clervaux, who had recently condemned Charles Belair to death, first threw off the mask by deserting. The evening before, being at Madame Leclerc's, he had said in a fit of passion, "I was free formerly; only to new circumstances do I owe it that I have raised up my reviled colour; but if I fancied that here the restoration of slavery would ever be thought of, that instant I would become a brigand."

Judge, if you can, of the position of Captain-general Leclerc; he knew the danger, he could not prevent it. The crews were not sufficient for the service of the ships. The garrison of the Cape did not comprise more than two hundred Europeans; there were in it fifteen hundred colonial soldiers.

On the night of the 13th-14th of September (1802), Pétion, that coolly audacious chief, threw all into confusion at the Cape, spiked the guns, and disarmed the European cannoniers."*

Two days after, Clervaux and Pétion made an attack on the Cape, but failed to capture it. So well were they received by Brigadier Anhouil that, thinking they were opposed by the fresh troops expected from France, they drew off their forces which, if pressed forward, must have been overwhelming, so superior were they in number to the defenders of the colonial metropolis. At the moment of the attack, Leclerc, as a measure of precaution, sent on board vessels in the harbour, whose crews had been greatly reduced by the fever, detachments of the colonial soldiers who had remained at the Cape. The sailors, panic-struck, cried out, "Let us kill those who may kill us." They fell on the black soldiers, and ruthlessly drowned of them more than a thousand.

Then Christophe, already prepared for defection, and lately standing, to use his phrase, *as a benevolent spectator,* in other words, watching the right moment, joined Clervaux. A few days after Dessalines threw himself into opposition.

The insurrection became general. The entire population was the enemy of France. The mother, the daughter, the child, as well as the father, and the brother, all were soldiers. The woods were their camps, dens their dwellings; the mountains [Page 247] their ramparts; they found their food in the spontaneous products of the earth; they transmuted into arms the instruments of agriculture. Stones hurled from the rocks served them instead of artillery. They threw their whole life into assaults, combats, and ambuscades. A new future was before them. "Death or liberty!" again became their rallying cry. Everywhere the insurgents repulsed, and laid waste the enemies of their freedom, They captured Poit-de-Paix, Gonaïves, Fort Dauphin. In the evacuation of the last place, General de Lacroix was obliged in his extremity to destroy powder and provisions to the value of two millions of francs. Escaping by sea to the Cape, he lost in the short voyage sixty-six sick persons, who were thrown into the sea. The first words which Leclerc addressed to him on landing them were, "General, what have you done? You bring a coloured population four times more numerous than your Eu-

---

*MÉMOIRES, VOL. II. 224, SEQ.

ropeans; you do not know then that they are tigers, serpents, that you bear in your bosom."

Leclerc felt that the colony was escaping out of his hands. Of all his conquests there remained only, in the North, the Cape, and Môle Saint-Nicholas, and in the West, Port-au-Prince, and Saint Marc. But for the colonists, who then appeared with arms in their hands, all was over.

At the prospect the Captain-general was greatly alarmed. He looked everywhere for succour. In his perplexity he sent to an enemy's camp to beg the aid of Christophe, offering him honours and riches. Christophe contented himself with replying, that he was rich and honoured enough in possessing liberty himself, and in securing the liberty of his colour.

Shortly, Christophe put himself at the head of the insurgents, and proceeded to attack the Cape. Then was Leclerc on the land side shut up within the walls of the capital. Scarcely did he possess vessels sufficient for flight.

Such was the condition of Hayti, when, in the first of November, 1802, the Captain-general, worn down by fatigue and pains, and overwhelmed with vexation, disappointment, and despair, breathed his last, as the final result of a sickness which had long threatened to prove fatal. A little before his death he expressed [Page 248] his regret for the errors committed by himself in the government. Regret now utterly vain; errors which had proved disastrous to all the great interests of the colony. Nor less disastrous to France was this iniquitous expedition. Of four-and-thirty thousand warriors, twenty-four thousand had perished, and eight thousand were in the hospitals; scarcely more than two thousand were fit for service.

Amid this thick darkness, and surrounded by these vengeful penalties, the Captain-general passed to a tribunal before which diversities of skin are unknown. Leclerc wanted neither sense nor manners. He possessed an easy eloquence which threw light on the discussions of his council-chamber. But he was little acquainted with the human heart; and was unable to interpret the peculiar character of Africans. In war he was active, uncertain, and presumptuous. Blindly obedient to the wishes of the First Consul, he made peace consist of a complication of troubles, divisions, treachery, and violence. By these deplorable crimes, he was reduced to the state of impotence which has been described. As he had none of the qualities of a great commander, a funeral oration pronounced in his honour before a few soldiers, who had escaped from the fever and the sword, was a mere harmonious assemblage of idle words.

Pauline, Leclerc's wife, affected the marks of extraordinary mourning, but she betrayed appearances by choosing for her companion one of the most handsome men of the army, and returned to her ordinary habits of luxury, pleasure, and voluptuousness. After having had her husband's body embalmed, she crossed the sea to France. When her vessel appeared at Marseilles, the inhabitants at the sight of the Consul's sister, a widow, so young, in tears, manifested their sorrow by decorating the port and the streets with crape and funereal garlands. The tokens of sadness had been commanded, but they had some reality, for many of them had seen her grow up to adolescence within their walls.

In mournful procession she entered Paris. Brothers, sisters, and wives, then shed true tears at the remembrance of sons, brothers, and husbands, whom they had lost in the expedition. [Page 249] Pauline herself let some tears fall when she saw her brother, who embraced her with joy and tenderness. Then she spoke to him eloquently of Saint Domingo as a land of fire, blood, and desolation. The Consul heard her in silence, and said, "Here is all that remains of that fine army—the body of a brother-in-law, of a general, my right arm, a handful of dust; all has perished, all will perish. Fatal conquest! cursed land! perfidious colonists! a wretched slave in revolt! These are the causes of so many evils." He concealed from himself for a moment that he had sent away so many brave warriors that they might not throw their bayonets across the road to the imperial throne, whither he was urged by his impetuous desires.

Soon his mind arose from that dejection, and in the immensity of the future which his genius embraced, he regarded the calamities of Saint Domingo only as an unlucky but useful incident. Had he not thrown into prison Toussaint, the chief and the soul of the revolt? The fever had nearly consumed its fuel; Rochambeau, whose character he knew, would terrify the island into obedience. Those wandering bands of insurgents, without a head, without union, divided among themselves, would desert the mountains to enjoy the pleasures of the cities. Besides, did he not possess the two heads of Saint Domingo, the South and the Spanish territory? Had he no more soldiers, no more ships? Let twenty thousand men fly over the ocean. Thus Bonaparte prepared for the loss of a second army. Blind ambition, reckless of its means, reckless of the misery it occasions! Meanwhile the First Consul deposited Leclerc's corpse amid much pomp in the Panthéon, and erected statues to his memory. The greater the calamities of Hayti, the more he endeavoured to efface the recollection of them by show and pomp, and by the aid of those arts which ought to transmit to posterity the memory only of truly great men.

[Page 250] *CHAPTER IV.*

Rochambeau assumes the command—His character—Voluptuousness, tyranny, and cruelty—Receives large reinforcements—Institutes a system of terror— The insurrection becomes general and irresistible—The French are driven out of the island.

AFTER the death of Leclerc, the command of Hayti passed into the hands of Rochambeau. That General was deformed in body, but of a robust constitution; his manner was hard and severe, though he had a propensity to voluptuousness. In his youth he had, under the eyes of an illustrious father, served the cause of independence in North America. He lacked neither ability nor experience in war. He possessed tender, domestic, and friendly affections. His good qualities would have accompanied him to the tomb, if he had not been called to the government of Saint Domingo. Regarding virtue as both lovely and requisite in private life, he judged it useless and even dangerous in public affairs, as if the laws of eternal justice depended on position and circumstances. Misled by this gross delusion, he feared not to give himself up to acts of violation, spoliation, and cruelty of all kinds. Blaming the tardy and hesitating administration of his predecessor, he resolved to employ all the resources of terror in order to establish his authority.

Masters who had been impoverished by the freedom of the slaves, saw with joy Rochambeau succeed a chief who, according to circumstances, espoused or betrayed their personal interests. But the blacks were disquieted when they knew that he had taken the helm. Independently of the massacre he had committed in the bay of Mancenille, they remembered that when merely a general, he had not scrupled to degrade them with the punishment of the lash; but what caused them greater alarm were some words addressed in a tone of pleasantry, to their wives at a festivity which he had given at Port-au-Prince. "You," he said, "are invited to dance at your interment." A [Page 251] hall hung with black, and lighted up by funeral torches, seemed to them the image of their approaching sanguinary end.

Despotism and sensuality have often been companions. In Rochambeau the one sharpened the appetite for the other, as though greediness of bodily pleasure welcomed the zest arising from the sight of bodily pain. No small part of his time Rochambeau passed at table, or on sofas, with Creole females, worshippers of pleasure, as well as most cruel towards their slaves. They spoke to him constantly of chains, prisons, the scourge and other punishments, in the midst of games, laughter, caresses, and senseless gratifications with which they intoxicated his soul. As his policy inclined him to violence, he willingly allowed himself to be overcome by the fascinations of these women, as well as by irritated proprietors, who continually pointed him to their houses in flames, and their slaves in revolt in the mountains. Thus did he listen only to counsels of hatred enforced by contempt and vice.

The fever had changed the character of the army. The heart of the soldier was worn by regret, fatigued by misfortune, and filled with trouble; no longer had the noise and glitter of arms, encampments, war, and victory, any attractions for him. A bitter and savage melancholy had succeeded to the hilarity and joy of courage and hope. Even officers of rank were seen to disown authority and to favour a revolt, which they judged legitimate. But Rochambeau, who required a blind submission, dismissed those the firmness of whose soul he doubted; thus giving free course to tyranny in order to oppose an effectual remedy to the evils he wished to put down.

Up to this time punishment and violence had been covered with a veil. Toussaint had not been arrested except as a result of a pretended conspiracy; a military tribunal had condemned Charles Belair. Those who had suffered death, had been taken with arms in their hands, or had kept up communications with the insurgents. In truth many women and children were in the number of the victims, but they were at least implicated by some accusation, and it was through fear rather than cruelty that disarmed soldiers had been drowned at [Page 252] the Cape. But from this time there was no longer any study of appearances; law, judges, and tribunals were ceremonies too circuitous and too tardy.

Meanwhile Rochambeau, who received in different detachments fresh troops, to the number of 20, 000 men, sent them under different circumstances against the revolters, whom he drove away from the country around Port-au-Prince, Mole Saint-Nicholas, and the heights which overhung the Cape. As he was most eager to signalize his command by some victory, he retook Fort Dauphin and Port-de-Paix without any memorable action. This was the term of his success. The blacks without regret, abandoned fortresses which to them seemed contemptible in comparison with their rocks. But in the degree in which they were repulsed at one point, they extended towards another, so that they only acquired accessions of strength.

But what was more for their encouragement and advantage, was that they were furnished with arms by English vessels. Rochambeau thought that there was no surer means to repress their ardour than to affright them by some extraordinary punishment.

The sea off the Cape was chosen to be the theatre of an execution, unparalleled in what is called civilized life. For fear that Maurepas, who had gained distinction under Toussaint L'Ouverture, after having embraced the side of France, should join the insurgents, Leclerc had written to him to come by sea, with his family and his troop, to take the command of the Cape, which he destined for him as a reward for his services. No sooner had he arrived than he and his soldiers were seized and disarmed. Rochambeau ordered preparations to be made for a barbarous punishment, in order to put the negro general to death, with his troop, consisting of 400 blacks. It was also put in deliberation whether death should be inflicted on his children, in order to prevent them from rising up to avenge their father.

After having been bound to the mast of a vessel, Maurepas was frightfully insulted. His wife, his children, and his soldiers were brought to be drowned under his eyes. The executioners were astounded when they beheld a father fix his dying eyes by turns on his children, his wife, and his companions in arms, [Page 253] undergoing a violent death; while they, on their part, turned their eyes away from a father, a husband, a general, whose countenance was disfigured by the tortures he was enduring. After being made to contemplate each other's sufferings, they were all tossed into the ocean. They died without complaining, in a manner worthy the champions of liberty. With a reversal of the order of nature, the father died last; he also suffered most.

Thus died Maurepas, whose character was a compound of frankness and severity. Thrice had he repulsed the French at the gorge of Trois-Rivières; he had at once the glory and the misfortune to go over to the French with victorious arms. The elevation of his soul equalled his valour. He preserved a tender feeling for the master whose slave he had been; he caused funeral honours to be paid to that master, and when his grave had been negligently prepared, he throw off his upper garment in order to perform the pious office properly. Among men of his own blood he was a powerful chief. A spirit of order and justice prevailed in his life. His riches, which were considerable, were given up to pillage. It would almost seem as if so much excellence were subjected to so much ignominy, expressly to show that while black men are capable of any virtue, white men are capable of any crime. Certainly, my narrative is replete with instances which, beyond a question, prove that moral as well as mental excellence is independent of the varieties of colour.

REVENGE OF THE FRENCH ON THE BLACKS.

This brutal punishment, preceded by vile perfidy, filled the camps of the insurgents with horror. That horror was augmented when Rochambeau, at the Cape, put to death five hundred prisoners. On the place of execution, and under the eyes of the victims, they dug a large hole for their grave, so that the poor wretches may be said to have been present at their own funeral.

Dessalines burning to avenge Maurepas and his fellow-soldiers, rushed like a lion on the Cape, and, in his impetuous and terrible march, he surrounded and made prisoners a body of Frenchmen, who, at the post called Belair, defended the approach to the city. Then, with branches of trees, that ferocious African raised, under the eyes of Rochambeau, five hundred gibbets, on which he [Page 254] hanged the same number of prisoners. Of these victims of vengeance, the greater number had been the Consul's companions in arms; they had assisted that bad great man to acquire his pretensions to a throne, and for their reward they had been sent out of his way to suffer an ignominious and painful death at the hands of a savage.

Rochambeau, who occupied himself less and less with war, continued to plunge into the delights of the table, and of voluptuousness with courtezans and wives of colonists who never ceased to stimulate his tyranny, and exact from him the restoration of their slaves. Then, while the insurrection, in the name of liberty, made head in the mountains, on the plains suspicion converted everything into crime. If you went abroad, you joined the revolters; if you stayed at home, you were waiting for them; if you manifested joy, you took pleasure in the public calamities; if you appeared sad, you grieved over the reverses of the revolt; if you wrote letters, you corresponded with the enemy; if you talked, you spread sedition; if you were observed to listen, you were a spy; if you failed to salute a white, you insulted a master: bravery was dangerous, weakness was complicity, innocence was stratagem. Interpretations were put on a gesture, a smile, a sigh; silence was accused of sedition, and even thoughts had no asylum in their last refuge, the human heart.

Such is the character of the tyranny which under the slightest pretext and often by mere hazard, threw its toils round a multitude of victims without distinction of age or sex, to effect their ruin. The number of sufferers was greatly augmented, because colonists by a species of rivalry denounced the peaceful slaves of other colonists, so that it became almost the sole business of Rochambeau to order or even to devise punishments; the sea and the land were covered with them. The unfortunate blacks were bound together and then thrown into the sea to perish: if they came up to the surface and made their way to the shore, they were in sport pursued and massacred. The executions were varied: now the blacks were beheaded, now they were dragged down into the depths by the weight of a shot tied to their feet; and now they were stifled by sulphur on ship-board.

[Page 255] Among the number of these victims were female priests, who worshipped African fetish idols. That veneration for the gods of their fathers was punished with death; so little does unbelief guarantee toleration. A French general, touched with compassion at the approaching death of one of these superstitious but well-meaning women, implored that her life might be spared. Rochambeau, taking into his hands the pigmy idols of her worship, said, "How can I save the life of one who worships these!" Yet during the fever these very women had bestowed every attention on sick French soldiers. Unhappy women, their charity had no other recompense than the punishment which is reserved for the vilest crimes. Base ingratitude of the commander! Here, again, on which side is the moral superiority? Oh, civilization, what crimes have been committed in thy name! Ye weak ones, whose "feeble knees" a Christian authority commands Christian men to strengthen (Heb. xii. 12), how have indignities and woes been heaped on your heads, simply because ye were weak, not only by sceptics and scoffers, but even by professed believers in a divine religion!

The numerous executions which began at Cape City soon extended to other places; Port-au-Prince had its salt waters made bloody, and scaffolds were erected and loaded within and without its walls. The hand of tyranny spread terror and death over the shores of the north and the west. As the insurrection became more daring, it was thought that the punishments had not been either numerous enough, violent enough, or various enough. The colonists counselled and encouraged vengeance as if it was their wealth.

All human passions were let loose. Never was such a spectacle of ferocity beheld. The calm, concentrated, impassible revolt which followed the death of Leclerc, had committed only particular acts of revenge; but at the sight of punishments so numerous and so horrible, insurrection roared and raged on all sides. Men, scarcely anything else than barbarians, made the mountains resound with this death song:—

"Open, ye sepulchres of our ancestors; ye dusty bones, shudder;
Vengeance! vengeance t reply the tombs and all nature."

[Page 256] With shouts of joy they ran to battle, and impatient to avenge their colour, they seized the enemies of their liberty, and cast them to the earth to perish. The South was once more on fire.

At the same time, at the Cape, at Fort Dauphin, at Port-de-Paix, at Saint Marc, at Port-au-Prince, and all along the shores, everywhere were whips, crosses, gibbets, funeral piles; and soldiers, colonists, sailors engaged in slaying, strangling, drowning human beings, whose only crime was their refusal to go back into slavery. Some had their bodies lacerated by the scourge; then they were fastened to posts in the vicinity of a marsh, that they might be devoured, half alive, by blood-sucking insects. Others were literally burnt alive, as if they had been martyrs for religion. Death thus appeared before the negro in its two most terrible aspects, extreme slowness and extreme rapidity. Others in greater number perished in the sea or on the scaffold. In the country, trees loaded with flowers and breathing perfumes, served as gallows, as if to put in broad contrast the goodness of God and the vileness of man. Countries created for peace, happiness, and joy, were thus desolated by human passions scarcely less baneful to those who fostered and indulged them than to those against whom they raged.

On the countenance of those who were led to death shone an anticipation of the liberty which they felt was about to grow on a land watered with the blood of their caste. They had the same firmness, the same resignation, the same enthusiasm as distinguished the martyr of the Christian religion. On the gibbets, in the flames, in the midst of tortures scarcely was a sigh to be heard; even the child hardly shed tears. The words "our country," "freedom," breathed quietly from their dying lips. They often encouraged each other to bear death manfully. A black chief named Chevalier, hesitated when he saw the instruments of his punishment. "What!" said his wife, "thou knowest not how sweet it is to die for liberty!" and without allowing herself to be touched by the executioner, she took the rope and ended her days. A mother said to her daughters who were going to execution, "Be glad, you will not be mothers of slaves."

The strength of soul which the blacks showed in their tortures [Page 257] was so surprising, that the whites ascribed the cause to some peculiarity of organization. It was pretended that the fibres of the blacks contracted with so much force that the sufferers became insensible to pain. Thus, by vain suppositions, an effort was made to rob the victims of the glory of their death. If the question was to make them slaves, then they were not men; if the cruellest punishments were to be inflicted on them, then they did not suffer. If they were not men, why make them do the work of men? If they did not suffer, why impose the punishments? Beasts may do the work which was laid on beings who were not men; and sufferings not felt, were inefficacious both as punishments and examples. But when did tyranny lack a pretext, or cruelty lack a palliation? In this case, the pretext and the palliation did but throw the enormity of the injustice into relief.

Ordinary expedients were too tame, or too slow, or not sufficiently efficacious. History was ransacked for others. Children, women, and old men were confined in sacks, and thrown into the sea: it was the punishment of parricides among the Romans. It was ascertained that three centuries before, in that same country, Spaniards had employed dogs to run down the innocent savages. Frenchmen of the nineteenth century rejoiced that they had at their command a resource so effectual, and I must add, so diabolical. Rochambeau, however, sent a vessel to the isle of Cuba to purchase dogs whose nature, under man's training, made them fit for the work of hunting human beings. When this ship appeared at the fort of the Cape, wives of the colonists went to receive them on the shore, and made the air resound with cries of joy; they put garlands on their necks, and strewed their path with flowers. Some degraded themselves so far as to cover those instruments of their vengeance with kisses. To what extravagances does slavery lead! An experiment must be made. In the courtyard of a convent a sort of amphitheatre was erected, which was filled with a multitude panting for negro blood. The victim was bound to a post. The dogs, sharpened by extreme hunger, were no sooner let loose, than they tore the poor wretch pieces. The raging animals disputed with each other the [Page 258] palpitating members, and the ground was dyed with human blood and canine foam. A report spread among the blacks, that at the last groan of that pitiable creature, the heavens opened, and received his soul.

This kind of death, with circumstances more or less frightful, became common, until cruelty, dispensing with all forms, disdainfully cast human beings to the dogs, who were kept in packs near the city; and when the appetite of the animals, satisfied with human flesh and gore, refused any longer to destroy, the sword finished the bloody work: showing that man's passions surpass in atrocity those of wild beasts. Indeed, language failed of terms to describe the crimes which the lust of unjust power perpetrated. New expressions were invented. The drowning of two or three hundred human beings was called "a good haul;" death on a gallows was "a step upwards;" to be torn in pieces by dogs was "to enter the arena." Some executioners gained celebrity; the name of Tombarel long continued to make men shudder. The sea and the rivers were stained with blood. The numbers of victims was so considerable that the inhabitants refused to eat fish, lest they should feed on blood of their own colour.

Many blacks, of whom some had witnessed these atrocities, and others, who, in the confusion, had, by swimming or flight, escaped from the hands of the executioners, went to join the ranks of the insurgents in different places. Often, under the shade of a tree, or under the point of a rock, these fugitives might be seen recounting to their companions the punishment they had witnessed, or suffered. How great soever the cruelty, it was exaggerated in their hyperbolical phraseology. The crowd listened with intense curiosity, silence, and horror; often the narrators were interrupted by questions respecting the fate of a child, or a sister, who had died on the gibbet, or had been tossed into the sea. It these frightful accounts, the auditors shed tears, but they were tears of vengeance. Some shouted, "Shall we go down into our tombs without having avenged them? No! their bones would repulse ours." Others, by gestures and cries, not satisfied with having carried fire and sword [Page 259] over the low lands, stirred each other up to deeds of carnage and devastation. Vengeance of a certain barbaric grandeur burst forth. In listening to one of these narratives, Paul L'Ouverture, the brother of Toussaint, learned, that, without any reason, his wife, who lived at the Cape, in the peace of her own home, had been drowned. He fell into a madness of revenge which grief nourished, and which nothing appeased. He captured, near Fort Dauphin, a shipwrecked vessel, on board of which were thirty French passengers. He took them, and having led them to one of the principal entrances to Cape City, he pitilessly immolated them all to the manes of his innocent wife, taking pains to put on a post an inscription, which stated that the death of a beloved partner had extorted from his grief a vengeance worthy of a proud, loving, and deeply afflicted soul. Truly, indeed, is revenge blind as well as ruthless. Who can describe, who can dare to contemplate the evils of slavery? Sixteen of the bravest generals of Toussaint L'Ouverture, chained by the neck to the rocks of an uninhabited island, breathed their last miserable sigh after wasting away during seventeen days. These abominable cruelties are not wholly without relief. Captains of ships, instead of casting the innocent victims put into their hands for the purpose into the sea, supported them at their own expense, and landed them on some of the neighbouring islands, or on some remote shore of Saint Domingo. None showed more humanity than Mazard, who employed as much zeal in saving victims as others did in destroying them. "I have," he said, "deceived your tyrants; my heart is lacerated to see the land and the sea covered with victims; go into the mountains, rejoin your people, that posterity may learn that savages dragged to servitude have founded a new state; but pity men's passions, and leave your revenge to time, to remorse, to heaven."

All the sea-captains did not act with the same elevation of soul. They did, indeed, save the blacks from death, but their conduct was dictated by a base avarice; they took them and sold them as slaves in some neighbouring island. On one of these occasions, the governor of Porto-Rico made this fine [Page 260] reply: "If they are slaves, I will not purchase them; if they are free men, you have not the right to sell them."

Nor was the army without examples of virtue. There were generals who, indignant at so many cruelties, uttered remonstrances, or disobeyed inhuman commands. Allix, who commanded at Port-au-Prince, refused ten thousand shot intended to be fastened to the feet of victims to freedom. This act of disobedience, which was really a virtue, Rochambeau punished by banishment. Other officers were punished for similar offences. Truly did the forcible eloquence of the Africans characterize the war as "a War of Cannibals."

Suddenly the south, which had been tranquil, awoke at the noise of the punishments which sent from the north and the west corpses to float on its shores. That province was peopled chiefly by men of colour, who possessed great wealth, and who showed themselves less than in other parts, enemies of the whites, with whom, notwithstanding the force of prejudice, they were united by marriage. When they saw that they themselves were not spared any more than the blacks, they ran to arms. The revolt began in the district of Petit-Troux, where, under the pretext of a conspiracy, of which nothing has ever become known, they had drowned Boudet, who had delivered up the fort Bizoton at the attack of Port-au-Prince. That punishment revolted public opinion the more because it involved ingratitiude. The revolt became general as soon as it had been resolved to put to death in the city of Cayes inhabitants of colour, who were in the police service, and who were charged with betraying signs of discontent. But how could punishment be inflicted on so many in silence? Recourse was had to the sea. The men were seized, disarmed, put into a ship, murdered, and thrown by night into the waves. But womanly love could not be blinded. Women, who had heard the voice of the carnage, demanded with tears in their eyes, that the massacre of their brothers and their husbands should not go unpunished. Then there appeared on the stage a new man, named Ferrou. Highly esteemed in peace, he was terrible in war. He was not a barbarian, his vengeance had some dignity. After having raised the country, he ordered all [Page 261] the colonists to be arrested, and to be conducted safe and sound to the village Coteaux, situate not far from the sea where his people had been destroyed. Not expecting clemency, the captives disdained supplication, and prepared for death. Ferrou addressed to them these words full of pride and bitterness: "Cruel whites, you hesitate not to sacrifice to your hate those who in this land are your defenders. Of what use is it that we are allied to you by the sweet and sacred bonds of nature, for our wives are your mothers and daughters? Not fearing the crime of parricide, you imbrue your hands in our blood. From this spot behold that sea in which, during a frightful night, under the pale light of the stars, you drowned a band of our people. What was their crime? To love you and to serve you. The winds and the waves bear back to us their livid bodies. They are brothers, husbands, companions, faithful friends in servitude, in war, in freedom. A just resentment commands us to sacrifice you; but go across that blood-stained sea, and join your own colour; behold in us enemies but not executioners." Ferrou then sent them in a vessel to Cayes, and forthwith made his arrangements for marching against the city.

Informed of this revolt, provoked by imprudent attacks, Laplume precipitately returned from the frontiers of the South, where he was engaged in checking the ravages of the terrible Lamour de Rance. Scarcely had he got back when he discovered the smoke of Ferrou's camp, in the vicinity of Port-au-Prince. He fell on him, and compelled him to retreat into the rugged mountains called La Hotte, whose decomposing rocks, breaking and bursting under men's feet, throw them into their abysses. But Ferrou knew the safe ways. Those he chose, and from them he rushed down to make an irruption into the plains near the town, Petit Goave. The body of troops employed in the defence of that city was in part composed of people of colour, and partly of Frenchmen—the former joined the devastator, the latter took to flight.

In order the more effectually to keep his eye on the insurrection which now covered three provinces, Rochambeau had fixed his residence at Port-au-Prince, still drawing after him a great [Page 262] number of women, with all the equipage of effeminate luxury. As soon as he had learned the disastrous news, he sent Nétervood by sea to recapture the city of Petit Goave. As he did not doubt of success, he gave his lieutenant a pack of hounds partly to pursue the insurgents with, and partly to devour the prisoners. Nétervood hastened on his errand, and made an attack. But the enemy, setting the city on fire, entrenched themselves in a fort, whence they dealt death on their assailants. Nétervood received a mortal wound in the midst of his soldiers, who were fast perishing, being placed between a burning town and a powerful stronghold. Flight by sea was the only resource; and the dogs, in the confusion dispersing abroad, added to the dangers and disgrace of the defeat. Thus Nétervood, eager for peril and combat, lost his life in the flower of his youth, in the dishonourable cause of slavery.

Bands of insurgents, inflamed by victory, occupied the long chains of mountains which run through the southern province. They formed communications one with another, and at their convenience and their pleasure rushed down into the plains in torrents which carried away whatever was before them. Dessalines put himself at the head of that great movement. Two powerful chiefs, Geffrard and Cangé, passed from the north to the south. They joined Ferrou, and in unison hastened across the mountains to ravage the fertile lands of Cavaillon, of Saint Louis, and of Cayes. Then they carried devastation over those of Jérémie.

These events threw consternation into the soul of Rochambeau. The insurrection threatened to pluck out of his hands the southern provinces. He had at first sent six hundred men to Laplume for the defence of Cayes; but that weak supply proving insufficient, he immediately directed toward Jérémie, vessels which were bringing from France a reinforcement of two thousand men. One moiety of these men reached Jérémie, and without delay prepared to set out for their destination. But from the peaks of his rocks Ferrou saw them, watched them, and prepared to cut them to pieces. Scarcely were the French ten miles from Jérémie, when they fell into an ambuscade. After [Page 263] a sanguinary conflict they were routed. A frightful slaughter ensued. The few that escaped, hurried back to Jérémie, where they spread the utmost alarm.

The other moiety who landed at Tiburon, were also taken in an ambuscade, and cut to pieces, near Coteaux. The few who escaped took refuge in Cayes, into which six hundred other soldiers had thrown themselves, who were to have formed a junction with the two defeated divisions.

Wherever the insurrection reigned scaffolds were erected. The cities of Cayes and Jérémie were afflicted with numerous executions, which drew more closely the bonds between the blacks and the coloured population, and more and more secured success to the cause of freedom.

Laplume, seeing that all was lost, embarked for France, where he died, without leaving means for the interment of his remains.

Rochambeau, on the brink of despair, made new efforts to put a stop to the insurrection. He took special pains to withstand the ravages of Dessalines, whom in a proclamation he threatened to flog to death, as the meanest of slaves. Men only laughed at the folly. Nevertheless, he succeeded in protecting from the continual incursions of that brute, the plain Cul-de-Sac, and Mirebalais, which furnished provisions to Port-au-Prince. At the same time he guaranteed the environs of the Cape from the frequent attacks of Christophe.

Meanwhile, Rochambeau experienced increasing difficulties in the low state of his exchequer. He sought remedies in stock-jobbing, and in exactions of all kinds. He drew on the United States bills to a very large amount, which his government refused to honour. He levied large contributions on cities that were half ruined. He imprisoned opulent persons, who obtained their liberation only by paying large sums of money; some had even to give up their property altogether. He attempted to justify these exactions by pleading the necessities of the public service. But he alienated the hearts of those who through interest remained attached to his party, to such a degree, that after having lost a second army, destroyed thousands of poor victims, and wasted much money, he fell into the same state of distress, [Page 264] misery, and abandonment, as that in which Leclerc was a short time before his death; with this difference, that under the latter the south had not been polluted or devastated by insensate passions and internecine war.

Rochambeau's efforts to stay the insurrection were utterly futile. Like a vast conflagration, it extended from the south to the north. If it went out at one point, it blazed up in another. Soon the war changed its seat. Masters on land, the Africans commenced hostilities on the seas, which they carried on the more advantageously because they were protected by the English. In light boats, with the aid of the tide and of oars, they went up and down the rivers, passed from the mountains into the ocean, and from the ocean into the mountains, spreading terror wherever they appeared. They attacked ships, massacred the passengers, and loaded themselves with plunder, which they carried back into their rocky fastnesses. Woe to the French who sailed toward those deadly shores. Two vessels, from Havre and from Nantes, fell into their hands; all on board were slaughtered. As on land so on water, the insurgents could not be reached; they hid their boats in forests; dispersed, re-assembled, defying alike the soldiers and the ships of war; and, almost with impunity, pursued at will their destructive career.

At the sight of an insurrection, which was master both on land and on the sea, Rochambeau was seized with an alarm that he in vain endeavoured to conceal. The Consul, who rewarded success only, was to be feared by a man who was overwhelmed in failure. Of what use so many victims, so many tortures, so many gallows, so many drownings, so many raging hounds? All this serves only to illustrate the strength of the insurrection, and the hopelessness of his cause. The moment that the General-in-chief was no longer in a state to make head against the rebellion, it began to insult and brave him, even in the cities which were his last places of refuge. His temper became more and more disquiet and fierce. The shades of his victims appeared to him in his dreams. Now he cried out that he would make Saint Domingo a vast cemetery, where at least slavery should bear sway. Now he declared he would re-establish [Page 265] liberty, which his cruelties had made only more precious to the inhabitants. Then, but too late, he grew angry at the artifices of the women who had him in their toils, and at the colonists who had misled him by their selfish counsels. Yet did he think it necessary for the security of his troops to continue the system of terror.

A situation so deplorable could no longer be kept concealed from Bonaparte. Rochambeau sent deputies to Paris, who reported that the revolt, somewhat calm after the death of Leclerc, having become active again, had spread from the. north to the south; that Rochambeau, in order to stop its progress, had employed the force of arms and the utmost terror; that these remedies had proved powerless; that the insurrection, animated by a fanatical spirit of liberty, had broken down every embankment; that at the head of the insurrection appeared in the west Dessalines, Christophe in the north, and in the south Ferrou; that after having laid waste the interior, the insurgents ravaged the coasts like pirates; that the colonists were in a state of extreme affliction, at seeing so great an armament overwhelmed with reverses; and that the only means of safety was another expedition.

Another expedition was impossible. Already had a bad feeling arisen between France and England. Soon the latter power declared war against the former. This rupture gave the finishing blow to the French cause in Hayti. On land, Rochambeau's troops were invested by the insurgents. At sea the English were supreme. Nevertheless, the French general maintained himself in his post with an intrepidity which would have done honour to a good cause. The sufferings of the besieged became extreme; rarely have woes equal to theirs been experienced. Rochambeau has related how pitiable was the existence of himself and comrades during this period, when placed between death and life; they appeased their hunger as well as they could by eating their horses, mules, asses, and even their dogs: yes, the very hounds they had obtained, in order to run down their foes.

Things remained in this condition until the middle of November (1803); then the besiegers forced some of the exterior 266 works, and prepared for a new attack. The inflexibility of the French commander was at length obliged to give way. Well did he know that an assault, if made, must succeed, and he feared to fall into the hands of his furious assailants. He offered to capitulate. The offer was accepted. On the 19th of November the articles were signed. The treaty stipulated that the French should evacuate Cap Français at the end of ten days, with all their artillery, ammunition, and magazines; that they should withdraw to their vessels with the honours of war and the guarantee of their private property; that they should leave their sick and wounded in the hospitals, whom the blacks should take care of until they were well, and that then they should be sent to France in neutral vessels. These conditions were more favourable than the invading army had a right to expect. The day on which this convention was signed, the French general sent two officers to treat with the commander of the English squadron for the evacuation of the Cape. The offered conditions were rejected. Others were proposed, which Rochambeau found inadmissible. His refusal had for its ground the hope that the season would soon compel the English to retire from the vicinity of the Cape, and so render his escape possible. Vain expectation. On the 30th of November the standard of the blacks waved over the Cape. Rochambeau felt compelled to throw himself on the mercy of the English. At the moment when the ships in which he had taken refuge were about to be sunk by red-hot balls prepared by the negroes, the ægis of Britain was thrown before them, and a frightful massacre was prevented. A short agreement having been hastily drawn up, Dessalines was informed that the vessels had surrendered to the arms of his Britannic Majesty. Not without difficulty did the vengeful and ferocious Dessalines consent to allow his prey to be thus plucked out of his hands. Shortly, a favourable breeze having sprang up, the three frigates and seventeen small craft that formed the French fleet at the Cape, set sail, according to the convention, under the French flag; then having tacked, they struck their colours and surrendered. The prisoners of war amounted to eight thousand.

[Page 267]Saint Marc, Cayes, Jérémie, Saint Nicholas, the Spanish territory, were successively abandoned by the French. The departure of the troops in the different cities was a painful scene. Families of the colonists and many other persons lacked vessels to fly from the fury of the irritated blacks. Wives and children were separated from their husbands and their fathers. The shores resounded with cries and lamentations. On land these were about to fall into the hands of persons who had been their slaves; on sea those were about to become prisoners to the English. A number entrusted their lives and their fortunes to fragile barks.

As they sailed from the island, Rochambeau, the soldiers, and the colonists saw the tops of the mountains glow with fire. Aforetime the blaze had been kindled for war and devastation; now the blacks lighted up their high lands in token of their joy. Freedom had been wrested out of the hands of their foes. Every heart beat with the thought. The dark past was wholly gone: the future was radiant with hope. "Freedom! freedom!" ran in joyous echoes from mountain-top to mountain-top, till the whole island shouted "Freedom!"

Thus ended this deplorable expedition. In less than two years sixty thousand persons fell: fifteen hundred were officers of superior rank; eight hundred were medical men; three and thirty thousand were soldiers, of whom not a sixth perished in battle. The attempt at subjugation cost the blacks more than twelve thousand men, of whom about four thousand found death at the hands of executioners of various kinds.

CHAPTER V.

Toussaint L'Ouverture, a prisoner in the Jura mountains, appeals in vain to the First Consul, who brings about his death by starvation—Outline of his career and character.

WHILE the cause of independence, forced at length on the aspirations of the natives of Hayti, was advancing with rapid strides amid all the tumult of arms and all the confusion of [Page 268] despotic cruelties, Toussaint L'Ouverture pined away and died in the dark, damp, cold prison of Joux.

The castle of Joux stands on a rock. On one side, the river Doubs flows at its base; on the other, the road of Besançon, leading into Switzerland, gives the stronghold the command of the communications between that country and France. The Château de Joux, built by the Romans, for their convenience in marching into Gaul, extended in the middle ages by the Lords of Joux, purchased by Louis XI., king of France, became under Louis XIV. a state prison. There Mirabeau suffered incarceration, in virtue of a *lettre-de-cachet*.

Toussaint L'Ouverture carried with him into his dungeon the conviction that he was to undergo a trial. In this conviction he sustained his soul. He felt confident of a triumph. His enemies he knew were numerous and powerful. The Consul, he suspected, feared as much as hated him. Yet what was his crime? Had not his authority emanated from the supreme power in France? By that power his position and his acts had been sanctioned. And if even he had offered resistance to the expedition, that opposition had been covered by an act of indemnity proclaimed by Leclerc. If solemn asseverations meant anything, if reiterated oaths retained their validity, he could stand before any tribunal in full confidence of an honourable acquittal.

But the First Consul was far from intending to give his prisoner the advantages of a trial. A trial was a public appeal to the great principles of law and right. In such an issue Bonaparte knew very well who would be the loser. There was another, and, for his purpose, a safer way. Toussaint was advanced in years. He had been accustomed to active pursuits. He was an African, and had lived only in tropical regions. His days, therefore, could be only few, and their number would be much abridged by confinement in a foul prison, under a chilling climate. Could he hold out through the coming winter? If he survived too long—why, other prisoners had passed away secretly; power has its secret strings and its swift remedies.

By a series of cunningly devised and coolly executed measures, [Page 269] Toussaint L'Ouverture was, ere many months, brought to his grave.

All communication with the outer world was forbidden him. He received no news of his wife and family. He passed his days alone with his servant; the presence of that faithful domestic was a support to him. That solace was taken away, and Toussaint was left alone. Yet was he not alone, for God was with him. In prayer his soul rose hourly to his Maker, and he received constantly new effusions of comfort and strength. Religious thoughts and observances carried his mind back to the country for which he had sacrificed everything. There, in imagination, he again saw the chapel where he and his family were wont to worship, and while the hymns of praise went up from its neatly-formed roof, he was drawn into sympathy with the worshippers, and with a moved heart and liquid voice, he joined his thanksgivings with theirs. Day by day, and often hours together, was he on his knees, seeking aid and finding support at the footstool of the heavenly grace, where never mortal knelt in vain.

But time passed on, and there were no signs of the expected trial. Hope sustained against hope began at last to fail. What! was he then a prisoner for life? If so, his sufferings, if severe, would not be long. Already he felt the chills of the nights of autumn—there alone, in that cold, dreary dungeon, no fire, little clothes, no companion, those long pinching nights. And then the winds bean to blow hollow and loud, as if they announced a worse time coming. How soon? How long? The winter must be at hand; his captivity may extend through its whole course; but can it endure, can life stretch out, till the genial breath of spring return?

One day, in the midst of Toussaint's gloomy solitude, a visitor was announced. A visitor! what, if it were his son Isaac! or if not he, perhaps an officer of justice to announce the coming trial, No, it was Cafarelli, aide-de-camp to the First Consul. "O then, here is an order for liberation; the prison doors will fly open, and I shall once more see my wife and children!" Alas, poor heart, no! the man comes from one whose soul is meaner than his own. Bonaparte thinks it a pity the treasures he [Page 270] fancies you have buried should be lost; and though he does not intend to give you your freedom as the price of the disclosure, yet he sends his aide-de-camp to trick you into some kind of confession on the point, which he may turn to account, and in the result of which, if it is enough, he may find some compensation for the millions he has lavished in Saint Domingo in making you his captive.

Toussaint, great in misfortune, gave for his reply, "I have lost something very different from money." Yes, thou hadst lost the liberty thou didst once enjoy; and, peradventure, in a moment of sorrow thou thoughtest thou hadst lost the sacred cause in which thou hadst put thy soul.

But mark this Consul's mean spirit. He had his victim there cooped up only too safely in that humid and infected prison. Still he was unsatisfied. Possibly the prisoner had money. If so, why its hiding-place must be ascertained, ere his lips are sealed in the silence of death. "Go then, Cafarelli, get the secret out of the old negro, and then he may be allowed to die."

Toussaint would not resign himself to his fate without an effort. There was only one tribunal, and that tribunal was a perjured one. Yet an appeal might have some effect. The following letter was therefore written:—

In the dungeon of Fort Joux, this 30 Fructidor, an, xi. (17th September, 1802.)

GENERAL, AND FIRST CONSUL,
"The respect and the submission which I could wish for ever graven on my heart—[here words are wanting, as if obliterated by tears]. If I have sinned in doing my duty, it is contrary to my intentions; if I was wrong in forming the constitution, it was through my great desire to do good; it was through having employed too much zeal, too much self-love, thinking I was pleasing the government under which I was; if the formalities which I ought to have observed were neglected, it was through inattention. I have had the misfortune to incur your wrath, but as to fidelity and probity, I am strong in my conscience, and I dare affirm, that among all the servants of the [Page 271] state no one is more honest than myself. I was one of your soldiers, and the first servant of the Republic in Saint Domingo; but now I am wretched, ruined, dishonoured, a victim of my own services; let your sensibility be moved at my position. You are too great in feeling and too just not to pronounce a judgment as to my destiny. I charge General Cafarelli, your aide-de-camp, to put my report into your hands. I beg you to take it into your best consideration. His honour, his frankness, have forced me to open my heart to him.

"Salutation and respect,

" TOUSSAINT L'OUVERTURE."

Days passed away, and no notice was taken of this epistle. The report of which it speaks was either suppressed or neglected. Dead to pity, Bonaparte watched for the consummation of the villany he had designed. It was customary to allow the commander of the prison five francs (about four shillings) a day for the subsistence of each prisoner; the First Consul wrote that three were sufficient for a revolter. More than sufficient for thy base purpose! Didst thou remember those words when thou didst beat thyself against the bars of thy own cage in the island of St. Helena, complaining daily of a table which, compared with thy allowance to "the first of the blacks," was a banquet of delicacies to "a dinner of herbs!"

While the process of gradual starvation was going forward, its unconscious victim, outraged by his sufferings, wrote this spirited epistle to his persecutor:—

In the dungeon of Fort Joux, this 7 Vendémiaire, an. xi. (20th September, 1802.)

"GENERAL, AND FIRST CONSUL,
"I beg you, in the name of God, in the name of humanity, to cast a favourable eye on my appeal, on my position, and my family; direct your great genius to my conduct, to the manner in which I have served my country, to all the dangers I have run in discharging my duty. I have served my country with fidelity and probity; I have served it with zeal and courage; I have been devoted to the Government under which I was; I [Page 272] have sacrificed my blood, and a part of what I possessed, to serve my country, and in spite of my efforts, all my labours have been in vain. You will permit me, First Consul, to say to you, with all the respect and submission which I owe you, that the Government has been completely deceived in regard to Toussaint L'Ouverture, in regard to one of its most zealous and courageous servants in Saint Domingo. I laboured long to acquire honour and glory from the Government, and to gain the esteem of my fellow-citizens, and I am now, for my reward, crowned with thorns and the most marked ingratitude. I do not deny the faults I may have committed, and for which I beg your pardon. But those faults do not deserve the fourth of the punishment I have received, nor the treatment I have undergone.

"First Consul, it is a misfortune for me that I am not known to you. If you had thoroughly known me while I was at Saint Domingo, you would have done me more justice; my heart is good. I am not learned, I am ignorant; but my father, who is now blind,* showed me the road of virtue and honour, and I am very strong in my conscience in that matter; and if I had not been devoted to the Government, I should not have been here— that is a truth! I am wretched, miserable, a victim of all my services. All my life I

---

* GAOU-GUINOU, TOUSSAINT'S FATHER, DIED IN 1804, HAVING COMPLETELY LOST HIS SIGHT. HE IS SAID TO HAVE LEFT THE WORLD UTTERING CURSES AGAINST WHITE MEN. WRONG AS THIS WAS, HE HAD ONLY TOO MUCH CAUSE FOR HIS WRATH.

have been in active service, and since the revolution of the 10th of August, 1790, 1 have constantly been in the service of my country. Now I am a prisoner, with no power to do anything; sunk in grief, my health is impaired."I have asked you for my freedom that I may labour, that I may gain my subsistence and support my unhappy family. I call on your greatness, on your genius, to pronounce a judgment on my destiny. Let your heart be softened and touched by my position and my misfortunes.

"I salute you, with profound respect,

(Signed) "TOUSSAINT L'OUVERTURE."

Alas! the First Consul has pronounced judgment, and the [Page 273] consequent sentence the prisoner is even now undergoing. That sentence is "slow death!" And then as you, Toussaint, shake with the cold of the northern blast, or sink overcome with sorrow on the moist, foul floor of your cell, or refuse with loathing the unsavoury food; and as your limbs part with their strength, and your heart flutters in debility, and your blood becomes thin and poor, and as you look to the winter's frost, snow, hail, and storm, with a vague distress and dismal forebodings—in each step of the process of slow death the Consul's verdict goes into execution, and another day, or another week, is taken from the brief number that remain to you.

Yet well and noble is it, that under the depression of your unhappy condition, while your heart sinks with the sinking of your ill-supported frame—it is well and noble that you descend to no mean flatteries, that you descend to no unworthy supplications, and that, retaining your own high manly spirit, you protest your innocence, proclaim your services, and charge your enemies with ingratitude.

Toussaint L'Ouverture then began to compose with his own hand a document, in which he entered into a systematic defence of his conduct. This document, the orthography of which is said to have been defective, was couched in correct and sometimes eloquent terms. By permission of the governor of the castle, it was copied by Martial-Besse, then one of his prisoners, and on the 2nd of October it was transmitted to the First Consul. The document contained the following passages:—"General Leclerc employed towards me means which have never been employed towards the greatest enemies. Doubtless, I owe that contempt to my colour; but has that colour prevented me from serving my country with zeal and fidelity? Does the colour of my body injure my honour or my courage? Suppose I was criminal, and that the General-in-Chief had orders to arrest me,—was it needful to employ a hundred carbineers to arrest my wife and children, to tear them from their residence without respect, and without regard for their rank, their sex; without humanity, and without charity? Was it necessary to fire on my plantations, and on my family, to ransack and [Page 274] pillage my property! No! My wife, my children, my household, were under no responsibility,—have no account to render to Government; General Leclerc had not even the right to arrest them. Was that officer afraid of a rival? I compare him to the Roman Senate, that pursued Hannibal even into his retirement. I request that he and I may appear before a tribunal, and that the Government bring forward the whole of my correspondence with him. By that means, my innocence, and all I have done for the Republic, will be seen.

"First Consul, father of all French soldiers, upright judge, defender of the innocent, pronounce a decision as to my destiny: my wound is deep, apply a remedy to it: you are the physician, I rely entirely on your wisdom and skill."

These appeals to the justice, honour, and humanity of the First Consul proved abortive. Bonaparte's mind was made up. His ear, therefore, was closed. Toussaint spoke to a foregone conclusion; his words were encountered by a fixed determination. That determination was so fixed, and so well known, that no one dared to speak in favour of the oppressed and doomed hero. Fear of the supreme magistrate occupied all minds around him, and gave to his will the force of law.

That precipitate and iron mind found the process of slow murder too slow. Solitude, cold, and short fare, were tardy in their operation. Their natural tardiness was not abated by the presence with the captive of his faithful servant. Mars Plaisir was therefore taken away by an express order of the Government. In parting from him, Toussaint L'Ouverture said, "Carry my last farewell to my wife, my children, and my niece. Would I could console thee under this cruel separation: be assured of my friendship and of the remembrance which I shall always preserve of thy services and of thy devotedness."

Toussaint, thou art still the same, still self-forgetful, still mindful of thy wife and family. The disinterested benevolence which made thee a patriot, and which the prospect of supreme power could not bribe into subjection, remains unchilled by the cold of the Jura mountains, and unsuppressed by bodily weakness, and unperverted by ingratitude and perfidy.

[Page 275]Mars Plaisir was loaded with chains and sent to Nantes, where he was put in prison. But unwelcome truths make their way through bars and walls, therefore was the good servant specially guarded and watched, lest, before his master's demise, he should disclose facts that might prove troublesome, or set in motion instruments that might traverse the designs of the tyrant.

The progress made in Hayti by the assertors of the national independence, kept Bonaparte in a constant state of solicitude. He could not conceal from himself that the escape of Toussaint from his dungeon was a possible event. He was well aware that his reappearance in Saint Domingo would make the reduction of the inhabitants impossible. Nay, the mere knowledge of his being still alive, while it encouraged the hope of his yet taking the lead of the soldiers of independence, served to keep up the courage of the insurgents, and to augment the difficulties of Rochambeau. His death, therefore, seemed to Bonaparte urgently necessary. Affairs were hurrying to a crisis in the West Indies. A blow must be struck. The trunk of the insurrection, the First Consul had it in his power to pluck up and destroy: at least, so he thought. Therefore the order went forth, "Cut it down: root it up." The manner was worthy of the deed.

The governor of the castle was chosen for the perpetration of the crime. Scarcely was he a man for the work. He had scruples of conscience. But nothing short of plenary obedience would be accepted. Besides, it was not a question of the dagger or the bowl. All that was wanted was a more decided system of privation. And that system he scarcely needed to work actively. When a prisoner is kept in close confinement, and must be got rid of, you have only to reduce his means of subsistence until death ensues as a matter of course. And if the process is too slow, it may be accelerated by a little well-timed neglect. To an attenuated and famished frame, the want of nutrition for a few days brings certain death. Let the ordinary pittance of supply then be forgotten, and your end is gained. And who shall dare to call an act of oblivion by the foul and offensive name of murder?

[Page 276]The governor twice took a journey to Neufchâtel, in Switzerland. The first time he entrusted the keys of Toussaint's cell to Captain Colomier, whom he appointed to fill his place in his absence. Colomier visited the noble prisoner, who spoke to him modestly of his own glory, but with indignation of the design imputed to him of having wished to deliver Saint

Domingo up to the English. His emaciated and feeble hands were engaged in writing a paper intended to disprove that groundless charge. The officer found Toussaint in a state of almost absolute privation. A little meal was his only food, and that he had to prepare himself in a small earthen jug. But Colomier had a heart: he pitied the destitution of a man who had had at his command the opulence of Saint Domingo. His humanity made him unfit for his office, and ascertaining that the captive accounted the want of coffee among his chief privations, he ventured at his own risk to furnish a small supply.

When the governor returned, he found that Toussaint L'Ouverture was still alive. In a short time he took a second journey to the same town, and for the same purpose; and as he suspected that Colomier's good nature had interfered with his duty, he said to him, on leaving, with a disquieted countenance, "I entrust to you the guardianship of the castle; but this time I do not give you the keys of the dungeons: the prisoners have no need of anything."

The governor returned on the fourth day. Toussaint was no more. He ascertained the fact. Yes, there he is—dead; no doubt whatever—dead and cold. He has died of inanition. And see, if you have courage to look on so horrible a sight—the rats have gnawed his feet!

The work is done—the crime is perpetrated. Bonaparte's will *is* law: his word is death. But murder is a word of evil sound. The world, with all its depravity, has a moral feeling, and that moral feeling it is impolitic to outrage. A veil must be thrown over the assassination.

"Toussaint is dead;"—"how came he by his death?"

The governor, on learning that his captive had breathed his last, carried some provisions into his dungeon. Who now can [Page 277] say that Toussaint had been starved to death? He died in the midst of abundance. This was the governor's own plea. But he deprived that plea of its effect by his eagerness to obtrude and make the most of it; and he betrayed his guilt by his looks and manner. Yes, he was distressed at Toussaint's sudden departure,—he bewailed the event. But hypocrisy ever overacts its part. Besides, the governor was not thoroughly depraved; and that which he would have men regard as the sadness of a virtuous heart in mourning, they saw to be the ragings of a conscience smitten with a sense of guilt; his checks put on a livid paleness; his steps were hasty and uncertain; his eyes were wild. Yes, here is a man deeply suffering under the stings of remorse. His nervous and agitated efforts to make it clear —very clear, beyond a question—that Toussaint has died of a natural cause, demonstrates that he knows more than he dares reveal, and has contracted a guilt that he would fain conceal even from his own eyes. But the keys of the dungeon were in his possession; and the words, "The prisoners want nothing," and the food recently carried thither; these facts—known to our authority,* and known to Captain Colomier, and known to other inmates of the castle—declare that murder has been committed. Yes, now we see why Mars Plaisir has been sent away. And now we see why this remote, solitary, wild and freezing prison has been chosen. And now we see why Toussaint L'Ouverture was entrapped. The series of crimes is consummated.

Still the question returns, "What will be the opinion of the world?" Medical men were called in. The head was opened; the brain was scrutinized. "It is apoplexy," the authorities said; and apoplexy was set down in the formal report made as to the cause of Toussaint's death. Possibly so; but what produced the apoplexy? Ask Captain Colomier—ask the mayor of the district. They were both required to state that death had taken place by some cause different from hunger, and they both refused!

[Page 278] Yes; what was the opinion of the world? The world believed and declared that there had been foul play. That belief gained prevalence in Saint Domingo, and added fuel to the flames of wrath which, without this new brand, burned with intensest fierceness, consuming the French army, and making their longer stay in the island an impossibility.

Thus, in the beginning of April, in the year 1803, died Toussaint L'Ouverture. A grandson of an African king, he passed the greater number of his days in slavery, and rose to be a soldier, a general, a governor. He possessed a rare genius, the efficiency of which was augmented by an unusual power of self-concealment. His life lay in thought and in action rather than in words. Self-contained, he was also self-sufficing. Though he disdained not the advice of others, he was in the main his own council-board. With an intense concentration of vitality in his own soul, he threw into his outer life a power and an energy which armed one man with the power of thousands, and made him great alike in the command of others and in the command of himself. He was created for government by the hand of Nature. That strength of soul and self-reliance which made him fit to rule, also

---

* See particularly Métral's "Histoire de l'Expédition des Français à Saint Domingue," p. 201, seq.

gave him subjects for his sway. Hence it was that he could not remain in the herd of his fellow slaves. Rise he must, and rise he did; first to humble offices, then to the command of a regiment, and then to the command of "the armies of Saint Domingo."

To the qualities which make an illustrious general and statesman, there were added in Toussaint's soul, the milder virtues that form the strength and the ornament of domestic life. Great as he was in the field and in the cabinet, scarcely less great and more estimable was he as a husband and a father. There his excellences shone without a shade. The sacrifice of his sons to the duty which he owed to his country, only illustrates the intensity of a patriotism which could extort so precious a possession from a father's hands.

But he had learned his duty from the lips of One who taught men to make the love of children and parents subordinate to the love of himself; and assured that he had in some special [Page 279] manner been called and sent to set the captive free, he, in a native benevolence of character which the Gospel enriched, strengthened, and directed, concentrated all the fine endowments of his soul on the great work of negro emancipation in the island of his birth.

His mind appeared in his countenance and his manner, yet only as if under a veil. His looks were noble and dignified, rather than refined;* his eyes, darting fire, told of the burning elements of his soul. Though little aided by what is called education, he, in the potency of his mind, bent and moulded language to his thoughts, and ruled the minds of others by an eloquence which was no less concise than simple, manly, and full of imagery. As with other men of ardent genius, he fused ideas into proverbs, and put into circulation sayings that are reported to be still current in his native land.But after all, he was greater in deed than he was in word. Vast was the influence which he acquired by the mere force of his silent example. His very name became a tower of strength to his friends and a terror to his foes. Hence his presence was so impressive, that none approached him without fear, nor left him without emotion.

If the world has reason to thank God for great men, with special gratitude should we acknowledge the divine goodness in raising up Toussaint

---

* All the likenesses of Toussaint L'Ouverture which I have seen except one, have the disadvantage of being in profile.

L'Ouverture. Among the privileged races of the earth, the roll of patriots, legislators, and heroes, is long and well filled. As yet there is but one Toussaint L'Ouverture. Yet how many of the highest qualities of our nature did that one unite in himself. But his best claim to our respect and admiration, consists in the entire devotion of his varied and lofty powers to the redemption of his colour from degrading bondage, and its elevation into the full stature of perfect manhood.

I do not intend to paint the Haytian patriot as a perfect man. Moral perfection once appeared on earth. It is not likely to [Page 280] have appeared a second time among the slaves of Hayti. Toussaint has been accused of harshness and cruelty. I am not prepared to affirm that the charges are without foundation. But it is equally true that his enemies have done their utmost to point out stains in his character. Unfortunately, the means for a thorough investigation are wholly wanting. It has also been said that he was an adept at dissimulation. But secrecy in his circumstances was both needful and virtuous; and if the study of secrecy on his part was undue, let the failing be set down against him at its full value. It has even been intimated that when in power he yielded to the fascinations of the accomplished creole women of the Cape. But the intimation, faint and indirect as it is, rests on no solid grounds. In truth, it was impossible that a man of the origin and aims of Toussaint L'Ouverture should have escaped the shafts of calumny, and, after all due abatements are made, enough of excellence remains to command our admiration and win our esteem.

While, however, the world has seen but one Toussaint L'Ouverture, this history sets forth many black men who were possessed of great faculties, and accomplished great deeds. And though the instance of their chief only shows what an elevation men with a black skin may possibly attain, there are in the general tenour of this narrative proofs very numerous and irrefragable, that in the ordinary powers and virtues which form the texture and the ornament of civilized life, an African origin and negro blood involve no essential disqualification.

Very clear, certainly, has it appeared that whether in its rights, its wrongs, its penalties, or its rewards, Justice—the ever-living daughter of the eternal God, and the ever-present and ever-active administratrix of Divine Providence—knows nothing whatever of the distinctions, the prejudices, the dislikes, or the preferences of colour. An injury done to a European ceases not to be an injury when the sufferer is an African. Nor are breakers of God's laws punished with less severity within the tropics than they are in the temperate zones. Slavery, which is the essence and the concentration of injustice—Slavery, which from its foundation to its top-stone is one huge and frightful accumulation [Page 281] of wrong of wrongs the hugest and the direst—Slavery, which is the worst form of treachery to man and treason against God, entails vengeance the most terrible, the most awful; vengeance not less sure than dreadful. Alas! that in the scourge the innocent should suffer as well as the guilty. The thought would sink the mind in grief, were it not attended by the conviction that "the hour cometh" when the righteous shall shine as stars in the firmament for ever and ever.

The family of Toussaint L'Ouverture received the news of his death with the deepest grief. They wept and wailed, and refused to be comforted because he was not.

Under a pretence that they contemplated escape, those innocent persons were transferred from Bayonne to Agen, where they found friends worthy of themselves.

When Saint Jean L'Ouverture heard of his father's death, he declared that he should not long survive him. The saying was too true. The effects of the climate on a naturally weak constitution brought him to the tomb ere he had quitted the period of youth. His death almost caused the death of his female cousin, from whom he received in his sickness the most tender and vigilant cares.

Shortly after, the family succeeded in obtaining the favour that Placide L'Ouverture should quit his place of detention and reside with them at Agen.

Madame Toussaint L'Ouverture, who was beloved and revered alike by her husband and her children, survived that husband and her youngest son for several years, without being able to overcome the grief which their loss occasioned, and which was so deep and constant as to undermine her faculties. She died, in 1816, in the arms of her sons, Placide and Isaac L'Ouverture.

The history of L'Ouverture placed by the side of the history of Bonaparte, presents a number of striking parallels. Both born in a humble position, they raised themselves to the height of power by the force of their genius and the intense energy of their character. Both gained renown in legislation and government as well as in war. Both fell the moment they had [Page 282] attained supreme authority. Both were betrayed by pretended friends, and delivered into the hands of embittered foes. Both were severed from their families. Both finished their lives on a barren rock.

The parallels have their contrasts. Toussaint L'Ouverture fought for liberty; Bonaparte fought for himself. Toussaint L'Ouverture gained fame and power, by leading an oppressed and injured race to the successful vindication of their rights; Bonaparte made himself a name and acquired a sceptre by supplanting liberty and destroying nationalities, in order to substitute his own illegitimate despotism. The fall of Toussaint L'Ouverture was a voluntary retirement from power, accompanied by a voluntary renunciation of authority, under circumstances which seemed to guarantee that freedom the attainment of which had been the sole object of his efforts; the fall of Bonaparte was the forced abdication of a throne which was regarded as a European nuisance, and descent from which was a virtual acknowledgment that he had utterly failed in the purposes of his life. In the treachery which they underwent, on one side, Toussaint L'Ouverture was the victim and Bonaparte the seducer; and on the other side, the former suffered from those who had been his enemies, the latter from those who in profession were his constant friends. And in the rupture of their domestic ties, Bonaparte was the injurer, Toussaint L'Ouverture the injured.

Nor is it easy to bring one's mind to the conclusion, that retribution was wholly absent in the facts to which allusion has just been made. The punishment is too like the crime to be regarded as accidental. Toussaint's domestic bereavement was requited by Bonaparte's domestic sorrows. The drear solitude of the castle of Joux was experienced over again at Saint Helena by him who inflicted the penalty. Strange to say, it was a friend of the negroes—namely, Admiral Maitland—that conducted the Corsican to his prison. And as if to make the correspondence the more complete, and the retribution the more potent, by an exchange of extreme localities, the man of the temperate regions was transferred to the tropics, to atone for his [Page 283] crime in transferring the man of the tropics to the killing frosts of the temperate regions. Resembling each other in several points of their calamities and pains, the two differed in that which is the dividing line between the happy and the wretched; for while, with Bonaparte, God was a name, with Toussaint L'Ouverture, God was at once the sole reality and the sovereign good.*

---

* See Note C, at the end.

BOOK IV.

FROM THE EVACUATION OF HAYTI BY THE FRENCH TO THE PRESENT TIME.

CHAPTER I.

Dessalines promises safety to the Whites, but bitterly persecutes them—Becomes Emperor of Hayti—Sanctions a wise constitution—Yields to vice and folly, and is dethroned and slain.

THE retirement of the French forces from the island of Saint Domingo, shortly after the death of Toussaint L'Ouverture, assured the natives of the essential goodness of their cause, and the genuine vigour of their strength. Aforetime, they had been making experiments; now, success gave them a consciousness of superiority. Even when robbed of their national hero, they had destroyed their foe and achieved their independence. From that moment, the blacks, who formed the bulk of the inhabitants, believed themselves invincible. Whatever Europeans were in Europe, in Saint Domingo they were clearly inferior to Africans. There had been a great trial of strength, and white tyranny, having been worsted in the encounter, must submit to its own law—the law of the stronger. In their hyperbolical language the blacks asked, "What fleet, what army, what warriors can in future bring us slavery? At their approach, should we not behold the form of a giant, the angry genius of our native land, raise the tempests with his powerful hand, and break in pieces and scatter their ships? The laws of nature obey his puissant voice; the plague, conflagration, prison, and famine, follow in his footsteps; but without the aid of this genius, whose arms are the elements, have we not souls hardened in adversity, and now [Page 285] more than ever panting for combat, for peril, for glory. The empire of our liberty can only grow, rise, and become grand."

But when they cast their eyes around them, they fall into melancholy, and waste away in regrets. Here is one who bewails the loss of a beloved wife that perished on the scaffold; there, another who cannot put away from his heart the image of a sister whom he saw thrown into the flames. Mothers weep for their infants crushed in their cradles. This man points out the tree which served as a gibbet for his father; another indicates the spot which is still stained with the gore of relatives, torn in pieces by half-starved hounds. One cries, "There is the sea, where I saw a whole band of our brothers perish." His companion attempts to calculate the victims, and makes their number amount to more than twenty thousand. On all sides, they see the perishing limbs or the dry bones of those with whom they own a community of nature: horrible images, which nourish in their souls a vengeance that, whether silent or clamorous, is alike fearful.

But if the past afflicts them, they are consoled by the future. Are they not about to offer to the world the singular spectacle of savages torn from the deserts of Africa, forming a new and well-organized state, which will dictate laws, promote civilizaton, receive ambassadors, form treaties, and make its flag respected by nations both near and remote? Thus, out of the bosom of Slavery would there arise a people, free, independent, and happy. Their origin, their adversity, their elevation, were unexampled in history. They had before them a great destiny. Besides, in their emancipation there was a guarantee of the emancipation of their race. Hayti free, the West Indies would not long remain in bondage; and when once the islands sang aloud in the joy of liberty, the Continent, at no very distant day, would send back the sounds in reverberations increased a hundredfold.

The colonists too, again, contemplated their condition; they were ruined, yet would they not relinquish hope. They were in exile, but they would not forego their desire to return. What! should slaves rule a land which their own ancestors had fertilized and civilized? Should slaves reap the harvests of wealth which [Page 286] they themselves had once enjoyed, and which of right belonged to them? Could France be insensible to the treasures of that mine whence it had already drawn so much wealth? Will not the Consul put forth his mighty hand, and resume possessions which are sufficient to enrich him? And surely they themselves had claims on his considerations. "See," they exclaimed—"see Saint Domingo a second time watered with our blood—with our blood, shed by the hands of slaves—the hands of our own slaves; our cities, our plantations, our edifices, are only heaps of ruins; and we ourselves, once the wealthiest of men, are houseless wanderers, condemned to live on charity." With Bonaparte, to be weak was to be in the wrong, and complaints were a kind of personal offence; the colonists had lost the game, and consequently were unworthy of attention: he listened to them no longer.

Saint Domingo, however, after having been the theatre of so many tragic scenes, was scarcely more than a desert inhabited by hordes of blacks, simple, ignorant, semi-barbarous, who knew the extremes of slavery and freedom; they had learnt much, because they had suffered much; they still preserved the youthful vigour of nature; but they had a task before them of the utmost difficulty, in comparison with which their strength was weakness indeed. Yet had they grounds of confidence. Among those grounds, their liberty was the chief; a liberty not bestowed, but acquired; a liberty fought for and paid for; a liberty, therefore, replete no less with strength than instruction. That liberty they owed to Toussaint L'Ouverture, who thus appeared to them as the founder of the state as well as the vindicator of their liberties. While fighting for the national freedom, and laying the foundations of the new policy, Toussaint had begun to form the men of his colour to the arts of peace, and to prepare them for developing the advantages which he put into their hands. Beneficial results would be slow to come, yet come they would. Under the fostering wings of liberty, and under the impulses of the undying mind and example of the national hero and patriot, letters and the arts, commerce and opulence, civilization and religion, would revive, and grow, and in time flourish.

After the departure of Rochambeau and the forces under his [Page 287] command, there remained in the island a number of Frenchmen, at Cape François and other towns. In part, their continued residence in Saint Domingo arose from their inability to find accommodation in the vessels which received their retiring fellow-countrymen. Some were not in haste to remove, hoping that they might by delay dispose of their property to a less disadvantage than was possible in the hurry of a compulsory and immediate departure. Others, again, were detained by a regard to domestic alliances into which they had entered.

It appears somewhat strange that any who had witnessed the tragic scenes of the recent terrible struggle, and who knew how the sensitive nature of the blacks made them prone to sudden and violent outbursts of vengeance, should have dared to risk their lives by tarrying on the scene of conflict. Few in number, and without organization, they were exposed to all the chances of reprisals, which lay in the sense of accumulated injuries and the consciousness of overwhelming numbers. At first, the political horizon was calm, and inspired them with some degree of hope or even confidence; but the promise of safety soon vanished. A proclamation, however, was put forth which was of favourable augury; it ran thus:

"IN THE NAME OF THE BLACKS, AND THE MEN OF COLOUR:

"The independence of Saint Domingo is proclaimed. Restored to our primitive dignity, we have secured our rights; we swear never to cede them to any power in the world. The frightful veil of prejudice is torn in pieces; let it remain so for ever. Woe to him who may wish to collect the blood-stained tatters.

You, proprietors of Saint Domingo, who are wandering in foreign countries, while we proclaim our independence, we in no-way forbid you, whosoever you are, to return to your properties. Far from us be such an idea! We are not ignorant that many among you have renounced their old errors, abjured the injustice of their exorbitant pretensions, and recognised the justice of the cause for which, during twelve years, we have shed our [Page 288] blood. We will treat as brethren the men who do us this justice; let them for ever reckon on our esteem and our friendship; let them return and dwell amongst us! May the God who protects us, the God of free men, prevent us from turning against them our triumphant arms. As to those who, possessed by senseless pride, interested slaves of guilty pretension, are blind enough to think themselves the essence of human nature, and declare that heaven made them to be our masters and our tyrants—let them never approach the land of Saint Domingo; if they come hither, they will find chains and banishment. Let them remain where they are; and tormented by a too well-merited wretchedness, and loaded with the disdain of the just men whom they have too long mocked at, let them continue their existence unpitied and unnoticed.

"We have sworn to show no mercy to those who may dare to speak to us of slavery. We shall be inexorable, perhaps cruel toward the troops, who, forgetting the object for which from 1789 they have not ceased to fight, may come from Europe to inflict on us servitude and death; nothing will be too dear to be sacrificed, nothing impossible to be executed, by men from whom it may be wished to snatch the first of all blessings. Should we be obliged to shed rivers of blood, should we, to preserve our freedom, be compelled to set on fire seven-eighths of the globe, we shall be pronounced innocent before the tribunal of Providence, who has not created men to see them groan under a yoke so oppressive and so ignominious.

"If in the different commotions which have taken place, some residents of whom we have no reason to complain, have been victims of the cruelty of soldiers or of planters, rendered by their past evils too blind to be capable of distinguishing good and humane proprietors from those who were insensible and cruel, we, with all generous minds, bewail their deplorable lot, and we declare, in face of the universe, whatever evilly-disposed persons may say, that those murders have been committed contrary to tile desires of our hearts. It was impossible, especially in the crisis through which the colony has gone, to prevent or to stop those horrors. Those who have the slightest knowledge of [Page 289] history, are aware that a people, when a prey to civil discord, even were it the most cultivated on earth, runs into excesses of all kinds, and that the authority of chiefs, too little respected in times of revolution, cannot punish all the guilty without continually creating new difficulties. But the Aurora of peace enables us to descry the light of a less stormy future. Now that the calm of victory has succeeded to the troubles of a terrible war, everything in Saint Domingo will take a new appearance, and henceforth its government will be the government of justice.

"Given at the Head-Quarters, Fort Dauphin, 22nd Nov. 1803.

(Signed) "DESSALINES. "CHRISTOPHE. "CLERVAUX."

These words were subscribed by the two great negro-chiefs and a powerful mulatto leader, men with some exceptions worthy of the sacred cause of which Toussaint L'Ouverture was the originator. Happy for that cause and for the island, had the spirit of this proclamation been observed. But Dessalines was by nature cruel. The gradual means of a peaceful policy were regarded by him as so many hindrances in his way. As slaves make the worst of tyrants, so Dessalines, who began life in the lowest condition of servitude, now that he had attained unbounded power, proved the most violent and the most unsparing of despots. And as in civil commotions the most depraved and the most daring snatch the lead from moderate and virtuous men, so Dessalines speedily set at nought Christophe and Clervaux, and entered on a sanguinary and destructive career, in which his soul had peculiar delight.

There were two special reasons which dictated the mild and just tenour of the preceding document. The population had been thinned by the ravages of war. The ranks of the army required to be recruited. Only in the possession of a strong military force could the rulers of the island feel completely secure. It was consequently important to check emigration, and procure the return of natives who had settled in the neighbouring islands and on the American continent. In order to augment his forces, [Page 290] Dessalines offered to give to the captains of American vessels the sum of forty dollars for every black or man of colour, whom they should land on the shores of Saint Domingo. If such a step looks like that purchase of men on which rests the servitude so strongly condemned in the proclamation, the offer which Dessalines among other commercial advantages made to Great Britain, namely, the exclusive possession of the slave-trade in the island, shows how little that half-savage understood the principles on which the freedom of the country reposed, and how prepared he was to augment his ranks by any means within his reach. Under the rule of one so ignorant and so violent, a pacific settlement of the disturbed, and to some extent conflicting interests of the island, was in no way to be expected.

Having, however, wrested their liberty out of the hands of its assailants, the blacks took such measures as were in their power for entering with advantage on their new and perilous career. The very name of the island was offensive to them. The designation, Saint Domingo, as given by white men, was a badge and a memento of the slavery out of which they had fought their way. The original name was still current among the native population in its more sequestered localities, and passing from mouth to mouth, was treasured in the hearts of thousands as a precious remnant of bygone and happy days. With that name old historic memories were connected, and family pride made that name a part of its own rude heraldry. Consequently one of the earliest determinations on the part of the blacks, was to revive the appellation of Hayti. The change was as politic as it was becoming. Under this favourite designation, on the 1st of January, 1804, the island solemnly assumed sovereign power. In the name of the people of Hayti, the generals and commanders of the army signed and promulgated a formal declaration of independence. That declaration contained an express renunciation of the authority of France. The subscribers swore one to the other to posterity, and to the world, that they would die rather than submit to European domination.

The solemn act was in every way proper and praiseworthy. But who was to be at the head of the new commonwealth? That [Page 291] the great actors on the occasion were military men, was more to be regretted than blamed in a people whose army had won liberty by their swords, and who were totally untrained to the procedures, usages, and authority of civil society. But lamentable was it that all those brave men should be willing or should be compelled to bend the knee to the ruffian spirit of Dessalines. Jean-Jacques Dessalines, however, was appointed Governor-general for life. Still more, the island just redeemed from bondage, even while proclaiming liberty, took to itself a new master, and gave to that ferocious soldier the power to establish laws, to declare war, to make peace, and even to appoint his successor. Little need we wonder if forthwith we find this Governor-general offering to our eyes the prototype of the President of the French Republic, who, from bloodshed and tyranny, has recently vaulted into an imperial throne. In one respect, history is only a series of repetitions. Ignorance, passion, and blind self-interest have ever been the prolific parents of servitude and despotism.

Having, by a show of mildness, gained the advantage which he sought, of securing time for affairs to settle, for the increase of his forces, and the acquisition of power, Dessalines, a few weeks after his appointment as Governor for life, threw aside the mask, and raised the cry of "Hayti for the Haytians," thinking by proscribing foreigners he should most effectually consolidate his own authority. For the furtherance of his self-aggrandisement, he published a proclamation, in which he said—

"Is it enough to have driven from our country the barbarians, who for ages have covered it with blood? It is not sufficient to have put down the successive factions who, in turn, have sported with the phantom of liberty which France put before their eyes. It has become necessary, by a final act of national authority, to secure the permanent empire of liberty in this country, which is our patrimony and our conquest. It is necessary to remove from that inhuman government which hitherto has held our minds in a state of humiliating torpor, every hope of being able again to make us slaves. The generals who led your forces against the tyranny, have not done enough. The [Page 292] French name still prevails in all places. Every object recalls the cruelties of that barbarous people. Our laws, our customs, our cities—in a word, everything bears the impress of France. What do I say? There yet remain Frenchmen in our island. For fourteen years, victims of our credulity and our toleration; conquered, not by the French armies, but by the artificial eloquence of the proclamations of their agents, when shall we be tired of breathing the same air as they? What have we in common with that sanguinary people? Their cruelty, compared with our moderation, their colour compared with our colour, the extent of ocean which separates us, our avenging climate—everything shows that they are not our brethren; that they will never be so; and if they find an asylum amongst us, they will become the instigators of troubles and divisions. Citizens—men, women, children, and old men, cast your eyes around you over this island; seek for your wives, your husbands, your brothers, your sisters—what do I say? seek for your infants, your infants at the breast, what has become of them? Instead of those interesting victims, the eye sees only their assassins; tigers, still covered with blood, whose frightful presence reproaches you with your insensibility, and with your slowness to punish them. Why do you delay to appease their shades? Do you hope that your remains will rest in peace by the side of those of your fathers, if you do not banish tyranny? Will you go down into your graves without having avenged them? Their bones will repel yours. And you, brave race, intrepid warriors, who, insensible to your private ills, have given life to freedom, by shedding your blood, know that you have done nothing, if you do not give to the world a terrible but just example of the vengeance which ought to be exerted by a brave people that has recovered its liberty, and is resolved to maintain it. Let us astound those who would dare to try to rob us of it again; let us begin with the French; let them tremble in approaching our shores, if not at the recital of the cruelties which they have committed, at least at the terrible resolution we are about to form, to devote to death every Frenchman who shall dare to stain with his sacrilegious steps this, land of liberty. Slaves—leave that odious epithet to the French nation; they [Page 293] deserve to be no longer free. Let us follow other footsteps; let us imitate other nations, who, directing their eyes into the future, and fearing to leave to posterity an example of cowardice, have preferred extermination, rather than to be struck out alive from the list of nations. Let us meanwhile be on our guard, lest a spirit of proselytism destroy our work. Let our neighbours live in peace; peace with our neighbours; but cursed be the French name; eternal hatred to France! Such are our principles. Let us swear to live free and independent, and to prefer death to slavery. Let us swear to pursue for ever the traitors and the enemies of our independence."

It cannot be denied that the prospect, however faint, of another effort on the part of France to subjugate and enslave the island—a prospect kept constantly before the eyes of the Haytian leaders, by the intrigues and entreaties of the colonists in Paris— offers some reason, if it affords no excuse, for the ferocity of this authoritative document; nor is it impossible that the stratagems put in play to operate on the French government, may have been viewed with approbation, if they were not secretly supported, by sympathisers in Saint Domingo. Still Dessalines was under a solemn pledge to respect the persons and the property of the French residents; and if any of them were, on valid grounds, suspected of tampering with the liberty of their fellow-citizens, they should have been prosecuted, and on being convicted, duly punished. But it may be doubted whether the fear of invasion, and the fear of internal treachery, were anything more than idle, or, at any rate, welcome pretexts for commencing a system of terror which Dessalines intended, and expected to turn to his own account.

The instigations employed by Dessalines to rouse the people to revenge, produced less effect than their author anticipated, for the army, as well as the inhabitants, were weary of bloodshed. In consequence, he resolved to accomplish his sanguinary designs by a military expedition. Traversing the towns where Frenchmen had remained, the monster put all to the sword, with a few exceptions, spared by acts of special grace. At the Cape, where [Page 294] the tragedy was enacted on the night of the 20th of April, the massacre was general; only about one-tenth of the inhabitants escaped. One fact brands Dessalines with perfidy as well as ruthlessness. A proclamation was published in the journals, declaring that the vengeance due to the crimes of the French had been sufficiently exacted, and inviting all those who had survived the butchery, to appear in the public square, that they might receive certificates of protection. Many came forth from their hiding places; immediately they were hurried to the place of execution, and shot.

The vindictive measures of Dessalines were far from being generally approved, even among his companions in arms. Christophe condemned them, but from a regard to his own safety, held his peace. Dessalines, however, took credit for the course he pursued, as appears from the following words, borrowed from a proclamation which he issued:—

"Crimes the most atrocious—crimes till then unknown— crimes which make human nature shudder—were committed by the French.

"At last the hour of vengeance has come, and the implacable enemies of the rights of man have received the punishment they deserved. My arm, raised above their heads, too long hesitated to strike. At that signal which the justice of God called forth, your hand, sternly armed, applied the axe to the root of slavery and prejudice. In vain had time, and still more, the infernal policy of Europeans, surrounded the tree with triple brass: you tore off the covering, which you placed in your hearts, and, like your enemies, you became cruel and pitiless.

"As an overflowing torrent, which breaks down whatever it meets with in its course, so your avenging fury bore away every obstacle. Let them perish—all the tyrants of innocence, all the oppressors of the human species!

"What! bowed down for centuries under a yoke of iron, playthings of the passions and of the injustice of men, and of the caprices of fortune; mutilated victims of the cupidity of the French;—after having, with unexampled patience and resignation, [Page 295] enriched those insatiable oppressors by means of our labours, we should have seen that sacrilegious horde make another attempt at our destruction; and we, whom they call men without energy and without courage, should not have plunged into their heart the dagger of despair! Intolerable. Where is the Haytian so vile, so unworthy of his regeneration, as to think that he has not fulfilled the decrees of heaven, in exterminating those sanguinary tigers? If there is one such, let him fly; may insulted nature drive him from our company—allow him to drag his infamy at a distance from ourselves! The air we breathe cannot suit his apathetic organs; it is the air of liberty,—it is pure, august, triumphant!

"Yes! we have given back to those anthropophagi war for war, crime for crime, outrage for outrage. Yes! I have saved my country, I have avenged America! The vow which I made in the face of heaven and of earth, is my pride and my glory. What to me is the opinion which will be entertained of my conduct by my contemporaries, and by future generations? I have done my duty; I approve my conduct—that suffices.

"But the preservation of my unfortunate brethren, and the testimony of my conscience, are not my only reward. I saw two classes of men, born to aid, protect, and cherish each other, mingled together in a part of the world, crying out for revenge, and disputing who should strike the first blow. Blacks, and men of colour, whom the perfidious policy of the

Europeans has so long sought to divide, you who now are united and form only one family, doubtless it was necessary that your reconciliation should be sealed with the blood of your murderers. The same calamities hung over your proscribed heads; the same ardour to smite your enemies has signalized you; the same destiny is reserved for you; and your common interests ought in future to render you inseparable. Preserve this precious concord—this happy union; it is the pledge of your liberty, of your success, of your felicity; it is the secret of being invincible.

"In order to strengthen this union, you must be reminded of the atrocities committed against our species. The premeditated massacre of the entire population of this island, resolved in the [Page 296] silence of the cabinet!—the execution of this abominable project was imprudently proposed to me, when it had already been commenced by the French, with the calm and the serenity of a countenance accustomed to such crimes.

"Guadaloupe pillaged and destroyed, its ruins yet smoking with the blood of its children—the women and the old men put to the sword! Pelage himself a victim of their perfidy, after having basely betrayed his country and his brethren! The brave and immortal Delgresse, blown up with the fort which he defended, rather than submit to their chains. Magnanimous warrior! that noble death, far from weakening our courage, will serve only to augment in us the resolution to avenge thee and to follow thee. The deplorable destiny of our brethren scattered in Europe, and (frightful forerunner of death) the terrible despotism exerted in Martinique! Unhappy people, would that I could fly to your aid and break your chains! Alas, an insurmountable barrier separates us; but perhaps a spark of the fire which inflames us, will kindle up in your hearts; perhaps at the report of this revolution, you, suddenly awakened from your lethargy, will, with arms in your hands, demand your sacred and inviolable rights.

"After the terrible example which I have given, may divine justice sooner or later send on earth men of strong minds, superior to vulgar weakness, for the terror and the destruction of the wicked. Tremble! usurping tyrants, pests of the New World; our poniards are sharpened, your punishment is at hand! Sixty thousand men equipped, hardened to war, obedient to my orders, burn to offer a new sacrifice to the manes of their assassinated brethren. Let that nation come, if it is senseless enough, or rash enough to attack me. Already, at its approach, the exasperated Genius of Hayti, rising from the depths of the ocean, shows his threatening form; he stirs up the waves; he excites the tempests; and with his puissant hand scatters and destroys hostile fleets. The laws of nature obey his formidable voice—plague, famine, fire, poison await his command. But why reckon on the aid of the climate and the elements? Have I forgotten that I command a people whose courage repels obstacles, and grows by dangers? Let those homicidal cohorts come! I wait for them [Page 297] with a firm foot and a calm eye. I freely resign to them the shores and the spots where towns were; but woe to those who come too near the mountains; better would it have been for them to be swallowed up in the depths of the sea, than to be torn to pieces by the furious hands of the children of Hayti.

"War against the tyrants—always war—war till death: that is my motto;—Liberty, independence: that is our rallying cry.

"Generals, officers, soldiers; differing from him by whom I was preceded, the ex-general Toussaint L'Ouverture, I have been faithful to the promise which I made you when I took up arms against tyranny, and as long as I live I will keep my oath. Never shall a colonist or a European set foot on this territory with the title of master or proprietor. This resolution shall henceforth form the fundamental basis of our Constitution.

"If other chiefs, after me, in following an entirely opposite course, shall dig their graves, and that of their fellow patriots, then you will have to accuse only the law of that destiny which shall have prevented me from rendering my fellow citizens free and happy. May my successors follow the plan which I have traced for them; it is the best system to consolidate their power; it is the greatest homage they can pay to my memory.

"As it is derogatory to my dignity to punish the innocent for the crimes of the guilty, a handful of whites, commendable for the sentiments which they have always professed, and who, besides, have sworn to live with us in the woods, have experienced my clemency. I direct that they be allowed to live, and that they be not maltreated.

"I again command and order all the generals of the departments to give succour, protection, and encouragement, to all neutral or allied nations, who may wish to establish commercial relations in this island."

The energy of this official document is terrible. What a volcanic soul was that of Dessalines! And if we are bound by every moral consideration to reprobate its spirit in the strongest terms, equally are we in justice bound to remember that this fury had been sharpened and intensified in those previous conflicts in which [Page 298] professed Christians were the aggressors. Nor, shocking and atrocious as is the revenge which here burns and rages, can it be denied that while some palliation may be found in the prevalent rumours that France was about to make another and yet more powerful attempt, so fierce a resolution and so fiery a wrath could not be without effect in deterring the enemy, and guaranteeing the shores of Hayti from another series of ravages and crimes.

A small French force remained in possession of Santo Domingo; and the Spaniards who, on the evacuation of the Cape, acknowledged the new government, had, under the impulse of the priests, been induced to break their promise of obedience to the blacks, and to espouse the cause of France. The subjugation of Spanish Hayti became the supreme object of importance with Dessalines. A few days before he entered on the campaign intended to effect his purpose, he published a proclamation addressed to the Spaniards, accusing them of treason, and calling on them to submit. "Yet a few moments, and I will overwhelm the remains of the French under the weight of my omnipotence. Spaniards! you whom I address, because I desire to save you; you who though guilty of desertion, may preserve your existence and find my clemency ready to spare you, it is yet time—abjure an error which may be fatal to you, break all the ties which bind you to my enemies, if you do not wish your blood to be mingled with theirs. I give you a fortnight from this date, to acquaint me with your final intentions and to gather under my flag. You know what I can do, and what I have done; think of your preservation. Receive the sacred promise which I give never to make any attack against your personal safety and interests, if you seize the opportunity of showing yourselves worthy of being numbered among the children of Hayti." On the 14th of May, Dessalines quitted Cap-Français, and having traversed the western and the southern provinces, advanced toward the east, and sat down to besiege Santo Domingo. After abortive attempts to overcome the resistance of the citizens, who hated the blacks, he judged it advisable to retire, and returned to Port-au-Prince. His return was soon followed by a fearful revolution which after some months made Hayti an empire, and placed on its throne one who, from the condition of a slave, had [Page 299] raised himself to be the first magistrate of a republic, now no more. The coronation took place on the 8th of October, 1804, about two months before a similar farce was enacted by Bonaparte. Though Dessalines had waded through blood to the throne, the clergy were among the first to salute him as emperor. The civil ceremony was followed by a religious service; a *Te Deum* was performed, and the new monarch led the choir, singing the words in the strongest voice there was in his majesty's dominions. The institution of the imperial dignity was accompanied by the grant of a constitution, which proceeding on the basis that the empire of Hayti was free, sovereign, and independent, proclaimed the abolition of slavery, the equality of ranks, the authority of the same laws for all, the inviolability of property, the loss of civil rights by emigration, and the suspension of those rights by bankruptcy, the exclusion of all whites, from the right of acquiring property, except those who had been naturalized; and the adoption of the generic name of blacks, for all the subjects of Hayti, whatever their colour. It was further declared that no one was worthy to be a Haytian, if he was not a good father, a good son, a good husband, and especially a good soldier. Parents were not permitted to disinherit their children, and every citizen was required to practise some mechanical art. The empire of Hayti, one and indivisible, contained ten military governments, each commanded by a general; every commander was independent of the rest, and was to correspond directly with the head of the government, who to the title of emperor joined that of commander-in-chief of the army. The last article of the constitution stated that Dessalines, the avenger and the liberator of his countrymen, was called to fulfil those functions, and that he would reign under the name of Jean-Jacques the first.

The title of majesty was conferred on the new emperor as well as on his august consort, the empress; their persons were declared inviolable, and the crown elective; but the emperor had the right to nominate his successor among a chosen number of candidates. The sons of the sovereign were to pass through all the ranks of the army. Every emperor who should attach to himself a privileged body under the name of guard of honour or [Page 300] any other designation, was by the fact to be regarded as at war with the nation, and should be driven from the throne, which then was to be occupied by one of the councillors of state chosen by the majority of the members of that body. The emperor had the right to make, approve, and publish the laws; to appoint and dismiss public functionaries; to direct the receipts and the expenses of the state, and the coining of money; to make peace and war; to conclude treaties; to distribute the armed force at his pleasure: he also possessed the exclusive prerogative of pardon.

The generals of division and of brigade were to form part of the council of state. Besides a secretary of state, there was to be a minister of finances and a minister of war. All persons were encouraged to settle their differences by arbitration. No dominant religion was admitted; the liberty of worship was proclaimed; the state was not to take on itself the support of any religious institution. Marriage was declared a purely civil act, and in some cases divorce was permitted. State offences were to be tried by a council to be named by the emperor. All property belonging to white Frenchmen was confiscated to the state. The houses of the citizens were pronounced inviolable.

The constitution was placed under the safeguard of the magistrates, of fathers, of mothers, of citizens, and of soldiers, and recommended to their descendants, to all the friends of liberty, to the philanthropists of all countries, as a striking token of the goodness of God, who in the order of his immortal decrees had given the Haytians power to break their bonds, and make themselves a free, civilized, and independent people. This constitution which, considering its origin, contains so much that is excellent, and which even the long civilized states of Europe might advantageously study, was accepted by the emperor, and ordered to be forthwith carried into execution.

The condition of the farm-labourer was the same as under the system of Toussaint L'Ouverture; he laboured for wages which were fixed at one-fourth of the produce, and that produce was abundant. The whip and all corporal punishments were abolished. Idleness was regarded as a crime, but was punished only by [Page 301] imprisonment. Two-thirds of the labour exacted under slavery was the amount required under the new system. Thus the labourers gained a diminution of one-third of their toil, while their wants were amply supplied. It was decreed that the black labourers could labour only in the divisions to which they had been aforetime attached; but if they had any reasons for changing, the commissioner of the district would give them permission. The greater number of the properties having been confiscated, were in the hands of the government; but they were let at an annual rent, and that rent was determined according to, not the extent of the soil, but the number of the labourers. The mulattoes, or quarterons, children of whites and mulattoes, who were very numerous, if they could show any relationship, whether legitimate or not, with the old white proprietors, were allowed to inherit their property.

The census of the inhabitants of the island in the parts subject to Dessalines, which took place in 1805, represented the population as then amounting to about 380, 000, with about 20, 000 from various causes not included. Of these 400, 000 the adult males were only a small proportion, so much had their ranks been thinned by war and massacre; the majority of labourers were women. Marriage, solemnized according to the rites of the Roman church, was almost universal, and its duties were, in general, well observed, in spite of the example of the emperor. The army consisted of 15, 000 men, of whom 1500 were cavalry; they were well armed and well disciplined, but badly clothed. The uniform was blue, turned up with red. All adult males fit for service, were four times a year drilled during several days. Emigration was put under the most rigorous restraints. An effectual system of self-defence was devised and executed, with a view to prepare against invasion.

In the midst of these outward and material arrangements, education was not neglected. Schools were established in nearly all the districts, and the negroes seeing what advantage was possessed by those among them who had received instruction, attached great importance to it, and there were few of them who did not at least learn to read and to write.

[Page 302]At the time of the insurrection of 1791, the emperor Jean Jacques was a slave under a black proprietor, named Dessalines, from whom he derived his own appellation. In 1805, that man was still alive; he dwelt at the Cape, and witnessed the elevation of his old servant to the imperial throne. He was accustomed to say, that the emperor had always been "a headstrong dog, but a good workman." Dessalines continued to entertain a great esteem for him, and made him his head butler. When asked why he had not given him a more honourable post, he replied that no other would have pleased him so much, as he was fond of good wine, and would drink for both. The emperor, although he had the best furnished wine-cellar in the island, drank scarcely anything but water.

Jean Jacques Dessalines, Emperor of Hayti, was small in person, but strongly made; of great activity, and indomitable courage. He knew not how to read, but he had learned to sign his name; as he was desirous of instruction, he employed a reader, to whom he listened with much attention. It has been affirmed that his military talents were superior to those of Toussaint L'Ouverture. However this may be, in all other respects he was greatly inferior to that unfortunate chief. Though open, affable, and even generous, he inspired fear rather than respect. He was remarkable for strange caprices, the evident effect of his personal vanity; now he was covered with embroidery and other ornaments, and attired with magnificence; yet often he appeared in public in the most wretched garb. But what was more singular and more ridiculous, he had the ambition to be accounted an accomplished dancer, and always had with him a dancing-master, who gave him lessons in his leisure moments; nor was it possible to pay him a more agreeable compliment than to tell him how well he danced, though he was very unskilful in that amusement, in which negroes ordinarily excel. He had daughters by his first wife, but no sons. His last wife had been the favourite mistress of a rich planter, from whom she had received a superior education. She was one of the finest negresses of the West Indies; her character was mild, and she often employed [Page 303] her ascendancy over Dessalines to soften his natural ferocity; unhappily, she sometimes failed in her benevolent efforts.

During some time, the Emperor Jean Jacques practised the cruelties to which his nature was prone only on the whites, but soon he spared not even his own colour. The suspicions of a mind disquieted as to his own authority, led him to put to death, without any judicial formalities, citizens and soldiers. Every effort he thus made to terminate his solicitudes, served only to augment them, His caprices, his atrocities, were carried to such a point, that the heads of his army conspired, and suddenly, on the 17th October, 1806, put him under arrest. In endeavouring to escape, he received a blow, which put an end to his life, and to the imperial government in the island of Hayti.

CHAPTER II.

Feud between mulatto and negro blood, occasioning strife and political conflicts— Christophe president and sovereign in the north—Pétion president in the south—The two districts are united under Boyer—Riché—Soulouque, the present emperor.

THE framers of the constitution under which Dessalines became the emperor of Hayti, in decreeing that the inhabitants in general should be denominated *blacks,* made a praiseworthy effort to extinguish the distinctions of colour which had occasioned so much calamity. But such distinctions are stronger than the words of which state resolutions consist, which have little power and durability, unless they are the embodiment not only of the national will, but also of the national character. Unfortunately, the distinctions in question, which rested on prejudices and antipathies deeply planted in human nature, had been aggravated by a long series of sanguinary contentions, and though now somewhat abated, still retained an influence both decided and noxious. It was a great, however pardonable, mistake to suppose that distinctions, which only ages, under the force of common institutions and good government, can effectually obliterate, could, [Page 304] within a few years, and amid conflicting social elements, be annihilated and disowned. And though their disavowal did something toward their extinction, and the counsellors who caused that disavowal deserve the gratitude of the friends of humanity, yet is there no ground for surprise, if their effort proved illusory. How small was its immediate effect, events will speedily show. The aristocracy of the skin retained in Hayti sufficient force to occasion jealousies, discord, and war among those who ought to have been united in one combined effort for the good of the country. But the mulatto blood could not brook the ascendancy of the negro blood. Its pride and its disdain were fed by long conflicts and inveterate animosities. Conscious of that individual superiority which ensues from a share in the influences of civilization, the mulattoes of Hayti despised the untaught and the rude crowd of black labourers by whom they were surrounded, and felt, that in submitting to their sway, they put themselves under the domination of a majority, whose authority lay exclusively in their numbers. Their natural position, they believed, was at the head of the Haytian government. Could they have peaceably taken that position, they would probably in a measure have forgotten their own party interests, and laboured for the diffusion, through the great body of the people, of the higher influences of civilization. But there was an alternative. They might have employed an elevated position for their own exclusive aggrandisement. This possibility the blacks could not disallow, the rather that hitherto they had found in the yellow blood the most virulent of the opponents with whom they had had to deal. Not without reason, therefore, did they look with suspicion and jealousy on all attempts at political elevation which were made by mulattoes. It is even to be feared that the blacks, under their distrust and fears, were much averse to the culture which education gives, and of which the mulattoes, who possessed some tincture of European civilization, were, in their eyes, the representatives. Thus the progress of the island, in those arts and attainments on which the good of society consists, was materially retarded, and the way paved for a renewal of strife and bloodshed, with their demoralizing effects.

[Page 305]On the death of Dessalines, the news of which spread joy among the inhabitants, the supreme power naturally fell into the hands of Christophe, who, with good reason, had long been recognised as the second chief in the state. Well acquainted with the great interests of which he undertook the care, and thoroughly experienced in Haytian warfare, Christophe, who enjoyed a high reputation for humanity and benevolence, and who, in addition to the domestic virtues, was actuated by a practical sense of religion, seemed to possess the best guarantees for a useful, if not a happy, career. Free from the vanity of his predecessor, he discarded the pompous title of Emperor, and took that of Chief Governor of Hayti. With befitting sagacity, he began his sway by directing his attention to the encouragement of agriculture and commerce. Specially desirous was he to see in his ports the merchant vessels of distant nations, and with that view he, on the 24th of October, 1806, put forth a proclamation, in which he promised neutral powers protection and favour.

While engaged in peaceful improvements, he suddenly found himself necessitated to prepare for war. The old feud between the negro and the mulatto blood broke out afresh. Unable to endure the supremacy of a negro who had been a slave, the mulatto Pétion resolved to put forward his claim to political power and dignity. Pétion possessed superior advantages. Having been educated in the military school of Paris, he was esteemed for his knowledge, and accounted the best engineer officer in the native forces. Christophe himself entertained a high opinion of his military abilities. The two competitors had recourse to arms. A battle was fought on the 1st of January, 1807, which issued in the defeat of Pétion. His successful rival pursued him to the gates of Port-au-Prince, his head-quarters. Hoping to complete his triumph, and so to consolidate his power, Christophe undertook the siege of that city, but was compelled to retire without effecting its capture. The hostilities led to little else than the enfeeblement of both parties. The black chief, however, established his power on solid foundations in the north, while Pétion succeeded in retaining a firm position in the south. Thus was the island once more unhappily divided between two [Page 306] authorities, each of which watched its opportunity for the overthrow of the other.

The war in which he had been engaged, and in which he had gained only partial success, made Christophe feel the necessity of augmenting his strength. The progress which he had made over the north, with a view to the assertion and establishment of his authority, had revived in him the knowledge that the negro character is by nature predisposed in favour of the monarchical form of government. He resolved, therefore, to take a step in that direction. On his return to Cap François he assembled a council, composed of generals and the principal citizens. On the 17th of February, 1807, that council decreed a new Constitution. At its head was Christophe, with the title of President. The office was for life, and carried with it the right to select, among the general officers of the State, a successor. The constitution abolished slavery, declaring every individual free that resided in Hayti. The Roman Catholic religion was established, with toleration of every other form of worship. Schools were opened in every district. Arrangements were also made for the administration of justice, the encouragement of agriculture and commerce, and the security of the neighbouring colonies.

The time occupied by these regulations was employed by Pétion in making preparations for a renewal of active operations in the field, while Christophe, on his side, was firmly resolved to extend his rule over the whole island. Soon was the country again rent and torn by intestine war. The conflict was long and dubious. Now the one chief, now the other, gained the advantage. Every defeat and every victory seemed to serve only to augment the fury and confirm the determination of both. During the collisions the country at large suffered greatly. Agriculture was hindered or arrested. Education was suspended. Wealth, instead of growing, decreased, and seemed likely to vanish. The two combatants became weary of a strife in which victory was baneful to the land over which they aspired to rule. At length the reduction of Môle Saint Nicholas by Christophe, a decisive blow to his competitor, put a period to the destructive hostilities, and afforded to the island time and scope to recover from its losses. The war [Page 307] was ended, but not the division. The two chiefs withdrew into their respective territories.

The time had now arrived when Christophe judged it desirable to complete his plan of self-elevation. In the spring of 1811 he assumed the title of King, with the almost unanimous consent, not only of the populace, but also of his chief men. He made Cap François the capital of his dominions, and proceeded to surround himself with all the pomp and parade of feudal royalty.

Meanwhile, Rigaud, having escaped from prison, landed in Hayti, and offered his co-operation to Pétion. It was eagerly accepted. But jealousy soon separated the two mulattoes, and Rigaud, having been appointed Pétion's commander in the south, retained his authority, and so gave rise to three rival powers in the island. Resolved to profit by this division, Christophe marched against Pétion; but the common danger brought about a union, and Christophe judged it prudent to retire. The peril over, the two men of colour again quarrelled. The city of Cayes was urged into revolt against Rigaud, who, in attempting to bring it back to obedience, lost his life. His rights, such as they were, fell to the share of his general, Borgella.

Pétion was about to take measures to dispossess him, when the unexpected approach of Christophe effected a reconciliation. The sable monarch, however, was driven back by Borgella, who now fought on the side of Pétion, aided by the mulatto general, Boyer, who is about to appear on the scene as the principal character.

With these events the conflict between the north and the south may be said to have terminated. As soon as his mind was free from the cares of warfare, Pétion, at the head of a republic in the south, applied all his powers, and not without effect, to the improvement of the condition of those whom be governed. Accessible and courteous to all, while Christophe affected grandeur and distance, Pétion gained general good-will, and turned his influence to account for the amelioration of his territories and the consolidation of his power. Labouring indefatigably, he did his utmost to ensure the due cultivation of the land, to administer justice, and to promote order. He was rewarded with great success, and came to be loved and revered; but he found his task [Page 308] one of great difficulty, and partly from want of power to give effect to his own views, and partly owing to prevalent ignorance and grossness of manners, he was often impeded in his efforts and frustrated in his hopes.

France had never given up the hope of resuming possession of Hayti. During the wars of the empire she had other occupation for her resources. But when Bonaparte had fallen, the old colonists recovered their hopes and resumed their efforts. They succeeded in getting a commission appointed. The report was so favourable as to throw the planters into a transport of joy. In 1814, three commissioners were sent to the West Indies, who were directed to transmit to the French Government the result of their inquiries relative to the condition of Hayti. Lavayasse, who was at its head, made overtures to Christophe and Pétion. From the former he received an indignant repulse; with the latter he succeeded in gaining an interview at Port-au-Prince. The commissioner, with very ample promises, invited the president to recognise Louis XVIII. The propositions were rejected. Disappointed in these pacific efforts, the colonists clamoured for war. Preparations were made, and a fleet was to sail in the spring of the year 1815. But before the time came Bonaparte was at large, and preparations for the battle of Waterloo absorbed all minds. Anxious to obtain all possible aid, that adventurer adapted his policy to his condition, and having once done his best to perpetuate slavery, he now decreed the abolition of the infamous traffic in human bodies and souls; and at the same time sent to Hayti propositions intended to win back the island. He retained the sceptre too short a time to receive a reply. As soon as the Bourbons were again restored, the colonists renewed their intrigues. In the middle of the year 1816 they succeeded in obtaining the appointment of commissioners, who were to assume the civil and military government of the island, tacitly superseding the actual authorities. They sailed to Hayti, and made an attempt to obtain a hearing, but in vain; they returned to France only to show how fruitless their mission had proved.

The unhesitating rejection of these overtures from France was the last important act performed by Pétion. That chief had long [Page 309] been drooping under the combined effects of disease and disappointment; his depression was witnessed by those whom he governed with sympathy and regret. Every means was taken to give his mind relief. But the disorder grew worse: he became suspicious, fancied conspiracies, distrusted his best friends, looked on the past with regret, and feared to encounter the future. In this melancholy, he finally put an end to his existence by voluntarily abstaining from food. He expired on the 29th of March, 1818, at the age of forty-eight, appointing, with general approbation, Jean-Pierre Boyer as his successor. His death occasioned general sorrow.

Jean-Pierre Boyer, a mulatto, born at Port-au-Prince on the 2nd of February, 1776, received in Paris the advantages of European culture; fought under Rigaud against Toussaint L'Ouverture; and in consequence of the success which the black leader obtained, quitted the island. Boyer returned to Hayti in Leclerc's expedition; he, however, separated from the French General-in-chief, and placed himself at the head of his own colour. Together with Pétion, he kept quiet in order to husband his strength, while Dessalines was expelling the French from the island. But when, on the death of Dessalines, Christophe, already master of the north, sought to take the south out of Pétion's hands, Boyer aided his fellow-mulatto to withstand the black ruler. Gratitude, as well as a regard to the common security, gave Boyer the President's chair on the death of Pétion. Raised to that dignity, he employed his power and his energies to complete those economical and administrative reforms with which he had already been connected under his predecessor. To labour for the public good was the end of his life. In this worthy enterprise he was greatly assisted no less by his knowledge than his moderation. Well acquainted with the negro and mulatto character, and conversant with all the interests of the state, he had it in his power to effect his purposes by mild as well as judicious measures.

Yet were the wounds deep which he had to heal; and he could accomplish in a brief period only a small part of that which it will require generations to carry to perfection.

While Boyer, with determination and firmness, and with the [Page 310] aid of superior men, was promoting the improvement of his republic, Christophe had painful experience that a crown is no protection against either internal or external troubles. His subjects began to find that the glitter of court apparel and high-sounding names is soon tarnished, and affords a poor repayment for its cost. The monarch was struck with paralysis, and confined within the Château de Sans-Souci, his favourite residence. What to him appeared a trifling incident occasioned his overthrow and death. An order for the degradation of a colonel who was loved by his soldiers caused the garrison of Saint Marc, consisting of 6000 men, to break out into revolt. On hearing of the insurrection, Christophe commanded 12, 000 men to march against the revolters; but those troops themselves proved hostile to their sovereign. The only force on whose fidelity he could count was his own body-guard. Them he reviewed as he lay in his litter; and having bestowed on each a gift of four dollars, he despatched them against the rebels. Midway they encountered the enemy, who came on with shouts of "Liberty for ever!" Whether this cry captivated their minds, or whether they were impressed with the inutility of opposition, Christophe's guard joined the soldiers of the Cape, and in one body marched against the residence of their former master. A report of the defection reached Sans-Souci before their arrival. As soon as it had come to the ears of Christophe, feigning to need repose, he withdrew into his chamber. Then he called his wife and his children, who ranged themselves around the bed on which he sat. He gave caresses to his daughters, asked for some linen, threw a mournful look on his son, and, without uttering another word, made a sign for all to retire. Then, having obtained some water, he washed his hands and his arms, as if he wished to purify himself, changed his clothes, covered his head with a handkerchief, and dismissed his servants. They had not yet shut the door, when they heard the report of a pistol. Returning into the room, they found Christophe dead; the ball had gone through his heart. His body was conveyed away by some soldiers to whom it was entrusted by the queen, to be carried to a place which she indicated; but the king of Hayti was, a few days afterwards, found half devoured [Page 311] by beasts on the edge of a forest, where he had been thrown without sepulture. Thus perished Henri, king of Hayti, after a a reign of nine years (1811-20).

Christophe was fifty-three years of age at the time of his death. He was a man of pure morals and cold in manner, who gave observers the idea of more depth of thought than he really possessed. English and French authorities have differed in regard to his character. The English, whose nation and commerce he favoured, have represented him not only as a man of the highest genius, but also as a monarch equally wise and just. Others have striven to set him forth as a sanguinary tyrant, and have found the cause of his downfal in the excess of his cruelties. Both views are exaggerations. With a mind little capable of continuous thought, Christophe possessed a strong and obstinate will. When once he had gained an elevated position, he manifested great energy of character. Having attained to the supreme power of a throne, he found himself placed between the exertion of absolute authority which he was compelled to maintain, and the necessity of improving the people, that they might take rank among the civilized nations of the world. The two duties were not easily reconciled. Anxious to augment by commerce the material strength of his dominions, and to develop its moral power by education, he imposed on the emancipated blacks a labour not unlike that of the days of their servitude, and called forth intelligence in the minds of a half-brutish people. The consequence was inevitable. Rigour produced discontent, and discontent received power from knowledge. Under the combined influence, Christophe fell. His life was not spent in vain. Not only did he render important services in the war of liberation, but even by his severity he compelled that industry to which negroes in their own climes are indisposed, and without which steady and continued progress in civilization is impossible.

On the cessation of the reign of Henri I., as Christophe was termed, General Paul Remain, Prince of Limbé, put himself at the head of affairs, and proclaimed a republic, while others declared in favour of Christophe's son. On the 15th October, 1821, the north and the north-west of Hayti formed themselves into a [Page 312] commonwealth, of which Paul Romain was nominated President. The chiefs of this government transmitted to Boyer the constituent act of their organization. Boyer sent it back unread, and refused all aid so long as the north should keep separate from the south. This state of division did not last long. On the 21st of October, Boyer took possession of Gonaïves without resistance. The next day he marched on the Cape, where the evening before, the principal inhabitants had met together to make preparations for his reception. He entered the city at the head of 20, 000 men, and on the 26th was proclaimed President. In the commencement of the year 1822, the Spanish part of the island acceded, of its own accord, to the new republic, and thus from Cape Tiburon to Cape Engano, Hayti was peacefully settled under one government.

While Hayti was thus making progress toward material prosperity, and preparing the way for rising from the bottom of the sink of human culture, its old enemies, the colonists, never ceased to put forward and enforce their claims. Abortive negotiations were the consequence. At length, in 1825, after the recognition of the independence of Hayti by others, the French, under Charles X., sold to its inhabitants the rights which they had won by their swords, for the sum of 150, 000, 000 of francs, to be paid as an indemnity to the colonists.

The form in which this act of emancipation was obtained, dictated by the historical claims and usages of the French monarchy, displeased the people; that displeasure was augmented by the large sum of money which they would have to pay to the planters. "Had not their enemies," they asked, "already exacted enough from them! Must they continue to labour for men who had ever shown the most embittered opposition to their interests?" Boyer's colour awakened distrust. "What is this ordinance," they said, "but an averment of the right divine of French despotism; and what is our acceptance of it but an acknowledgment of French sovereignty? We are betrayed by our old foes, the men of colour. We must withstand the predominant influence of mulatto blood." This jealousy threw serious obstacles in Boyer's path. His reformatory measures were [Page 313] obstructed. His efforts to promote agriculture, on which depended alike the wealth and the civilization of the country, encountered resistance, as if they were designed for the gradual restoration of slavery. The civilizing influences which his own culture and the good of the country equally demanded, were withstood by the brutishness of a suspicious Africanism which was indisposed to learn, to labour, and to obey. One consequence of these oppositions was inaction on the part of the Government. Boyer's reign has been characterized as "a long slumber." Certainly his power for good was curtailed, and he found that the less be attempted, the more was he at his ease. Of course under a system of comparative neglect the island made little progress. Large portions of the country fell out of culture, for life is easily supported in the West Indies; and in the decline of industry, education made little way. Thus did the prejudices of colour still prove adverse to the real good of the island. Nevertheless, Boyer had on his side powerful allies—peace and time. Twenty years of tranquillity had so softened men's minds that robbery and murder were unknown. The pacific contact of the two castes in a measure produced their fusion; the black party with its extreme opinions daily grew less as fathers and grandfathers passed into the grave; and Boyer and the intelligent men whom he had around him, hoped that the time had arrived when they could effectually put an end to barbarism.

But a young party made its appearance, a party of progress as it was called, but really a party of extravagance. The new generation, filled with extreme democratic ideas, accused the President and his government with encouraging the very brutishness which they were labouring to put away. Impatient of the slow movement of the country which Boyer had been compelled to accept, and which he would have gladly accelerated, the heady reformers were loud and bold in demanding changes, for which the people were unfitted, and which could end in nothing but disappointment. That a nation is not born in a day, is a truth of which they knew nothing. It was to no purpose that the President pointed out to these ardent reformers whose leaders were men of mulatto blood, and possessed of some culture, that they were [Page 314] endangering the public weal by awakening the passions of the ignorant populace. The suggestion indicated fear on the part of the Government. The opposition then was likely to prove successful. Africanism, too, learned that it was feared, and hence rose into a more threatening attitude. How formidable it might prove was seen in the devastations which it committed in the city, when, in 1842, the Cape was laid in ruins by an earthquake, and one half of its inhabitants were destroyed. The population of the country rushed into the town, and spent a fortnight in pillage and plunder; saying to the ruined proprietors: "It is the good God that gives us this; yesterday was your day; to-day is ours." The opposition made its appearance in the legislative hall. It was driven thence by the force of *coups-d'état*. It revived in the country in the form of conspiracy. The conspirators gathered around an ambitious man of small ability, Hérard-Rivière, a commander of artillery, who was put forward by an ambitious man of talent, Hérard-Dumesle. A manifesto was sent forth, in which Hérard-Rivière was placed at the head of the executive government. Fighting ensued. Boyer, in disgust, quitted the island (13th March, 1843), and embarked for Jamaica, after taking leave of the inhabitants in language which did not want dignity.

After the departure of President Boyer, various pretenders to the supreme authority came forward, and for a time disorders more or less prevailed. These disorders were not wholly without advantage. Around

Guerrier gathered sympathies in favour of national unity; Accaan united men in a common effort of defence; and Pierrot strengthened the feeling of a common need of conciliation and regard to law. Hence an important fact came into view, namely that the moral, economical, and political fusion of the two colours was not only not impossible but in part accomplished. The great question now was to find a man capable of developing the consequences of this new state of things, a man who should unite in his policy the good qualities of the system of Christophe with that of Pétion and Boyer, and who, energetic like the former, should be humane, liberal, and civilizing, like the two latter. The national sentiment looked to General Riché and made no mistake. Uniting to the ascendancy which he derived [Page 315] from his skin,* the intelligence and almost the instruction of the mulatto chiefs, Riché for a moment realized the ideal of a Haytian government. He repressed the barbarous element without at the same time crushing the element of culture, and he had both the power and the will, to open the country to foreign capital, and to organize native labour. He had done little more than enter on these important improvements, when he was carried off by a sudden malady, universally regretted, two days previous to the first anniversary of his elevation. Public opinion designated as his successor the black Generals Paul and Souffrant, who appeared equally desirous and equally able to continue the policy of Riché. The Senate, whose duty it was to elect the president, was divided between the two competitors, when a third candidate was proposed, who was elected on the very ground that as no one thought of him, no one offered him opposition. On the 1st of March, 1847, General Faustin Soulouque, the present ruler of Hayti, was appointed its president.Soulouque was a large, good-natured negro, who, from the year 1804, when he was the house-servant of General Lamarre, had passed through all the events of his country without leaving any trace of himself whether good or bad. In 1810 Lamarre was killed, while defending the Môle against Christophe, and Soulouque, who had become his master's aide-de-camp, was charged to carry his heart to Pétion. The latter made him lieutenant in his mounted guard, and bequeathed him afterwards to Boyer, as a piece of furniture belonging to the presidential palace. In his turn Boyer appointed him captain, and attached him in particular

---

* RICHÉ WAS WHAT IS CALLED A GRIFFE—THAT IS, THOUGH HE HAD WHITE BLOOD IN HIS VEINS, HE WAS, IN APPEARANCE, IN NO WAY DISTINGUISHED FROM A BLACK.

to the service of Mademoiselle Joute, who had been the lady president of two successive presidents. From that time until 1843, Souloque had remained completely forgotten; thenceforward every change made him more prominent. Under Hérard he became a chief of squadron, under Guerrier, a colonel, and under Riché, a general and superior commander of the palace guard. The new president was, at his election, two-and-sixty years old, though he did not seem to be more than forty. The negro peculiarities of [Page 316] feature appear in him in a subdued form. His eyes have a mild aspect. The general expression of his countenance is placid. He manifested singular timidity when he entered on his dignified office, and really possessed a modesty which subsequent events have done much to wear away. In Souloque the inferior element of Haytian life has its representative and its encouragement. Grossly ignorant, he is also absurdly superstitious. His vanity exceeds all bounds, and led him in the year 1849 to assume the title of Emperor. In this silly step he took for his model Napoleon Bonaparte, according to whose court and camp Souloque formed his own. The details are too trivial to deserve enumeration. Only let not the folly be imputed to the hue of Souloque's skin. If Hayti has its emperor, that sovereign borrowed the idea from France.

CHAPTER III.

CONCLUSION.

My narrative has come to a close. In looking back on the series of events of which I have spoken, I am impressed with the necessity of guarding against two extremes. Of these, the one degrades the African to the level of the brute; the other sets him on an equality with the Caucasian. The negro is a man; equally is it true that the negro race is inferior to the highest style of man. Individuals belonging to that race have risen very high in the scale of civilized life. Toussaint L'Ouverture commands our respect and admiration. But the race at large cannot be accounted equal to some others, if only because as yet it has no history. Qualities there are in the negro blood of a very valuable nature. Peculiarly is it favourable to the development of the domestic affections. It involves a strong attachment to place as well as kindred. But the very excess of its emotional nature unfits it for elevated thought, continuous industry, and lofty achievement. It is no disparagement to the Africans to say that they have realized but [Page 317] a small amount of social good in the Island of Hayti, since the outbreak of its insurrectionary movements. With its legacy of slavery degradations, envenomed prejudices, conflicting interests, and sanguinary wars, the island, within the last seventy years, has had a most rugged and perilous path to tread, in which it may be safely affirmed, the most cultivated of European nations would have experienced great difficulty to hold itself erect. And after what, in this old world of ours, we witnessed in the year 1848, we surely have no right to be severe in our judgment, even of the Emperor Soulouque. There is, however, in the preceding history —in the patriotism of Toussaint, in the firmness of Christophe, in the moderation of Boyer, and in the wisdom of Riché, with the good results of which those eminent rulers were severally and unitedly the authors,—there is enough to assure the impartial, that in dark-coloured blood there is no incapacity for either government or social and civilized life, and to inspire and warrant the hope, that Hayti will gradually, if slowly, rise to take a position among the first nations of the earth.

Before the sixteenth century, the African races were little known in the Christian world. Since then they have been brought into close contact with white men. A fusion has ensued. That fusion in Hayti has gone far to render pure African blood somewhat rare. A similar result is rapidly taking place in the United States. In this intermingling of two diverse streams, Providence seems to intend the improvement of both. The union involves the personal freedom and the social elevation of the blacks. It will also in time issue in a higher moral culture on the part of the whites. We shall learn to do justly by the weak; they will be aided to rise out of an existence little more than sensuous; while, in cases in which the two streams flow together in the same veins, the black may obtain nerve and hardihood, and the white may be enriched and mellowed.

Between two parties who may thus confer benefits on each other, there is no reason, and ought to be no room, for prejudice and misunderstanding. Children of the same great and good Parent, and objects of the same redeeming love, they have each a work on earth to perform, they have each a mind to [Page 318] cultivate and a soul to save, and can gain the approbation of their Creator and their Saviour, only so far as they interchange succour and promote common good, and aid and forward the grand drama of human life.

Persons who view great social questions in their bearing on material interests, will be disposed to inquire what has been the result of emancipation in Hayti on the products and commerce of the island. Statistical evidence shows a considerable diminution. If that diminution is real, it is the measure of relief from labour which his freedom has brought to the slave; it is more— it is the measure of his lessened punishments and his lessened sufferings. And if the negro can with little labour supply all the wants of which he is sensible, who has a right to augment his toil by compulsion? If our stock of sugar is less, it is an ample compensation to feel that the amount of human happiness is more; and if the negro is content, let us show our dissatisfaction, not by coercing him, but by raising him by gentle, persuasive, and attractive means to feel and acknowledge other and higher wants; and then, of his own accord, he will impose on himself additional labour. Should he, however, continue to prefer his native banian, with ease and repose, to our beef, purchasable only by long and severe toil, I see no ground whatever on which we may justifiably interfere with his mode of life, still less why we are at liberty to compel him to toil for our pleasure or our advantage.

NOTES AND ILLUSTRATIONS.

NOTE A.

ON THE COLOURED POPULATION.

Coloured population means sometimes the collective mass of blacks and of coloured men; but we more frequently understand by the words, *coloured population, coloured caste, coloured people, coloured men,* those who are neither black nor white; we also give them the general denomination of *the mixed races.*

The collective or particular acceptation of coloured population derives its signification from the phrase in which it is used.

M. Moreau de Saint-Méry, in developing the system of Franklin, has classed under general heads the different shades which the mixed population of colour present.

He supposes that man altogether forms 128 shades, which are white among the whites, and black among the blacks.

Setting out from this principle, he proves that we are so much nearer to or farther from the one colour or the other, as we either approach or remove from the number 64, which is their middle term.

According to this system, every man who has not eight shades of white, is considered black.

Proceeding from this colour towards white, we distinguish nine principal stocks, which have again varieties among them, according as they retain more or less shades of the one colour or of the other.

The Sacatra

Approaches nearest to the negro, is produced in three different ways, and can have from eight to sixteen shades white, and from 112 to 120 shades black.

The offspring of the sacatra and the negress has . . . . . 8 WHITE. . . . . .
120 BLACK.
The offspring of the male and female sacatra . . . . . 6 ". . . . . 112"
The offspring of the griffe and the negress . . . . . 16 ". . . . . 112"

[Page 322] *The Griffe*

Is the result of five combinations, and can have from 24 to 32 shades white, and 96 or 104 black.

The offspring of the marabou and the female sacatra, has . . . . .
32 WHITE. . . . . . 96 BLACK.
The offspring of the male and female griffe . . . . . 32 ". . . . . 96"
The offspring of the negro and the female mulatto . . . . . 32 ". . . . . 96"
The offspring of the negro and the female marabou . . . . . 24 ". . . . . 104"
The offspring of the griffe and the female sacatra . . . . . 24 ". . . . . 104"

The Marabou

Has in his five combinations, from 40 to 48 shades white, and from 80 to 88 black.

The offspring of the male and female marabou has . . . . . 48 WHITE. . .
. . . 80 BLACK.
The offspring of the quarteron and the negress . . . . . 48 ". . . . . 80"
The offspring of the mulatto and the female griffe . . . . . 48 " . . . . . 80'"
The offspring of the mulatto and the female sacatra . . . . . 40 " . . . . . 88"
The offspring of the marabou and the female griffe . . . . . 40 ". . . . . 88"

The Mulatto,

In his twelve combinations, varies from 56 to 70 shades white, and keeps from 58 to 72 of them black. Thus, there is a mulatto such as to approach nearer to the white than any other, by 14 parts.

The offspring of the quarteron and the female sacatra has . . . . .
70 WHITE. . . . . . 58 BLACK.
The offspring of the mamalouc and the female sacatra . . . . . 68 ". . . . . 60"

The offspring of the white man and the negress . . . . . 64 ". . . . . 64"
The offspring of the métif and the female sacatra . . . . . 64 ". . . . . 64"
The offspring of the quarteron and the female griffe . . . . . 64 ". . . . . 64"
The offspring of the male and female mulatto . . . . . 64 ". . . . . 64"
The offspring of the sang-mêlé and the negress . . . . . 63 ". . . . . 65"
The offspring of the quarteron and the negress . . . . . 62 ". . . . . 66"
The offspring of the mamelouc and the negress . . . . . 60 ". . . . . 68"
The offspring of the métif and the negress . . . . . 56 ". . . . . 72"
The offspring of the quarteron and the female sacatra . . . . . 56 ". . . . . 72"
The offspring of the mulatto and the female marabou . . . . . 56 ". . . . . 72"

The Quarteron.

His twenty combinations give from 71 to 96 shades white, and from 32 to 57 shades black.

The offspring of the white man and the female mulatto has . . . . .
   96 WHITE. . . . . . 32 BLACK.
The offspring of the male and female quarteron . . . . . 96 ". . . . . 32"
The offspring of the sang-mêlé and female mulatto . . . . . 95 ". . . . . 33"
The offspring of the quarteron and the female mulatto . . . . . 94 ". . . . . 34"
The offspring of the mamelouc and the female mulatto . . . . . 92 ". . . . . 36"
The offspring of the white man and the female marabou . . . . . 88 ". . . . . 40"

[Page 323] The offspring of the métif and the female mulatto . . . . .
   88 WHITE.. . . . . 40 BLACK.
The offspring of the sang-mêlé and the female marabou . . . . . 87 ". . . . 41"
The offspring of the quarteron and the—— . . . . . 86 ". . . . . 42"
The offspring of the mamelouc and the—— . . . . . 84 ". . . . . 44"
The offspring of the white man and the female griffe . . . . . 80 ". . . . . 48"
The offspring of the métif and the female marabou . . . . . 80 ". . . . . 48"
The offspring of the quarteron and the female mulatto . . . . . 80 ". . . . . 48"
The offspring of the sang-mêlé and the female griffe . . . . . 79 ". . . . . 49"
The offspring of the quarteron and the—— . . . . . 79 ". . . . . 50"
The offspring of the mamelouc and the—— . . . . . 76 ". . . . . 52"
The offspring of the white man and the female sacatra . . . . . 72 ". . . . . 56"
The offspring of the métif and the female griffe . . . . . 72 ". . . . . 56"

The offspring of the quarteron and the female marabou ..... 72 "..... 56"

The offspring of the sang-mêlé and the female sacatra ..... 71 "..... 57"

The Métif.

We find in his six combinations from 104 to 112 shades white, and consequently, from 16 to 24 shades black.

The offspring of the white man and the female quarteron .....
  112 WHITE...... 16 BLACK.
The offspring of the male and female métif ..... 112 "..... 16"
The offspring of the sang-mêlé and the female quarteron ..... 111 "..... 17"
The offspring of the quarteron and the—— ..... 110 "..... 18"
The offspring of the mamelouc and the—— ..... 110 "..... 18"
The offspring of the quarteron and the female métif ..... 104 "..... 24"

The Meamelouc.

The five ways in which he is produced, stand in the relation of 116 to 120 parts white, by 8 to 16 parts black.

The offspring of the white man and the female métif has .....
  120 WHITE...... 8 BLACK.
The offspring of the male and female mamelouc ..... 120 "..... 8"
The offspring of the sang-mêlé and the female métif ..... 119 "..... 9"
The offspring of the quarteron and the—— ..... 118 "..... 10"
The offspring of the mamelouc and the female métif ..... 116 "..... 12 "

The Quarteron.

His four combinations vary from 122 to 124 shades white, and from 4 to 6 shades black.

The offspring of the white man and the female mamelouc has .....
  124 WHITE...... 4 BLACK.
The offspring of the male and female quarteron ..... 124 "..... 4"

The offspring of the sang-mêlé and the female mamelouc ..... 123 "...5"
The offspring of the quarteron and the—— ..... 122 "..... 6"

[Page 324] *Sang-mêlé*

Is produced in four ways; and varies from 125 to 127 parts white, and from 1 to 3 black.

The offspring of the white man and the female of the sang-mêlé has ... .. 127 WHITE.. ..... 1 BLACK.
The offspring of the white man and quarteron ..... 126 "..... 2"
The offspring of the male and female sang-mêlé ..... 125 "..... 2"
The offspring of the sang-mêlé and the female quarteron ..... 125 "..... 3"

The sang-mêlé, by continuing its union with the whites, at last passes into white colour.

According to the aforesaid system, whoever reaches the 8th degree, finds that he has 8191 white parts to one black part, which is really no difference, because numbers of individuals of southern Europe, in Spain, in Provence, in Italy, in Turkey, and in Hungary, have in their blood more than 164th part black.

Doctor Franklin was the first to conceive this system, which shows the infinite power and goodness of the Creator; thus the species always reforming itself by varieties, is renewed at the end of a score of generations, without retaining any of the organic elements which would debase it.

Philosophy has made use of this observation in order to make us comprehend the nothingness of hereditary pride. This pride males us believe that in spite of nature we retain the pure blood of our ancestors to the sixteenth generation, whereas we have only a small portion of it. It is a good or an evil, infinitely divided in the common existence of our race.—- *Translated from Pamphile de Lacroix.*

NOTE B.

The immediate causes of the insurrection are given by *Gustave d'Alaux* in the *Revue des Deux Mondes,* vol. viii. Nouvelle Pèriode, pp. 776 *seq.*

"The planters took the initiative in the revolution. Not less devoid of foresight than the aristocracy of the mother country, they warmly accepted and patronised the ideas which gave birth to 1789. The enfeeblement of the monarchical authority, was for them the relaxation of a system which excluded them from the high colonial positions, and forced their pride and their habitual despotism to bend before the discretionary power of the agents of the mother country. Civic equality was the complete assimilation of the colony to France, the free exercise of the means of action which their immense riches seemed to secure them. Without waiting for the authority of the government, the colonists formed themselves into parochial and [Page 325] provincial assemblies, and sent to Paris eighteen deputies, who were admitted some as of right, the others as petitioners. Much excited by this first success, these pretensions to political and administrative equality were soon, in the colonial aristocracy, transformed into an avowed wish for independence. The provincial assemblies delegated the direction of the interior affairs of the colony to a sort of convention, which met at Saint Marc, and that convention, in which the influence of the planters predominated, declared that they were constituted in virtue of the powers of *their constituents,* contrary to the opinion of the minority, who proposed to say, "In virtue of the decrees of the mother country."

But by the side of the colonial aristocracy were the whites of the inferior and the middle class, who in ardently adhering to the revolutionary doctrines which they had fomented, intended to deduce therefrom all their logical consequences. Offended at the disdain of the planters, those two classes hailed in the new ideas the coming of civil and social equality. Between the feudal oligarchy which the planters saw in their dreams of independence, and a share in the conquests already realized by the liberalism of the mother country, those classes could not hesitate, and gave themselves wholly to France. The provincial assembly of the north, almost entirely composed of lawyers whom the convention of Saint Marc had alienated by certain regulations tending to lessen their fees, gave the official signal of the reaction. Forthwith the planters changed their tactics. They pretended to renounce their projects of independence, armed themselves against the authority of the mother country with demagogical ideas, and thus succeeded in acquiring a numerous party in the dregs of the white population; but Peinier, the governor, supported by the sound part, of the colonial tiers-état, broke up and dismissed the insurrectionary assembly of Saint Marc.

A third element appeared on the scene, and took in regard to the whole white population the part which the tiers-état (the people) had in regard to the planters. While the colonists were disputing respecting liberty and equality, the freed-men had not kept their ears closed. More than others they had a right to see a benefit in the revolution; for by the fact that their colour (two thirds of them were of mixed blood), their education, their quality of free-men and of proprietors, brought them into proximity to the white caste, it was for them specially that the dark susceptibility of colonial prejudice took pleasure in making the demarcation harsh and offensive. The decree of the 8th of March, conferred on them indeed political rights; but that decree raised in all the ranks of the white population such a condemnation that the governor himself concurred in preventing its execution. In vain the freed-men took up arms in favour of the mother country in the struggle sustained by the governor against the colonial aristocracy. After the victory the governor showed the freed-men no favour for their efforts, and carried disdain so far as not to allow them to wear the white cockade, which distinguished the royalist party. The mulattoes abandoned that party; and a new decree, by which the constituent assembly retracted the decree of the 8th of March, completed the rupture. Then came a third decree, which restored their political rights to the freed-men, and that occasioned fresh resistance on the part of the whites. The demagogical party revolted against the government; the aristocratical party, or those who were [Page 326] for independence, offered the colony to England; the royalist party, quite as hostile to the mulattoes as the two others, found nothing better to hold the planters in respect than to covertly arouse the blacks; and the mulattoes, who on their side had made a new armed attempt to support their rights against the white caste, gained all the advantage of this intervention of the blacks, among whom they even made numerous recruits. In the midst of the intricacies of the contests which ensued, one fact is of special consequence: feeling that their only point of support was in the mother country, the new citizens (the freed-men) had the tact or the good faith to remain faithful to her. There thus came a time when they became for the commissioners charged with the pacification of the island, that which the white *tiers-état* had been for Governor Peinier, namely, the only colonial auxiliaries under French influence, so that the final triumph of the authority of the mother country had for a necessary result the preponderance of the men of colour."

NOTE C.

The following is the view taken of the struggle for negro freedom by CHRISTOPHE, who was himself concerned therein; the passage is taken from a manifesto, published in 1814, by that warrior, then King of Hayti, and threatened with a new invasion by the whites.

"We have deserved the favours of liberty, by our indissoluble attachment to the mother country. We have proved to her our gratitude.

"At the time when, reduced to our own private resources, cut off from all communication with France, we resisted every allurement; when, inflexible to menaces, deaf to proposals, inaccessible to artifice, we braved misery, famine, and privation of every kind, and finally triumphed over our enemies both within and without.

"We were then far from perceiving that twelve years after, as the price of so much perseverance, sacrifice, and blood, France would deprive us in a most barbarous manner of the most precious of our possessions—liberty.

"Under the administration of Governor-General Toussaint L'Ouverture, Hayti arose from her ruins, and every thing seemed to promise a happy future. The arrival of General Hedouville completely changed the aspect of affairs, and struck a deadly blow to public tranquillity. We will not enter into the detail of his intrigues with the Haytian General Rigaud, whom he persuaded to revolt against his legitimate chief. We will only say, that before leaving the island Hedouville had put every thing into confusion, by casting among us the firebrands of discord, and lighting the torch of civil war.

"Ever zealous for the re-establishment of order and of peace, Toussaint-L'Ouverture, by a paternal government, restored their original energy to law, morality, religion, education, and industry. Agriculture and commerce were flourishing; he was favourable to white colonists, especially to those who occupied new possessions; and the care and partiality which he felt for them [Page 327] went so far, that he was severely censured as being more attached to them than to people of his own colour. This negro wail was not without reason; for some months previous to the arrival of the French, he put to death his own nephew, General Moise, for having disregarded his orders relative to the protection of the colonists. This act of the governor, and the great confidence which he had in the French government, were the chief causes of the weak resistance which the French met with in Hayti. In reality, his confidence in that government was so great, that the general had disbanded the greater part of the regular troops, and employed them in the cultivation of the ground.

"Such was the state of affairs whilst the peace of Amiens was being negotiated: it was scarcely concluded when a powerful armament landed on our coasts a large army, which, attacking us by surprise, when we thought ourselves perfectly secure, plunged us suddenly into an abyss of evils.

"Posterity will find a difficulty in believing that, in so enlightened and philosophic an age, such an abominable enterprise could possibly have been conceived. In the midst of a civilized people, a horde of barbarians suddenly set out with the design of exterminating an innocent and peaceable nation, or at least of loading them anew with the chains of national slavery.

"It was not enough that they employed violence; they also thought it necessary to use perfidy and villany,—they were compelled to sow dissension among us. Every means was put in requisition to carry out this abominable scheme. The leaders of all political parties in France, even the sons of the governor Toussaint, were invited to take part in the expedition. They, as well as ourselves, were deceived by that chef-d'œuvre of perfidy, the proclamation of the first consul, in which he said to us, 'You are all equal and free before God and the republic;' such was his declaration, at the same time that his private instructions to General Leclerc were to re-establish slavery.

"The greater part of the population, deceived by these fallacious promises, and for a long time accustomed to consider itself as French, submitted without resistance. The governor so little expected the appearance of an enemy, that he had not even ordered his generals to resist in case of an attack being made; and when the armament arrived, he himself was on a journey towards the eastern coast. If some few generals did resist, it was owing only to the hostile and menacing manner in which they were summoned to surrender, which compelled them to respect their duty, their honour, and the present circumstances.

"After a resistance of some months, the governor-general yielded to the pressing entreaties and the solemn protestations of Leclerc, 'that he intended to protect the liberties of every one, and that France would never destroy so noble a work.' On this footing, peace was negotiated with France; and the governor Toussaint, laying aside his power, peaceably retired to the retreat he had prepared for himself.

"Scarcely had the French extended their dominion over the whole island, and that more by roguery and deceit than by force of arms, than they began to put in execution their horrible system of slavery and destruction.

"To hasten the accomplishment of their projects, mercenary and [Page 328] Machiavellian writers fabricated fictitious narratives, and attributed to Toussaint designs that he had never entertained. While he was remaining peaceably at home, on the faith of solemn treaties, he was seized, loaded with irons, dragged away with the whole of his family, and transported to France. The whole of Europe knows how he ended his unfortunate career, in torture and in prayer, in the dungeon of the Château de Joux.

"Such was the recompence reserved for his attachment to France, and for the eminent services he had rendered to the colony.

"At the same time, notice was given to arrest all suspected persons throughout the island. All those who had shown brave and enlightened souls, when we claimed for ourselves the rights of men, were the first to be seized. Even the traitors who had most contributed to the success of the French army, by serving as guides to their advanced guard, and by exciting their compatriots to take vengeance, were not spared. At first they desired to sell them into strange colonies; but as this plait did not succeed, they resolved to transport them to France, where overpowering labour, the galleys, chains, and prisons, were awaiting them.

"Then the white colonists, whose numbers have continually increased, seeing their power sufficiently established, discarded the mask of dissimulation, openly declared the re-establishment of slavery, and acted in accordance with their declaration. They had the impudence to claim as their slaves, men who had made themselves eminent by the most brilliant services to their country, in both the civil and military departments. Virtuous and honourable magistrates, warriors covered with wounds, whose blood had been poured out for France and for liberty, were compelled to fall back into the bonds of slavery. These colonists, scarcely established in the possession of their land, whose power was liable to be overthrown by the slightest cause, already marked out and chose in the distance those whom they determined should be the first victims of their vengeance.

"The proud and liberty-hating faction of the colonists, of those traffickers in human flesh, who, since the commencement of the revolution, had not ceased to impregnate the successive governments in France with their plans, their projects, their atrocious and extravagant memorials, and everything tending to our ruin,—these factious men, tormented by the recollection of the despotism which they had formerly exercised at Hayti, a prey to their low and cruel passions, exerted all their efforts to repossess themselves of the prey which had escaped from their clutches. In favour of independence under the constitutional assembly, terrorists under the Jacobins, and, finally, zealous Bonapartists, they knew how to assume the mask of any party, in order to obtain place and favour. It was thus by their insidious counsels they urged Bonaparte to undertake this iniquitous expedition to Hayti. It was this faction who, after having advised the expedition, furnished the pecuniary resources which were necessary, by means of subscriptions which were at this time commenced. In a word, it was this faction which caused the blood of our compatriots to flow in torrents,—which invented the exhausting tortures to which we were subjected; it is to these colonists that France owes the loss of a powerful army, which perished in the plains and marshes of Hayti; it is to them that she owes the shame of an enterprise which has fixed an indelible stain on the French name.

[Page 329]"Immediately, the greater part of the people took up arms for the preservation of life and liberty. Even this first movement alarmed the French, and appeared to General Leclerc so important as to cause him to summon a special meeting of the colonists, in order to adopt measures suitable to bring about a better state of affairs; but these colonists, far from desisting from their atrocious principles, notwithstanding the imminence of the danger, unanimously exclaimed, 'If there is no slavery, there is no colony!'

"Members of the council, it was in vain that we raised our voices to prevent the total ruin of our country; in vain we represented to them the horrible injustice of again casting so many free men into slavery; in vain (for we knew the spirit of liberty which animated our compatriots) we denounced this measure as the certain ruin of the country, and that it would detach it for ever from France: it was all in vain. Convinced that there no longer remained any hope of conciliation, and that we were compelled to choose between slavery and death, then, with our weapons in our hands, we undeceived our compatriots, whose whole attention was directed towards us, and we unanimously seized our swords, resolved either to drive those tyrants from the land for ever, or to die.

"General Leclerc had already announced the conquest of the island, and had received from almost all the maritime towns of France (where resided the chief advocates of slavery), letters of congratulation on his pretended conquest. Ashamed of having given rise to such deceitful hopes, mortified at not being able to achieve the detestable enterprise, and mistrusting the approach of another terrible war, despair shortened his days and dragged him down to the grave.

"Amid this long tissue of crimes which marked the administration of General Leclerc, we will merely point out his conduct towards the Haytian general, Maurepas, which could not but excite the commiseration even of the most cold-hearted. Maurepas, a man of gentle and agreeable manners, esteemed by his fellow-citizens for his integrity, was one of the first to join the French, and rendered them the most signal services. Nevertheless, he was suddenly carried off to Port-au-Prince, and taken on board the admiral's vessel, which was then at anchor near the Cape coasts; and then, having been bound to the mainmast, in mockery they put two epaulettes on his shoulders, fastened them on by nails such as they use in naval carpentry, and covered his head with a general's hat. In this frightful condition, these savages, after having given free vent to their ferocious joy, precipitated him, with his wife and children, into the sea. Such was the destiny of this virtuous though unfortunate soldier."—*Histoire de l'Ile d'Hayti*, par Placide Justine, p. 391—Paris, 1826.

NOTE D.

The efforts made by Christophe for the instruction of the people are described in the following passages, which are laid before the reader, the [Page 330] rather because they afford encouragement to those who may be desirous of aid in raising Hayti to its proper condition:—

"He (Christophe) had already learnt, by means of his correspondence with some English gentlemen, that the Lancasterian system, being singularly adapted to the education of youth in the rudiments of knowledge, had been acted on with great success in this country;—he also knew that a society had been formed for the purpose of establishing schools on this system, and for preparing young men to superintend them, and it was further stated, that if he was desirous of introducing it into Hayti, that society would readily furnish him with schoolmasters duly qualified for the work. In consequence of this information, he caused an application to be made to the British and Foreign School Society for such a number of instructors as was thought necessary to commence the undertaking; and all matters relating to their salaries and other expenses being arranged, six teachers, who had been previously engaged in superintending schools in England, sailed for Hayti.*

"On their arrival at Cap François, which was in 1816, Christophe afforded them every possible facility, and at the same time exempted them from the disagreeable regulations to which the other white residents were subject. Thus encouraged, they proceeded in the prosecution of their object with great diligence and application. Buildings were prepared under their inspection; books, and every other necessary apparatus, were provided; and in a short time, schools were established at Cap François, St. Mare's, Gonaives, and other towns, containing nearly 2, 000 pupils. In these schools, the Haytian youth were taught reading, writing, the elements of arithmetic, and English; and after they had made considerable progress in the latter, the business of the school was conducted in that language. The object of this regulation, it was stated, was to introduce English into general use; for so thoroughly did Christophe detest the French, that he was anxious to abolish everything that indicated their former possession of the island; to accomplish which, he was determined to leave no means untried.

Among the first things which I visited, after my arrival in Hayti, was the school established at Cap François. The place appropriated to this purpose was a large building, situated in a retired and elevated part of the town, and was as properly arranged and as perfectly furnished with all the necessary apparatus, as the best schools conducted on this system are prepared in England. This school contained from one hundred and fifty to two hundred boys, from eight to sixteen years of age. When I entered the room, they were regularly divided into their classes, all busily engaged at their lessons; and their evident attention and application could not fail to strike a visitor. The sight of so many young negroes, employed in acquiring the rudiments of learning, would have been, to any one, as interesting as it was novel; to those who feel a just concern in the welfare of the African race, it was peculiarly so; nor was it possible to witness it, without recollecting how different would have been their condition had they been enslaved, and rejoicing at the change which had led to such beneficial results.

---

* SOON AFTER THE SCHOOLS WERE ESTABLISHED IN HAYTI, AND THE UTILITY OF THE SYSTEM BEGAN TO APPEAR, CHRISTOPHE PRESENTED THIS SOCIETY WITH ONE HUNDRED GUINEAS.

[Page 331]"The master of this school, who was an intelligent young man, had conducted it from its commencement, and his ability and attention appeared from the perfect order which prevailed throughout. My inquiries of him respecting those placed under his instruction related to the following particulars:—Whether they displayed common aptness for learning; whether they readily remembered what they acquired; and whether they were capable of the application expected from boys in general of their age? To these questions he replied, that among so great a number as were committed to his care, there were, of course, several whose incapacity prevented them from making any great progress, but that the majority learnt without much difficulty, and many even with considerable facility; that with regard to their memory, their gradual advancement from one branch to another, and their readiness in recollecting small pieces of poetry or prose, which they were occasionally required to learn, were satisfactory proofs of its being sufficiently retentive; and at the same time adding, that they required no more powerful stimulus to application and diligence than is necessary for youth in general.

"In answer to a question respecting the general character of his pupils, he further stated that they were far less obstinate and refractory than he had expected to find them. The facility, he said, with which they became familiarized to the mechanical part of the system, was surprising; the necessity of inflicting severe punishment, he stated, was not frequent; if a few were disobedient and inattentive, he observed, others were no less diligent and submissive; and pointing to the state of the school at that moment, he hoped, he said, its order and regularity were indications of its flourishing condition, as well as of the docility and submission of the boys.* He concluded his answers by assuring me that, on the whole, he found the young negroes and mulattoes as apt to learn and as ready to remember as he had found the youth of our own country."At this period, all the boys of the school could read and write; many of them were acquainted with the introductory rules of arithmetic; and some spoke the English language

---

* SINCE MY RETURN TO ENGLAND, I HAVE VISITED THE CENTRAL SCHOOL OF THE BRITISH AND FOREIGN SCHOOL SOCIETY, IN THE BOROUGH-ROAD, LONDON; AND GRANTING, AS EVERY ONE MUST, THAT IT IS CONDUCTED WITH ADMIRABLE ORDER, YET I CONFESS I COULD NOT PERCEIVE ITS SUPERIORITY, IN POINT OF GENERAL DISCIPLINE, TO THAT CONSISTING OF THE HAYTIAN YOUTH AT CAP FRANÇOIS.

with considerable ease and propriety. At the request of the master, I called several of his pupils indiscriminately, and proposed to them questions, according to the classes in which they stood; and the result of this examination was a conviction that, whatever may be affirmed of the stupidity of the negro, he is no further inferior in intellect to others than the system of slavery renders him. Of this I received a further confirmation by subsequent trials. I directed a certain number of these lads to commit to memory select pieces of English and French, some in poetry and others in prose; and promised to encourage them by bestowing appropriate rewards on those who should repeat these pieces most readily and correctly. At the expiration of the time appointed them for learning, they each recited their respective portions with so much ease and propriety, [Page 332] that it was difficult to determine to whom the prizes should be adjudged, and the only satisfactory mode of arrangement appeared to be that of increasing the number, so as to give to each boy a trifling reward. A short time afterwards, I heard them repeat the same pieces, and they rehearsed them with nearly the same readiness and correctness as they had previously done.

"One of the elder boys of this school was particularly pointed out, as distinguished from his schoolfellows by his great aptness for learning, and for the progress he had made in some branches not usually included in the Lancasterian system of education. He was an interesting looking lad, about sixteen years of age, and occasionally undertook, in the absence of the master, the superintendence of the school. Being desirous of ascertaining the extent of his acquirements, I requested him to call at my lodgings for the purpose of examining him. On his compliance with this request, I first proposed to him a few questions in the Single Rule of Three: these he answered with perfect ease. I then proposed others in the different cases of Practice: these also he performed with equal facility. After this I tried him in the simple and compound rules of Vulgar and Decimal Fractions, and found him no less familiar with them; but the Square Root somewhat puzzled him, and in the Cube Root, he felt totally unable to proceed. His next trial was to translate a paragraph from one of the pieces in Enfield's Speaker into French, which he did without much difficulty, and, as far as I was qualified to judge, with a great degree of accuracy. He was then requested to give in writing a translation of a page of Bossuet's 'Histoire Universelle' into English, and was furnished with a dictionary for his assistance. About this part of his examination, he employed considerable time, and appeared to bestow on it special attention and care; he repeatedly corrected his translation, copied it several times before he appeared satisfied, and even then hesitated to hand it to me. But when completed, it far exceeded my expectations; for though it contained one or two Gallicisms, in point of sense and grammatical construction, it was remarkably correct. Finally, he pointed out, on a map, the boundaries of the four quarters of the globe, the situation of his own country, with its latitude and longitude, the limits of the European nations, with their capitals, the principal islands of both hemispheres, and the more remarkable mountains, gulfs, and lakes, with a readiness as surprising as it was satisfactory; at the same time answering the questions proposed to him respecting the religious and peculiar manners and customs of different nations with like facility and accuracy. During the whole time his manners were perfectly unassuming; it was also evident that he had been especially assisted and encouraged, and that his progress was proportionably rapid and sure; and I confess that the result of this examination afforded me as much gratification as any circumstance I witnessed during my stay in the island.

"While the school at Cap François was in this flourishing condition, and presented such satisfactory proofs of the capacity and application of the Haytian youth, those established at Gonaïves, St. Marc's, Fort Royal, and at other places, were, I understood, (for I had not an opportunity of visiting them,) in a state equally encouraging and prosperous. The young negroes admitted into them were stated to have exhibited similar proofs of their possessing a ready apprehension and a retentive memory; and while, by their [Page 333] progress, they afforded the utmost satisfaction to their teachers, their facility of acquirement rendered the labour of instruction far less difficult and tedious than had been anticipated.

"In the meantime, a 'Royal Board of Public Instruction,' had been established, for the purpose of superintending the education of youth, and of extending the present system, whenever it should become necessary. It consisted of two dukes, five counts, and four barons, some of the most intelligent and active of Christophe's adherents, and therefore the best qualified to undertake the duties which their situation involved.* In the first account of their proceedings, published in the Haytian Gazette, they declare it as their belief that 'Instruction, when founded on the true principles of liberty, religion, and morals, is one of the most fruitful sources

---

* DE LIMONADE AND DUPUY WERE OF THE NUMBER.

of public prosperity, and essentially contributes to the good order of society, and obedience to the laws.' And in conformity with these views, they express their resolution 'to give regular organziation to this important branch of the administration, and to establish suitable regulations for its superintendence.'" The more especial objects of this Board were, to provide that 'education be founded on good principles,—viz., those of religion, respect for the laws, and love to the sovereign; to confirm the regulations already ordained for this purpose, and to appoint such others as should be deemed expedient; to maintain order, discipline, and the observance of the rules, in the national establishments for public instruction already existing; and to found new schools, and colleges, or academies, whenever it should appear necessary.' To facilitate the accomplishment of these objects, 'three inspectors were nominated for each establishment, chosen from among the respectable residents of the neighbourhood where it was situated; whose business it was to visit the places of instruction, and to correspond with the Board on all things relating to their appointment. In addition to which, one of its own members was selected to make similar visits, at stated periods, and to render an account of the state of the schools, and of the progress of education, as reported by the inspectors and masters.' In pursuance of the same objects, it was further determined that the Board should, every six months, present to the king a report of the progress of public instruction, with the names of the masters most distinguished for their attention and care; and that, more especially, to encourage the students of the different establishments, annual prizes, granted by his majesty, should be awarded to those who, by their diligent and successful application, should merit particular distinction.

"Conformably with the general design of the 'Royal Board,' when the schools had been some time in operation, and the elder boys had acquired the rudiments of knowledge, it was resolved that another establishment should be founded for their further instruction, denominated the Royal College; an appellation, perhaps, somewhat misapplied, the institution being similar to the grammar schools, or to the more respectable academies in England. Cap François was fixed on for its situation, that place being the capital of the kingdom, and possessing greater advantages than any other. While a suitable building was preparing for the purpose, a proposal was made to two English [Page 334] gentlemen, through the same medium by which the Lancasterian schoolmasters had been procured, inviting them to Hayti, to superintend the institution, and offering them a liberal remuneration for their services, which proposal was accepted. The students were then selected from among the more meritorious of those who had previously distinguished themselves by their conduct and acquirements; and thus the college (if such it must be called) was established, without either difficulty or delay.

"A considerable number of the Haytian youth were now instructed in Latin, English, and French composition, history, geography, and mathematics, and were assisted in these pursuits by tutors whose attainments fully qualified them to direct their studies. The classical professor, on whom at first devolved the entire charge of the college, devoted himself to a task at once laborious and irksome, with the utmost zeal and diligence. He strove to simplify his instructions, so as to render them intelligible to the slowest understanding; he varied his method of teaching according to the different capacities of his pupils; he assisted them in their difficulties, and encouraged them by his mildness and persuasions; and being a clergyman of the Anglican church, he added to his usual engagements that of occasionally instructing them in the doctrines and precepts of the Christian religion. Nor was the mathematical professor less indefatigable in his endeavours to promote the improvement of those committed to his charge. He was a gentleman of considerable scientific attainments, highly respected by Christophe and the Board of Instruction for his superior qualifications, and esteemed for his amiable disposition and obliging deportment by all who had the happiness of his acquaintance. Though unaccustomed to the education of youth previously to his arrival in Hayti, his intimate knowledge of mathematics, accompanied by a correct judgment, enabled him to adopt a method of instructing his pupils perfectly adapted to their abilities and attainments; and while he endeavoured to initiate them into the elements of science, he was not forgetful to encourage them by the most powerful motives. Desirous at the same time of employing his leisure hours in the promotion of some useful object, he occasionally delivered lectures on mechanics and chemistry; and being provided with the apparatus necessary for the purpose, he illustrated their principles by suitable experiments.

"Under the tuition of these instructors, the students made considerable advances in those branches of learning to which the attention was now directed. The majority were able, in a short time, to construe the more easy Latin authors without much difficulty; they wrote English and French with ease and correctness; and they especially delighted in the study of history and geography, and regarded it rather as a recreation than as a task. The mathematics alone they found so difficult as to require every possible encouragement to induce them to proceed. But if they made slower progress in this than in other pursuits, it arose more from the peculiar application it requires, than from any defect in their mental powers. They possessed, it was evident, the ability to learn; but had not always resolution to persevere in a study so dry and abstract, and, to those who have not a genius peculiarly adapted to it, so utterly uninviting. Yet a few, who were distinguished from the rest more for their patient application than for greater quickness of parts or strength of memory, steadily [Page 335] persevered; and having overcome the first difficulties, which to their fellow-students had appeared insurmountable, they afterwards advanced with considerable ease; and at length became as familiar with the elements of geometry and algebra as they were with their previous acquirements.

"Among other circumstances connected with their progress in this branch of learning, the following may not be uninteresting. During the period that the late Sir Home Popham was appointed to the Jamaica station, he paid occasional visits to Cap François. On the last of these visits to that place, whilst on his return to England, he made particular inquiries respecting the college, and went, in company with Baron de Dupuy, to see it. He was exceedingly pleased on entering, at observing the order and regularity with which it was conducted; and was still more gratified by the evident progress of the students. Being informed by Dupuy that, among other things, the mathematics also were taught, he was curious enough to try the proficiency of the class, by pointing out some geometrical propositions for them to demonstrate. They readily constructed the diagrams, and gave the demonstrations with correctness and facility; and the admiral appeared singularly gratified with this unexpected proof of the ability and acquirements of negroes."*

THE END

[Page 336]
LONDON:
SAVILL AND EDWARDS, PRINTERS, CHANDOS STREET,
COVENT GARDEN.

---

* Harvey's "Sketches of Hayti," pp. 200-215.

NEW BOOKS FOR FEBRUARY.

Illustrated London Library.
(VOLUME 6.)

Lares and Penates; or, Cilicia and its Governors. Being a Short Historical Account of that Province, from the Earliest Times to the Present Day. Together with a Description of some Household Gods of the ancient Cilicians, broken up by them on their Conversion to Christianity, and first discovered and brought to this country by the Author, WILLIAM BURCKHARD BARKER, M.R.A.S., many years resident at Tarsus in an official capacity. Edited by WILLIAM FRANCIS AINSWORTH, F.R.G.S., F.G.S. Demy 8vo, price 6s. cloth; calf, marbled edges, 10s. 6d.

National Illustrated Library.
(VOLUME 24.) Now complete,

The Iliad of Homer. Translated into English Verse by ALEXANDER POPE. A New Edition, with Notes, Illustrations, and Introduction, by the REV. THEODORE ALOIS BUCKLEY, B.A., Chaplain of Christ Church, Oxford; Editor of Translations of Homer, Æschylus, Sophocles, Euripides, &c., &c.; Author of "Great Cities of the Ancient World," "History of the Council of Trent," &c., &c. Two volumes, cloth, 5s.

*** This Edition of Homer's Iliad is copiously embellished with Flaxman's Illustrations.

In morocco extra, for SCHOOL PRIZES. Two vols. 15s., or two vols. in one, 10s. 6d.

New Educational Works.
JUST READY.

The First Six Books of Euclid, with numerous Exercises. Printed on a new plan, with accurately executed Diagrams. Demy 8vo, cloth, price 2s.

The Illustrated Practical Geometry. Edited by ROBERT SCOTT BURN, Editor of the Illustrated London Drawing Book. Demy 8vo, cloth, price 2s.

First Lessons in Arithmetic, on a New Plan. By HUGO REID, late Principal of the People's College, Nottingham, and Author of numerous Educational Works. Demy 8vo, cloth, price 2s.

Mechanics and Mechanism. By ROBERT SCOTT BURN. With about 250 Illustrations. Demy 8vo, cloth, price 2s.

N.B.—THE ILLUSTRATED LONDON GEOGRAPHY, with Coloured Plates, can now be supplied, price 3s., or plain, 2s.

The Illustrated Library of the Best Works of the Best AUTHORS OF ALL NATIONS, IN ALL DEPARTMENTS OF LITERATURE. Beautifully and uniformly printed in royal octavo, with two or more first-class Illustrations to each number, and a handsome cover.

SIX NUMBERS have already appeared—
1. SCOTT'S "LADY OF THE LAKE," AND "LAY OF THE LAST MINSTREL." 1s.
2. GOLDSMITH'S "VICAR OF WAKEFIELD," AND SAINTINE'S "PICCIOLA." 1s.
3. ANSON'S "VOYAGE ROUND THE WORLD." 1s.
4. IZAAK WALTON'S "LIVES OF DONNE, WOTTON, HERBERT, HOOKER, AND SANDERSON." 1s.
5. ALISON'S "ESSAY ON TASTE." 1s.
6. STERNE'S "TRISTRAM SHANDY." 1s. 6d. (168 pages.)
7. FABLES OF LA FONTAINE. Translated from the French, by E. WRIGHT. 1s. (February Number.)

Cheap Series of Illustrated Novels.

Crown octavo, about 300 pages, elegantly bound in cloth, 2s. 6d. per Volume.

UNABRIDGED AND ILLUSTRATED EDITION.

Uncle Tom's Cabin.

By HARRIET B. STOWE. Now ready, sixth edition, price 2s. in wrapper; or, 2s. 6d. cloth, gilt. *Unabridged Edition, Embellished with Eight Fine Engravings.*

Lady Felicia.

By HENRY COCKTON, Author of "Valentine Vox," "Sylvester Sound," &c. Post 8vo, with Illustrated Frontispiece and Title, elegantly bound in blue and silver, price 5s.

"From the office of the *Illustrated London Library* is issued 'Lady Felicia,' a novel, by Henry Cockton, author of 'Valentine Vox,' 'Sylvester Sound,' &c. The book is more animated and less diffuse than the generality of novels."—LITERARY GAZETTE.

"This is an agreeably-written novel; and few of the lovers of fiction who may commence its pages will be likely to relinquish their pursuit until they arrive at the grand *dénouement*. . . . . . . A more fascinating specimen of womankind than Lady Felicia has seldom been introduced to us through the medium of romance; and there is also much to attract in her arch, lively, and attached maid, Fidèle. Then, the genuine warm-hearted uncle, Cys, and Chubb, 'who, although a coarse person, held nearly half the mortgages in the borough,' are extremely well drawn."—NAVAL AND MILITARY GAZETTE.

The Squanders of Castle Squander.

A New Novel. In Two Volumes. By WILLIAM CARLETON, Author of "The Black Prophet," "Traits of the Irish Peasantry," &c. &c.

"It will be strange indeed if we do not get at the truth of the state of society in Ireland through the country's novels."—THE SCOTSMAN.

Ivar; or, the Skjuts-Boy.

From the Swedish of EMILIE CARLEN, Author of "Woman's Life," "The Birthright," &c.

"We tell our readers confidently, whether they be of the rougher or gentler sex, that a perusal of this story, abounding with (to us) novel sketches of Swedish animate and inanimate nature, with incidents always relevant and entertaining, with life-lessons conveyed charmingly, will give them very pleasing satisfaction, and much soothing mental comfort."
OBSERVER.

"This tale bears the same national features as the 'Neighbours' and 'The President's Daughters,' and will find acceptance with the same class of readers. Miss Carlen enjoys a high reputation in Sweden, and, judging by this volume, she is worthy of it. Her sketches of female character are exquisite; as chaste and true to nature as the most perfect statue ever formed by the master chisel of Canova."—ECLECTIC REVIEW.

UNABRIDGED AND ILLUSTRATED EDITION.

The White Slave: a Tale of Slave Life in Virginia.

Third Edition. Edited by R. HILDRETH, Esq., Author of "A History of the United States."

LONDON: INGRAM, COOKE, & CO., 227, STRAND.

[Advertisement]

www.ingramcontent.com/pod-product-compliance
Lightning Source LLC
Chambersburg PA
CBHW030335240426
43661CB00052B/1641